THROUGH
THE LION GATE

THROUGH
THE LION GATE

A History of the Berlin Zoo

GARY BRUCE

OXFORD
UNIVERSITY PRESS

OXFORD
UNIVERSITY PRESS

Oxford University Press is a department of the University of Oxford. It furthers
the University's objective of excellence in research, scholarship, and education
by publishing worldwide. Oxford is a registered trade mark of Oxford University
Press in the UK and certain other countries.

Published in the United States of America by Oxford University Press
198 Madison Avenue, New York, NY 10016, United States of America.

Library of Congress Cataloging-in-Publication Data
Names: Bruce, Gary, 1969- author.
Title: Through the lion gate : a history of the Berlin Zoo / Gary Bruce.
Description: New York, NY : Oxford University Press, 2017.
Identifiers: LCCN 2016052215 | ISBN 9780190234980 (hardback)
Subjects: LCSH: Zoologischer Garten (Berlin, Germany)—History. |
Zoos—Germany—Berlin—History. | Zoos—Political
aspects—Germany—History. | Berlin (Germany)—Social life and customs. |
Berlin (Germany)—History. | BISAC: HISTORY / Europe / Germany.
Classification: LCC QL76.5.G32 B433 2017 | DDC 590.7343/155—dc23 LC record
available at https://lccn.loc.gov/2016052215

1 3 5 7 9 8 6 4 2
Printed by Sheridan Books, Inc., United States of America

For Gabriel and Naomi

CONTENTS

ACKNOWLEDGMENTS

GIVEN THAT THIS BOOK WAS a significant departure from my previous projects, I relied to a great extent on the help of others. Over the course of the five years that I spent in Berlin archives, several of which I had not worked in previously, I received first-rate assistance from dedicated staff. Undine Beier was my first point of contact at the Bundesarchiv and helped me navigate the labyrinth of documents therein. At the Landesarchiv Berlin, Bianca Welzing-Bräutigam spent countless hours locating invaluable historic sources, such as the Berlin zoo's first visitor's guides. Nils Seethaler at the archive of the Berlin Society for Archaeology, Ethnography, and Pre-History placed at my disposal virtually all of the photographs in the society's substantial collection, three of which have found their way into this book. Although I regret I was not permitted to view documents held by the Berlin zoo, I am nevertheless grateful for the assistance of Martina Borchert in locating rare historic photos of the zoo and to the Berlin zoo for allowing me to reprint the photos without charge. Dr. Vera Enke of the Berlin-Brandenburg Academy of Sciences Archive kindly facilitated my visit there. I was fortunate to be able to fund these many trips due to a generous grant from the Social Sciences and Humanities Research Council of Canada.

The time and distance from Berlin required me to hire two on-site research assistants. Adrian Mitter helped to locate, but more importantly decipher, some of the nineteenth-century holdings on the zoo located at the Prussian Privy State Archives. But his assistance reached far beyond this one task. He was constantly on the lookout for seldom-used or unusual sources on the zoo, such as the memoirs of some of the early trappers involved in the animal trade. The current book has much greater texture due to Adrian's efforts. Jolanta Turowska undertook the herculean task of scanning and collating hundreds of pages of newspaper reports on the zoo's ethnographic exhibits which are located in the newspaper division of the National Library in Berlin. Her unrivaled thoroughness and deep intellect were tremendous assets on this research project, as they were on my last book.

I am extremely thankful to Herr Gödicke, a recently retired keeper at the Berlin zoo who has undertaken considerable research on the zoo's history, for his insights and assistance with making contacts. I will always remember with fondness our many chats after hours in his service quarters on the zoo's grounds, the stillness of those northern European summer evenings interrupted by the sounds of animals rather than traffic for a change. I am also thankful to two other scholars of the Berlin zoo, Curtis Christopher Comer and James Scott, who have given freely of their advice. Alan McDougall at the University of Guelph assisted me with attendance figures for East Germany's top soccer division, while Mat Schulze at the University of Waterloo helped with the occasional tricky translation.

My PhD students, Alan Maricic and Jennifer Redler, have not only been terrific intellectual companions but also contributed directly to the book. Jennifer learned more about Knut than she probably wanted to know and offered outstanding proofreading and keen insights into the manuscript's content as well. I turned, frequently in a panic, to Alan for research assistance on every manner of topic, questions that he answered with ease and professionalism. I look forward to following the career of these two very promising historians.

I consider myself extremely fortunate to work with a group of historians at the University of Waterloo who are deeply dedicated to their teaching and research. For their insights and friendship, I am grateful to Geoff Hayes, John Sbardellati, Ian Milligan, Ryan Touhey, and Dan Gorman. I owe a special thanks to Dan for alerting me to the colonial insights found in *Tintin in the Congo*. Patrick Harrigan provided sage advice and a constant reminder that as a species (if not individually), humans pale compared to dogs. Susan Roy offered both her knowledge and academic resources on the Nuxalk Nation (Bella Coola), which aided my understanding of the Canadian context of this indigenous group exhibited in Berlin. Jim Blight and janet Lang provided evidence as convincing as any historic document that the Berlin zoo's iconic hippo was a massive cultural phenomenon when they showed me the stuffed animal of Knautschke (complete with his landings, a tonic for all ailments) that they were drawn to purchase during a trip to Berlin during the Cold War. Jim and janet's perseverance and contagious good-humor in the face of adversity, and their own meticulous historical research, have been great influences on me.

Twice now I have had the distinct pleasure of working with the editorial staff at Oxford University Press. Nancy Toff's eye for narrative and her intuitive understanding of the reader's point of view greatly improved the manuscript. I also appreciated two qualities that she possesses in abundance that make her such an effective editor: candor and humor. Elda Granata was of tremendous assistance in locating photos for the book and securing the copyright for them. I also wish to thank the copyediting team and Oxford's anonymous reviewers for their very useful suggestions to improve the manuscript.

My greatest debt is, as ever, to family and friends. My parents gave me the opportunity to study history in the first place, for which I am constantly grateful. My mum has shared in the ups and downs of this project from the outset and has provided welcome feedback on many aspects of it, including the cover photo. The interest shown in my work by my brothers and sister has sustained me much more than they know. Although it has been some time now, at moments like these I think even more often of my father, who would have been so pleased to see this book. Matthias Putzke, Sven Lauk, Samuli Siren, Ulrich Poppelbaum and Anne Löchte, Hartmut and Barbara Mehlitz, and their respective families continue to make me feel welcome in Berlin. Closer to home, Henry and Sam have been welcome additions on this journey. Gabriel wakes me from my complacency on a daily basis to recognize the magnificence of the natural world. As he has shown me on numerous occasions, one need not go far afield to encounter the mysteries of nature; there is a lengthy voyage of discovery at the base of every tree.

And already I draw inspiration from Naomi, who conveys a sense of the wonder that surrounds us through her raw gestures and in her endearing, wide-eyed, wordless looks.

Finally, this book, and much besides in my life, would be vastly diminished without Bec, with whom I am so very lucky to be writing our own history.

Introduction

ON A NIGHT TRAIN FROM Nice to Berlin in 1928, two men sat mesmerized by the companion who shared their compartment. One was Gustav Brandes, the director of the Dresden zoo; the other was the author Paul Eipper, whose descriptions of the unusual passenger caused great anticipation in Germany. "[He] already has a fully formed personality. He's aware of and interested in everything around him," wrote Eipper. "He stands at the window with an air of curiosity, the sturdy forearms resting in such a way that the muscles on his strong back stand out. His completely round head rises with hardly a transition from his very wide shoulders.... He petted me and kissed me, put his arms around my neck, and lovingly nibbled my ear."[1]

Following his arrival at the Berlin zoo, Bobby, the three year-old gorilla and at the time the only gorilla in European captivity, became a sensation. Tourists from home and abroad crowded around his pen in amazement, as his trainer brushed him, greased his hands and feet, fed him, and played hide and seek with him.[2] In one of the earliest zoo booklets for children, the cover picture shows the zoo director, a positively beaming Ludwig Heck, with Bobby clinging to him as if he were his child.[3] Growing to an astounding 262 kilograms, Bobby was a behemoth, the heaviest gorilla in any zoo, and the first one to be raised in captivity from youth to adulthood.[4] Scientific commissions came from great distances to study what was once thought an impossibility: a long-standing exhibit of a live adult gorilla. When he died in 1935 after a

The gorilla Bobby in his pen at the Berlin zoo. From his arrival in 1928 until his death in 1935, Bobby was the zoo's star attraction, and he remains as the image on the zoo's official logo. *Berlin Zoo Archive*

brief illness that attracted top doctors in vain to the zoo (later diagnosed as appendicitis), Germans were devastated, and newspapers across the country lamented the loss.[5] Because of his enormous popularity, Bobby was immediately taxidermied and displayed in the Berlin Museum of Natural History. Eighty years after his death, and much as in life, Bobby surveys the large crowds from behind his display case with a look of concern tinged with weariness.

Bobby had cost the Berlin zoo a fortune. Not only was there a steep purchase price of 15,000 marks paid to the French officer serving in Cameroon who had cared for Bobby, but he also had to be transported from Africa to Marseilles, where he stayed for several weeks to acclimatize himself, a common practice at the time for animals brought from Africa.[6] He then required transport from France to Berlin and needed dedicated attention once he arrived, with particular attention to his diet.[7] But the outlay was hardly a gamble. Germans had been enticed through the lion gate in large numbers for decades to see the natural wonders on display in the Berlin zoo. Bobby only added to the zoo's aura.

Centuries ago, many Europeans would have found it utterly bizarre that a population wept at the death of an animal. The fact that today we are not surprised at the German reaction to the loss of Bobby says a great deal about the perception of animals in our era, in particular our increased awareness that throughout history, the fates of humans and animals have been entwined. We have hunted them for sustenance and then, later, for fun. At some point, although when and how it came about remains a riddle, we determined that the tamer ones could live among us and be raised for food.[8] We have used animals as transport over vast, foreboding landscapes like deserts[9] and to drag our weapons of war. We even welcomed them into our homes, initially as an antidote to the cold, isolating, life of the city. As we moved away from the intimacy of the countryside and into the crowded metropolis, we longed for the loyalty of dogs and cats when our fellow city dwellers let us down.[10]

And from long ago, we also captured them and put them on display to satisfy our own curiosity. Ancient civilizations from Babylon, through Greece and Rome, to the Aztecs and Incas kept wild animals in captivity. European rulers in the Middle Ages and early modern period continued the trend, the latter fueled by overseas explorers who returned with animals from distant lands for the rulers' living cabinets of curiosity. In 1752, the Holy Roman Emperor Francis I established at his Schönbrunn palace one of the most historically significant menageries. Modest at the outset, his collection grew quickly as royal families from around Europe and elsewhere, eager to curry favor with the emperor, lavished him with some of their most unusual animals.[11] One of the favorite pastimes of Maria Theresa, the emperor's wife, was to eat breakfast in the palace's central pavilion while observing the animals, which soon included several elephants.[12] Vienna's animal collection became more publicly accessible over time and remains today the oldest display of animals in continuous existence.

The first modern zoo, however, appeared in Europe some forty years later in Paris, when the writer Jacques-Henri Bernardin de Saint-Pierre helped to establish an animal collection at the Jardin des Plantes. "Modern" in this context denotes an emphasis on animal classification and taxonomy rather than sheer exoticism and should not be confused with advanced understanding of keeping animals in captivity. During its initial years, the Paris zoo put on lavish concerts for its elephants believing that the music would entice them to mate.[13] Unlike royal menageries, the modern zoo was to be scientific and accessible to a broader audience than simply those whom the king fancied. National (or in some cases civic) pride also prompted the educated elite to establish zoos, as would be the case later on with national collections of art. In his appeals to his contemporaries to assist him in founding the Paris zoo, Saint-Pierre spoke of the "dignity of the nation."[14]

Following Paris's lead, the Zoological Society of London established a zoo in Regent's Park that set the standard by which other zoos were compared for centuries to come. Tapping into Britain's vast colonial network, the London zoo was able to display a tremendous variety of exotic animals and, just as important, to replenish the supply when the animals died, which they did in large numbers in those early years. Apart from exhibiting the might of the British empire, some members of the London zoological society also hoped that certain animals could be acclimatized to England's natural environment and be made to mate with indigenous domesticated animals.[15] For two pounds, a British breeder could borrow a zebra from the zoo and try to infuse his herd of horses with its exotic genes.[16]

Well-to-do Dutch eager to show off the Netherlands' scientific prowess and its overseas expansion established the second zoo in continental Europe in 1838. It was soon a vibrant cultural center, membership in which became a status symbol for the thousands of Amsterdam's citizens who supported the zoo.[17] Belgium followed in the footsteps of its neighbor several years afterward, establishing a zoo in Antwerp. The fascination with zoos then took hold of Germany in a manner unparalleled in Europe. Berlin's zoo was established in 1844 and, unlike Amsterdam and Antwerp, was immediately open to the public rather than being the exclusive purview of a closed scientific society; it was the lone German zoo for fourteen years, but then six more German cities joined with Berlin in rapid succession: Frankfurt (1858), Cologne (1860), Dresden (1861), Hamburg (1863), Munich (1863), and Hannover (1865).[18] By 1905, Germany had far more zoos than any other country in Europe—nearly triple its closest competitor, Britain.[19] Germany was well ahead of the United States, too, opening its seventh zoo in Hannover more than a decade before the first US zoo opened in Philadelphia. The rapid rise of zoos in Germany is all the more astounding considering that in the vast majority of cases, private citizens—doctors, bankers, professors, scientists—rather than royalty pushed for a display of exotic animals in their cities.

Zoo foundings throughout western Europe and North America occurred during an era of urbanization. As people traded the farm for the factory and animals vanished from daily life, many leading citizens worried about the negative effects of this distancing from nature. Zoos, they believed, could provide an important antidote and contribute to the moral upbringing of the nation. Through a quiet contemplation of the stunning variety of animal life, zoo-goers would be led toward God, and thus to a more ethical life.[20] Whether this lofty aim ever materialized is unknowable, but for many zoo-goers, it was precisely the ability to escape the squalor and crowds of the city that attracted them through the gates. Whatever the motive might have been—intellectual curiosity, escapism, casual entertainment—the zoo allowed people to dream of another place, far away from the urban center, where animals roamed in a state of nature. If wonder, as Descartes describes it, is a "sudden stirring of the soul," then animals in zoos became objects of wonder, among the few sights in the city that were not man-made.[21]

Given the focus on the human purpose of zoos, most zoo founders did not dwell on the ethics of placing wild animals behind bars, believing that animals did not have sufficient self-awareness to recognize their captivity, nor could they experience human emotions even if they were to understand their lost freedom. In their view, animals were simply soulless creatures that acted on instinct. Although he lived several centuries earlier, Rene Descartes's dismissal of animals would nevertheless have struck a chord among many zoo founders: "The reason why animals do not speak as we do is not that they lack the organs, but that they have no thoughts."[22]

By the turn of the century, Europeans were no longer at ease with this understanding of animals. The notion that animals experience human emotions, known as anthropomorphism, began to gain traction. Increasingly, Europeans questioned the premise that only humans had the capacity to solve problems, form friendships, and even love. In 1908, puzzled by the demise of almost all gorillas shortly after they arrived in European zoos, the German zoologist Alexander Sokolowsky believed there could be no other explanation: Sadness about their imprisonment sapped them of their will to live.[23] The narrative of dominance, of the "conquest of nature," that was present in the early years of the Berlin zoo, gave way in the late nineteenth century and into the twentieth to a respect for, and fervent desire to protect, the other species on Earth. As was the case with Bobby, the Berlin zoo fostered a profound attachment between Berliners and the animals in their zoo, to the point that Berliners themselves rescued the zoo from certain closure on four separate occasions when the city's coffers were depleted.

The changing view of animals is revealed in striking fashion in *Tintin in the Congo*, which appeared in 1930 as a serial in the children's supplement to the Brussels newspaper *Le Vingtième Siècle*. Educators today often employ the comic strip outlining the adventures of the Belgian reporter Tintin and his dog Snowy to demonstrate the paternalistic, colonial attitudes of the era. European dominance and mockery of Africans abound in the story. To solve a dispute between two locals about the ownership of a straw hat, for example, Tintin tears the hat in half and gives each one a half, a solution that delights the adversaries. "White man very fair," exclaims one as he walks away with a broad smile.[24]

These clear images of European superiority were accompanied by Tintin's dominance of the Congo's wildlife. Hiding behind some bushes, Tintin sees a gazelle poke its head up over a small mound. Tintin shoots at it several times but appears to miss the animal, which continues to stand in the same location. Frustrated, Tintin empties several more rounds into the animal before it finally falls behind the mound. When Tintin reaches the animal, he sees a pile of fifteen gazelle corpses. Tintin realizes that as he killed one gazelle, another took its place. "Well, at least we'll have enough fresh meat!" he exclaims. Immediately after shooting the gazelles, Tintin kills a monkey, slices it open, and crawls into its skin so that he can infiltrate the monkey troupe that has captured his dog Snowy. Tintin is later seen proudly walking with massive elephant tusks on his shoulders.

When the book was reissued in 1975, the only change that the publisher requested related not to the racist depictions of Africans, which remain as they did in the original version even in the most recent edition, published in 2005, but to one scene in particular involving animals. Concerned about public sensitivities, the publisher requested that Hergé rewrite the panels where Tintin places dynamite into a hole he has drilled in the skull of a living rhinoceros and then explodes the animal. In the updated version, the rhinoceros is scared by a rifle Tintin has accidentally discharged and scurries off.

The reissue of *Tintin in the Congo* tells us that the public mindset had changed: It could accept the 1930s racial attitudes depicted in the book but not the grotesque killing of an endangered wild African animal. But it is not the animals that changed over time. We have. In the *New York Times* of August 10, 2014, the editorial writer is alarmed about the poaching of rhinoceroses in South Africa: "The threatened extinction of this magnificent creature obviously cries out for stronger international countermeasures."[25] There is, however, an obvious question: Why does it matter if the rhinoceros goes extinct? The *New York Times* does not feel compelled to provide an answer. In our era, it is self-evident that this large African animal, which most North Americans have not seen in the wild, enhances life on earth. It the mid-nineteenth century, it would have been by no means self-evident that there was merit in preserving the animal. Large mammals went extinct on a regular basis in the nineteenth century; few people cried out. The study of animals in human history tells us much more about how humans make sense of their world than it does about the animals themselves.[26]

When I first embarked on this topic, I was pleased to find that little had been written about the Berlin zoo and certainly almost none of what had been written was in English.[27] The initial excitement about writing on a topic few had researched soon gave way to the usual anxieties of historians—why has almost no one written about my topic? Considering some of the colossal economic, societal, and political forces at play in German history—to say nothing of individual personalities—was the Berlin zoo trivial? I was aware that David Blackbourn and Geoff Eley made German zoos a legitimate topic of study in their pathbreaking 1984 book, *The Peculiarities of German History*. The bourgeois push for zoos in the nineteenth century was further evidence, in their view, for the quiet revolution that took place in Germany. Although the rising middle classes may not have succeeded in obtaining political power, they nonetheless achieved their civilizing and moralizing goals through their countless associations and public institutions, including zoos.[28] But perhaps that was all there was to say about zoos.

My concerns mounted as I reread some of the outstanding histories of Berlin, looking in vain for references to the zoo. Alexandra Richie mentions it in passing when she describes the sad scene that Russian soldiers uncovered as they entered the zoo during the Battle of Berlin, but otherwise her magnificent account bypasses the subject.[29] In Wolfgang Ribbe's exhaustive two-volume history of the German capital, the zoo does not merit even a footnote.[30]

Prepared for the worst when I entered the archives, I was intrigued—but not yet convinced—by some basic facts around the Berlin zoo, and German zoos in general: Alexander von Humboldt, Germany's greatest naturalist and an iconic figure in Germany today, was an ardent proponent for establishing a zoo in the German capital. In the latter half of the nineteenth century, Berlin's largest restaurant was in the zoo. Germany had more zoos than any other European country at the dawn of the twentieth century. During its exhibits of "exotic" humans at the end of the nineteenth century, as many as 100,000 people visited the zoo on one day, nearly 8 percent of the city's entire population. The Nazis accorded zoos a special exemption from wartime austerity measures, and the director during that era, Lutz Heck, seemed to have resurrected a long-extinct animal. Evidently, the Nazis' warped ideas about eugenics and selective breeding applied to both the human and the animal world. In the postwar period, the East Berlin zoo alone—and there were five other zoos in East Germany—attracted bigger crowds than the entire Oberliga, East Germany's top soccer division. West German zoos similarly far eclipsed the Bundesliga, West Germany's top soccer tier, in visitor statistics.[31]

As the evidence mounted that the Berlin zoo was not simply a sideshow, I began to see the larger implications for it in Berlin's history. The fact that an exotic animal like an elephant was present in the Berlin zoo as early as 1857 meant that there had to be an intellectual curiosity about the broader world in the first place, a sufficient German presence abroad to arrange transportation, and an audience at home that was interested enough to come out and see the animal. And it was by no means self-evident how the zoo-goers would react. In the various political regimes in German history, zoo backers put exotic animals on display for reasons that reflected their own priorities. At their most benign, the organizers urged the visitors to expand their horizons by observing these animals from all over the world, seeing this as part of the zoo-goers' education as "whole" persons (*Bildung*), and even suggesting that they emulate the family loyalties on display in the animal world. At the most radical, the Nazi zoo highlighted the perils that awaited animals who mixed their genes with those of other species and thereby spread the mad Nazi message about race. The unknown, however, was how Berliners would respond to the animals on display and the implied messages of the zoo officials. Cultural offerings are always a dialogue between the user and the provider, and in many instances Berliners took away a softer message than the one the organizers intended.

The story of the Berlin zoo is not only about the educated, worldly, middle-class Germans who molded the zoo in their image nor about those ideologues who abused it shamelessly. It is also the story of the animals and humans on display and how they shaped Berliners' attitudes about their world. Rostom the elephant, Knautschke the hippo,

Okabak the Inuit elder, and Evi the sun bear came to be integral characters in Berlin's history. The profound impact of the zoo on Berliners, from creating in them sympathies with the natural world to an openness to the lands and peoples beyond Germany's borders, can hardly be considered inconsequential. It is time to bring the zoo in from the periphery of Berlin's history. There simply was no other institution in the city—professional soccer club, theater, museum, or hospital—that was so beloved, that exerted such a powerful influence on attitudes toward the natural world, and that was as much a part of daily life for Germans from all socioeconomic backgrounds over such a long period of time as the Berlin zoo.

I

Out from the Island of Peacocks

HAVING BEEN THOROUGHLY DEFEATED BY the French at the battles of Jena and Auerstadt in October 1806, the Prussian king Friedrich Wilhelm gathered his family together and began the humiliating flight from Napoleon's revolutionary armies. Several months later, the Prussian royal family, including two young boys, the future kings Friedrich Wilhelm and Wilhelm, arrived at their comfortable but far from regal quarters: a merchant's house in the city of Memel, deep in east Prussia. The beloved queen Luise, terribly weakened by the journey, took months to recover. It would be three years before the royal family returned to the Prussian capital and three years more before the French had been driven back across the Rhine and their self-proclaimed emperor dethroned.

With Napoleon safely ensconced in his island prison, Friedrich Wilhelm III arrived in Paris to survey the capital of his defeated foe and to discuss the postwar settlement. Considering the pressing matters at hand, he undertook a curious outing a day after his arrival. The triumphant Prussian king went to the zoo.[1] This was not, to be sure, just any zoo, but the first modern zoo,[2] the menagerie in the Jardin des Plantes, where during the revolution the king's animals, just like French citizens, had been freed from their noble overlords. The revolutionaries had placed some of the animals in the Jardin, but other captive animals—and not for the last time in European history—found themselves on the tables of the hungry citizens.[3] The remaining collection, which included lions, zebras, antelopes, and two elephants that the French army brought back from a menagerie in the Netherlands, captured the Prussian king's imagination.[4] During his several months' stay in Paris, Friedrich Wilhelm III visited the zoo frequently.

Inspired by what he had seen, Friedrich Wilhelm III returned to Berlin and began to establish a menagerie, as had many regents in the German lands. Unlike the majority of his contemporaries, however, the Prussian king wanted his display of exotic animals to be open to the public.[5] Located on the Island of Peacocks in the Havel River, a short distance from the royal palace in Potsdam and a pleasant day-trip from Berlin, Friedrich Wilhelm's menagerie initially housed peacocks, birds of prey, and monkeys. Later, deer, buffalo, boars, foxes, wolves, and bears would join the king's animal display—many of which he fed with his own hand.[6] Although the king occasionally gave in to his subjects' thirst for the exotic, as was evident in the kangaroos on display, his preference was for "aesthetic" animals that complemented the tranquil nature of the island. As a case in point, he asked the owner of a traveling menagerie for a "non-predatory" animal, as he phrased it, in return for the Brazilian ocelot he had received as a gift.[7]

Twelve years after its establishment, the Island of Peacocks housed more than 800 animals and had become such a popular destination for Berliners that it had its own train station. The king even felt compelled to limit access to three days per week so as not to overwhelm the animals.[8] Theodor Fontane, that brilliant observer of the Brandenburg region that surrounds Berlin, was awestruck by the vista before him when as a child he undertook his first trip to the king's menagerie: "The Island of Peacocks! As if in a fairy tale, the image from my childhood days rises before me: A castle, palm trees, and kangaroos; parrots squawk; peacocks perch on high branches or turn a cartwheel. Aviaries. Fountains. Tree-covered meadows. Winding paths that go everywhere and nowhere. An island full of riddles, an oasis. A carpet of flowers in the middle of the [Province]."[9]

Christian Ludwig Brehms, an unassuming pastor from Renthendorf who was also an amateur ornithologist, was similarly struck when he visited the island in 1832. His report, a rare glimpse of animal life on the island, captured the astonishment of the many Berliners who visited the island. He marveled at the animals. Their size surprised him—the bear was much larger than he thought, the hunchback ox much smaller—as did their movements, sometimes slow and deliberate like the kangaroo, sometimes in odd patterns, like the lion who refused to cross to the far reaches of his enclosure. Above all, Brehms, like many others, was shocked by the fact that the animals were alive. The most common experience that Germans of that era would have had with animals from beyond Germany's borders would have been with static, taxidermied animals on display in a contrived setting in a museum. But here the animals were in motion, eating, leaping, lunging, and howling. "The strangest part of the island for me," Brehms stated in his report, "was the living animals.... The kangaroos I found very interesting. They jump about their open grassy space, but seek refuge in a small building during thunderstorms. Here one can observe very clearly how these animals jump with their hind legs. And these jumps are tremendous. Even odder to me was their slow walk. They position themselves on their front legs and tail, and slowly bring their hind legs forward. The tail in this process represents a fifth leg. It almost looks like when someone is on crutches."[10]

Although the Prussian king was a sentimental man with a genuine concern for animals, he had little knowledge of how to keep animals in captivity. In the early nineteenth century, such knowledge resided primarily with the odd collection of showmen who ran traveling menageries. Strange and wondrous animals had been appearing in Europe from the fifteenth century, when an Egyptian noble family provided a gift of a giraffe to Lorenzo de' Medici. That famous giraffe makes an appearance in Renaissance artist Piero di Cosimo's 1490 painting *Vulcan and Aeolus*, currently hanging in the National Gallery of Canada, to symbolize how Europeans saw the unusual creature as proof of the richness of God's earthly creations.[11] One can scarcely imagine how awestruck Hamburgers would have been in 1638 when a traveling menagerie brought to town an Asian elephant (the much larger African elephant would not appear in Germany for another 200 years), or in 1746 when a rhinoceros was put on display in a fishing hut on Berlin's Spittelmarkt near the central canal, prompting school-children throughout the city to sing in the streets: "In order to see the rhino roam, I resolved to leave my home."[12] In 1776, the Dutch East India Company delivered to William V's menagerie in Holland the first orangutan ever to be displayed in Europe.[13] The most intriguing of the apes, the gorilla, long thought to be mythical, would not be exhibited alive in Europe until 1855 and remained a rarity well into the twentieth century. Over the course of the eighteenth century hundreds of circus-like menageries fanned across the continent, bringing Europeans a burst of the exotic in what were otherwise predictable lives in a circumscribed world.

The king turned to the traveler, scientist, and regular observer of traveling menageries Martin Hinrich Lichtenstein to help him with his collection of animals. He, along with Alexander von Humboldt, was to become the driving force behind Germany's first zoo. A physician by training, Lichtenstein was part of a generation of well-to-do middle-class Germans drawn to explore and engage with the broader world. In his account of his travels in South Africa in the first years of the nineteenth century published shortly after his return to Berlin, he writes of what drew him to a colony that was at the time a five-month sea voyage away in favorable winds:

> An unconquerable inclination to try my powers amid the vicissitudes and toils of wandering through new climes and under a different heaven; an ardent desire to be acquainted with a country upon which, even in my boyish years, my imagination had eagerly dwelt, and since my arrival at a maturer age I had always had an unbounded curiosity to explore, induced me to offer my services to the governor, who, a short time before his departure, was seeking out a tutor from Germany for his son, then thirteen years of age.[14]

Lichtenstein spent the next four years as tutor and the attending physician to the governor of the Dutch Cape Colony in South Africa, exploring vast reaches of the colony, observing indigenous peoples, and collecting species. From his lengthy account of his time in Africa (nearly 1,300 pages over two volumes), a picture emerges of a wide-eyed young man, profoundly curious about animal life on earth and about other peoples. He diligently recorded native languages in his field notebooks, which formed the basis of embryonic dictionaries he published upon his return. He genuinely admired much about the area, from local basketmaking to the wide rivers and majestic peaks, which he was eager to climb. As if a visitor in a fairy tale land, Lichtenstein related countless anecdotes from his travels, one of a man who was 120 years old, another of a deaf and dumb "genius" who miraculously produced beautiful woodwork without patterns to follow, and many other tales of witch doctors. He described in minute detail every local custom he encountered, including the elephant hunt. According to his account, when a hunter killed an elephant, locals approached the animal and gently whispered in its ear that its death was unintentional. They then cut off the trunk and buried it while chanting: "The elephant is a great lord, and the trunk is his hand."[15]

The naturalist Martin Hinrich Lichtenstein, along with Alexander von Humboldt, pushed for a zoo in the German capital. The king appointed him the first director of the Berlin zoo. *Berlin Zoo Archive*

His fascination with the fauna he encountered would lead to a lifelong professional occupation with animals. In South Africa, he kept a flock of flamingos in his camp and delighted in netting butterflies, his favorite species.[16] Having witnessed a native ritual in which local hunters trapped a panther in a pit and then set hyenas upon it, Lichtenstein wrote of the animal:

> Two of the dogs bit the throat, so that the panther within 15 minutes showed no further sign of life. Until that point he defended himself with his claws and wounded one dog so badly that it died the following day. At the dissection of the animal, I found all muscles of the throat and neck to have been ripped apart, but the hide itself, which is extremely tough and protected by thick hair, did not have a single hole. Since it was intact otherwise, I bought it from the owner of the land for the usual price of 10 Thalers and took as a "bonus" for my own collection the skull and other unusual parts.[17]

Lichtenstein's clinical descriptions of animals were not entirely different from his descriptions of human life, albeit laced with his era's mindset of racial hierarchy. He ranked tribes along a spectrum of civilization. He admired the Hottentots for their "ear for music,"[18] but other tribes were the object of his scorn, most notably the "Bushmen," whom he describes viciously:

> There are likely no other savages on this Earth, whose entire physical being is closer to that of an animal, whose needs, concerns, pleasures are simpler, and who are more incapable of culture, than the Bushmen. What is certain is that you will not find another savage people, who possess a similar level of animal rawness combined with cunning. They never encounter their foe in an open field. A gunshot suffices to chase hundreds of them away, and whoever should run at them armed with a truncheon need not fear any resistance from them. On the contrary: Their way of waging war is to ambush their opponent with an arrow to the back.[19]

Lichtenstein is somewhat kinder to the Caffre peoples, but his account still rings, unsurprisingly, with European superiority:

The universal characteristics of all the tribes of this great nation consist in an external form and figure varying exceedingly from the other nations of Africa. They are much taller, stronger, and their limbs much better proportioned. Their color is brown—their hair black and wooly . . . .

Their language is full-toned, soft and harmonious, and spoken without clattering . . . . In peace addicted to indolence; frugal and temperate, loving cleanliness and ornament, and respecting wedded faith. They have in general good natural understandings; but the most sensible are, notwithstanding, addicted to the grossest superstition.

These may be called the characteristic features of the nation at large. While in them will be recognized a more than half uncivilized race, the Caffres must be acknowledged a very distinct people from their next neighbors the Hottentots . . . ; the latter are much lower in stature, poor in understanding and in speech, without government or laws—without any distinction of property: such a race are as distinct from the Caffres, as a Muslim from a Briton.[20]

After his return to Berlin, Lichtenstein enjoyed a reputation in the capital as someone—indeed, the only German—knowledgeable about the southernmost lands of Africa.[21] He also rapidly earned a reputation as Prussia's leading zoologist, although the discipline as such did not yet exist. His substantial personal collection of insects and plants obtained in Africa formed the basis of the zoological museum that he established a few years later at the university. Soon, anyone of stature with any question whatsoever related to animals turned to Lichtenstein. The great writer J. W. von Goethe repeatedly referred to Lichtenstein all matters animal related. When an acquaintance asked Goethe about the type of fur adorning an elegant woman in a restored painting, Goethe wrote to his correspondent: "We have closely examined the spotted hide that hangs over her shoulder. We have identified three similar examples in portraits from the beginning of the 16th century. Go ahead and ask Professor Lichtenstein—and tell him I sent you—whether he is aware of a small panther, roughly as big as a medium-sized cat. I tend to think that we are dealing with young animals whose hides arrived in Upper Italy through Venetian trade."[22]

In recognition of his expertise, the king called Lichtenstein to a professorship of natural sciences at the recently established University of Berlin, vaulting him to a place of prominence in Berlin society. He and his wife could often be found in some of Berlin's most prestigious salons, hobnobbing with artists, public servants, diplomats, and fellow world travelers.[23] In an 1839 painting by the court artist Franz Krüger, Lichtenstein was featured as one of Berlin's most prominent citizens, along with princes, artists, and military figures whose names adorn streets and plazas in today's Berlin: Johann Gottfried Schadow, P. J. Lenné, Karl Friedrich Schinkel, Wilhelm von Humboldt, and Friedrich von Savigny.[24] Lichtenstein was the embodiment of that segment of middle-class Germans, still politically powerless in the pre-1848 era but possessing increasing economic and cultural clout.

Lichtenstein's close friend and the other driving force behind the zoo was Alexander von Humboldt, the greatest German naturalist of his era. Much like his contemporary Charles Darwin, who would credit Humboldt with inspiring him to voyages of exploration, Humboldt sailed into Latin America's remote bays, collected rare species, recorded volcanic tremors, studied the Amazon River basin, and scaled mountains, including one in the Andes that, in this era before Everest had been conquered, geologists thought was the tallest mountain in the world.[25] Unlike most scientists of the day interested in rigidly classifying species, Humboldt sought to understand plant and animal life in its broader ecological context, taking account of soil, climate, currents, and elevations. He was a scrupulous observer, carting along scores of velvet-lined boxes with the latest scientific instruments in order to observe the big and the small, from the cosmos to the insect world. No fewer than eleven species and twelve geographic features are named after him.

Laden with species and soil samples from his voyage to Latin America, Humboldt returned to Berlin in 1805 a hero, "our conqueror of the world," as Goethe called him.[26] Friedrich Wilhelm III appointed him to the prestigious Academy of Sciences and a professorship at the University of Berlin. Upon his return to Berlin in 1827 from living in Paris, Humboldt was again the toast of the city, lecturing several times a week to a packed audience of hundreds at both the university and the local Music Academy. These wildly popular lectures caused scenes of pandemonium on the days they were held. "As newspapers announced the lectures," writes the historian Andrea Wulf, "people rushed to secure their seats. There were traffic jams on the days of the talks with policemen on horses trying to control the chaos. An hour before Humboldt took the podium, the auditorium was already crowded." Humboldt's brother, Wilhelm von Humboldt, exulted that Berlin had never seen anything like it.[27] His standing continued to rise, with an appointment in 1829 as privy counselor to the king and the accompanying title of "Excellency."[28]

Nearly two decades later, with the publication of his most important work, *Kosmos*, Alexander von Humboldt was again in the limelight. The first two volumes appeared in 1845 and 1847, and three subsequent volumes in 1850, 1858, and 1862. *Kosmos* struck a chord, selling out within two months of publication despite its sophisticated, oftentimes laborious writing style. The 1847 volume was the bestselling book of its day and the only book to breach the milestone of 10,000 copies.[29] Demand for the book was so great that agents tore open shipments of it destined for London and St. Petersburg so that they could supply local German bookstores.[30] To recognize his singular popularity, the king Friedrich Wilhelm IV commissioned a commemorative medal with an image of Humboldt on one side and the Sphinx on the other.[31]

Lichtenstein and Humboldt were fellow members of the Society of German Nature Researchers and Physicians (Gesellschaft deutscher Naturforscher und Ärtze), one of the many middle-class societies that sprang up around Germany in the first half of the nineteenth century. Lichtenstein's zoological knowledge complemented Humboldt's findings from his voyages, leading both to conclude that a more formal zoological display in the capital would serve to educate Berliners about the natural world. In July 1833, Lichtenstein approached the king, requesting funds to support a research trip to gather information on the London zoo. The choice of London is not at all surprising. The metropolis of 1.5 million inhabitants, nearly five times as many as in Berlin,[32] with trade and colonial networks that covered vast areas of the globe, was home to a collection of exotic animals that would not be seen on the Continent for years. The menagerie of the London Zoological Society located in Regent's Park housed animals that were the stuff of legend elsewhere: chimpanzees, orangutans, elephants, giraffes, rhinos, and hippos.[33] In requesting the king's support, Lichtenstein reasoned that the time was ripe to expand the collection on the Island of Peacocks, as advancing trade patterns made the acquisition of exotic animals a practical possibility that it had not been even a few years before. Alluding to England, Lichtenstein attempted to pique the king's interest: "Through the expansion of world traffic in shipping, a whole host of rare animals never before seen alive in Europe have been brought here."[34] Lichtenstein offered further justification of his trip in the importance of natural history for an informed population: "There is an increasing tendency in the English nation toward natural history. This tendency in the upper classes is thanks to one of the most splendid of institutions: the menagerie of the London zoological society, in which not only several thousand non-European creatures have been kept alive, but where many have been successfully bred." Lichtenstein further believed that his familiarity with England's model would ensure a successful outcome: "As a result of my three previous trips, I have become familiar with the language and traditions of England. I am also acquainted with the leading men in my field. Indeed, two years ago I was elected an honorary member of the London zoological society."[35]

As his letter reveals, the desire for a zoo in the Prussian capital was the result of a confluence of events. Shipping lanes became more crowded as Europe developed a sophisticated global trade network. Upper-class Germans open to the world saw the benefits of a zoo for science and for the education of their fellow citizens. Not to be underestimated is the extent to which rivalry with England added momentum to the push for a zoo. The subtext of Lichtenstein's revealing letter is that—as odd as this might sound today—Prussia was falling behind England because it lacked a zoo. It is telling that Lichtenstein framed his London trip in terms of trying to keep up with England: "Everywhere I see useful scientific instruments and scientific institutions that we must get to know right away if we do not wish to fall behind."[36] The Munich zoologist and scientific journal editor Johann Andreas Wagner echoed this sentiment years later on the eve of the founding of the Berlin zoo, lamenting: "What a wonderful opportunity [the zoo] has afforded English zoologists. How poor and limited in contrast are German zoologists without this resource."[37]

Lichtenstein's letters from London, a "world emporium" as he called it, are infused with a boyish enthusiasm that recalls his southern

African days nearly two decades prior. Shortly after his arrival, he wrote: "I feel perfectly well and find myself surrounded by the most astonishing things in the discipline of natural history . . . . When I head out in the morning, I frequently do not know where I should turn first, and return in the evenings intoxicated, and unable to record even the most important of what I have seen."[38] Lichtenstein crisscrossed England, immersing himself in the wonders of the natural world on display. He followed up a trip to the Greenwich observatory with a visit to the Surrey zoo to learn how to keep animals in captivity; then it was off to the British Museum, the private collection of the Bruton Street Society, and animal collections in Manchester and Liverpool.[39] "Not only the number, but the rarity and beauty of the animals on display is astounding," Lichtenstein exulted in a letter back to a royal courtier. "Odd, newly discovered species from the furthest reaches of the earth which one had experienced only as drawings in zoological texts, are already exhibited alive here."[40] As the reference to the "furthest ends of the earth" makes clear, Lichtenstein was awestruck by the trading power and global networks that allowed England to acquire such exotic animals. He makes the point again, in macabre fashion, in reference to the plight of London's monkeys: "Last year in London, almost all of the monkeys fell ill during the summer and by the fall most had died of a lung infection, just as they do in Germany. Such a loss hardly registers here, as ships arriving in the spring from warm parts of the earth can replenish the supply of monkeys at a reasonable cost." Again, less aghast at the death toll than impressed by England's global resources, Lichtenstein noted with a hint of jealousy that the Tower of London, which also housed a small collection of exotic animals, allowed its monkeys to die from cold in the winter and simply replaced them in the spring, as it was cheaper to do so than heat their cages.[41]

Lichtenstein's letters to his wife, in contrast to those he wrote to the king, dwell on the banalities of his daily routine, as one might expect, but they also offer an uncensored glimpse into what he believed to be the most important results of his trip. Above all, Lichtenstein was interested in acquiring British scientific instruments and British learning in the form of books. The ship with Lichtenstein's collection that left Britain's shores for Hamburg at the end of his British stay contained five micrometers that he purchased for his colleagues at the Academy in Berlin, a large number of books, and, in his words, a "very pretty" taxidermied collection of birds and a few mammals.[42]

His return trip to Berlin took him through Leyden and Frankfurt in order to view collections of various colleagues. (He also used his first stop on the Continent to take a jab at the British, writing to his wife: "I must tell you how well I feel. All of the reservations which I felt among the egotistical British in their fog and coal fumes, disappear here among my dear cordial Dutch.")[43] In Leyden, he studied a collection of plants and animals that Dr. Phillip Franz von Siebold, a German botanist and physician, had brought back from Japan. In Frankfurt he pored over the magnificent natural history collection of Eduard Rüppell, a German naturalist and frequent traveler to Africa, who had recently returned from Abyssinia. Having seen various collections, he concluded that the Berlin zoological museum (the precursor of Berlin's natural history museum, and distinct from the zoo) lagged others in terms of "splendor and value of the collection," but that, on the other hand, Berlin outshone its contemporaries in a category close to his heart—the ability to educate its visitors: "In functionality of the exhibit and the way it is organized to educate, [the Berlin zoological museum] eclipses them all. No other is its peer when it comes to consistent cleanliness and precision of nomenclature."[44] At least one prominent individual who delighted in the museum might have agreed with Lichtenstein's assessment: Charles Bonaparte, nephew (but hardly an admirer) of the deposed emperor and an avid amateur ornithologist, twice undertook the trip from Paris to Berlin to study the Berlin zoological museum's bird collection.[45]

Immediately following his 1833 trip to London to observe Europe's flagship zoo, Lichtenstein prepared a proposal for the establishment of a zoo in Berlin, but little came of it. It would take two further developments to make the zoo a reality—the establishment in Amsterdam of the first zoo on the European mainland and a new king on the Prussian throne. The Amsterdam zoo, known as Artis (the short form of Natura Artis Magistra, Latin for "nature is the teacher of art"), was a spectacular success, awash in funds that far surpassed those allotted to Amsterdam's art museums. Founded by prominent figures in banking and trade, Artis became a cultural center for Amsterdam's elite and a bold statement about Dutch colonial and commercial power. The zoo published journals for an international audience, held lectures for its members, hosted concerts, and established a library that had more than 5,000 volumes by 1862.[46] Unlike the Berlin zoo, which was open to the public from its inception, Artis was restricted to members until the mid-nineteenth century, when the general public was permitted entry (although the price effectively kept out the working class until the early twentieth century).[47] Nevertheless, as an elite cultural institution, it boosted Amsterdam's international reputation in the arts and sciences and became an important symbol of the city. The national art museum, home to the masterpieces of Vermeer and Rembrandt, would not be founded until nearly fifty years after the establishment of the zoo.

The death of Friedrich Wilhelm III in 1840 and the ascension to the throne of his eldest son provided the second impetus for the establishment of a zoo in Berlin, not the least because of the very close friendship between the king and the ardent supporter of the zoo, Humboldt. When he was heir to the throne, the future Friedrich Wilhelm IV selected Humboldt as his traveling companion, first to Russia in 1830 to visit Friedrich Wilhelm's sister, the wife of Tsar Nicholas I, and the following year to Warsaw.[48] By the time Friedrich Wilhelm IV had ascended the throne, Humboldt was dining with him almost nightly.[49] At the elegant—and by the standards of the time, modest—palace of Sans Souci, Friedrich Wilhelm IV reveled in Humboldt's friendship, granting him a permanent audience without the need to go first through other members of his court. The long conversations between Humboldt and the king meant that Humboldt could catch up on correspondence with his many friends and acquaintances only late at night, after the king had retired for the evening. And given Humboldt's prodigious letter writing, he was often up very late. As he lamented in a letter to the great Romantic poet August Wilhelm Schlegel on his tardy correspondence: "It is not that I suffer from a lack of good will, but rather that 3,000 letters to both parts of the world arise annually from my pen. I can never get to bed before two in the morning."[50] Humboldt was even permitted to use a bedroom in the king's summer residence of Charlottenhof, which was made famous many years later as the site of the post–World War II Potsdam conference.[51] The king's residence was teeming with prominent poets, historians, sculptors, and diplomats, but with the exception of the painter August Kopisch, none had the ear of the king as Humboldt did.[52] The noted historian Leopold von Ranke, the composer Felix Mendelssohn, the sculptor Bertel Thorvaldsen—all had to give way to the king's favorite naturalist. In one letter, the king even addressed his learned friend, at the time eighty-one years old, with the very familiar: "Salve! Alexandros!" (Humboldt was, on the other hand, careful never to take such liberties, always employing "Your Majesty" in his correspondence.)[53] When the king suffered a stroke toward the end of his life, Humboldt was one of the few people permitted an audience with the ailing monarch.[54]

The friendship between Humboldt and the king sprang in large part from the king's fascination with the natural world. Many evenings at the palace were taken up with Humboldt reading from his *Kosmos* manuscript to a small group of people, including the king, who hung on Humboldt's every word, and Leopold von Gerlach, a Prussian army general and the king's adjutant, who invariably fell asleep.[55] Apart from this shared interest, however, Humboldt and the king made an odd pair. Humboldt sided with the liberal aspirations of the increasingly powerful bourgeoisie for a constitution containing a catalogue of basic rights, including freedom of the press and a *Landtag* (provincial assembly) elected by universal male suffrage that would have considerably limited the king's powers. He also fought for rights for Jews, vehemently opposing an 1847 law that would have barred Jewish teachers from non-Jewish schools. It was nowhere more evident that his heart "beat with the democrats," as he himself said, than in 1848, when he emerged on the balcony of the palace to the cheers of the crowd who had gathered in the square below demanding constitutional change. The fighting that ensued after overzealous soldiers botched the king's order to clear the square peacefully resulted in the deaths of 200 Berliners. Humboldt took part, as did Germany's leading novelist Theodor Fontane, in a massive funeral for the "March heroes."[56] As it turned out, the fighting in Berlin, the bloodiest in any German city other than Vienna, went, in the short term, for naught.[57] One of the revolutionaries' key demands, universal male suffrage, which the king had granted in 1848, was replaced the following year by a watered-down three-class voting system that remained in place through World War I. Berlin's conservative mayor and symbol of the old regime, Heinrich Krausnick, removed amid jubilation in 1848, returned to his position in 1851 and went on to run the city for another eleven years.[58] The revolutionaries, for now, had been thoroughly defeated.

Although Friedrich Wilhelm IV was deeply saddened by the bloodshed, he had little sympathy with the political aspirations of the demonstrators, a stance that dismayed liberals who held out such hope when he came to the throne in 1840. Liberal expectations were not unfounded; one of the king's first acts was to call the Grimm brothers, dismissed from Göttingen University because of their support of constitutional rights, to the Prussian Academy of Sciences.[59] His personality also inspired liberal hopes. Indeed, Friedrich Wilhelm would not match most history students' idea of a Prussian monarch. A "Romantic on the throne," as scholars have dubbed him,[60] he had little inclination to things military, preferring to paint in quiet solitude rather than to strategize about geopolitics. His leading biographer puts it plainly: "He was the least martial monarch in Prussian history."[61] Somewhat unusually for the time, he genuinely loved his wife, Elise, although their marriage would remain childless, eventually allowing his brother to become the first emperor of a united Germany. He much preferred to stand in front of an audience where he might exercise his extraordinary gift for public speaking than to join in the kingly sport of hunting, which he made every effort to avoid. He was a dreamer, an unwavering supporter of the University of Berlin, which rose to glorious new heights under his patronage, and the last Prussian king to personally influence art and architecture of his day.[62] He was intimately involved in the establishment of Berlin's magnificent Neues Museum of antiquities, one of the most important projects of his reign and one that provided him a great deal of personal pleasure.[63] The director of Berlin's state museums rivaled Alexander von Humboldt for time spent in the presence of the monarch.[64]

Recognizing the opportunity presented by a new king on the throne, one who was so fond of Humboldt, Lichtenstein drafted a memorandum entitled "Thoughts on the Founding of a Zoological Garden in Berlin," based in large part on his observations in England during his 1833 trip. Of crucial importance to Lichtenstein was the zoo's role in education, conservation, and animal husbandry. He was adamant that the zoo not serve simply to satisfy the curiosity of visitors but that it breed "attractive and useful" animals, including crossing indigenous animals with foreign ones in order to improve German farming. Without this practical purpose, he believed, the zoo would have little chance of success.[65]

The concept of acclimatization, whereby foreign species would be adapted to local conditions and bred with domestic species for the improvement of domestic agriculture, had taken hold in Europe during the first half of the nineteenth century. Acclimatization required an inordinate amount of trial and error, but the prevailing view at the time was that successful breeding would provide a distinct advantage to Germany. "Should we succeed in naturalizing in Germany even one new animal," wrote the Frankfurt zoologist David Friedrich Weinland, "then the years of effort will have been worth it."[66] The idea of domesticating foreign animals was based in experience. Europe had witnessed many successful experiments in introducing non-indigenous animals for both pleasure and service, including the turkey, peacock, silver and golden pheasants, canaries, guinea pigs, and camels—not to mention crops like potato, tobacco, and corn.[67] It is telling that two of the zoo's most important founders, Peter Joseph Lenné, the landscape architect and director of royal gardens, and Lichtenstein, were members of the Prussian Acclimatization Society. The Berlin zoo was not alone among early zoos in forwarding domestication as a rationale for keeping exotic animals. A significant portion of the London Zoological Society wanted foreign animals domesticated for "English parks and tables."[68] Although breeding to maintain and expand the Berlin zoo's collection of exotic animals soon took place of prominence, acclimatization did not entirely disappear from the zoo's landscape until at least 1945.[69]

Although Friedrich Wilhelm IV was not as intrigued by animals as his father was, he gave permission to Lichtenstein in 1841 to develop with Humboldt and Lenné a proposal for a zoo in the Prussian capital.[70] They suggested that the zoo be established in the Tiergarten, just outside the city gates, where a facility for breeding pheasants and accompanying buildings already existed. The site was appealing in other ways, too. As a vast area of trees, grass, and ponds, it provided visitors with the opportunity to stroll, to enjoy the tranquility, and to take the air.[71] The zoo was eventually to be self-financing, primarily through the sale of shares, but the founders were aware that this day was still some time off. In the meantime, they requested from the king a loan of 15,000 thalers, a donation of the animals on the Island of Peacocks, and free use of the service buildings at the pheasantry. The king agreed to all three requests, although he made it clear that he would be unwilling to provide additional funds to support the zoo; the zoo would have to make a go of it on its own.[72]

The zoo's founders had the good of Berliners at heart. They hoped that the display in the Prussian capital of live animals from around the world would promote an interest in nature, and even inspire visual artists. They envisaged regular lectures by zoologists on animals in the zoo's collection and relaxing social spaces where Berliners could unwind. "We recommend serving refreshments," wrote one zoo founder to the king. "One station could serve various types of beer (but not spirits), another warm drinks, and a third confectionaries."[73] Many Berliners were also excited about the prospect of smoking at the zoo, an act that had been banned since 1787 on squares and streets of the capital.[74] This social component of the zoo, where Berliners could stroll, listen to bands, dine at the zoo's restaurant, Berlin's largest, cannot be overlooked. Throughout its history, the zoo was a place where Berliners came to see animals and Berlin society equally on display.

Prominent in the founders' arguments for a zoo was scientific research, although it must be said that many in the scientific community viewed the study of live animals with skepticism. The Berlin Academy of Sciences rejected Lichtenstein's plea for support of his zoo project, believing that little knowledge of life on earth could be gained by the passive observation of live animals. What mattered was anatomy, not behavior.[75] Nevertheless, in a letter to the king expressing his profound gratitude for the king's support of the zoo, Humboldt left no question as to the zoo's scientific role: "I express to you once again gratitude for your noble support of an institute that holds such promise for the sciences."[76]

The zoo founders did not simply pay lip service to this goal but engaged from the beginning in research on the animal collection. The zoo's first research project was meant to unravel the mystery of a kangaroo's birth. For years, the movement of a kangaroo embryo from the womb to the pouch had puzzled observers. Lichtenstein tasked the zoo's veterinarian with producing a report on the subject, but after years of observation he still could not determine how the tiny embryo appeared in the mother's pouch. He might have been comforted by the fact that it would be another century before researchers observed the embryo climb from the vagina to the pouch under its own strength and not, as was the common speculation, with the assistance of the mother.[77] Apart from zoo staff, many other researchers observed zoo animals in those early years, including university faculty and students and museum scientists.[78]

After nearly a decade of negotiations with the sovereign, the city of Berlin, and prominent Berliners, Lichtenstein and Humboldt finally had acquired the land and finances to begin building a zoo. A year prior to the zoo's grand opening in 1844, gardeners, diggers, and masons busied themselves preparing an enormous, untamed, area of the former royal hunting grounds for the arrival of animals.[79] The considerable area of the future zoo—until 1899, the Berlin zoo had the largest area of any zoo in the world[80]—needed to be fenced off and ponds built. Lenné's crew planted rose bushes and more than 4,000 trees.[81] Dozens of workers built bridges across the creeks that crisscrossed the Tiergarten, constructed from scratch a new building for the kangaroos, and set on new foundations two eagle's huts that had been transported from the Island of Peacocks. They dug a pit for the lions and fenced in the buffalo enclosure. And, of course, Lichtenstein needed to acquire animals for the zoo and transport them to Berlin. He traveled to Le Havre in France, the port of entry for so many global wares, where he purchased from animal traders for the sum of 866 thalers a raccoon, an agouti (South American rodent), several loris (Asian primate), and cockatoos. These animals, the first ever to be purchased for the zoo, were transported by water to Hamburg, before being placed in horse-drawn carriages for the five-day trip to Berlin. As the enclosures at the zoo were not yet ready for them, they spent the next few months at the Island of Peacocks.[82]

Shortly before the zoo opened, calamity struck: its prized possession, a lion, died on the Island of Peacocks before it could be transported to the zoo. It would be another two years before a lion made an appearance in Berlin, this one a gift from an unlikely source. Richard Lepsius, the greatest Egyptologist of his day, famous for raising the Prussian flag atop the Great Pyramid, donated it to the zoo following his 1845 expedition to Sudan.[83] Lichtenstein, well aware that the Berlin zoo could not do without a crowd-enticing display in its inaugural year, went to Hamburg, where he purchased monkeys from merchants on the city's docks. He did worry, however, about how long they would survive: "A large building for monkeys," he wrote in the summer of 1843, "tops the list of priorities. It would be not only the main draw for the public, but would allow the animals to live longer, and would make possible scientific research on them."[84]

Lichtenstein's concerns about the longevity of the animals were no doubt a reflection of his time in London, where monkeys succumbed to lung infections on a regular basis. The challenge for Lichtenstein was to balance the income from an entertaining animal like a monkey against the exorbitant costs of keeping them. The proposed monkey house alone was to cost nearly a third of the entire sum the king had provided to establish the zoo. As a result, and given the tight financial situation that was to be expected in the first years of the zoo, Lichtenstein sought out animals that fit within the zoo's budget but would still intrigue visitors: water birds, who would sit around the newly constructed ponds; beavers, with material on hand for their engineering feats; amphibians; and insects.[85]

In order to cover the staggering costs of acquiring and caring for exotic animals, the zoo founders turned to a model increasing in use in the early nineteenth century that took advantage of a middle class growing in prosperity: the joint-stock company. Between 1851 and 1857, Prussia alone witnessed the establishment of 119 joint-stock companies, a reflection of the remarkable industrial transformation taking place there.[86] Well-to-do middle-class Germans delighted in providing capital to entrepreneurs and saw their shares as a status symbol, making a point of bringing them up in conversation with their peers.[87] The joint-stock company was one way that the middle class could flex muscle that had been denied them in the political arena. The zoo founders' desire for a joint-stock company was not without controversy, however. Fearing that it would change the emphasis from scientific research to sheer profit making, the king made clear in his order of February 13, 1843, that the society to oversee the zoo was quite specifically *not* to sell shares. The founders were able to obtain approval for the joint-stock company only by embedding into the company's statutes explicit provisions that the zoo existed for the well-being of science and society and not to turn a profit for shareholders. Expansion of the animal collection, breeding programs, scientific research, youth education—all of these were to come before profits.[88]

And perhaps for that reason, the sale of shares in the zoo flopped. The founders hoped that putting 500 shares on the market, at a cost of 100 thalers each, would fill the zoo's coffers with at least 30,000 thalers. They were sorely disappointed. Even though the initial shareholders were some of the most prominent people in town, such as the mayor, Franz Christian Naunyn; the director of the gas works; the director of the royal museums; the founder of a school for the blind and an individual whose tireless efforts singlehandedly improved the lives of Berlin's blind people, August Zeune; and a tobacco manufacturer, there were simply not enough of Berlin's wealthy upper class.[89] Where was, for example, August Borsig? One of Berlin's most successful industrialists, he established a plant just outside Berlin's Oranienburger gate in 1837 that became Europe's largest producer of steam locomotives.[90] In barely a decade, his operation had grown rapidly, covering ten times the area of the original factory. Berliners nicknamed the area of town that housed his sprawling group of factories "Land of Fire" after the numerous smokestacks and chimneys that spewed flames day and night.[91] Although we do not know why Borsig refused to purchase shares, the fact that one of Europe's wealthiest individuals did not financially support the zoo reveals the major challenges that Humboldt and Lichtenstein faced in establishing Germany's first zoo.

Of the first 500 shares, just over 100 had been sold a year after they were put on sale,[92] and a high percentage were bought by individuals on the state's payroll.[93] In a letter to the king, the founders lamented the lack of support among Berlin's industrial upper crust: "The participation in particular of the richest and highest-standing residents of the royal capital has been far less than anticipated."[94] And the founders were correct to point the finger at the higher-income earners. In 1898 a share in the zoo would have cost a factory worker a year's wages,[95] but there were plenty of industrialists, like Borsig, enjoying a windfall.[96]

All other German zoos of the nineteenth century followed Berlin's lead and adopted the model of the shareholding company to raise capital, frequently because the absence of royal support left them no other choice. This was true in Dresden, Frankfurt, Halle, Leipzig (which was not initially a shareholding company but became one to finance expansion twenty years after it opened),[97] Hamburg, Cologne, and, somewhat later, Nuremberg.[98] Other cities proved more successful in raising funds from their residents. Frankfurt, for example, overshot its goal by nearly 80 percent on its first offering and had nearly twice as many shareholders as in Berlin.[99] Even the much smaller Hannover, where the sales of shares were disappointing to the zoo founders, still managed to outraise Berlin.[100]

The lack of income from shares, combined with decent but not over-whelming crowds, led Minister of Culture Johann Eichhorn to plead with the king for an infusion of 25,000 thalers—10,000 more than he had initially provided—and an annual subvention of 15,000 thalers for the next ten years. He justified his request on the basis of the exorbitant costs of running a zoo. Food alone accounted for two-thirds of the entire budget, nearly triple the costs of salaries. The zoo founders were desperate to obtain a large, exotic animal like a giraffe or an elephant in order to attract crowds, but the acquisition and upkeep of an elephant was nearly 9,000 thalers, an amount that would cover the maintenance costs of all other animals combined.[101] Added to this was the desperate situation of housing the animals. "Our resources do not even cover costs that must be incurred," wrote Minister Eichhorn to the king in the summer of 1846. "Above all here I would mention a new, roomier and healthier building to house the animals in winter. Only a new building will reduce the all-too-high incidence of death among animals."[102] In their plea to the king, the founders were anxious to demonstrate that they had observed that most desired of Prussian qualities—thrift. They pointed out that the zoo had begun feeding the animals horsemeat instead of beef. (In 1855, the zoo would establish an abattoir with the sole purpose of slaughtering horses for animal feed.) And as a mere five keepers tended the nearly 300 animals, the zoo could also hardly be accused of overspending on staff.[103]

The zoo also had much to boast about, as the founders made clear in their appeal. In the first two years, more than 6,000 people had come through the gates. The relatively robust attendance was partly the result of the fact that the zoo was open to all, not just to a select group of the upper class as was the case in the London zoo,[104] and partly due to the many subsidized educational visits. In an act of egalitarianism remark-able for the era, pupils and students from every level of education and socioeconomic background were able to take advantage of discounted rates. As one of the founders explained: "We have received no less than

9333.27 Thalers through admissions, although all shareholders receive free entry for themselves and their families, and all educational establishments, from universities to elementary schools to schools for the poor, are accorded entry either at reduced rates or completely free."[105]

Volksaufklärung, or enlightenment of the population, came to occupy a place of prominence in the zoo's mission, as the founders repeatedly made clear in their letters to the king. Educating the general public was itself a reflection of the liberalizing tendencies among the German elite, who believed that individual education was the key to political empowerment. Exposure to the natural world and contemplation of non-human life were to expand an individual's mental horizons and contribute to their political emancipation.[106] Founders hoped that Berliners might reflect on their own political reality following an afternoon spent observing an almost mythical otherworld that they had previously not ever imagined.

Believing that rising attendance would solve the zoo's financial woes, the king denied the minister of culture's request for a long-term commitment of royal funds.[107] The timing, then, could hardly have been worse when in 1846 an epidemic wiped out a considerable portion of the zoo's collection, including its most valuable animals: the sole lion, two leopards, two kangaroos, a bear from North America, a llama, three marsupials, a Brazilian porcupine, two deer and a stag, eight monkeys, both giant tortoises, a crocodile, two peacocks from Java, four rare parrots, and many other birds.[108] No one at the time could have imagined that the zoo, in a desperate financial situation and lacking any major popular animals, would go on to an uninterrupted existence of 170 years. Given that the zoo had lost the majority of its popular animals to disease, the king responded positively to a renewed request for financial support. For a brief time in 1847, the zoo's fortunes seemed to turn. Lichtenstein giddily reported in the summer of that year: "The cages are once again full. Even a harbor seal swims again in the pond.... A considerable number of beautiful and rare parrots, an aviary with African songbirds, a genuine golden eagle, and two falcons are acquisitions from abroad that have entered the zoo since the spring." These animals would be joined by several star attractions in the fall that fell into the lap of the zoo. The French general in Algiers, Jussuf, presented two young lions to the king of Prussia in September, along with two adult ostriches and two gazelles.[109] The lengthy journey from the animals' home country to the Prussian capital is a reminder of the slow pace of transportation in the nineteenth century compared to our world. After a sea voyage of several days, the animals arrived in the port of Marseilles in April, where they resided for nearly four months awaiting further transportation by horse and carriage to Strasbourg. By the time they had arrived in Berlin, the animals had been en route for nearly six months.[110]

The glory of 1847 turned out to be short-lived. A poor harvest in the surrounding countryside led to the price of foodstuffs doubling from a few years earlier. In Berlin, crowds attacked the stalls that potato vendors had set up on various city squares, cutting open their sacks and making off with the potatoes.[111] These potato riots were a prelude to the revolutionary events of March 1848, when Berliners took to the barricades demanding more participation in government. Street fighting and political upheaval unsettled Berliners, who eschewed the capital's cultural attractions. Attendance at the zoo plummeted. The zoo directorship believed that the residents of the capital were staying away for financial reasons and so introduced the "cheap Sunday," which offered half-price admission on Sundays and holidays. But the measure was not enough to solve the problem, as 1848 witnessed the worst attendance in the four-year history of the zoo. Although attendance would improve in the coming years, for the next several decades the zoo was in dire financial straits that lasted until the surge in Berlin's population in the 1860s and its elevation to imperial capital following unification. The king was forced to bail out building projects in 1849, 1850, 1852, and 1853, the latter the most expensive intervention for a capital project at the zoo to date, when he paid 6,000 thalers for a building to house the big cats.[112] His last subsidy to the zoo, 5,000 thalers for a building to house cattle, came in 1857.

Despite its financial woes and an animal collection that rose and fell, the zoo from the outset continued its efforts to educate Berliners about the natural world. In those early years of the zoo, however, nature was presented less as an object of wonderment than as something to be conquered. It would be difficult to argue that the founders of the Berlin zoo were concerned about the welfare of animals, beyond the simple fact that they needed animals in the zoo for their broader educational and scientific goals. To be sure, Lichtenstein was aghast that some visitors were placing burning cigarettes in the hands of monkeys, but he also promoted social dinners where "surplus" zoo animals were served up. For example, in 1846 shareholders were invited to the zoo to dine on zebu, an Asian humped cattle. The actor Louis Schneider's memory of the evening suggests that the guests enjoyed themselves enormously: "In 1846, the Association of Share Holders in the Zoological Garden, to which I belonged, held a gala at which the meat of a zebu cattle was consumed. For the lively and jocular evening, I wrote a humorous after-dinner speech. My talk had such an effect, that newspaper reports the following day spoke of the jokes as something quite wonderful."[113] Even the king heard about Schneider's after-dinner speech and requested that he repeat it for him, which Schneider was reluctant to do given that it contained some off-color remarks designed to wrap up a "happy and boisterous" evening, as he called it. This joviality that accompanied the consumption of a zoo animal, an act unthinkable in Europe today, helps to capture the era's belief in the servitude of animals.

Early zoo visitor's guides also reflect this view that animals existed to be dominated by humans. Whenever possible, descriptions of the animals refer to their savage behavior. The jaguar is "extremely dangerous" to cattle, which it "kills and drags into the bushes." The hyena is "so strong it can carry off a man." The leopard is "bloodthirsty and cruel." Hunting a chamois [mountain goat-antelope] could be "very dangerous." A buffalo "has a drooping head, a nasty look and a sunken neck and can be dangerous if it glimpses red clothing." On occasion, the emphasis on their "wildness" approaches the absurd, as in the description of the young lion pair: "These two lions used to live with a dog in the enclosure, but recently they killed it." Even the hamster had a "nasty bite." The guides convey the message that these savage animals had been subdued by their human masters and can now be safely observed. This sentiment comes out clearly in the way the zoo visitor's guides go out of their way to indicate animals that can be tamed, some of which stretch credulity. It could well be that the Rocco chicken from South America "is easily tamed," but the claim that a raccoon "can be as tame as a pet" or that a jaguar, if obtained at a young age, "can be raised like a dog" suggests that the author never tried to do so. The visitor's guides also take pleasure in highlighting that bears can be taught "dancing and other antics."[114]

The visitor's guides and information plaques gave visitors the impression that animals were not wonders of nature with an intrinsic value that enhances life on earth, but rather they represented a "wild" that had been put in its place by human hand. A visitor to the Berlin zoo in 1846 would come away with the impression of base, savage animals that were now safely behind bars and could be contemplated at leisure by onlookers. They were not in the least romanticized. It would have been apparent to any zoo-goer in the mid-nineteenth century that nature had been conquered.[115]

The zoo was in this way a culmination of centuries of interest by Europeans in a nature that, in their view, humans needed to study, catalogue, de-mystify, and control. Natural history began to emerge as a scientific discipline in Europe at the end of the eighteenth century, spurred in large part by two individuals who undertook the arduous task of naming and ordering life on earth: Georges Louis Leclerc (later Conte de Buffon), director of the Jardin du Roi, and Carl Linnaeus, a Swedish naturalist who was the originator of the two-word Latin description of an animal to denote genus and species (such as *Homo sapiens*). He believed that a systematic categorization of earth's creatures would reveal a balanced and harmonious system—and the hand of God—and thus proceeded to give names to every known species on Earth, a total at the time of 4,378.[116] Following directly in the footsteps of Buffon and Linnaeus was Charles Lucien Bonaparte, the nephew of the emperor, who died before he could compile a list of all 7,000 bird species.[117] Their approach informed the manner in which animals would be exhibited in a zoo—by taxonomy and common traits rather than the method of ecosystem typically used today.

The eighteenth century witnessed regular expeditions sent out by European courts to gather information about the world beyond the seas. The House of Habsburg sent an expedition to the West Indies in 1754, another to North America in 1783, and a third to Africa to collect live animals and plants in the same year.[118] Perhaps the most significant of these voyages was that of James Cook, who circumnavigated the globe twice, once beginning in 1768 and the second in 1772, bringing him to New Zealand, Chile, South Africa, and the South Pacific. Although gathered on voyages sponsored by the British Crown, much of the knowledge about the flora and fauna resided in Germany in the persons of Johann Reinhold Forster and his son Georg, the naturalists who accompanied Cook on his second voyage.[119] The elder Forster returned to Germany after his time with Cook to become professor of natural history at the University of Halle and director of the botanical gardens there. Lichtenstein would later help to ensure that Forster's magnificent descriptions of the animals he encountered would see the light of day, editing his *Descriptiones animalium*, which appeared in 1844.

What began as a steady stream of exotic animals and plants entering Germany from the cargo holds of ships of exploration in the eighteenth century became a deluge in the nineteenth century. Soon, no overseas voyage of exploration was complete without a naturalist on board. Charles Darwin's great theories, it should be remembered, were based not primarily on his five-year voyage across the seas but on careful study over twenty years of the extensive collections in London and Cambridge.[120] Lichtenstein played a key role in arranging for many of Prussia's expeditions abroad, including a voyage to British Guyana in 1840, which returned in 1844 with plant, soil, and mineral samples as well as several exotic species. Humboldt was anxious to see the large electric eel that had been captured, an animal that had fascinated him on his own South American voyage years earlier, but he would be sorely disappointed. After a sea voyage of several months, the ship carrying the eel docked in Southampton, England. A sailor accidentally bumped the barrel containing the eel as it was being unloaded, knocking it to the ground and killing the eel.[121] Other animals from the expedition found their way to the Berlin zoo, however, including a giant snake, a cayman, several kangaroos, and the prize of them all, a South American eagle, an animal, Lichtenstein noted with satisfaction, that the London zoo did not yet possess.[122] Another German researcher, Johann Jakob von Tschudi, returned from his voyage to Peru in 1842 with a turtle for the zoo.[123]

The most striking example of a naturalist mission abroad, however, must be that of Christian Gottfried Ehrenberg and Wilhelm Hemprich through the Near East between 1820 and 1825, also arranged by Lichtenstein and Humboldt. They returned with a collection that staggers the imagination: 34,000 animals and 46,000 plant samples in more than 100 crates.[124] The vast majority of this mammoth collection resided for 120 years in Berlin's zoological museum before it was obliterated during an aerial bombing in February 1945. Hemprich paid a price that so many explorers paid, dying of fever at the end of his voyage, but Ehrenberg continued his explorations, joining Humboldt on his journey through Siberia to the border of China in 1829.[125]

The German public learned of these voyages of discovery through popular publications, clubs, and societies, an astounding number of which dealt with aspects of the natural world. Nature societies simply became part of the civil society landscape. Their collections formed the basis for some of the world's greatest, and most popular, natural history museums, including the British Museum, which opened in 1881, and the Museum of Natural History in Berlin, founded in 1889. The number of natural history museums rose exponentially in the following decade, so that by the turn of the century Germany had 150 natural history museums, while Britain and the United States had 250 each.[126] But there were also geographic societies, homeopathic societies, tourist societies, bird protection societies, Alps clubs, and countless others.[127]

Natural history magazines and journals, targeting the lay reader rather than the scientist, enjoyed rapid growth. The first major natural history journal, *Die Natur*, appeared in 1852, its articles focused on detailed descriptions of animals and sophisticated comparisons of species. Its popularity would carry it for the next fifty years before it closed in the early twentieth century.[128] *Die Gartenlaube* (The Garden Arbor), a natural history journal founded in Leipzig in 1853 by the book dealer Ernst Keil and in which the Berlin zoo was prominently featured, had a circulation of more than 382,000 in 1875—the largest circulation of any periodical in Germany.[129] One of the star contributors to *Die Gartenlaube* was Alfred Brehm, a zoologist who had explored Egypt and Sudan, an enormously successful author of the natural world, later director of the Hamburg zoo and subsequently the first director of the Berlin Aquarium.[130] *Die Gartenlaube*, along with other family journals like *Buch der Welt* and *Westermanns Monatshefte*, enthralled readers with new discoveries about animal behavior, updates on popular animals in European zoos, and travelogues about exotic peoples, flora, and fauna overseas.[131] *Isis*, the well-respected journal of the Dresden nature society of the same name, enjoyed robust circulation. Perhaps most important, these journals were all lavishly illustrated, piquing popular curiosity in the natural world.[132] Popular publications like these were no doubt carried aloft by the rapid increase in literacy in the German lands, which rose from 25 percent at the beginning of the century to 75 percent in 1870 and reached close to 100 percent on the eve of World War I. Not surprisingly, newspapers flourished, too. In 1780, there were 700 newspapers in Germany. A century later, there were more than double that number.[133] Between weeklies and dailies, a reader in Berlin in 1862 had the choice of 90 newspapers.[134]

Although the excitement around natural history was more pronounced in Germany, other countries in this era witnessed a spike in popular outlets for natural history. A journal similar to *Die Gartenlaube* appeared in England in 1832 with the delightful title *The Penny Magazine of the Society for the Diffusion of Useful Knowledge*.[135] John James Audubon's book *The Birds of America* swept through the United States at the same time, and the first Dutch journal of zoology, published by the Amsterdam zoo, would appear a few years later.[136]

The central figures in the early years of the Berlin zoo, Humboldt and Lichtenstein, had themselves all undertaken expeditions to the far reaches of the earth. Upon their return, they actively sponsored others to do the same, filling the cages of the zoo and the display cases of the natural history museum with exotic flora and fauna, from British Guyana to Peru, from the Mideast to Siberia. During their trips to London and Paris, Humboldt and Lichtenstein were surrounded by other German scholars who had sought out Europe's worldly metropolises. Founding members of zoos elsewhere also had firsthand experience with exotic nature, including Alfred Brehm, Hamburg's first zoo director, who had spent five years in Egypt and Sudan. As is clear from an entry in his journal, his time abroad left with him a deep appreciation for animal life: "I had God's sun and his holy nature. I had in my encampment my own little world. How many pleasures brought me my tame ibises and the other large animals; oh, how the monkeys flatter me, how Bachilda, my tame lion, caresses me .... She follows me around like a dog, shares nights in the camp with me, and is so well-behaved. Through these lions I've learned that animals can replace humans."[137]

The first scientific director of the Frankfurt zoo, David Friedrich Weinland, became director of the laboratory at the Museum for Comparative Zoology at Harvard in 1855, before traveling to Canada and then on to Haiti, where he studied the coral reefs. Although he did not have much direct contact with animal life in Haiti, he did manage to keep a pet raccoon during his stay. Farther afield, the Paris Jardin founder Bernardin de Saint-Pierre had been influenced by his time in Mauritius, while Sir Stamford Raffles relied on his experiences during his five-year stay in Malaya and later as deputy governor of Java when he established the London zoo.[138]

This interest in the natural world beyond Germany's borders occurred at a time when Germany was preoccupied with trade routes and overseas markets for its products. Liberals in the Frankfurt parliament urged the king to adopt a national overseas policy that would secure markets for German businesses, many of which were expanding overseas willy-nilly. The Meubrinck silk factory exported to Mexico and Brazil, while the Sußmann & Wiesenthal cotton plant supplied Asia and the Americas. The Treu & Nuglisch perfume factory shipped its products to Hungary, Italy, and Turkey. There was more to Germany's interest in securing overseas markets than solely to improve the domestic economy, however. A sense of establishing Germany as a global presence, as a "brand," permeates the desire to engage with the burgeoning overseas trade. As early as 1815, Joachim Nettelbeck captured the spirit of the age with his pronouncement that Prussia must be "great, blooming, and respected on the other side of the world's oceans."[139] In his monumental *History of Prussian Politics*, Johann Gustav Droysen talked of "Germany's Duty in the World," which was but an updated version of Nettelbeck's thoughts. In the second half of the nineteenth century, German scholars and adventurers, businessmen and diplomats, by their very presence abroad, brought a message of Prussia's rise to greatness to the far reaches of the globe. This same class of citizens returned home with an awareness of the vastness and diversity of the globe, one that found an outlet in the Berlin zoo.

In many ways the image of Richard Lepsius, the noted Egyptologist, raising the flag of Prussia on the Great Pyramid of Giza, captures the zeitgeist. His 1842 expedition, financed by the king, was a triumph for Prussian science and helped to develop the realm of cultural politics. The zoo, like Lepsius's flag raising, was also a badge of honor for Prussia, an institute to promote Prussian science and learning, and a way of keeping up with England in the international arena—a gap that was brought home in the tales of the many Germans who visited the world's fair in London in 1851. In this regard, it is perhaps not so surprising that Prussia's representatives overseas undertook herculean efforts to support the zoo. The Prussian consul in Alexandria, Egypt, secured a number of animals, including lions, leopards, ostriches, and monkeys, for the zoo in the Prussian capital. In St. Louis, Missouri, the Prussian counsel obtained a young wapiti for the zoo. Count Schlieffen, later chief of the Imperial German General Staff and the originator of the 1905 military plan for an invasion of France, donated to the zoo its first two giraffes.[140]

Lichtenstein, who personified the worldly German drawn to the lands beyond Germany's borders, led the Berlin zoo for the first thirteen years of its turbulent existence until his death at the age of seventy-seven on a postal ship while returning from a conference in Stockholm in 1857. The sudden loss of the Berlin zoo's first director necessitated a search for a successor to assume the leadership of what was still Germany's only zoo. Hartwig Peters, an individual with a remarkably similar biography to Lichtenstein, became the second director in the zoo's history. An efficient administrator but uninspiring leader, Peters would enter history as a caretaker zoo director between the brilliant originator Lichtenstein and the dynamic Heinrich Bodinus, under whom the Berlin zoo exploded into a cultural phenomenon.

Also a physician by training, Peters had succeeded Lichtenstein as professor of zoology at the University of Berlin. He, too, developed an interest in the natural world based on voyages of exploration. His beautifully illustrated account of his six-year voyage to East Africa, *Naturwissenschaftliche Reise nach Mossambique*, is breathtaking in its detailed descriptions of the enormous variety of animal life that he encountered: mammals, birds, amphibians, fish, and insects. To recognize this encyclopedic book about one of his country's possessions, the king of Portugal named Peters an officer of the Order of Santiago.[141] In the tradition of Linnaeus and Buffon, Peters was above all concerned with describing animals not by behavior but by physical features, both inside and out. Taxonomy and classification of species were his overriding interests. So, for example, he brought with him on his voyage South African rhinoceros skulls to compare with the rhinoceros of eastern Africa. On a meerkat, he was intrigued in particular by the coloring: "The skin of the face, nose, eyelids, and cheeks are of a black-violet color; the lips, chin, and the inside of the ears have white and yellowish-white hairs.

The green coloring on its back fades to gray as it approaches the sides, and individual hairs here are white and black or white and gray.... The soles of the hands and feet are black."[142] Organs and the digestive tract were the focus of his description of the hippopotamus: "When one opens the stomach cavity, at first one sees nothing but the thick coils of the tremendous stomach, and in front of it the flat, 2 foot wide spleen. Under the spleen is a section of intestine." He then described in great detail the length, width and shape of the animal's kidneys, pancreas, and other internal organs.[143]

Peters was typical of nineteenth-century zoologists, interested in a "thick description" of the animal and its place in the pantheon of species rather than in animal behavior or preservation. For his purposes, as for other zoologists of his era, it was more advantageous for the animal to be dead, which is also the reason that taxidermy was a growth field in the nineteenth century.[144] In his lengthy account of his time in Africa, Peters is matter-of-fact about the demise of animals. He boasted of how hippos were hunted: "One catches them either by trapping them in holes, or harpoons them in water. The latter is not without danger and requires great strength and nimbleness."[145] He was nonplused by the fact that 10,000 elephants per year were being killed in Mozambique for the ivory. It seemed to him that there were still plenty of elephants.[146]

Peters was equal parts adventurer and scientist. For as much as he compiled information on hundreds of animals and brought back ship-holds full of samples, his justification to the minister for educational and medical affairs for state subvention of his book pointed to the ordeals of travel: "I allow myself once again to point out that my scientific trip to these dangerous climates was the only successful one of all those that over centuries had travelled there. According to most reports, the last scientists to accompany the missionary Livingstone perished from the deadly climate there."[147]

When Peters became director in 1857, the zoo was in a state of flux. Attendance was increasing, thanks in part to the first elephant on display, but it was still drawing below expectations. Peters, in the hopes that an infusion of new animals would attract more Berliners through the gates, acquired for the zoo two camels, lions, tigers, leopards, a black panther, a family of mandrills, and—a first for the zoo—flamingos and a zebra. He also undertook a major building project, adding a bird pavilion to the zoo's landscape in 1862.[148] Despite his efforts, the animal collection continued to decline due to harsh winters and a still rudimentary veterinary knowledge. Peters himself believed that even if animal losses had not plagued his directorship, the entertainment competition in the German capital would have still presented an enormous challenge to the zoo. In a telling memorandum, Peters outlined the issues unique to the capital's zoo:

> The zoological garden is the oldest of all zoos in Germany, established 25 years ago under favorable conditions like no other, and with support of the state, support which continues to this day. No other zoo received such a beautiful, vast, park-like terrain at no cost.
>
> So when, according to those with knowledge of these things, this same zoo lags behind all others in its achievements, in the condition of animals and in scientific results . . . it seems necessary to determine the reasons for such an unfavorable result.
>
> It cannot be denied that one of the reasons lies in the fact that Berliners have a wide variety of food and entertainment venues, more than any other German city, to distract them from the zoo. This cannot in any case be the sole reason, given that in other cities, like Hamburg and even more so London, where there is no shortage of entertainment venues, the zoological gardens are not dependent on state support, but rather deliver desirable financial results.[149]

Peters was, of course, correct that Berliners had many ways to spend their leisure time. The zoo competed with opera, the Berlin Music Academy, and a burgeoning theater scene. The comedian Beckmann enthralled patrons at the Theater in der Königstadt, the first private theater in Berlin.[150] At the Café Kranzler on the corner of Unter den Linden and Friedrichstrasse, young aristocrats tasted the latest eastern delicacy sweeping the capital—Russian ice cream. The middle class indulged in cakes and coffee at more than 100 coffeehouses or sampled wine at the many wine bars and increasingly talked of the need for political change in the conservative capital.[151] Berliners made their way to the district of Charlottenburg for the "Turkish tent," a salon-like meeting point for artists and philosophers, or to Treptow to feast on eel with a side of cucumber salad. An annual highlight was the Stralsauer Fischzug, the largest *Volksfest* in Berlin, where residents of the city watched puppet shows, rode the carousel, and whiled away the time over coffee and sausage in the food tents.[152]

For most Berliners in the first decades of the zoo's existence, these diversions won out over a long trip to the zoo, still located outside the city and lacking iconic exotic animals or, as zoo managers refer to these species with widespread appeal, "charismatic megafauna." London had rhinos, hippos, giraffes, and chimpanzees. Berlin had none of these. The rudimentary cages and low standards of hygiene also seemed to put off many Berliners. *Die Gartenlaube* claimed that the monkey pavilion was suitable only for those visitors "willing to subject their nose and lungs to the greatest of tortures" and compared the zoo to a "penitentiary for animals."[153]

A turn in fortune for the zoo was around the corner, though, one which was brought on by two major changes. The first was beyond the zoo's control: the population explosion and riches that attended Berlin when it became the capital of the German empire in 1871. The second was the zoo board's programming decision to put on display that most charismatic megafauna of them all—human beings.

2

The Human Zoo

ON THE EVENING OF SEPTEMBER 7, 1872, thousands of Berliners stood shoulder to shoulder on the square in front of the royal palace. Across Unter den Linden, Berlin's main thoroughfare, at the foot of the Berlin cathedral, gas lamps lit up the large, grassy area known as the Lustgarten. The armory across the Spree River—along with the cathedral, a museum of antiquities, and the royal palace, the fourth pillar of Prussian power on display in the royal quarter—glowed orange from the special illumination. As an orchestra played the national anthems of Germany, Russia, and Austria-Hungary, the moment for which the crowd had assembled arrived. Kaiser Wilhelm I of Germany, Kaiser Franz Joseph of Austria-Hungary, and Tsar Alexander II of Russia emerged onto a palace balcony just as the latest invention, electric street lighting, caused the darkness in the square below to disappear in an instant.[1] The cry of the newspaper boy captured the excitement at the presence in the German capital of the leaders of Europe's largest Continental empires: "Come closer ladies and gentlemen! Get your paper! See the Austrian and Russian emperors and our William—he's the handsomest of the three! Just a penny and you get all three emperors! Every detail! Come closer, ladies and gentlemen! Just a little penny for three emperors! Such a thing hasn't been seen in the history of the world!"[2]

The meeting of the three emperors was a show of solidarity in the face of a revolutionary tide that had proved stubbornly persistent since 1848.[3] Equally important, it was an opportunity for the German emperor, fresh off a resounding victory over France in 1871, to show off his splendorous imperial capital. The orchestra and electric lighting for the emperors' arrival were but a prologue. Kaiser Wilhelm I saved Berlin's latest jewel for last.

The following morning, the emperors and their entourages set off from the palace, Kaiser Wilhelm and Kaiser Franz Joseph occupying the first carriage followed by Tsar Alexander and his wife Augusta in the second carriage. Germany's crown prince Friedrich Wilhelm joined the group, along with the grand dukes of Baden, Sachsen-Weimar, and Mecklenburg-Schwerin.[4] Ten thousand people awaited them at their destination and cheered loudly as the convoy arrived. Heinrich Bodinus, the zoo director, escorted the emperors into the zoo—past a pond with waterfowl, by the carnivore pavilion, and on to the palm tree–lined foyer of the Antilopenhaus (antelope pavilion). There, the three emperors enjoyed a chilled beer and a "simple" breakfast (no doubt so that it could be consumed before the animal stench put a damper on things), and they lavished "unqualified praise" on Bodinus for his beautiful zoo.[5] The noted animal painter Heinrich Leutemann was practically giddy that the emperors had visited the zoo, speculating that they would be astonished at the zoo's collection.[6] After a few hours in the zoo, the emperors continued on to Potsdam where they visited the royal palace and garden complex. To express his gratitude for the hospitality he received in Berlin, Alexander later donated two European bison (wisents) from his own hunting grounds to the Berlin zoo.[7]

The 2,000-square-meter Antilopenhaus, built at a cost of 60,000 thaler, was by all accounts magnificent.[8] The Berlin daily *Vossische Zeitung* advised visitors from the countryside that there was "no more captivating image" of Berlin than the Antilopenhaus.[9] It alone was chosen for postwar rebuilding after the devastating aerial bombardment of November 22, 1943. The fourteen-meter-high interior courtyard, above the entrance of which hung Paul Meyerheim's monumental painting *The Antelope Hunt in the Sudan*, was topped by a glass ceiling that allowed the palm trees to grow around the central fountain, giving the impression of the reception hall of an oriental palace. Ivy climbed

Emperor Franz Joseph I of Austria-Hungary, Tsar Alexander II of Russia, and Kaiser Wilhelm I of Germany gather for breakfast in the foyer of the House of the Antelopes at the Berlin zoo in 1872. Kaiser Wilhelm I was eager to show off the zoo to his visitors. *Berlin Zoo Archive*

up the pillars to the roof. Beyond the three emperors' meeting, artists, politicians, and leading industrialists sought out the palm courtyard of the Antilopenhaus, including during the Nazi era when it played host to the first panda exhibited in Europe.[10] Visitors to the Antilopenhaus could either look down on the giraffes, antelopes, and zebras from a suspended walkway that ran around the interior or come close enough to touch them through iron bars in the main foyer.[11]

From the four gold-capped minarets, any visitor would have immediately recognized in the zoo's newest building an expression of the "Orient," the first time that the zoo signaled visually the origins of the animals contained within. The Berlin architectural firm Ende & Böckmann, which would design and erect many of the zoo's iconic buildings, brought into being Bodinus's conception for the Antilopenhaus, stating: "The outer appearance of the building should inspire the visitor, and, building on his own imagination, cause him to believe that he is seeing the penned-in animals in their native environment."[12] Witnessing the success of the Antilopenhaus in Berlin, the Hannover zoo built a similar mosque-like structure for its giraffes, antelopes, and camels.[13]

The Antilopenhaus and other lavish pavilions like the elephant pavilion that the board had built in 1873 were a sign of newly united Germany's wealth. "In which other time," asked August Woldt, the popular author who wrote about Germany's world explorers, "other than this one, with its blessings in the billions, could one even think of building an elephant house, for the trifling sum of about 340,000 marks?"[14] To put this sum in context, in an era when major European cities were tripping over themselves to build grandiose hotels to flaunt their riches, Berlin's Grand Hotel, the precursor of the iconic Hotel Adlon, cost half as much.[15]

Woldt's reference to "blessings in the billions" is likely referring to the 5 billion mark indemnity that France was required to pay Germany following the Franco-Prussian war.[16] Germany also reaped the rewards of the textile industry and iron-ore deposits of newly annexed Alsace-Lorraine. But the zoo board did not need to rely exclusively on these outside sources of revenue. Working closely with Carl Hagenbeck, the board undertook a radical departure from its previous programming and began hosting ethnographic displays of "exotic" peoples from around the world, exhibits that drew Germans to the zoo in unprecedented numbers. For the first time in its history, the zoo found itself awash in funds.

The animal tycoon Carl Hagenbeck stands beside a cage at the zoo. A savvy entrepreneur, he furnished the Berlin zoo with animals and humans for its displays. His zoo near Hamburg, which allowed animals to roam in open enclosures rather than be confined in cages, set the stage for modern zoos. *Landesarchiv Berlin, F Rep 290 0074699*

Part impresario, part brilliant but scrupulous entrepreneur, Hagenbeck emerged from the gritty St. Pauli district of Hamburg to become fabulously wealthy from trading in exotic animals. His father was part of a modest international animal-trading dynasty that was in the embryonic stages of supplying Europe's zoos; Carl's father's business partner, the London animal trader Charles Rice, married Carl's sister. The partnership would be relatively short-lived, as Rice died at the hands of one of his jungle cats while preparing him for display in the ballroom of a Berlin restaurant.[17] Recognizing how business was increasingly crossing borders, Hagenbeck's father encouraged Carl to learn English and French at an early age, language skills that would serve him well in his many dealings with the United States.[18] And indeed, he spoke a perfectly passable, if bookish, English.

Following directly in his father's footsteps, Carl Hagenbeck entered the animal trade, an increasingly lucrative enterprise thanks to the seemingly unquenchable thirst of Europeans and Americans to see exotic animals. When Hagenbeck first entered the animal-trading world, there were eight zoos in Germany and nineteen others in Europe. By the time he left it, a further sixteen zoos had been established in Europe and twenty-one in the United States.[19] Zoos were not his only clients, however. Hagenbeck supplied almost all of Europe's fifty traveling menageries as well as the leading circuses of the day—Carl Merkel and Ernst Renz in Germany, Ringling and Barnum and Bailey in the United States.[20]

Hagenbeck's rise to fame led him to several audiences with the kaiser, moments in his life that he cherished. Having received flowers from the emperor while lying on his deathbed in April 1913, Hagenbeck whispered "Mein Kaiser, mein Kaiser" and then expired.[21] Nicknamed the "king of the animals," Hagenbeck traveled more than 50,000 kilometers a year trading in exotic species, earning the respect of scientists across the Continent who named after him newly discovered species of kangaroo, giraffe, and mountain goats. In a 1913 US survey of most recognizable names in the world, Carl Hagenbeck ranked fourth.[22] His "panorama zoo" in Stellingen outside of Hamburg, in which animals were displayed in herds in their habitats rather than in individual cages by their taxonomy, revolutionized zoos across the globe. When

Thomas Edison visited Hagenbeck's zoo in 1911, he remarked in the guestbook: "The animals are not in the cage, they are on the stage!"[23] Hagenbeck was a household name in Germany in his time, as famous as Ferdinand Graf Zeppelin or Werner von Siemens.[24] "Hagenbeck is not a proper name," wrote the playwright Carl Zuckmayer, "but rather, like Alaska or the Wild West, the expression of a mysterious, unexplored land, where one yearns for adventure."[25]

Arguably the most important contact Hagenbeck would make for his future success was the Italian animal trapper Lorenzo Casanova. At a meeting at the Dresden zoo in 1864, Hagenbeck entered into a contract with Casanova for him to acquire animals for Hagenbeck, a transaction that would cause the Hagenbeck name to become known around the world. "Casanova opened the door for a series of adventurers," recalled Hagenbeck in his memoirs, "who searched in the bush, in the forest and on the steppes, for wild and rare animals, and who brought the name Hagenbeck from pole to pole, from the south seas to Siberia."[26]

In 1870, Hagenbeck traveled to Suez to accompany back to Europe his first shipment of animals acquired by Casanova. Arriving by train in the port city whose new canal would greatly aid his work, Hagenbeck saw elephants and giraffes awaiting transport in railway wagons at the station, the giraffes, he thought, craning their necks as if to greet him. But it was the sight on the square behind his hotel that would remain a lifetime with the twenty-three-year-old.[27] There, as if Noah had opened the doors on Mount Ararat, he saw "elephants, giraffes, antelopes and buffalos, tied to a palm tree. Sixteen large ostriches ran free in their midst. In 60 transport crates, artistically stacked among every manner of equipment, barrels, and awnings, thirty spotted hyenas, lions, leopards, panthers, lynxes, and African civets jumped around and roared. Monkeys and parrots clamored about the weather. And alongside them all, marabus swaggered with gravitas, birds of prey screeched, and young rhinoceri grunted."[28]

Transferring the assembled animals to the awaiting ship proved almost as challenging as their capture. Hagenbeck was deeply unnerved by the sight of the animals "dangling between sky and water" at the end of the pier's steam crane.[29] With more than 150 animals in tow, Hagenbeck returned to Europe, delivering his cargo to zoos in Vienna, Dresden, and Berlin—the last being the recipient of the largest number of animals on that transport, where the zoo director, Bodinus, eagerly awaited Hagenbeck's African rhino, the first to be displayed in Europe since the Roman era.[30]

That first shipment of animals would soon be dwarfed by subsequent ones. The reporter for a Frankfurt newspaper documenting Hagenbeck's animals awaiting shipment in Alexandria conveyed his astonishment:

> A dust cloud arises. A jumble of animal sounds can be heard—the bellow of the cattle, the trumpet of the elephant, the terrifying roar of the lion. Added to this is the noise of hundreds of people, screaming and gesturing wildly. 150 Nubians, each an experienced hunter, accompany the caravan. More than 150 camels carry all manner of equipment on their backs, as well as groceries, and large drinking bowls for man and animal. Then you notice the 25 donkeys and several hundred goats, who supply the milk for the younger animals. Of the 400 sheep that started out with the caravan, only a few remain as they had to be consumed along the way.... Majestic and resigned, 14 elephants lead the pack ... 20 ostriches strut proudly around; 7 lions are contained in strong cages. Amidst them all are 11 giraffes, 5 buffalos, 20 antelopes and gazelles, 4 anteaters, leopards, 25 hyenas, lynx, monkeys, eagles, vultures, and twelve cages of small birds pulled by camels.[31]

Hagenbeck's animal-trading network extended around the globe, from local trappers in Korea, Japan, Brazil, Calcutta, Australia, and Chile to shipping and railway barons, to buyers in the new world, and to German diplomats. The American trapper Frank Buck, whose tag line "Bring 'Em Back Alive!" captured the imagination of a generation of American youth, once said that "every German consul in the smallest part of Asia or Africa had been a Hagenbeck agent on the side,"[32] a statement that was barely an exaggeration. This sophisticated network, a clear example of how globalization is not a recent phenomenon, allowed Hagenbeck to transport animals around the globe. In 1908, Hagenbeck delivered a pair of hippos from Africa to the newly established zoo in Buenos Aires, Argentina—both Africa and Argentina thousands of kilometers away from his headquarters in Hamburg. Hagenbeck repeated this type of delivery again and again, providing animals to new zoos in Calcutta, Tokyo, and Adelaide, Australia.[33] Indeed, the sheer volume of animals that Hagenbeck traded is staggering. In 1883 alone, he exported 67 elephants from Sri Lanka,[34] but that was a pittance in his overall shipments to Europe between 1866 and 1886: more than 1,000 lions, 400 tigers, more than 1,000 bears, 300 elephants, 26 rhinos, 150 giraffes, tens of thousands of monkeys, and more than 100,000 birds.[35]

Not only do these numbers tell a story about the European fascination with exotic animals; they also reveal the changes that were wrought by the mass consumerism, larger bureaucracies, technological advances, and increasing trade networks characteristic of the age. Hagenbeck's enterprise would not have been possible without the explosion in railway networks, the surge in the number of large public and private institutions that could host such animals, and the increase in leisure time and disposable income that allowed average Europeans to visit the zoo or watch a traveling menagerie. These were the golden years for Europeans, when department stores like Harrod's and Galeries Lafayette were bursting with shoppers, when huge sports stadiums first appeared (although their heyday would be in the twentieth century), when wax museums such as the Musée Grevin in Paris became sensations, when public transportation infrastructure boomed, and when the working class could begin to consider going on a holiday. A clear sign of the times was Berlin's first travel agency, which opened its doors in 1876 offering mail coach service to European holiday destinations like the Rhine and Switzerland and, for the more adventurous, Russia.[36] Zoos directly benefited from the huge numbers of people who were looking for something to do with their money, a situation that was a first in European history.

Given the exorbitant costs associated with obtaining and transporting wild animals, zoos today acquire new animals either through breeding or trade with other zoos. Most animals in today's zoos have never seen the wild. Hagenbeck's era was very different. He relied on both local guides and European adventurers who captured the animals in a manner that most today would consider abhorrent. Joseph Menges, a plucky explorer who had participated in Charles Gorda's 1884 White Nile expedition, was one of Hagenbeck's key suppliers, spending fourteen years on the African continent capturing animals for shipment to Europe. Another Hagenbeck supplier, until his death from malaria while on an elephant-catching expedition in Zanzibar, was his own brother Dietrich.[37]

It is from Hans Shomburgk, however, that we have some of the most vivid—and unsettling—accounts of the capture of animals. A commercial elephant hunter with a passion for natural history, he wrote his memoir *Wild und Wilde im Herzen Afrikas* (Savages and Beasts in the Heart of Africa) in 1910 after his four-year journey through Africa. One of the key episodes in the book deals with the capture of the elephant Jumbo (only one of the many elephants in captivity that would be given this name), which would become one of the "jewels," according to Hagenbeck, of his zoo near Hamburg. After several days of tracking a herd of elephants, Schomburgk suddenly came upon a female elephant and her young bull. "The mother noticed me," Schomburgk wrote. "An enormous animal. Still, I was able to fire a shot at the root of her trunk. She collapsed, affording me the opportunity to deliver a deadly shot . . . . Naturally, the young animal stayed by its mother . . . . As I was waiting for my people to arrive, I observed how the poor, small baby continually paced around its mother and shoved her with its trunk, as if it wanted to wake her up and continue their journey."[38] Unperturbed, Shomburgk took a photo of Jumbo and his dead mother and published it in his book. This was not a case of local trappers running amok; Carl Hagenbeck himself was, of course, fully aware that the adult animals would be killed in order to take the offspring.[39]

More than the simple acquisition of animals, trappers displayed a yearning to dominate nature, relating in their accounts in far more detail than necessary the bloody nature of their kills. These hunters marveled at the fact that humans, who once cowered in the presence of lions and elephants, had now turned the tables. As Schomburgk wrote: "It is impossible for me to describe just how proud I was to sit myself down on the first elephant I had slain by myself."[40] Even more telling of his attitude toward his conquest than this sense of accomplishment is that he chose to sit on the animal. In another photo from his memoir, he rides a bicycle triumphantly over a dead elephant.[41]

Another trapper, Hugo von Koppenfels, recalled letting out a "massive German hurrah that rattled throughout the jungle" when he saw his first gorilla fall.[42] Schomburgk, Koppenfels, and other trappers were in awe of the ascent of humans and their ability to impose their will on the animal world. They exhibited, as historian Harriet Ritvo has said so marvelously about British collectors of exotic animals, an "overpowering urge to overpower."[43] Although over time Hagenbeck came to be more concerned about the welfare of animals, he too initially had few qualms about collateral damage during his captures. In one instance, sixty-eight walruses died at his hands so that he could acquire five for his zoo.[44] The idea of human dominion over nature was echoed in other German circles. The leading German animal painter of his day, Heinrich Leutemann, whose paintings still fetch a high price at auction, was excited at the prospect of elephants serving at the behest of humans: "It was a true pleasure to be able to see these noble, powerful animals being put to a dignified use. And when one sees them remove large tree trunks, which they do in different ways but always very cleverly, then one gets a sense of just how useful these giants of the animal world can be if put in the service of men."[45]

Utility was not always at the root of animal subservience to humans. Simultaneously with the explosion of zoos, the animal entertainment industry boomed. People flocked to see animal tamers standing calmly beside a lion, the animal's wildness removed, seemingly now more a part of the urban world than the steppes it left behind. Hagenbeck once boasted to the eminent anthropologist Rudolf Virchow that he could tame an elephant to be "ride-ready" within forty-eight hours.[46] Hagenbeck put his prowess in animal training on display at the Chicago world's fair of 1893, where he and his 1,000 trained animals were the talk of the town. Americans could scarcely believe the sights before them: a lion riding on the back of a donkey; a lion standing on the back of an elephant, which in turn was riding a tricycle; chimps playing the harmonica and violin. His caravan of animals stayed on in the Americas, touring for several years under the title "Hagenbeck's trained animals."[47]

The ambition to dominate nature was not limited to conquest of the animal world, of course. Many highly educated Europeans saw the natural environment, including waterways, fields, moors, and bays, as objects to be molded on humanity's anvil. The physicist Hermann von Helmholtz spoke for many when he declared to the Association of German Natural Scientists and Physicians in 1844 that what united them was the belief that science would "make the reasonless forces of nature subservient to the moral purposes of humanity."[48]

Hagenbeck's animal empire rose and fell with the broader economy. After an economic boom in Germany from 1850 to 1870, the following twenty years were dismal, the economy faltering in part due to squandered reparations from France after the Franco-Prussian war and in part due to a mismanaged currency reform. But the popular mindset also played a role. Germans became pessimistic about the future, thereby spending less and helping to bring about the economic crisis that they feared.[49] Hagenbeck's animal-trading business began to feel the pinch of the economic slowdown. In the late 1870s, zoos in Dresden and Hannover did not buy a single animal from him, while those in Hamburg and Leipzig could only afford several hundred marks' worth of animals. Animal purchases were down at zoos in Frankfurt, Düsseldorf, and Breslau, too. "Business is bad," Hagenbeck wrote to a friend in 1878, "very bad." [50] Hagenbeck weathered the worst of the depression thanks to purchases from the Berlin zoo, which continued to buy from him in large quantities, and from a new market with untold potential—the United States. In 1878 he sold his first giraffes to Barnum and Bailey, and the following year delivered his first shipment to the Cincinnati zoo. A robust US demand for Asian elephants helped buoy him in the 1880s. He was also able to sell a few elephants to an unlikely client—opera companies in Berlin and Milan, who in the case of the latter used the animal for the triumphal march in Verdi's *Aida*.[51]

Still, the cautious Hagenbeck realized that he would need to branch out from animals if his business was to survive. When a friend suggested to him that he allow some Lapps to accompany his shipment of reindeer from Scandinavia to Hamburg in 1875, Hagenbeck entered into the lucrative world of recruiting "exotic" humans for Europe's museums, festivals, and, especially, zoos.[52]

Ever since the voyages of overseas exploration, Europeans had brought foreign peoples—some willingly, most not—to Europe and had paraded them in front of curious onlookers. Columbus, returning to Spain in 1493 laden with every manner of treasure from the Americas to present to the Spanish royal couple, left no question as to which of his loot was the most fascinating: "I presented the treasures I had brought with me: previously unknown, brightly-coloured birds, rare animals and plants, gold in various forms—nuggets, raw chunks, and jewelry. What amazed the majesties the most, however—just as had been the case with ordinary people—were the Indians, who stood there motionless, as if they were not made of flesh and blood, but were copper statues."[53] Columbus's hopes that these members of the Arawak peoples would learn Spanish and become cultural emissaries between Europe and the Americas were dashed when the Native Americans, in a state of shock from their voyage, lost the ability to speak.

Inuit peoples were among the most common to be showcased in Europe, having been displayed in Bristol in 1501, in Antwerp in 1567, in London in 1577, the one "success" from Martin Frobisher's otherwise failed attempt to find the Northwest Passage, and again in London in 1772.[54] In the 1820s, ship captain Samuel Hadlock of Maine toured a troupe of Inuits through Europe, taking them to London, Hamburg, Leipzig, Dresden, Prague, Vienna, and Berlin.[55] While in the Prussian capital, they were painted by one of Berlin's most recognizable figures, Johann Schadow, president of the royal academy of arts.[56] One historian has summarized the long history of Inuit on display elegantly: "Every generation, it seems, saw its Eskimos."[57] In the mid-nineteenth century, a pygmy tribe from Central America, promoted as "Lilliputian Azteks," was presented to a host of notable dignitaries, including the Berlin zoo founders Alexander von Humboldt and Hinrich Lichtenstein, the king of Prussia, the queen of England, Napoleon III, and the US vice president Millard Fillmore.[58]

One of the most famous humans ever to be put on display was Saartje Baartman, a South African "Hottentot" woman suffering from steatopygia, a condition that leads to enlarged buttocks. She was exhibited in Paris for fifteen months beginning in 1810, mercilessly exposed to ridicule as the "missing link," suffering endless humiliation as an object that visitors were encouraged to touch to verify her authenticity.[59] The indignity did not end with her death. Paris's Musée de l'Homme displayed her skeleton, genitals, and brain until 1974.[60]

"Exotic" peoples did not necessarily even need to be alive to draw a crowd. At the special request of the Austrian emperor, an Ethiopian servant to several Austrian princes was "taxidermied" and displayed in Vienna's Natural History Museum wearing a belt and crown of ostrich feathers. Not far away, visitors could have seen stuffed displays of animals that had originally been housed in the nearby royal menagerie.

Beside them stood one of their zookeepers, who, because of his mixed race, had been stuffed like the animals he watched over.[61]

By the late nineteenth century, European city dwellers could view "exotic" people from around the globe several times a year. In the forty years beginning in 1875, there were more than 300 ethnographic shows in Germany alone, one-third of which were produced in affiliation with Carl Hagenbeck.[62] Although zoos were a preferred venue for show-casing these individuals, museums, annual fairs like Oktoberfest, circuses, world's fairs, industrial exhibits, and panopticons (unscientific museums of curiosities and oftentimes wax figures) also displayed non-Europeans. In Berlin, Castan's Panopticon, a cabinet of the unusual to satisfy even the strangest tastes for the human body, exhibited anatomical oddities, human embryos, wax figures of all sorts, from criminals to the royal family, and "exotic" humans. Small groups of Australians, Zulus, Tunisians, Sioux, and whirling dervishes were displayed alongside torture instruments and skeletons in the dark, eerie passageways.[63] Other European sites, not confined by space, were able to host much larger human displays, such as the Paris world's fair of 1878 that hosted 400 natives from Indochina, Senegal, and Tahiti, or the colossal British Exhibition in Wembley stadium in 1924 that involved 15,000 people.[64] Although there were exceptions, like the exhibition of pygmies at New York's Bronx zoo in 1906, US zoos in general did not display humans.[65] Other entertainers, such as Buffalo Bill, it seemed, had cornered that market. His Wild West Show, complete with "Indian village," was one of the star attractions at the 1893 Chicago world's fair.[66]

Having witnessed the popularity of a show of Inuit in Paris earlier in 1878, the Berlin zoo director Heinrich Bodinus signed a contract with Carl Hagenbeck to host at the zoo these same Inuit, a small troupe of six individuals: Okabak and his wife, their two children aged one and three, and two young male relatives. Eight sled dogs accompanied the group.[67] The ad in a Berlin daily announcing the show was a small one that did not match the scope of the event, reading simply: "Zoological Garden: Eskimo Family from Jacobshafen on the west coast of Greenland. Entry: 1 Mark, children half price."[68] Compared to future shows, this first display of humans, obtained by the world-renowned Norwegian Arctic expert Adrian Jacobsen, was modest. Nevertheless, the Inuit family, who, in its provisional dirt hut, made traditional crafts

A group of Inuit from Greenland and their sled dogs pose for a picture in the Berlin zoo in 1878. Okabak and his wife and their two children are in the background while a young male relative looks out from the provisional enclosure that the Inuit constructed. The group was the first of the "human zoos" in Berlin. *Archive of the Berlin Society for Anthropology, Ethnography, and Pre-History, FS 04170*

and ran its sled dogs along the sandy banks of the artificial pond in the snowless zoo, captivated the imagination of Berliners, including Kaiser Wilhelm I, who watched with great interest, then increasing fear, as Okabak demonstrated his skill in a kayak, rolling himself under water for what seemed to the kaiser an impossibly long time before righting the kayak and launching spears from the middle of the water to targets on shore.[69] The kaiser's son, the crown prince, visited the seal fur–clad family on several occasions, entering the makeshift hut to see how the diminutive family lived.[70] For weeks, Berliners streamed to the zoo to see the northern peoples.

It is difficult to know for certain how Germans reacted to this first human zoo, but contemporary newspapers suggest that it was a mixture of delight, genuine curiosity about peoples who inhabited the world beyond the oceans, and a paternalistic superiority over a primitive "other," the latter demonstrated by a story reported in the *Leipziger Illustrirte Zeitung*: "Okabak has provided evidence while here that he can write.... His Majesty the Kaiser wished to see for himself.

According to an interpreter, Okabak wrote the following on a piece of paper: 'Okabak and his family are grateful for this honored visit, and hope that God blesses the Kaiser's house.'"[71] Members of the Berlin Society for Anthropology, Ethnography, and Pre-History later vigorously discussed Okabak's writing sample, hoping to determine whether his script offered telltale signs of racial differences from Germans.[72]

The major German daily *Vossische Zeitung* also reflected this dual interpretation of the visitors to the imperial capital. On the one hand, the newspaper displayed an elitist curiosity about the Inuit who, while at the zoo, lived in earth huts and "had to do without whale blubber" but also expressed a certain degree of admiration for individuals who were able to live in "the most inhospitable regions of our earth."[73] The newspaper also exhibited deep concern regarding the welfare of the sled dogs that the Inuit had brought with them. Given the lack of snow in northern Germany that year, the Inuit were to display the animals' penchant for pulling, not on snow, but on the "Brandenburg sand," an activity that the newspaper thought should be brought to the attention of the Animal Protection Society to ensure the safety of these small "beasts of burden."[74]

The most important venue for German researchers interested in the physiology and cultures of humans was the Berlin Society for Anthropology, Ethnography, and Pre-History, which took a strong interest in the ethnographic exhibits. Founded in 1869, the society counted some of Berlin's most prominent academics among its members, including the historian Leopold von Ledebur, the botanist Alexander Braun, and the ethnographer Adolf Bastian. By 1884, the society had about 520 members.[75] The face of the society, however, was the complex figure of Rudolf Virchow, its founding president. A physician by training, Virchow was also politically active, co-founding with Theodor Mommsen and Hermann Schulze-Delitizsch the Progressive Party, which would go on to become the strongest party in the Prussian diet. Opposed to socialism and to Bismarck's conservatism, Virchow championed a state in which parliament, rather than chancellor and emperor, would wield political power.[76] Virchow was also central to the Darwinian debate about the origins of humans, which dominated most of the 1880s. Pitted against Ernst Haeckel, a Jena zoologist who popularized Charles Darwin's ideas in Germany, Virchow and his fellow anti-Darwinists won a singular victory when the school board removed biology from the Prussian school curriculum.[77]

Members of the Berlin Society for Anthropology were a constant presence at the zoo, barely able to contain their excitement at having ethnographic specimens dropped in their laps. When one thinks of what anthropologists had had to rely upon to study other peoples up to this point, it is no wonder that Virchow and those around him were thrilled about the shows. Following the 1873–76 expedition sent out by the German African Society to explore the central African state of Loango, for example, Paul Güssfeldt, the expedition's leader, provided to ethnologists and anthropologists back in Germany drawings that he had made of the people he encountered.[78] But now, Berlin anthropologists could study other peoples in the flesh, in their own backyard. Virchow gave regular talks to the society on almost every group that the zoo exhibited. He described in detail the Inuit peoples in the zoo, relaying skull measurements, smoothness of skin, the length of feet and forearms, and skin tone. Their dark skin, reminiscent of the Africans recently in the zoo, puzzled Virchow: "If one takes the Parisian Color Table [a scale of human skin color developed by the Anthropological Society of Paris], one would be tempted to believe that such a dark skin tone suggests that [the Inuit] were related to Africans in some fashion. Their color is a deep red-brown, achieving 28–30 on the Parisian Color Table."[79] Given that the leading theories of the day suggested that Africans' dark skin color resulted from exposure to sun and heat, the reasons for the Inuit to have a similar skin tone eluded Virchow.

During the tenure of the Inuit show, one of the society's members, Alexander Horn von der Horck, obtained four plaster masks of the adults, a feat made all the more difficult because the Inuit had had a trying experience in Paris when similar masks were fashioned. Okabak initially offered Horck 20 francs to avoid the "torture" of having another mask of his face made, but later he agreed to undergo the process on Horck's assurance that Berlin had more sophisticated methods than Paris. Okabak, according to the society's report, marveled at the procedure that produced a mask that captured even the stubble of his beard without any of the pain he had experienced in Paris.[80]

Although we lack hard numbers, there are indications that the first Inuit show at the Berlin zoo drew large crowds. The *Vossische Zeitung* reported that after the public was informed that the Inuit show would be in town until March 29, "crowds grew day by day, coming to observe the goings-on of this well-meaning group of humans staying in the zoological garden."[81] Berliners brought with them so many food baskets for the visitors that their overflowing contents of oranges and jams often rotted before they could be eaten, prompting the newspaper to urge Berliners to show their appreciation for their guests by giving them a cash tip instead.[82] Newspapers referred to the Inuit family as Berlin's "premiers amours."[83]

The Inuit made additional stops in Cologne, Dresden—where they were presented to the king and queen of Saxony—Hannover, and Hamburg, where they attracted more than 44,000 visitors over the Easter weekend. Before embarking on the return voyage to Greenland, they were put on display in the Berlin zoo for a few more days, an unplanned stay in the German capital that speaks to the enormous public interest in the show.[84] In alerting Berliners to their last chance to see the Inuit, a Berlin daily waxed sentimental:

For only three more days will the Eskimos be with us on their return journey to their northern home .... Margareth or Magog with their black, slanted eyes will once again impishly say goodbye to their old Berlin friends, this time forever. Okabak will, for the last time, traverse the waves on the small lake in his kayak made of sealskin, his hunting call ringing out .... For a few days, then, you will be able to observe a most interesting part of northern life. After that, however, the desolate earth palace [constructed by the Inuit] will stand alone; it will be the last reminder of its inhabitants .... Then new life will bloom from the ruins, as May is approaching and on the site of those simple huts, the melodies of the summer concert series will fill the Emperor's City.[85]

The Inuit show of 1878 paved the way for a half century of human exhibits at the Berlin zoo.[86] Shortly after the Inuit had left town, the zoo management booked a group of Nubians from northeast Africa who would prove as fascinating to Berliners as the Inuit had been, not the least because of their skin color. Newspaper reporters rarely missed an opportunity to point out the contrast with white Europeans. In the first article announcing the forthcoming arrival of the group, the author wrote enthusiastically about the physical specimens: "The company consists of 16 interesting, slender, well-built male negroes with chocolate brown skin and beaded hair, and one well-proportioned Nubian woman."[87] Journalists otherwise described the Nubians as "half-naked brown figures," "brown sons of the desert," "dark sleepers," and "dark statues."[88]

The Nubian show was considerably larger than the Inuit one, comprising ten men and one woman, and a sizable collection of animals, including five elephants, four rhinos, eight giraffes, three cattle, three zebus, two ostriches, three donkeys, five young lions, two monkeys, and several sheep and goats. Onlookers were astounded as the caravan made its way from Berlin's main train station, along Mühlenstrasse, over Oberbaum bridge, and then by the canal to the zoo, where the zoo director welcomed them.[89] One journalist reported that the sight of the caravan elicited an "excitement in school children beyond compare" and betrayed his own fascination with the lone female in the group, whom he described as "a Nubian beauty, a tattooed woman with a gold nose ring."[90] The first evening in the zoo brought together the Nubians and Berlin society, including the promoter Carl Hagenbeck, in the Great Hall of the zoo restaurant for an elaborate "Nubian Soirée." Following a dinner that took place amid much "laughter and joking," the Nubians and Berliners played games and music long into the night.[91] The following day, the Nubians put on a display of their hunting skills, reminiscent of the "ancient, fearless, hunters" of prehistoric times, as one Berlin daily described it.[92]

Berlin newspapers painted the Nubians as a primitive, simple people, similar to Europeans of the distant past when life was a constant struggle with nature and animals. Unlike urbanized Europeans, the papers suggested, the African mental and physical makeup was formed by nature. Journalists employed the term *Naturvolk* (people of nature) to describe the Nubians and referred on a regular basis to the hostile climate from which they came. Their "hot-blooded" temperament was understandable given their "harsh environment," their "strapping, steeled" bodies a result of the desert climate.[93] Observers took great pleasure in the contrast of urbanized, sophisticated Berliners with the African people and their animals. "What a colorful image for the public!" wrote the

Vossische Zeitung of an excursion by the Berlin Society for Anthropology to the zoo. "Professors and elephants. Privy councilors and Nubians. Doctors and Giraffes. All in a lively jumble!"[94] The zoo management played to these stereotypes, at one point offering up a dead sheep for the Nubians to roast over an open fire. Thousands of Berliners watched and then ate the chunks of meat on knives that the Nubians presented to them.

A "Nubian fever," as one newspaper phrased it, had gripped Berliners. Anyone who showed up to see the Africans in the German capital after noon had little chance of coming close to them. Because more than 10,000 Berliners visited the zoo on each of the first two days of the show, the zoo director had to have the iron fence around the gazelle house moved to accommodate the huge crowds.[95] By day four of the show, more than 50,000 people had come to the zoo.[96] On the first Sunday of the exhibit, an astounding 62,000 people attended the Nubian show, arriving by foot or horse-drawn trolley.[97] Publishing houses took out large ads in Berlin newspapers advertising their picture books on the Nubians in the zoo.[98] The following year, a zoo board member explained simply why 1878 had been such a good year financially for the zoo: "The Eskimos and Nubians had an enormous appeal."[99] Well aware that the Nubians had enchanted Berliners, director Bodinus arranged for a torchlit parade through the zoo of both "his" Nubians and those visiting from the Frankfurt zoo.[100] The three dozen Nubians making their way through the dark zoo, illuminated only by torches, the metropolis receding into the night, seemed to transport Berliners to the faraway African continent.

Members of Berlin's academic community shared in the excitement, spending countless hours photographing the Nubians, observing, talking, and listening to them. Noted language researchers wrote down their words. They took hair samples. They took plaster casts of various body parts, allowing them to compare population groups long after the exhibited people had left town. Anthropologists determined, for example, that the feet of the Bella Coola, aboriginal people from British Columbia, were nearly identical to those of Japanese; in both cases, the toes did not spread when bearing weight.[101] Above all, though, Berlin academics measured the humans in the zoo. They took cranial, nose, and foot measurements; they measured the length of their forearms

The Bella Coola group from British Columbia, Canada, wear their traditional regalia for a portrait made at the photography studio of Carl Günther. Berliners were not as enamored of this group as some of the other peoples on display. *Archive of the Berlin Society for Anthropology, Ethnography, and Pre-History, FS 03948*

and lower legs; they measured the distance between the eyes and the distance from fingertip to fingertip. Each individual was subjected to about thirty-five measurements.[102] Rudolf Virchow was the most zealous of the "measurers," at one point postponing a long-planned trip to Egypt so that he could spend more time measuring the Lapps on display at the zoo.[103]

The presence of Nubians and Lapps in Berlin permitted anthropologists to study an issue that was at the forefront of the profession, namely, whether the ability to distinguish color was a product of civilization. Although the scientists were puzzled that the Nubians did not have a unique word for "blue," employing instead the generic term for "dark," they determined that the retinas of Nubians and Lapps (who did not have the same difficulty with blue) were indeed able to distinguish colors. This finding flew in the face of a prevailing theory, forwarded by an obscure German ophthalmologist, Hugo Magnus, and the far less obscure William Gladstone, the once and future prime minister of Great Britain, that humans had passed through evolutionary stages toward color recognition.[104] In a talk to his assembled scientists, Virchow discussed this revolutionary finding:

> You are well aware that Mr. Gladstone and Herr Magnus believed that even in Homer's time the Greeks were not able to distinguish among certain colors, and that only the progress of civilization led to a sense of color or, as Herr Magnus would have it, led to the development of the organ of color, the retina. Our testing has demonstrated that their view must now be completely abandoned.[105]

It is little wonder that at its year-end assembly, the Berlin Society for Anthropology reported that the "most exciting occurrence" for its members that year was the "display of foreign peoples, organized by our member from Hamburg, Herr Carl Hagenbeck."[106]

In 1879, a group of Nubians, mostly from the same tribe as the previous year's group, arrived at the Berlin zoo. They provided another spectacularly successful exhibit, drawing more than 40,000 visitors on one day, Sunday, September 7, and a total of 200,000 in the course of a month.[107] The presence of one female Nubian among the group, the sixteen-year-old fiancée of a man twice her age who supposedly paid 40 marks to purchase her, contributed to the popularity.[108] Newspaper ads promoting the Nubian show continually highlighted the female presence. Even the popular Berlin clothing store, the Golden 110, named after its address on Leipziger Street, marveled at the female Nubian in a poem contained in one of its newspaper ads:

> Hagenbeck, that noble knight
> Once again brings Nubians to Berliners' sight.
> And not only desert sons are on display.
> No. A brown female beauty makes the day.[109]

When Hagenbeck brought the show to Breslau, he had the caravan parade through town between the train station and the zoo to generate excitement. In the first wagon, the places of honor were occupied by Carl Hagenbeck, the zoo director Franz Schlegel, and the lone Nubian female.[110]

Although the Nubians themselves were largely responsible for the soaring zoo attendance—local newspapers suggesting that extra viewing platforms be installed to accommodate the crowds[111]—the large snakes on display for the first time in Berlin were an added attraction. The reptiles drew crowds so large that on one Sunday the security barrier buckled under the weight of the heaving mass, causing the bewildered viewers to nearly topple into the snake enclosure.[112]

After the Nubians had a successful run at the zoo, it was time for them to leave. To the surprise of the zoo's administrators, many of them refused.[113] Defending themselves with whips and knives, they declared through their interpreter their intention to remain in the zoo. All efforts at negotiation came to naught due to, according to a Berlin daily, the "stubbornness of the wild group." The zoo director, Bodinus, called in security forces who then proceeded to usher the Nubians onto awaiting carriages and remained with them on their journey to the train station. The *Vossische Zeitung* was coy as to the motives behind the Nubians' resistance, focusing on the sequence of events rather than what led to the confrontation in the first place, but one line of the report was suggestive: "Enthusiastic female admirers of these Sons of Nature accompanied them to the train station."[114] Years later, Adrian Jacobsen confirmed in his memoirs that the Nubians were loath to leave Berlin because it meant parting from their girlfriends.[115] A throwaway line in a newspaper report about the Chilean natives who were put on display in the zoo in 1881 also suggests that relationships formed between the Nubians and Berliners: "It is somewhat less likely that the *Feuerländer* [People from the Land of Fire] will work magic on the hearts of the female Berliners, as the [Nubians] did two years ago."[116]

As far as we can tell, erotic attraction to the peoples on display occurred on a regular basis, and it is likely that many more of these instances occurred than are revealed by the existing accounts of their visits. When the Bella Coola, an aboriginal group from British Columbia, were in town, one male from the tribe strolled proudly through the streets of Berlin with his German girlfriend on his arm.[117] Hagenbeck, too, noted how European females responded to some of the non-European men on display: "A young, gigantic hunter who, in spite of his 'tender' age of 19, measured over 6 feet tall, wreaked havoc on the hearts of European women."[118] The connection between erotic and exotic is, of course, not new, but striking is what such interactions say more broadly about the popular reception of the foreigners. Far from distancing "civilized" Germany from the uncivilized world, these shows served to bridge the divide, breaking down rather than confirming stereotypes and contributing to an emotional, if not always romantic, bond between Berliners and the people on display. And these bonds, it should be said, developed contrary to the organizers' efforts. Hagenbeck avoided wherever possible recruiting participants who could speak English (foreign German-speakers were so few as not to be a cause of concern) and prohibited them from leaving the zoo during the show, a ban that was difficult to implement in practice.[119]

The other major ethnographic display of 1879, the Lapps of Scandinavia, was not as "exotic" as some of the other groups, but Berlin scientists used their "plainness" to make a point about the scientific merit of the shows. "Anthropology does not aim to showcase only those people whose appearance will cause a fright," leading members of the Berlin Society for Anthropology wrote, "those with spikes in their ears, nose rings, or tattoos on their body. Rather, it is much more interested in spreading knowledge about the various branches of humanity and the relationships between races."[120] The scientific community also took pride in making the displays of humans in the zoo tasteful. Instead of parading the visitors before the public out of context in circus-like fashion, zoo officials allowed the Lapps to build huts as they would at home, to be displayed authentically.

Jacobsen, the zoo's liaison with northern peoples, had recruited the first Inuit to the zoo, and when he arrived in Greenland in 1880 to recruit a new group of Inuit to tour Germany, locals treated him to a hero's return. Inuit paddled out to Jacobsen's galleon *Der Eisbär* (Polar Bear), a vessel equipped especially for the transport of ethnographic troupes. Scores of kayaks bumped into each other in the churned-up waters around the vessel, as the kayakers were all hoping to be "noticed and recruited." Jacobsen's champion Carl Hagenbeck wrote later in his diary, "Okabak, Kojange, and Kokkik, the Eskimos who were in Europe three years ago, were now well-to-do people, and have long inspired the wish among their acquaintances to share in the same good fortune."[121] When they were invited aboard, the Inuit, according to Hagenbeck, could not resist the melodies of the organ grinder on the ship, dancing in improvised balls, taking up every open space on deck, tripping over steel planks, pulling themselves up again, laughing, and dancing some more.[122]

Although he had many willing subjects, Jacobsen was unable to reach a compromise with the Danish government to bring them to Germany, forcing him to look elsewhere for a show troupe. Setting sail for the West, Jacobsen arrived in Hebron in Labrador, a fifty-year-old Moravian mission. When he encountered a group of missionaries who advised their charges against the voyage to Europe, Jacobsen headed farther north, to "uncivilized" Inuit territory. There, with the help of a trader from the Hudson's Bay Company, he recruited an Inuit family of three and five of their acquaintances, including the interpreter Abraham, who agreed to the trip in return for a year's supply of provisions for his ailing mother in Labrador.[123]

At the end of August, the *Polar Bear* set sail for Hamburg amid roiling seas, an inauspicious beginning on a journey away from a homeland that the Inuit would not see again. The passengers were violently ill for the first eight days of the voyage. Paingo, the mother of the lone teenager in the group, took comfort in tobacco whenever the captain informed her that Hamburg was still a long way off. Nearly a month later, the *Polar Bear* encountered a ferocious storm as it entered the North Sea, leading Tigganiak, the shaman of the troupe, to stand on the bow and bid the seas to calm. Even the European sailors wondered about his powers when the storm subsided shortly afterward.[124] At the end of September, the eight-person troupe, ranging in age from one to approximately fifty (Paingo's age was not known for certain), finally docked in Hamburg, where the Inuit were exhibited for a month before continuing on to Berlin, Prague, Frankfurt, Darmstadt, Krefeld, and Paris.[125]

Through a stroke of good fortune, the diary of the interpreter Abraham found its way from Europe to the Moravian mission in Labrador after the tour, where it was bundled up with other records from the area and sent to the archives of the American province of the Moravian church in Bethlehem, Pennsylvania.[126] Abraham's account is one of the very few records of these shows from the perspective of a participant. His first impression of the German capital was what might be expected, a comment on urbanization and the absence of nature: "In

Berlin it is not beautiful because with all those people and trees it is impossible . . . . The air is constantly buzzing because of the walking and driving."[127] We know from Abraham's diary that the Inuit presence in Berlin caused such a sensation that at one point crowds ripped down the fencing in order to approach them. "One day a big gentleman came to see us," wrote Abraham. "He had many gentlemen with him. They came into our enclosure to see the kayak but immediately everything was filled with people and it was impossible to move anymore . . . . Since [Jacobsen and Schoepf] failed to achieve anything they came to me and sent me to chase them out. I did what I could. Taking my whip and the Greenland seal harpoon, I made myself terrible. One of the gentlemen was like a crier. Others quickly shook hands with me when I chased them out. Others went and jumped over the fence because there were so many."[128]

As much as the show organizers wanted to prevent any contact between the performers and locals, that border was very porous, as the above incident illustrates. Occasionally, the performers were permitted outside the zoo. In Prague, for example, the Inuit gathered around a pond in the city to hunt a seal that had been brought from Holland. A large and boisterous crowd erupted in deafening applause and a band filled the air with music when Abraham finally harpooned the animal. Zoo visitors also brought food to the Inuit, the fresh fruit and other "good-tasting things" very pleasing to Abraham.[129]

By January 1881, five months after their arrival in Europe, all the Inuit were dead. As there was no European doctor in Labrador, Jacobsen had opted to have the troupe immunized upon arrival in Hamburg, but because he became ill, he did not arrange for this immunization immediately. Sara, the four-year-old, died in Krefeld from smallpox, a disease that affected the others with ferocious rapidity, such that the immunization they eventually received in Paris was ineffectual.[130] For the remaining members of the troupe, the journey that began in Nachvak, Labrador, ended at the Hospital St. Louis in Paris. A letter from Abraham to a friend at the Moravian mission in Canada provides a sorrowful account of his own impending demise: "My dear teacher Elsner, pray for us that this sickness be removed, it if be His will; but His will be done. I am a poor man like the dust."[131] An early chronicler of the events minced no words, pointing a finger at Hagenbeck and

Jacobsen for having butchered the "poor creatures" in order to make a "Roman holiday."[132]

Afterward, Jacobsen claimed that the deaths of the Inuit caused him much soul-searching: "Did I really have to lead these poor brave people from their homeland only to find their grave in foreign soil? How did everything come to pass so differently from my intention?"[133] Abraham's diary paints a picture of a much different Jacobsen, however, one who did not shy away from corporal punishment. "Something sad happened to us," wrote Abraham in his diary. "Our companion, the single man Tobias, was beaten with a dog whip by our master, Jacobsen. Mr. Jacobsen was very furious because Tobias did not do what he was told."[134] Given Abraham's account, it might be fair to question the sincerity of Jacobsen's remorse.

Even before the deaths of the Inuit, the displays of humans in zoos—and particularly in zoos—had caused discomfort in certain circles. The large regional daily, the *Magdeburger Zeitung*, ran an article under the headline "The Eskimos in Berlin's Zoological Garden," which outlined the matter succinctly: "We are fully prepared for the fact that our point of view will be mocked and dismissed as sentimental. Nevertheless, we want to register our view. Should these 'interesting' humans be put on display, then our own sense of 'race propriety' should prevent us from allowing our equals to be viewed in a zoo."[135]

Virchow did not share the author's concerns, responding viciously:

The author's line of reasoning is basically that—and this is the point I would really like to touch on—there is no academic rationale behind the shows, and that for the vast majority of spectators there is little more than a raw curiosity. The author likes to insert the phrase "It is nevertheless interesting" from time to time, as if that were a criticism. In so far, it appears that it is not clear to the author that "interest" can be varied, that certain things are interesting in terms of a curiosity.... Yes, as a matter of fact, these notions of humanity are of interest to anyone who has even a passing desire to be informed about the place of humans in the natural world....

Anyone who is unable to comprehend this, anyone whose education is so minimal that they do not see that these are the greatest questions that humanity can pose, anyone who believes that these questions should not be on the daily agenda, anyone like that should not be permitted to write opinion pieces. At a minimum, the editors should think twice before taking such a gossip-monger into its columns.[136]

The exchange of letters reveals a divide that frequently emerged between a sympathetic public, who did not share the academic world's view of a racial hierarchy, and scholars who found it acceptable to display humans in a zoo. Virchow is perhaps the best example of an academic who did not see the people on display as the equals of Germans. In his utterly emotionless account of measuring the Inuit, he wrote:

It might interest you to hear about Frau Bairngo's episode which I recently witnessed. You will have all seen by now how shy the daughter is; she looks like a caged animal. The mother isn't as sensitive, but she too is intensely wary. . . . It was exceptionally difficult to carry out the measurements on her, unlike others. I started with the simplest measurements and tried to gradually convince her that nothing bad would happen. But each new act caused her more anxiety and as soon as I started with body measurements, she started to tremble and got very agitated.

During the measurement of her armspan, when I extended her arms horizontally, she suddenly suffered an attack. She pushed her way under my arm and started to tidy up around the room in a way that I had never seen before, even though I had been for years the attending physician at a prison and had seen the most peculiar kinds of rage-induced seizures. At first I thought that she would go into convulsions, but it quickly became clear that this was not a physical seizure, but rather a psychological one, similar to those experienced by people in a fit of rage. Even among our people are those who, when in a fit of rage, run around a room destroying everything and do the oddest things. . . . This case was very similar. She jumped around the room in a crouching position, throwing chairs and tables in all directions. While she bounded around the room, she did not make the least effort to head out the door or to approach the others in the room. She leapt howling from one corner to the other; her hideous face looked deep red, her eyes blazed, foam appeared around her mouth. Suffice it to say it was a disgusting sight. . . .

The seizure lasted about 8–10 minutes. Then, all of a sudden she was quiet. She laid her head on the table and stayed in this position for a few minutes before righting herself and saying in her native tongue: "I'm better now." Since she was still trembling, I decided not to continue with the measurements.[137]

The tragic end of the Inuit show in 1881 did little to change what had become a profit maker for zoos that was too successful to be discarded. In October of that year, Carl Hagenbeck arranged for a group of *Feuerländer* (native Chileans from Tierra del Fuego) to be brought to the Berlin zoo from Chile. His sales pitch to the Berlin zoo, which referenced the display that the Paris zoo had held of this same group from Chile, revealed both the significant profits involved in these exhibitions and his crass showmanship: "It is a fact that these people are real cannibals. To demonstrate the power that the label 'man-eater' holds, let me mention that the income of the *Jardin d'Acclimitation* [in Paris] last month was around 150,000 francs."[138] Even though the Chileans lacked the animals that had accompanied the Nubians, their presence was still a boon for the Berlin zoo, drawing 37,000 visitors in one day and accounting for the majority of the zoo's profits in 1881. Hagenbeck was likely correct that people were drawn to the group by his promotional advertising, which employed sensational terms like "cannibals" and "a primitive people from a bygone era."[139]

Newspaper feature articles on the forthcoming show were laced with fascination and horror: "They know no government. They move up and down the coast without a chief, eating fish, berries, and the carcasses of seals and whales. When it is necessary to do so, they don't hesitate to eat humans. Their language consists mostly of raw, short, guttural noises."[140] And from *Die Gartenlaube*: "Men, women, and children go about completely naked. They don't even know the cleansing properties of water."[141] A columnist from the Leipzig *Illustrierte Zeitung* seemed himself to be speechless when he described the Chileans in town: "Impassive and speechless, they squat around a flickering pile of wood."[142] Heinrich Leutemann, a nineteenth-century biographer of Hagenbeck, came to the defense of the native Chileans, but this action alone suggests that the image of them in the media as creatures only one step removed from the apes was widespread. "Even a cursory look at them," Leutemann wrote, "provides irrefutable evidence that these savages are in no way the depraved figures that one has become accustomed to reading about."[143] One Berlin newspaper described them as "the lowest rung of civilization" and urged that they not be thought of as the "Eskimos of the south," given that the Eskimos were, in the newspaper's view, much higher on the chain of civilization.[144] Like the Inuit from Labrador, this group also met a tragic end. Five of the eleven died from lung infections or stomach issues, causing Hagenbeck to abruptly break off the show in Zurich and send the remaining participants back to Chile.[145]

The death toll from these shows now stood at thirteen, but the public, organizers, and host institutions were too caught up in their own excitement, curiosity, and enormous profits to consider the high cost that other people were paying for their own enjoyment. After a quiet 1882 in which no ethnographic shows took place at the Berlin zoo, or, for that matter, anywhere else in Germany, 1883 was a blockbuster year, with the Berlin zoo hosting three shows involving far more participants, far more visitors, and far more money than any of the previous shows. A group of twenty-two Calmucks, Mongolian nomads, and their animals resided in the Berlin zoo for three weeks in July 1883. The zoo took out a splashy ad in a major Berlin daily to whet the appetite of Berliners:

CALMUCKS! CALMUCKS!
The Calmuck encampment in the Zoological Garten!!
10 Men, including 2 religious leaders in their magnificent regalia!
8 Women, in their picturesque national costumes
4 Children, 18 Camels, 8 horses, 8 foals, 8 fat-tailed sheep!!
Religious ceremonies!
Displays of horseback riding!
Milking of female horses!
Babies who smoke![146]

In contrast to the *Feuerländer*, whose show was a subdued affair, the Calmucks put on elaborate displays of singing and dancing, riding camels and horses, and lassoing. They also re-enacted a traditional wedding ceremony and moved their encampment from one part of the zoo to another. In the "Decampment for the steppes," the Calmucks took down their improvised tents, bade the camels to kneel, loaded them, and formed into a procession, two holy men leading the way, men on horses following, women and children on camels at the rear, and all around the procession sheep and foals gamboling.[147]

An ad that the clothing store, the Golden 110, took out in a Berlin newspaper captured some of the excitement around the Calmuck show. Calling them "Our Calmucks," the marketers at the clothing store took advantage of the foreign peoples in town to promote their high-end fashions:

Berliners are now really out and about
And have diversions by the mile
Nothing could be finer though
Than with our Calmucks to while!
The men: Kind. The women: Slim
Their hair is very woolly.
Two holy men are also here.
As I said, it's all very chummy!
Only about one thing was I shy,
I say this in truth,
That they, while otherwise well dressed,
Had so little on.
I asked the old one why this was so
To which he shed a tear
And spoke plain: We don't have the Hundred Ten!

The personable Calmucks' lively displays likely contributed to the show's achieving the highest single-day attendance of any to date, a success that Hagenbeck noted in his memoir: "I can still remember the joy that I experienced when I received from Berlin a telegram with the following message: 'So far, about 80,000 visitors. Traffic can only be managed through the use of a large number of security people on foot and on horseback.' These 80,000 had visited the zoo on one single day, by 4 P.M. By the time evening arrived, that number had risen to 93,000."[148] In fact, the zoo was overflowing at 7 A.M. on that first Sunday of the Calmuck show, requiring extra viewing platforms to be installed on top of the carnivore pavilion and straining the food and beverage services which, by the end of the day, had poured nearly 23,000 liters of beer.[149] When the Calmucks returned to the Berlin zoo four years later, none of their appeal had waned. On several Sundays during their stay, the Calmucks put on seven different shows daily—almost hourly—to accommodate the throngs. The crowds that gathered for the Calmucks outside both of the zoo's entrances were so large that one newspaper reported a passersby would be forgiven for thinking that a mass migration of Germans (*Völkerwanderung*) was occurring.[150]

It is worth pausing to consider these attendance figures. Berlin's population at the time of the Calmuck show was approximately 1.3 million, meaning that 7 percent of the entire population—every man, woman, and child—went to the zoo to see the nomadic Asian peoples on a single day.[151] With a seating capacity of 74,000, a sold-out Olympic stadium in today's Berlin, the largest venue in the city, would pale in comparison. Getting to the zoo had become somewhat easier with the introduction of the S-Bahn, the city train, in the 1860s and electric trams in 1881, but the transportation infrastructure was still rudimentary. It would have been a mild ordeal for most visitors to get to the zoo; although Berlin had expanded, the zoo was still on the outskirts.

Several months later, Berliners headed in similar numbers to the zoo, this time to see fire-eaters, snake charmers, and elephants. The group consisted of twenty-one Sinhalese people from Ceylon, today's Sri Lanka, and included children ranging in age from four months to four years; there were also ten elephants, eight zebus, and several other animals. The troupe stayed in the zoo for nearly eight weeks. On one Sunday, nearly 100,000 people visited the show, mesmerized by the snake charmer and amazed by the elephants that could transport tree limbs weighing 2,000 pounds.[152] The spectacle attracted members of the royal family, including the princess of Schleswig-Holstein and the three daughters of the crown prince.[153] Although there was a certain amount of self-promotion involved, it was no exaggeration for Hagenbeck to claim that the show had "cast a spell" on the public.[154]

The Sinhalese show was popular throughout Europe, returning year after year to major cities across the continent including Berlin in 1884. One of the most striking scenes during that show occurred when the Sinhalese visited the "cannibals" from New Zealand who were being exhibited in Castan's Panopticon. After an initial moment of astonishment, they tried briefly to communicate in English before performing traditional dances for each other. They then left the panopticon to marvel at the streets of Berlin lit up by gas and electricity.[155] Two years later in Paris, the show attracted more than 1 million visitors in six weeks, an average of 23,000 a day.[156] Following on the success of the Sinhalese show, the Berlin zoo board entered into discussions with Carl Hagenbeck for a new, larger show, consisting of fifty-one Sinhalese, more than double the number of people in the first show. In response to Hagenbeck's concerns about the zoo's ability to accommodate a group that size, the board agreed to convert one of its aviaries, essentially sacrificing its animals, the heart of its initial mission, in favor of the human animal.[157]

Berlin academics used the display of Sinhalese at the zoo to educate the public through a series of newspaper articles. Anthropologists described Sinhalese marriage practices, beginning with weddings, where the bride was typically between ten and twelve years old, half the age of the groom, and the wedding ceremony was performed by pouring water over the fingers of bride and groom that had been bound together. In the interior of the country, the academics felt it important to point out, the people practiced polyandry, whereby several brothers had the same wife.[158] They said of the Sinhalese: "Conviviality and hospitality are only practiced at weddings and other major social occasions. The tender sentiments of love and friendship are foreign to them. In their place are hatred and a constant desire for revenge . . . . They have learned to hide, especially from Europeans, their deceitful ways." [159] Other scholars dismissed Sinhalese science as the "most basic" and, although they were officially Buddhist, one author thought it would be more accurate to describe their religion as "superstitious."[160] Still, Berlin academics, including Heinrich Becker, recognized the relatively high placement of Ceylonese on their imagined hierarchy of civilization. They noted with approval that most men could write (the women and children could not) and that they could do so in beautiful penmanship. Their language was "sweet-sounding." "All told," concluded the author, "we recognize here a people of paradise, not in a vulgar sense of living care-free among the animals. Rather, a people of culture who, even if not travelling at the same pace as ourselves, has started down the path, so much so that we need not be ashamed that our races are related."[161]

Given the resounding success of these ethnographic spectacles and their frenzied anticipation by the public, the failure of the Bella Coola show is notable. A dismal draw particularly in Berlin, the display of aboriginal people from British Columbia, Canada, deeply disappointed its organizers, who had undertaken enormous efforts to arrange the show, and the institutional hosts who had expected large profits.[162] One of the show's main promoters, Adrian Jacobsen, described in his memoirs the reaction to the Bella Coola as "cool."[163] A typical Sunday, usually the day with the highest attendance, drew 5,600 people to the Bella Coola show in Kroll's Theater in Berlin, a far cry from the 100,000 who viewed the Sinhalese show at the Berlin zoo on a comparable Sunday.[164]

Jacobsen, the same northern explorer who had arranged the show of Labrador Inuit that ended so tragically, had become interested in a show of northwest coast aboriginal people while collecting artifacts in Canada for the Royal Museum of Ethnography in Berlin. The Bella Coola, a people residing in the area around the town of the same name in what is today the Nuxalk Nation, had first come into contact with non-aboriginal people when George Vancouver encountered the group during his explorations of 1793. Sporadic contact after this first encounter gave way to sustained engagement between non-aboriginal people and Euro-Americans when the Hudson's Bay Company opened a permanent trading post in Bella Coola in 1867, the year of Canada's confederation.[165] Upon his return to the Prussian capital, Jacobsen contacted his friend and former business partner Carl Hagenbeck, who agreed to finance the show. As Jacobsen had already committed to another artifact-gathering expedition, this time in Siberia, Hagenbeck employed Jacobsen's younger, inexperienced brother Filip, who was living among the Bella Coola for his anthropological research, to recruit the group. Although he had learned Chinook in previous trips to the area, Filip was unable to reach an agreement with the Canadian aboriginal people, causing his brother Adrian to cut short his Siberian expedition and head for the west coast of Canada, which in itself was an extraordinary journey.[166] Jacobsen left Vladivostok in April 1885 for Korea and then traveled to Nagasaki, where he boarded the liner *City of New York* bound for

San Francisco, arriving two weeks later. He then traveled north along the coast to his final destination, Bella Coola.

In return for passage to Germany and $20 per month wages, the nine male Bella Coola agreed to accompany Jacobsen back to Germany and once there to perform for the public in terms outlined by the contract:

> The said parties of the first part agree with the said John Adrain [*sic*] Jacobsen that they will forthwith proceed with the said John Adrain Jacobsen to Germany and will there at such place or places as the said John Adrain Jacobsen may determine and between the hours of eight and twelve o'clock in the forenoon and between half past one and six in the afternoon inclusive of Sundays according [to] the best of his skill and ability in concert with the other parties of the first part and under direction of the said John Adrain Jacobsen exhibit himself before the Public in the performance of Indian Games and recreations in the use of Bows and arrows in singing and dancing and speaking and otherwise in showing the habits manners and customs of the Indians and will during the term of the engagement hereinafter mentioned behave himself reasonably and respectably.[167]

The Bella Coola then began a journey halfway around the world. Arriving in Portland by ship, they embarked in a train for their cross-continental journey to New York City, with stops in Minneapolis and Chicago. The steamship *Werra* of the North German Lloyd line delivered them in ten days to Bremen, the first stop on a tour that would include twenty-seven German cities.[168]

By all accounts, the Bella Coola show was highly entertaining. Newspapers reported in glowing terms on the dances the group performed, including the Thunder Dance and the Cannibal Dance—according to the papers a tribute to their human-eating ancestors—and on the beautiful masks and costumes. The group put on archery displays and potlatch festivals, while their shamans "cured" the ill.[169] The Bella Coola also had a flare for showmanship. One of their acts involved the "burning" of a shaman, whereby one of the group was put into a box and, according to the Breslau newspaper, the box was "tossed onto the fire, where after a while it burst into flame…. What a sight! There, in the glowing remains, was a charred head and body parts. The

A group of Nubians from what is today Sudan pose with their weapons in 1878. Berliners turned out in droves to see these first people of color to be put on display at the zoo. *Berlin Zoo Archive*

deception was striking.... With a loud cry from the garden, the shaman reappeared, healthy and unscathed, and joined his friends. Not even those standing close to the performance could solve the riddle of the burning."[170]

One of the most dramatic incidents involving the Bella Coola took place during the show's stop in Berlin. One evening after the theater had closed, the Bella Coola were performing a sacred dance, one that tolerated no error, when the youth Pook-Pook stumbled and fell. Believing that the god Manitou had been insulted by the miscue, the Bella Coola chief ran at Pook-Pook, his tomahawk at the ready. Only a rapid intervention by Captain Jacobsen, who had witnessed the entire event, saved the youth. The journalist covering the incident praised the captain, the embodiment of civilization, who saved the savages from themselves: "A real murderous lot, these Coola-Indians! And what a romantic role played by Captain Jacobsen!"[171]

On the whole, the show failed to draw, causing several host institutions to complain to Jacobsen about the lack of income. The host in

Weimar wrote in January 1886: "The business this evening has been bad. Only 7 marks." In Berlin, the show was so poorly attended that it ended two weeks early. What's more, the entire exhibit of artifacts that had accompanied the show was stolen as it sat packed up in a back room of Kroll's Theater awaiting transport.[172]

Having spent nearly a year in Germany, the Bella Coola in July 1886 embarked from Bremerhaven for North America. Jacobsen's brother Filip, who had been unsuccessful in his attempts to recruit the Bella Coola, greeted them upon their arrival back in their hometown in British Columbia, a place in which he had decided he would spend the rest of his days. Indeed, he was so effusive about the natural beauty of the area in his articles in American newspapers that Norwegian colonists from Minnesota moved to the area and established a utopian religious community.[173]

Scholars have pointed to a number of possible reasons for the failure of the Bella Coola to connect with the public, foremost among them German preconceptions of "Indian." Lacking horses, feathered head-dresses, and red-toned skin, the Bella Coola did not match the portrayal of Indians that Germans had come to know in literary works, like those of James Fenimore Cooper, of *Last of the Mohicans* fame. (The well-known German author of the "Wild West," Karl May, did not come to prominence until the 1890s, after the Bella Coola had been to Germany.) One reporter cautioned: "If you are not to be disappointed, you must put away all preconceptions, formed perhaps by Cooper, of Indians."[174] Jacobsen, it appears, had brought over the "wrong" Indians, northwest coast residents lacking the trappings of the Plains Indians.

The failure of the Bella Coola show is only partially explained by the fact that the showmen did not match the fictive reference points of Germans. After all, it would be difficult to argue that literary depictions of Plains Indians (which were mostly absent from Cooper's works any-way) would have come to stand in the German mind for "all Indians."[175] And other reference points were lacking. The extravagant, over-the-top Buffalo Bill Wild West shows—showcasing more than 200 perform-ers, re-enactments of stage coach hijacking, lasso displays, and other "cowboy fun"—were five years away from their first appearance in Germany. Moreover, the Bella Coola show itself was highly entertain-ing, and the Bella Coola certainly looked exotic, sporting feathers (if not the elaborate headdresses of the Sioux), magnificent bird masks, and traditional clothing with northwest aboriginal motifs, and possessing elongated skulls, a feature that the leading Berlin anthropologist Rudolf Virchow referred to as "the deformation of their heads."[176] The show opened in the Kroll Theater to a packed house of invited dignitaries, including members of the Geographic Society, the Anthropological Society, and the Colonial Society. The crown prince was unable to attend but sent his adjutant in his place.[177] In short, they more than fulfilled the three criteria that Hagenbeck had already determined were critical to a show's financial success: foreignness, physical distinctions, and a "picturesque way of living."[178] Moreover, no German could have reasonably expected another opportunity to interact with a Canadian aboriginal person in his or her lifetime.

The Berlin public may well have perceived the show as mundane not because of any cultural preconceptions but simply because of the extravagant shows that had preceded it. The Bella Coola troupe fol-lowed in the wake of the Sinhalese, the most spectacular of all the ethnographic shows, with more than fifty participants, ten elephants, fire-eaters, and snake charmers. Before that, the Calmuck show, with its dozens of animals and wedding re-enactments, had caused a stir, to say nothing of the ostrich-riding Somalis who were put on display in the Berlin zoo in 1885.[179] The all-male troupe of Bella Coola, the first show in Berlin since the initial one in 1877 not to have children, and devoid of a single animal, paled in comparison.[180] It is true that the animal-less Chilean group drew well, but they showcased women and children, and Hagenbeck marketed them as authentic cannibals. The Bella Coola, in contrast, only performed a cannibal dance.

Given the paucity of sources, it may be impossible to know for cer-tain how Berlin compared to other cities in this regard, but there are suggestions that the show performed worse in Berlin than elsewhere. Berlin was, for example, the only city where the show was canceled early. Other cities seemed to have had somewhat better success, as in Cologne, where Jacobsen reported: "Business here is very good. Castan [the host] has nothing to complain about. Last Sunday we had about 4,000 people, and we're expecting roughly the same today."[181]

A further mundane issue, but one not without consequence, affected the Bella Coola's time in Berlin: The winter of 1886 was miserable.

Newspapers are replete with reports of the worst winter on record. Twenty-three days in January 1886 were "frost days," and nine of those were "ice days" when the temperature did not reach zero degrees Celsius. A vicious snowstorm buffeted Berlin on January 21 and 22.[182]

It appears that Berlin, accustomed to extravagant shows, had become spoiled. Apart from Jacobsen's comments about the show's success elsewhere, there is other evidence about Berlin's fussy tastes. A re-creation of a Dinka village in Hamburg, involving nearly forty members of that African tribe, attracted large crowds, prompting the Berlin zoo to request the group for one month in the late summer of 1895. According to newspaper reports, the show, featuring "black giants from equatorial Africa," was "stranger" than any show that had come before. Audiences were further enticed with the description of the Africans as having "frighteningly wild faces." [183] Despite agreeable weather, the show failed to draw the same way it had in Hamburg. The chair of the Berlin zoo's board, Franz Duncker, of the prominent Berlin bookselling family, intimated that for Berlin—and especially Berlin—static exhibits of peoples no longer excited the public. In his oral report to the board, he said about the Dinka village: "On the whole, experience has taught us that for these types of performances there is in the Berlin population no longer the same interest that once existed. Only extraordinary offerings, ones that are today extremely hard to acquire, can be expected to be successful."[184] It was now going to take a more extravagant show to get residents of Europe's newest imperial capital to leave their homes, especially during a miserable winter.

Although the Bella Coola did not attract the public as other shows did, they were exceedingly popular with Germany's academics. Franz Boas, the future expert on northwest coast aboriginal peoples and pioneer of American anthropology, spent much time studying the language of the Bella Coola while they resided in Berlin and presenting his findings to the Berlin Society for Anthropology, Ethnography, and Prehistory.[185] Captivated by what he had seen in Berlin, Boas traveled to North America to study its aboriginal people, initially teaming up with Frederic Putnam, curator of Harvard University's Peabody Museum, to study the Kwakwaka'wakw people of the northwest coast. He then traveled to British Columbia, collecting Bella Coola tales in Victoria for a number of years before venturing into the Bella Coola valley itself.

Having amassed Bella Coola stories and created a catalogue of their dance masks, Boas published his findings in 1897 in a seminal work, *The Mythology of the Bella Coola Indians.*[186] Carl Stump, a psychology professor at the University of Berlin and music ethnographer transcribed seven songs that the Bella Coola performed for him, while Rudolf Virchow impressed upon Germans the singular opportunity afforded by the visit of the Canadian aboriginal people: "By virtue of the deformation of their heads, the peculiar formation of their faces, their quite singular language, their highly developed artisanship, they are immediately rendered conspicuous among the multitude of American native peoples. For this reason they afford one of the most interesting objects for the observation of every thinking human being."[187] By this time, anthropologists in many instances had come to rely solely on Hagenbeck's troupes for their understanding of other peoples. The entries on the Chilean *Feuerländer*, the Nubians, and the "Eskimos" in the standard anthropological work of the day, Friedrich Ratzel's *Völkerkunde*, were based exclusively on the shows. Similarly, Virchow's studies of groups brought to Berlin formed the basis of Johannes Ranke's monumental two-volume work *Der Mensch.*[188]

One reminder of the failed Bella Coola show remains in Berlin to this day. The totem pole that the Bella Coola fashioned during their stay continues to form the backdrop of the buffalo enclosure.[189]

The next show to rival the success of the spectacular Sinhalese show of 1883 was the Samoan show of 1900. The previous year, Samoa had become a German colony, drawing to a close Germany's brief and belated period of acquiring lands overseas. Samoa, a small group of islands in the south Pacific, joined the African colonies of Cameroon, Togo, German Southwest Africa, German East Africa, and the Bismarck Archipelago lands of German New Guinea and parts of the Carolina, Mariana, Marshall, and Solomon Islands as German colonial possessions. Billed in a publicity blitz as an exhibit of "our newest countrymen," the show, consisting of nine men, ten women, and a five-year-old, was an extravaganza. The landscape painter Berthold Gerbsch provided the thirty-meter-wide and nine-meter-high backdrop while palm trees and freshly sown grass were brought in to cover the terrain on which the exhibit took place. The zoo's marketers invited Berliners to witness the "unusual and never before seen Samoan practice of roasting an entire pig between leaves and glowing rocks."[190] The dances, coconut harvesting, and songs of the Samoans in Berlin struck a chord with the public. "Our new countrymen from the south sea," proclaimed a zoo publication "have in the course of time gained the sympathy of all visitors, through their melodic songs, their graceful dance movements, their charming appearance, and their cheerful disposition."[191]

Kaiser Wilhelm II was among those captivated by the colonials on display, ordering them to interrupt their show at the Berlin zoo and head to Kiel where he intended to show off his German warships. The Samoans performed traditional dances; laid gifts at the feet of the kaiser, crown prince, and other dignitaries who had gathered at the royal palace in Kiel to welcome them; and generally expressed humility in the presence of the "powerful ruler of the German empire." After about an hour, the kaiser took leave of his "new brown subjects," as one newspaper described them. [192] When it came time for the Samoans to leave Berlin, high-ranking officials from the Foreign Office and from the Colonial Office presented gifts of pocket watches and gold chains to the men; brooches, rings, and silver chains to the women; and toys to the children.[193]

Alfred Kerr, one of Berlin's most colorful essayists, also raved about the colonial peoples on display: "Samoa is German! As this message flew through Germany in November 1899, likely every German heart beat with satisfaction …. Those on display in western Berlin are a kind, lovely, light brown … people."[194] Indeed, Germans were awestruck by the physical beauty of the Samoans. Newspapers referred to them as "beautiful figures, in every respect,"[195] reported on their "magnificently developed muscles,"[196] and described them as "beautiful marzipan dolls covered in chocolate."[197]

The Samoan show was the first and last of the exhibits of people from Germany's colonies. Perhaps somewhat counterintuitively, the Colonial Society opposed the shows, criticizing them for "burdening [the visitors] with civilization." Ludwig Heck, the director of the zoo at the time of the Samoan show, responded directly to the criticism, urging members of the Colonial Society to take in the show for themselves and to witness the harmless exchanges between Germans and Samoans. He emphasized that the Samoan show, like all of the zoo's ethnographic shows, was informed by science and should not be compared to the

freak shows taking place across town where there had been alterca-
tions between Europeans and "the wild ones."[198] He added: "You might
then even endorse our view, that these exhibits of our newest countrymen foster rather than harm our colonial aspirations. Politically for the
Samoans, these shows are not to be underestimated, for they will leave
here not only with handsome profits, but certainly also with an excellent
impression of the capital, and of the greatness and power of Germany.
The sight of our troops and their equipment at the last parade rendered
them practically speechless."[199] Heck's pleas fell on deaf ears. The following year the Colonial Society banned the exhibit of peoples from
the German colonies because it believed that exposure to Germany
was negatively influencing native people's views of their new colonial
overlords.

Heck's protests to the Colonial Society may have been based in part
on an exaggerated view of the show's academic qualities, but compared
to other human exhibits in town at the same time, the Samoan show
was positively highbrow. Barnum and Bailey's show on the Ku' damm,
Berlin's main shopping street, boasted "1000 men, women, horses,
dwarfs, tattooed people; a woman with long hair and a full beard; a
child with a dog's head; men without arms; jugglers."[200] At Castan's
Panopticon, visitors were invited to see a Hindu boy without arms and
legs, and a young girl with the head of an orange.[201]

The keen popular interest in the zoo and the staggering crowds at
the ethnographic shows can be explained in part by the era's general
thirst for a glimpse into unknown parts of the globe. "The [Nubians
on display]," wrote the *Neue Hannoversche Zeitung,* "excite us, and put
thoughts in our heads of those African deserts and countries, the study
of which has caused so many academics to travel there."[202] Beginning
with Richard Lepsius's 1842 archaeological investigation of Egypt, the
first African expedition financed by the Prussian state, the hodgepodge
of adventure seekers, geographers, and explorers who visited what was
for Europeans the most mysterious continent began to take on institutional form. Geographers formed themselves into the German Society
for Research on Equatorial Africa in 1873, a group comprised of young
and courageous individuals who fanned out across the vast continent.
In the second half of the nineteenth century, some 100 young Germans,
typically in their late twenties, frequently with advanced degrees from

While on display at the Passage Panopticon in Berlin in 1906, Maria Fassnauer, also known as Mariedl, demonstrates her height of seven feet compared to that of an average man. The Berlin zoo management was eager to distinguish its "scientific" ethnographic exhibits from these types of displays, which it considered freak shows with no educational value. *Archive of the Berlin Society for Anthropology, Ethnography, and Pre-History, FS 00792*

the University of Berlin, headed for Africa, nearly a third of whom died there.[203]

Some of these expeditions had the express purpose of fostering a German colonial presence in Africa, such as Carl Peters's trip in 1884 under his newly established Society for German Colonization, which was integral in establishing German East Africa, today's Tanzania.[204] Others, such as the 1873 Loango expedition, aimed to explore equatorial Africa while bringing to Europe what many people at the time thought to be a purely mythical creature—a gorilla.[205] The expedition got off to a disastrous start when its ship wrecked off the African coast, destroying valuable scientific instruments on board. Determined to salvage the expedition, the eight explorers waded ashore and established a small camp. One member of the group, Julius Falkenstein, purchased a young male gorilla from a Portuguese trader, which he then sold to the aquarium at the Berlin zoo, only the second live gorilla to be displayed on the European continent.[206] The aquarium management arranged to have the rare animal paraded through town on its way to the aquarium, a spectacle that prompted the aged Charles Darwin, Britain's foremost naturalist, who had published *On the Origin of Species* sixteen years earlier, to send a letter of congratulations to the aquarium director.[207]

"M'Pungu" succumbed to a lung infection less than two years after his arrival, an affliction that in the nineteenth and first half of the twentieth century killed virtually all gorillas in captivity. Still, the presence in Berlin of a live gorilla, no matter how brief, combined with the publication of Darwin's landmark *On the Origin of Species*, meant that apes became for a time the city's most popular topic. In an article in a popular natural history journal, Julius Falkenstein, who, upon his return from his African adventure, wrote of Berlin's enthusiasm for primates: "Who hasn't heard talk of apes over the past few years? Who hasn't himself talked about them many times over? Who wasn't most interested to hear that the king of the anthropoids had finally made it alive to Europe?"[208]

Regardless of whether the motive for exploration was scientific or political, the explorers' tales ignited the imagination of the Berlin public, who bought their works in droves. *Through the Dark Continent* by the British Congo explorer Henry Stanley, who found David Livingstone in what would become German East Africa, was translated into German in 1878. Thereafter, *Die Gartenlaube* featured Stanley's adventures in Africa on a regular basis.[209] Hermann Wissmann's 1881 account of his trek across the African continent, *Unter deutscher Flagge quer durch Afrika von West nach Ost* (Under the German flag across Africa from West to East) went through eight editions in its first thirteen years.[210] Heinrich Barth's *Travels and Discoveries in North and Central Africa* was pared down from its initial five volumes to cater to the general public.[211] The tireless campaigner against animal experimentation Ernst von Weber wrote a blockbuster, two-volume account of his time in Africa.[212] Adolph Thamm's diary of his voyage in the south seas to the new German colony of Samoa, part travelogue, part adventure tale, paints a picture of exquisite natural beauty, of lush vegetation and plentiful coconut and banana trees, and the occasional skirmish with the local inhabitants. Its appeal was no doubt all the greater because the author drowned on the return voyage. His brother Otto Thamm published Adolph's diary and letters posthumously under the matter-of-fact title *Von Kiel bis Samoa: Reise Erlebnisse des am 16.März 1889 ertrunkenen Obermatrosen Adolph Thamm* (*From Kiel to Samoa: Travel adventures of the senior sailor Adolph Thamm, drowned on 16 March 1889*).[213]

Aware of the increasing public appetite for real-life adventure tales, the *Vossische Zeitung*, Berlin's oldest newspaper and arguably Germany's national newspaper until the Nazis forced it to cease publication, commissioned Professor Karl Steinen, a researcher of Brazil and its peoples who had led an expedition there in 1887, to write a regular column for the newspaper giving updates along his journey to the Marquesas. Coincidentally, one of his first stops was in Clayoquot Sound in British Columbia, where he visited Filip Jacobsen, brother of Adrian, who had arranged for the shows of Inuit and Canadian aboriginal people at the Berlin zoo. Steinen expected to find Filip leading a simple life akin to the Bella Coola whom he had joined but was taken aback to find him surrounded by goods "like on Friedrichstrasse" in Berlin, including a tandem bicycle for female riders. Steinen was deeply dismayed by the encroachment of European civilization, lamenting the loss of mask-making ability among the local artists and the steady decline of the aboriginal population. In a similar vein, the popular magazine *Die Gartenlaube* printed articles on a regular basis from participants in major African expeditions, like the one to Loango in 1873, complete with enticing pictures of the adventurers' campsite, raft leaning up against a tent, sextants resting on spindly tables, measuring instruments on tripods, a small desk on which to record the wonders one encountered, and in the distance a charming African village.[214]

Having read of the explorers' daring encounters with peoples in faraway lands, a Berliner at the end of the nineteenth century could then leave her residence and take the tram line to see people from around the globe. There were times when she would have even been overwhelmed by the choice of human displays in town, like the winter of 1886 when she could have headed over to Kroll's Theater to see the Bella Coola aboriginal group from Canada or down the street to Castan's Panopticon to see the display of Sioux. If North American aboriginal peoples weren't her cup of tea, the Berliner could head across town to see a family of African pygmies at the Concordia Theater, the father of whom, at four feet, six inches, newspapers noted, was a "giant in his land."[215] Scarcely a few months later, our Berliner could have visited the show of thirty-three Calmucks at the Berlin zoo or the Hagenback Transvaal show a stone's throw away on Savignyplatz. At the nearby Passage Panopticon, she could see the Bedouins, dervishes, belly dancers, and snake charmers that the Panopticon marketed as "desert children." Berlin had indeed become "The World in Small" as the tagline for Castan's Panopticon read. Anytime any group of non-European peoples so much as passed through town, Berliners were abuzz, like this incident in 1888: "A group of dark-skinned Africans passed through the Friedrichstrasse train station yesterday. They were on their way to Warsaw, accompanied by Herr Hagenbeck. Their leader, a mulatto, wore shiny, magnificent rings on his fingers. The group looked like something out of a painting in their European travel outfits .... The men drank the Bavarian beer offered to them by onlookers and appeared to become very merry."[216]

The friendly gesture of alcohol stood in contrast to the way that many in Berlin's academic community responded to the peoples on display in the zoo. Leading figures in the Berlin Society for Anthropology, Ethnography, and Pre-History viewed those on display as primitive peoples, far below Germans on an imagined civilizational hierarchy, a glimpse into the past, and a curiosity to be gazed upon not terribly different from the animals that shared their enclosures. Rudolf Virchow embodied this viewpoint, leaving little doubt as to his belief in German superiority. On Inuit ability in math, he wrote: "Nothing solidifies the impression that the Eskimos are a lower race as does their difficulty with numbers." And likewise about their tools: "You will also see that nearly all of their tools for hunting and fishing are so similar, that one has the impression that you are looking at a small museum of pre-history."[217] Newspaper editorials continually emphasized the physical differences between Germans and those on display—height, hair, size of feet, and always, always, skin color. The Sinhalese from Ceylon ranged from olive brown to dark brown.[218] The Araucanians were "olive brown. The Calmucks were a "deep yellow."[219]

Newspapers and other popular outlets contained frequent references to the bare feet and simple clothing of those on display. One of Berlin's premier clothing stores, the Golden 110, took out large ads in Berlin dailies almost every time an ethnographic group was in town, using the rudimentary clothing of the guests as a reference point for the clothing riches that awaited customers at the store. The ad during the Sinhalese show ran as follows:

A horrible story!
More horrible has likely never happened—
It has touched me deeply—
In the zoological garden—that's where I saw it—
A Sinhalese. He's freezing!
Herr Hagenbeck—do you not have a humane bone?
To put on display half naked people in autumn
Is a bit too much!
Lions, bears—all creatures
Have pelts—and quite a bit of them—
Only your poor Sinhalesen
Are lacking a light overcoat!
Purchase at a bargain the best and warmest clothing.
The "Golden 110" exists out of pure humanity.[220]

A similar ad ran about the Bella Coola on display at Kroll's Theater:

> At Kroll's near the Brandenburg Gate
> Are Indians now on display.
> On Monday the countess Lola
> Saw for herself the Bella-Coola
> "Ah," she sighed, "the redskins
> really are a well built lot,
> One in particular
> Has a pair of civilized legs
> And dances so airily and gracefully
> As if Herr Engel [the owner of Kroll's Theater] was instructing him;
> There's only one thing that I find embarrassing:
> He is questionably dressed
> And reveals his wardrobe to be lacking.
> So follow this advice, Herr Engel,
> And send the wild man
> To the "Golden Hundred Ten"
> Because its glorious clothes will fit
> Even the wildest races of people.[221]

Newspapers tended to portray the exotic peoples in a similar vein to the marketers at the Golden 110, frequently using the terms "primitive" and "uncivilized," but most commonly they employed "savage" (wild). In a newspaper report praising Carl Hagenbeck, the organizer of most of these shows, the author wrote matter-of-factly: "It is certainly a very difficult task to acquire people of a wild or half-wild tribe to be put on display in civilized lands. Herr Hagenbeck deserves our recognition for his efforts."[222]

At the same time that German observers emphasized the lack of civilization among other peoples, they did not entirely dismiss the merits of their way of life. They waxed nostalgic, almost envious of the global guests because of the simpler life that they represented, one that was free from the burdens of civilization and more in tune with nature. Prior to the arrival of the Sinhalese at the Berlin zoo in 1884, Heinrich Becker wrote a lengthy article in the *Vossische Zeitung* entitled "The People and Landscape of the Old Paradise" that reveals in striking fashion the nostalgia for a past where people were closer to nature. The bygone "paradise" included animals who lived off the land, not from the hand of humans, and farmlands fertile enough to be tilled without plows. "The people of the East," the author wrote, referring to the Sinhalese, "had to come here to us, to remind us of their homeland, to present themselves to us as original peoples, so that we might reflect on the place from which our forefathers rode out, until, after endless migrations, they lost themselves in this Germanic land of fog."[223] The author clearly saw in the people from Ceylon a kindred spirit, the progenitor of the current German population: "Their dancing eyes, their lively language, the grace in all their movements which is most on display when they dance, remind me of Persians, Turks, and modern Greeks. Their color reveals the influence of the sun. Otherwise, there are hardly any differences between these Hindus and the great races of Europe."[224]

Newspaper journalists and other observers therefore did not by any means solely disparage the peoples on display but were more often than not effusive in their praise of certain qualities. They described Okabak, the patriarch of the first Inuit group, as a "dignified leader" and a "philosopher."[225] The *Vossische Zeitung* wrote glowingly of the Nubian horse-riding skills, attributing their prowess to an anatomical advantage: "It is a well-known fact that a distinct advantage of uncivilized peoples over even us is that each of their toes can be put to use. In our culture, the heavy use of boots has distorted the foot."[226] "This wild, unforced, training-free manner of riding," continued the editorial, "marks the Nubians as authentic, dark brown Centaurs. And as unforced as the riders are the animals themselves."[227] Newspaper writers further described the Sinhalese as "frugal, tidy, and resourceful."[228]

This combination of condescension and admiration, of fear and attraction, was most evident with the Chilean *Feuerländer*, the group touted as the most primitive on earth, representatives of a cannibal group numbering about 2,000 who were a throwback to the days of hunters and gatherers. According to Berlin's largest daily, they went about naked in their homeland and had an "empty expression," but they were also "peaceful" and "brave." Another reporter acknowledged that these "poor stepchildren of nature possessed admirable qualities."[229] Indeed, newspaper writers often singled out bravery and prowess in warfare and the hunt as admirable traits. One newspaper author thought it worthy of mention that the Araucanians a South American tribe, had demonstrated "outstanding bravery" in their fight against the conquistadors.[230] Even while the Golden 110 ads mocked the dress of the foreigners, they revealed these visitors to be, on some level, their equals, in that it was possible for them to wear European clothing.

Journalists heaped scorn on the Calmucks for the "comical" way that the "children of nature" used cutlery but also wrote approvingly of their ability to play chess. Heinrich Berghaus, geographer and author of numerous anthropological works, described in glowing terms in a series of lengthy articles in the *Vossische Zeitung* their ability to overcome adversity as they migrated vast distances across eastern Russia toward Mongolia: "The suffering brought on by extreme cold and heat. The relentless attacks of merciless enemies. Hunger. Thirst. None of these could prevent this people from migrating across a stretch of land that is, as the crow flies, 1/8 the circumference of the earth. In reality, though, it was much further than that due to the number of detours they would have had to make."[231]

Carl Hagenbeck, who had organized the human zoos for nearly three decades and worked in close collaboration with the people on display, so much so that he knew many of them by name, illustrates the contradictory thoughts about the visitors from abroad that existed even in the same individual. On the one hand, Hagenbeck was condescending toward them, recalling long after the shows had concluded: "Oh, how some of those smiling dark heads return to my memory. How their puzzled black and brown faces, eyes wide open, beheld the incredible wonders of our culture. Where are you now, you Africans, Indians, you red sons of the prairies, you Eskimos, you Patagonians from the glacial world of Tierra del Fuego, you who trusted me to lead you into the land of the white people, you who were gazed upon by millions, as if you were a magical animal?"[232] On the other hand, Hagenbeck reflected on the fact that people, regardless of culture, faced similar life challenges: "As the Eskimos were preparing to leave [the Stelligen zoo], they ran into the *Feuerländer* from the southern tip of the Americas, the last representatives of the stone ages, who were arriving at the zoo. Both the Eskimos and the *Feuerländer* had one mother each with an infant and, in friendly motherly competition, they compared their children.

Captain Jacobsen translated the entire lively debate about the eternal problem on both sides of the equator: How do I feed my children!"[233] For as much as Hagenbeck and others in his circle did not doubt the superiority of Western civilization, they were nevertheless aware, perhaps even somewhat unsettled, by the fact that Germans shared a common humanity with those on display.

It appears that the human zoo provoked thoughts in the general public—as distinct from academics—well beyond a simplistic fascination with harems, skirmishing Bedouins, seal hunts, pig roasts, and other stereotypical imagery of exotic foreigners.[234] Writing in 1955, long after the end of the human zoos, Alfred Lehmann, who would go on to become one of Germany's most noted ethnographers, reflected on the role the shows played in his own life: "I can say in my case that visiting these ethnographic exhibits in my childhood, especially after about 1897, not only contributed substantially to widening my horizons, but also instilled in me the desire to study ethnography."[235]

It would be an oversimplification to think that Germans saw the humans in their zoos as victory trophies, or worse, as the freakish genetic anomalies that one would find in the circus. Newspapers and Berlin learned societies portrayed them as relics of a world about to be lost, a more innocent world, one of warriors with innate fighting skills, a world in harmony with nature where animals were integrated into daily life and not objects of curiosity in a zoo. To the general public, it was by no means clear that the loss of that world was for the better. In Rudyard Kipling's 1890 short story "The Mark of the Beast," a mysterious leper bites the character Fleete, who then slowly turns into an animal. "I've been gardening, botanizing, you know," Fleete says to a fellow European in India. "The smell of the earth is delightful."[236] For many Germans mired in the grit of late nineteenth-century urban life, where the smell of the earth could only be imagined, Fleete's utter delight at a return to nature would have struck a chord.

In 1855, Friedrich Gerstäcker, a German novelist as well known in Germany as Kipling in Britain, published an article entitled "Civilization and the Wild" that remains one of the most remarkable commentaries on the concept of civilization and a devastating critique of nineteenth-century Europe. Far from convinced that Europe was the more advanced civilization, Gerstäcker took pains to point out the number of similarities between the different cultures. He reminded Europeans who mocked Native Americans for putting feathers in their hair to consider the attire of a European admiral. And he laid bare the serious shortcomings of European society: "We have not become better people because of civilization," Gerstäcker wrote. "We criticize them for being bloodthirsty, for killing their children, and for attacking neighbouring territory. We beat our chest and thank the good Lord that we are not like them. At the same time, with the help and blessing of the Churches, we make every effort to improve our murderous machines, guns, bombs, etc.... No, civilization has not improved humans." Gerstäcker continued with a fatalism worthy of Stefan Zweig:

> We must not disparage the Wild, heap scorn on its peoples as heathens and cannibals, then pretend that we are something special. Those peoples are still in a developmental stage: They are children, who require little more than a place to eat and play (the same place, incidentally, where *we* would like to set up our wardrobes and dressers) and when they are finally in their graves, these quiet sons of far-away lands, we will give them a eulogy and lament that we did not think a bit sooner to be more gentle with them. But then it will be too late. Their history will be forgotten. We have better things to do than dwell on extinct races. And then the world will be civilized.[237]

In the human zoo, we see a reaction to the turbulent modern world and an emotional longing for utopia. Huge numbers of Berliners (for certain shows, almost every single Berliner) left the grime of the city behind and strode through the lion gate to find the simplicity and harmony of the first garden. In late nineteenth-century Berlin, El Dorado was not a mythical golden city but a grass village. Even the grass and wood used to re-create the villages in the zoo frequently came from Germany's colonies, almost as if such materials were a quaint relic, no longer available in the urbanized Germany. Adolf Bastian, founder of academic ethnology in Germany, typified this view, undertaking an eight-year trip to Australia, the United States, India, South Africa, and Angola with the express purpose of finding in the non-industrialized world a way to heal the trauma of modern civilization.[238] Even Carl Hagenbeck's humorous comment about monkeys in his zoo contains an underlying criticism of German society: "The big monkeys have strong nerves. No wonder. They don't smoke, drink, or work, and spend all day in the fresh summer air."[239] It is not the case that the German public realistically thought of adopting the more primitive lifestyle; that was simply not an option. But in seeing their own reflection in the mirror held up by the peoples on display, Germans recognized the ugliness of their urban landscape and their crushing workloads, and they saw how terribly distant they had become from nature and one another.

3

To the Zoo! Animals and Society in the Imperial Capital

WHILE WAITING FOR THE NEXT exhibition of South Asians, Inuit, Pacific Islanders, Chileans, and other peoples from around the world, Berliners continued to visit the zoo in large numbers, not least because the zoo housed some of the city's most exciting architecture. Although the Antilopenhaus was the first iconic building of the Berlin zoo, it would soon be joined by a new, larger, more spectacular building that would rival the Brandenburg Gate as the defining symbol of Germany's largest metropolis. The architectural firm Ende & Böckmann, also responsible for the Antilopenhaus, built the pachyderm pavilion, colloquially known as the Elephantenpagoda, in 1873 at a staggering cost of 300,000 marks. As the German name suggests, the pavilion resembled an Indian pagoda, a nod to the country of origin of most of the zoo's elephants. At nearly twenty meters in height, its two main towers dominated the skyline around the zoo. Inside, there were colorful mosaics and stalls for elephants, rhinos, hippos, and tapirs.[1] *Die Gartenlaube*, the most successful of the illustrated magazines aimed at Germany's new and rapidly growing middle class,[2] reported that the pachyderm pavilion was so magnificent that "Buddha himself" would have felt comfortable there, adding that "a glance at the building would be enough to delight

The elegant House of the Antelopes (which also housed giraffes and zebras), built in 1872, was the first of the Berlin zoo's buildings to visually signify the lands from which the animals came. It marked the end of simply caging wild animals and showcased the increasing importance of educating visitors. *Berlin Zoo Archive*

even the most cold-blooded person."[3] It was not entirely surprising that the pachyderms would be singled out for the palatial enclosure. The nineteen animals contained in the stylized pagoda were by far the most valuable in the zoo's possession, worth nearly 126,580 marks, almost double the value of the zoo's bird collection, which numbered in the thousands.[4]

The 1901 ostrich pavilion, styled as an ancient Egyptian temple complete with hieroglyphics so accurate that they were used to instruct students of Egyptology, continued the pattern of exotic buildings to match the exotic animals and provided a bookend to the neighboring elephant pagoda. Scenes of ancient Egyptians interacting with ostriches, including farming and hunting them and offering their eggs to the pharaoh, adorned the lavish building, constructed at a cost of 104,000 marks.[5] But it was the ceiling of the interior courtyard that attracted the most attention. Painted against a blue backdrop was the Egyptian sky god held aloft by the earth god. The stars of the northern hemisphere

The 1873 elephant pagoda, built for the enormous sum of 300,000 marks, became a symbol of the wealth of late nineteenth-century Berlin. Because elephants were still relatively rare in European zoos, the architects designed the building in a manner that tended to keep the elephants isolated from one another rather than allowing them to socialize in larger spaces, as is common in today's zoos. *Berlin Zoo Archive*

and a copy of the celestial circle of animals from the Egyptian city of Denderah circled around the two gods.[6] The Berlin daily *Vossische Zeitung* speculated that the ten African ostriches must have been utterly thrilled to end up at the Berlin zoo's ostrich pavilion rather than live the humdrum ostrich existence that awaited them otherwise.[7]

With its oriental architecture, the zoo was an exotic dreamland where ordinary Berliners could imagine themselves in parts of the world they would likely never see. "How pleasant to rest on a bench on a mound," wrote one Berliner describing the area near the Antilopenhaus, "and dream of being far away. Far away from Berlin."[8] "Ever since the king of Württemberg had a Moorish, fairy-tale castle built for him in Stuttgart," zoo director Bodinus explained in justifying the eastern-themed Antilopenhaus, "and since the grandiose plan was put in place in Egypt to build the Suez Canal, everything Moorish has been seen as ultra-modern."[9] What is striking about these two statements is the positive associations of the "Orient." It signified progress, modernism, and tranquility. The region in this view is, to be sure, romanticized, but the connotations are far different from the supposed Western views of the East that formed the basis of Edward Said's controversial 1978 book *Orientalism*. Said argued that major Western political and intellectual thinkers over the course of centuries had both promoted and internalized a message of a culturally inferior "East," the result of which was an intellectual rationalization of colonial rule. "Orientalist" became a curse word, shorthand for a colonizer and proponent of the "rise of the West." There is, of course, value in assessing the views of Dante, Shakespeare, Euripides, and Walter Scott on the Mideast and in particular on the Islamic world, and there is likely some truth in Said's claim that they helped contribute to the notion of an "Orient" as distinct from an "Occident." The idea that the West, broadly speaking, held a "low opinion"[10] of the East, however, finds little resonance in Germany, which is curiously absent from Said's account. On the contrary, in late nineteenth-century Berlin, the East was viewed as worthy of emulation, as "ultra-modern" and a place of which one could dream. It is difficult to imagine the Antilopenhaus, which excited an interest in the part of the world it was supposed to portray, as a sign of Western cultural superiority. Moreover, as Germany's most popular attraction, the Berlin zoo was a bellwether for the formation of German cultural attitudes. Far more people saw the Antilopenhaus and formed opinions about the Islamic world on its basis than ever read the works of, for example, Professor Theodor Nöldeke, Germany's leading historian of the Qur'an.

The harsh urban reality that visitors left behind magnified the dreamland aspects that they encountered through the zoo's gates. "He who wants to flee the dust and bustle of the city should rush to the zoological garden," one commentator wrote in *Die Gartenlaube*. "There he can have his morning coffee, then lunch with his friends, and in the afternoon see assembled before him the wonders of this beautiful world."[11] Whiling away the day in the natural splendor of the zoo, its exotic buildings and animals transporting the visitor to faraway lands, was an enticing prospect for many who knew only the city, and the number who fell in this category increased enormously at the end of the nineteenth century. Germany's population rose from 41 million to 65 million between 1871 and 1914, or about 58 percent. At the start of that period, only 4.8 percent of the German population lived in a large urban area (defined as having a population over 100,000). By the beginning of World War I,

Zoo visitors gather around the bandshell in 1905. Concerts, held regularly until the end of World War II, helped make the zoo a focal point for Berlin society. *Landesarchiv Berlin, F Rep. 290 II 6646*

that figure had risen to 20 percent. Perhaps the most revealing statistic about the shift away from rural life during this era is that *every second German* moved to the city.[12] This phenomenon resulted in making Berlin, with its 26,000 basement apartments and shantytowns on the outskirts, one of the most crowded cities in the world.[13] Even the mayor, it was said, could not find a suitable apartment.[14]

Beyond escapism, the zoo offered another major enticement to its visitors: It was a social—indeed *the* social—gathering point of the city. Paul Lindenberg, journalist, writer, and editor of *Die deutsche Rundschau*, taking stock of the imperial capital in 1888, wrote: "Elegant society loves to rendezvous [at the zoo] . . . . Over there a group of young women in ultra-modern, airy, bright, elegant dresses. Over here an officer troop, strolling about, rattling their sabers. There a group of students with colorful caps, and everywhere people of every nationality, speaking their native tongue: French, English, Italians, Americans, Turks."[15] The music from two military bands added to the atmosphere. "Truly," reported Lindenberg, "it is difficult to tear oneself away from this patch of earth."[16] The zoo became the most popular recreation destination of Berliners, attracting thousands per day and even as many as 100,000 during special exhibits like the human zoo. A prominent Berliner remarked at the time that in summer there was only one answer to be expected when asking friends where they were headed: "Naturally, to the zoo!"[17]

And many of those visitors found their way to what would become the zoo's fourth showcase structure, the restaurant. The two-story neo-classical restaurant built at a cost of 110,000 marks had two covered verandas, terraces that reached to the Neptune pond, and the splendid Kaisersaal, where high society held its balls.[18] On many days, the 12,000 chairs and 5,000 tables, the 15,000 coffee cups and 40,000 plates were insufficient for the crowds who had come to relax and listen to a concert while watching the water fowl emerge from their Turkish-themed huts to play in the fountains.[19] To cater to its patrons, the zoo restaurant had more than 200 waiters at the ready.[20]

Due to the windfall from the human zoos and auxiliary sources of income like the restaurant, the zoo director Heinrich Bodinus was able to undertake a significant expansion of the zoo's animal collection. Populating the zoo with common, unexotic animals would have been

Patrons dine at the zoo restaurant in 1931. With its six kitchens, in-house bakery, and seating for 10,000 guests, the restaurant at the Berlin zoo was a center of social life in the German capital. *Berlin Zoo Archive*

a relatively easy affair, but to put on display young, healthy, marquee animals required large sums of money. At 30 marks, every zoo could afford the lowly raccoon. A Russian bear was also inexpensive at roughly 100 marks, but for the more popular polar bear, zoos had to spend more than ten times that amount. Even having paid the hefty sum of 1,500 marks, a zoo would have to expect a polar bear at least ten years old. Of the big cats, leopards were a relative bargain at roughly 600 marks. Lions were a different category altogether at 2,000 marks apiece, as were the rare Indian tiger and the jaguar, both of which cost 3,000 marks. The prized, and most expensive, animals of any zoo, however, were the elephant and the rhinoceros. A five-year-old rhino and an eight-foot-high elephant cost roughly the same amount: 10,000 marks,[21] or the equivalent of ten times the annual salary of a skilled mason.[22]

Beginning in 1884, the zoo's collection also benefited tremendously from Germany's acquisition of colonies. On a regular basis, German colonial administrators from the South Pacific and Africa donated animals to the Berlin zoo, including a rare marsupial squirrel from the Bismarck Archipelago[23] and domesticated sheep and pigs from Togo as well as more exotic animals such as meerkats, mangabeys, baboons, and leopards.[24]

German East Africa proved to be the most lucrative colony for the zoo, however, furnishing leopards, ostriches, hyenas, panthers, and various species of birds.[25] Occasionally, the zoo received gifts from well-to-do Germans abroad, such as Dr. Beeck, who sent an ocelot to the zoo from his station in Paraguay.[26] Through these various pipelines, the Berlin zoo had become by 1892 one of the largest and most diverse in existence, housing 2,365 animals representing 885 species.[27] The Hannover zoo, in comparison, housed 948 animals from 280 species at the same time, while the Frankfurt zoo, Berlin's nearest German competitor, housed 1,336 animals in 243 species.[28] Most astonishing of all, Berlin had almost caught up in terms of size of the collection to the world's flagship zoo. The London zoo had scarcely 200 more animals than Berlin by 1894.[29]

The steady supply of animals from the colonies helped to offset the stubbornly high losses due to death during this era of still rudimentary veterinary knowledge. Given the costs of acquiring certain animals and the financial bonus from their ability to draw in the public, it is understandable that animal deaths caused zoos great anxiety. The days of the London zoo simply replenishing its supply of monkeys annually were long over. In 1893, the Berlin zoo suffered devastating losses of some of its marquee animals: a chimpanzee, an orangutan, a panther, a giraffe, and a hippo. The apes had died from an infection of the intestine, the giraffe from a leg that it had broken at the shallow pool, and the panther while giving birth.

The zoo's board was originally mystified by the hippo's death. On October 8, 1893, the hippo ate its meal as usual but refused to eat the following day. Since Nina had experienced temporary loss of appetite in the past, the keepers paid little mind to the unusual behavior until a few days later when it became clear that something was amiss. They offered all manner of food to the animal but to no avail. On November 5, four weeks after the first indication that Nina was ill, the hippo collapsed in the water and died. The zoo director, Ludwig Heck, immediately ordered an autopsy, which revealed the cause of death to have been a child's rubber ball lodged in the digestive tract. Although there was no indication of how the ball found its way into the hippo pen, some zoo officials speculated a member of the public had tossed it in while feeding the animal. For some zoo professionals, this was ample reason to suspend the practice of letting the public feed the animals or, at the very least, to have a keeper oversee public feeding.[30] They were in the minority. Feeding the animals was part of the attraction for the public, an activity the zoo encouraged to strengthen the bond between animal and human. Reflecting on her childhood visits to the zoo, Hildegard von Bülow, a rural resident and frequent visitor to the zoo who published her observations in a leading popular journal, recalled her fondness for feeding the animals. "I brought along old bread, apple peels and the like," she wrote "to spread some cheer among my friends." Should visitors forget to bring food for the animals, they could purchase it in small bags for 10 to 20 pfennig at the zoo.[31] Zoos did not completely ban the public feeding of animals for another seventy years.

At this stage, the zoo's emphasis remained on acquiring as many species of animals as possible both to educate the public and to facilitate research. For those purposes, cages, rather than enclosures with contrived wilderness, were well suited. Although it is difficult to imagine from today's perspective, it made perfect sense for zoos from that era to have just one example of each of forty different species of deer, each in its own cage.[32] Zoo officials expected visitors to acquire knowledge about taxonomy and relationships among various species of animals and not simply satisfy an idle curiosity. Visitors were to come away, as one zoo observer of the day said, with an understanding of "every possible link in the grand possession of organized life."[33] Education was, after all, central to the mission of Germany's increasingly powerful middle class, who considered base entertainments without an educational component to be in distinctly poor taste.[34]

In the last decades of the nineteenth century, two subtle shifts in German zoos occurred relating to the nature of the collection and to the mindset around animals. In the first shift, zoo directors increasingly focused on collecting indigenous fauna. During the Berlin zoo's fiftieth anniversary celebrations in 1894, several of the distinguished invited guests praised the zoo's leadership for turning its attention to German animals.[35] The trend was evident in other German zoos, such as Hamburg and Frankfurt, each of which erected aviaries to display German birds exclusively.[36]

The second shift related to attitudes toward animals. Alongside the triumphalist view that humans had tamed wild beasts and could now look upon them at their leisure, which was so in evidence in the zoo's early visitor's guides, an increasing number of articles in the popular and scientific press were suggesting that animals could experience sensitivities and emotions as humans did, that they were more than a disposable object of entertainment. Alfred Brehm's monumental ten-volume *Life of Animals*, published between 1863 and 1869—a work that ranks alongside Pliny's *Natural History*, Aristotle's *Inquiries on Animals*, Louis Leclerc's *Histoire naturelle*, Oliver Goldsmith's eight-volume *History of the Earth and Animated Nature*, and Humboldt's *Kosmos* as one of the greatest tracts ever written on the natural world—spurred in large part a more sympathetic view of animals. Brehm's work explored in minute detail the behavior and anatomy of virtually every known animal.[37] Distinguished by its stunning ink drawings of animals in motion— leaping, crouching, prowling—by the leading animal artists of the day, Ludwig Beckmann and Robert Kretschmer, *Life of Animals* was a sensation in Germany.[38]

Like Aristotle, Brehm imparted to animals human emotions, a term known as anthropomorphism. His animals were variously "sad," "defeated," or "reproachful." His description of the death of a horse was

A woman approaches the recently opened elephant gate in 1899. At that time, the elephant gate, located in Budapest Street, was the main entrance to the zoo. The lion gate was built ten years later around the corner on Hardenberg Square. *Landesarchiv Berlin, F Rep. 290 II 12378*

typical: "He died from his wounds like a hero, quiet and calm." Many of Brehm's contemporaries subscribed to his views, describing animals in ways that they might use to portray humans as well rather than as soulless, disposable creatures. Articles in *Die Gartenlaube* pointed out various behaviors among animals that were virtually identical to those of humans, such as how animal mothers protected their young out of love.[39] When the new aviary at the Berlin zoo was constructed in 1901, the keepers took extra care to incorporate flora such as blueberry bushes and heather so that the animals might, as a Berlin daily suggested, "forget that they were in captivity."[40]

Popular views of apes had undergone the greatest transformation, from terrifying, quasi-mythical beasts to close human relatives who loved their children and enjoyed a joke. In 1855, when the first gorilla was exhibited in Europe, Catholic writers portrayed it with horns on its head and labeled it "Martin Luther." Even the *Brockhaus*, Germany's most respected encyclopedia, described the gorilla in 1894 as "one of the most monstrous creatures one could imagine."[41] Some fifteen years later, readers might be forgiven for thinking that the Berlin aquarium director Oskar Heinroth's obituary for Rolf was for a boy rather than an orangutan: "He knew how to win the charms of even Berlin's most elegant ladies.... At meal time, he went hand in hand with his keeper to a table by the wall. There he sat down with legs crossed as they do in the orient. By a hand motion in the direction of the food cabinet, he indicated his desire for a cup of tea. Having emptied the cup, and eaten some fruit and white bread, he was ready to play and joke around."[42] Alfred Brehm, in keeping with his firm belief in the human qualities of animals, wrote of the chimpanzee:

> He thinks himself better, of a higher standing, than other animals, especially other apes. He differentiates between human adults and children. He respects the former but adores the latter. He likes a good gag, both with animals and humans.... He is not only curious, but possesses a thirst for knowledge.... He is wily, headstrong, but not stubborn. He demands his due without being bossy. He has moods. Today he is spritely and cheerful, tomorrow sad and morose.[43]

On an international level, governments reflected the increasingly popular concern for animals by enacting animal protection laws. Britain passed the Elephants' Preservation Act of 1879, which prohibited the killing of wild elephants in Asia unless they threatened human life or property. In South Africa, lawmakers curtailed the hunting of buffalo, quaggas, zebras, hares, and antelopes and established the first game reserves.[44] In May 1900, Germany, England, France, Italy, Portugal, and Spain signed an international convention on the protection of hunted animals that imposed stiff penalties on those illegally hunting elephants, zebras, and other big game animals, as well as those in possession of ostrich and crocodile eggs.[45]

On a local level, the strange case of the Berlin zoo's rogue elephant laid bare the changing view of animals. At Easter 1881, the Prince of Wales, the future king Edward VII, presented his nephew, future kaiser Wilhelm II, two Indian elephants from the London zoo on the occasion of the kaiser's wedding. Wilhelm in turn donated the elephants to the Berlin zoo.[46] Early on a Sunday morning two years later, while sweeping out the cages of the two large elephants, the forty-six-year-old zookeeper Krüger crossed back and forth over Rostom's breakfast of hay, angering the elephant. Stopping only momentarily from eating, Rostom plunged his right tusk into the shocked keeper and pushed him against the wall with colossal force. A second keeper whipped the elephant away from his fallen colleague, but he could do little else than remove the corpse of the long-time zoo employee and father of seven. For the second time in the zoo's history, an elephant had killed its keeper. Boy, the zoo's first elephant and one of Lichtenstein's proudest accomplishments, had trampled his keeper to death in 1867.[47] The Berlin zoo's investigation into Rostom's past revealed that he had killed a keeper at the London zoo years earlier. Perfidious Albion, it appears, was up to her old tricks.

The zoo's first decision regarding Rostom was, wisely, to suspend children's rides on the animal. It then deliberated his fate, concluding that the animal should be euthanized. This was not the twenty-first century, however, when methods of euthanizing even the largest animals are well understood. As recently as the nineteenth century, no one in Europe really knew how to kill an elephant. In 1826, the English had attempted to put down the elephant Chunee of the Exeter Exchange menagerie, then the most popular zoological attraction in London, because of his unruliness and had botched it horribly. Lying in a heap but still alive following a volley of 152 bullets from a firing squad, its agonized trumpet attracting throngs of onlookers, Chunee finally mercifully expired when one of the participants plunged a harpoon into the wounded beast. Had that option not succeeded, the executioners stood at the ready with a cannon.

An outpouring of grief followed the terrible scene, immortalized in a play that ran in London's Sadler's Wells Theatre, *Chuneelah: or, The Death of an Elephant at the Exeter 'Change.*[48] Another tragic element was added to the story when the autopsy revealed that the cause of Chunee's aggression was a toothache. The Exeter Exchange sold his nearly 2,000 pound hide to a tanner and his carcass to the Royal College of Surgeons, whose members butchered it in a public spectacle. His skeleton, installed in a place of prominence in the Hunterian Museum in Glasgow, an object of intense interest for over a century that brought the sad story anew to subsequent generations, was destroyed in a German aerial bombardment in 1941.

Sixty years after the Chunee incident, the Berlin zoo board, having decided that the elephant Rostom was to be put down, elected to do so by strangulation, a decision that caused a public backlash at home and anguish overseas. A member of the British royal family pleaded in a letter to the kaiser: "Hear that the fine large elephant uncle Bertie gave the zoological garden here is to be strangled. If true, cannot something be done to prevent this? If the poor animal must be destroyed, of adopting other means?"[49]

In Berlin, the zoo's decision was met with anger and suspicion. At boisterous public meetings organized by the Berlin Animal Protection Society, where zoo directors refused to appear fearing that the audience would not be open to "someone who thought differently," attendees vilified the zoo. Passions ran so high at these meetings that the zoo board speculated that soon a police presence like those at meetings of the working class would be necessary to ensure the public's safety. It might even be time, board members mused, to establish a Berlin Society for the Protection of Humans from the Berlin Animal Protection Society.[50] The Animal Protection Society's board suspected above all that the zoo scientists' thirst for an elephant cadaver on which to conduct experiments was at the heart of the decision to kill the animal. Describing it as a "vivisection in optima forma," the society's board publicly questioned the "pseudoscience" emanating from the zoo.[51] Berlin dailies, skeptical of the need to kill Rostom, sided with the society. Ordinary Berliners flooded the zoo with letters of protest.[52]

The emperor, a man who shared his brother's passing interest in animals but not his father's passion for them, was concerned by the growing anger in the streets and the intervention of the British royal family. He instructed the zoo to defer killing the elephant until his envoy had a chance to meet with the board.[53] Clearly angered by the public outcry against its plans but resolute, the board responded with a lengthy letter to the king justifying the need to kill the elephant and the choice of strangulation. The board pointed to the elephant's surly demeanor and his unpredictability and suggested that he was deranged. "Every visitor," the board explained, "notices the incessant swaying of his head back and forth."[54] Since no other zoo would take him because of his violent past and since space at the zoo was at a premium, the board concluded that there was no other option than to kill the "ugly, contrary, and expensive glutton." How to do so was another matter altogether. As one member of the zoo board wrote:

> Four killing options stood before us: electric shock, shooting, poisoning, and strangulation. Although it is the cleanest and smoothest option, we abandoned the option to kill by electric shock almost immediately, as we had received advice from expert witnesses that our machine would likely not achieve the desired result.... The option of shooting we also dismissed after a brief deliberation, as we had deep misgivings, more from a humanitarian than practical standpoint....
>
> For this reason, we have been busy corresponding even more vigorously with experts in the field about the possibility of poisoning the animal. After several surveys and experiments, even one of our leading pharmacologists and poison specialists declared that he was not in a position to offer us a poison with rapid and certain results. Since an insufficient amount, or a slow-acting poison, would mean an unimaginable torture for the animal, we regrettably dismissed the use of poison, leaving us with the strangulation option.... It is humane. In that moment that the animal loses consciousness, the tremendous weight of the collapsing body causes its neck to break.[55]

(The quick dismissal of poisoning is somewhat surprising, given that the first Berlin zoo director, Lichtenstein, had euthanized an unruly elephant at a menagerie in Potsdam by putting in his water bucket a combination of hydrogen cyanide, rum, and sugar.)[56]

The zoo board, recognizing the benefit that would accrue to themselves and other scientists from an intact elephant, wrote in terms that leave doubts about their emphasis on the "humanity" of the strangulation option and suggest that the Berlin Animal Protection Society's criticisms were not unfounded:

> Thus, [strangulation is] thankfully the fastest and least painful death. To say nothing of the fact that the cadaver remains completely intact and useable in its entirety for scientific purposes. This was a consideration for us as well as for all level-headed thinkers, since to have at one's disposable the fresh, healthy cadaver of a large elephant is a rarity. We could name a whole host of more or less well-known academics who would be overjoyed to have such an unusual, and therefore valuable, subject for their scientific studies.[57]

Having received the king's tacit assent to euthanize Rostom, the zoo management moved ahead with the strangulation. The first clumsy attempt failed when the rope slipped through the amateur pulley device that zoo workers had rigged up. The zoo then turned to local companies to develop an elephant strangulation machine, making it clear that the elephant would be alive when it entered the machine.[58] The rope itself was subcontracted to a master rope maker who was to fashion it out of hemp.[59] Although no images exist of the strangulation machine that the zoo desired, it appears from the description in this correspondence that it was to be upright, so that the animal's weight would be used against it.

Unfortunately, the archival sources on Rostom's fate become thinner after the initial flurry of correspondence. In March 1890, five months after the zoo had made the decision to kill the elephant, the zoo was still clearly in a fight to justify its decision. The zoo director, Ludwig Heck, pleaded with the emperor to ask the Prince of Wales, who was visiting the German capital, to publicly endorse the killing of the "rogue elephant Rostom,"[60] adding that the zoo board would be "exceptionally obliged" should the emperor facilitate its request. Whether or not the heir to the British throne stepped into the fray is unknown, but what is known is that Rostom remained alive until February 1892, when he died from natural causes.[61] The elephant strangulation machine was never built.

Within a few months of Rostom's death, the Stuttgart zoo faced a similar situation. A pattern of violent behavior by the male African elephant Peter caused the zoo director, Adolf Nill, to conclude "with a heavy heart" that the animal would have to be euthanized. Given Berlin's experience, he opted to have the animal shot. Nill, son of the zoo's founder and nothing if not a capitalist, charged admission to witness the elephant's death, scheduled for November 7, 1893, at 2:00 P.M. In a lengthy editorial, the newspaper *Schwäbische Merkur* criticized the zoo's decision to sell tickets to the elephant's execution:

> Local papers have invited the public to a "grand spectacle" at Nill's Zoo next Tuesday afternoon. At that hour, the shooting of the sick elephant is supposed to take place. We are aware that the owner wishes to mitigate the loss of such a valuable animal. Still, it injures our sensibilities that the killing of this poor chap, for years the darling of the zoo's visitors, is to be made into a spectacle for the public's gaping eyes. In our country, there are laws which outline that large animals can be slaughtered only in closed quarters . . . . It is true that the upcoming tragedy in Nill's Garten will be free of torture. Without doubt. Nevertheless, we would have wished and expected, that at a minimum, women would not be permitted entry.

The newspaper hoped that Stuttgarters would be dignified, and refrain from witnessing how "a noble animal descends into death."[62] Although the sources do not specify the number in attendance, we do know that a crowd gathered to watch Adolf Nill's rifle bring down the elephant in one shot.

The cases of the elephants Rostom and Peter illustrate the embryonic ideas of animal welfare that reached from the British royal family to concerned citizens of Germany. In both Stuttgart and Berlin, a growing number of citizens believed that animals deserved a modicum of dignity. Notably, the Berlin Animal Protection Society, with its modest but growing membership of 2,165 in 1888,[63] had little objection to keeping animals in captivity or to the principle of zoos in general, but it was deeply concerned that an animal not be killed unnecessarily. It is striking, for example, that when the society reorganized itself in 1890, it demonstrated concern solely for the treatment of pets, domesticated animals, and birds. As the society's five organizational units—dogs and cats, horses, birds, animal transportation, and slaughter practices—reveal, zoos were the last thing on its mind.[64]

When the society renamed itself in 1919 as the League for Radical Ethics, it adjusted its priorities again, focusing its fight against vivisection, cruelty to animals, hunting for the sole purpose of pleasure, and the consumption of meat.[65] The league's promotion of vegetarianism took on almost radical levels and vastly outweighed concerns for exotic animals held in captivity. In a similar vein, zoos hardly registered with the other major European animal protection society. The British Royal Society for the Prevention of Cruelty to Animals targeted pet cruelty, ill treatment of draft animals, vivisection, and bringing an end to animal sports like dog fights, but it, too, paid little mind to zoos.[66]

The end of the nineteenth century, then, was an era of transition, when the public increasingly viewed all animals, whether in captivity or not, as creatures whose presence enhanced the human experience and who had a certain emotional capacity rather than as objects over which humans should have dominion. By the dawn of the twentieth century, a growing number of Germans believed that people should not starve dogs or make them fight, scientists should not subject animals to surgery without an anesthetic, zoo boards should not strangle elephants, and entrepreneurs should not profit from euthanizing an elephant. Fifty years earlier, hardly anyone would have given a second thought to animals put in these situations.

As the cultural shift in the perception of animals played out around it, the Berlin zoo continued to experience a golden era, as did the city in which it was located. The Berlin zoo remained a flagship cultural institution in Germany's flagship city, setting the pace for other zoos. The first exhibition of "exotic" peoples at a German zoo took place in Berlin, opening the floodgates for exhibits at other zoos. The Dresden zoo's first show of humans occurred in 1878 and included the six Inuit who had been displayed at the Berlin zoo. It was as if other zoos in Germany were waiting to see whether Berlin approved of such shows before hosting their own.[67] By the end of the nineteenth century, the Berlin zoo was a splendorous focal point of the imperial capital. While other zoos struggled with the vagaries of the economy, sometimes suspending animal purchases entirely, the Berlin zoo remained Carl Hagenbeck's largest client, buying annually until 1910 between 10,000 and 35,000 marks' worth of animals. The Berlin zoo, the only one that could consistently afford the big-ticket animals—elephants, rhinos, hippos, and giraffes—accounted for between one-third and three-fourths of Hagenbeck's income.[68] Berliners responded to the zoo's many attractions by turning out in large numbers, vaulting Berlin to second place among European zoos in attendance:

Moscow	93,574 visitors (1889)[69]
Halle	100,000 (1890)[70]
Dresden	189,302 (1892)[71]
Frankfurt	239,629 (1898)[72]
Hamburg	387,776 (1891)[73]
Berlin	611,278 (1874)[74]
London	662,649 (1893)[75]

Berliners seemed to enjoy their newfound status as a first among equals. Local newspapers boasted that even the peoples on display in the human zoos believed that they were in better hands in Berlin than in other German cities. When the patriarch of the Lapps reluctantly agreed to undergo Virchow's numerous measurements, for example, the *Vossische Zeitung* saw an opportunity for Berlin boosterism: "Most Lapps gladly allowed themselves to be manipulated. Only Saupa, the father of the family, bristled somewhat. Nevertheless, he was much more patient than in any other German city."[76] Berlin's intellectual circles clearly believed that their city was different, a notch above other German cities of the era, distinguished in particular by its academics. Unlike in other German cities, the daily *Vossische Zeitung* claimed, the Nubians could be addressed in their native tongue because of the presence of many African experts, like Brehm, Hildebrandt, Ascherson, Fritsch, and Hartmann, who spoke their language. "Berlin has become after all," the newspaper reported, "thanks to Virchow and others an eminently anthropologically minded city. We see these things, these people and scenes that Herr Hagenback presents to us, with different eyes from elsewhere."[77]

Berlin's view of itself was laced with a certain hubris, born out of its advantageous financial situation. Other zoos did not enjoy the population base or the donation of animals that Berlin did. As a result, they were forced to seek income in base entertainments. The Leipzig zoo, for example, hosted a variety of freak shows: Peter Spanner, a "skin man," who suffered from an affliction that left him with elasticized skin that he could pull from his neck over his face; Krao, a woman from Laos who was billed as the "missing link" because of the thick hair that covered her body; and Irene Woodward, an American woman with tattoos covering every inch of her skin.[78] The Frankfurt zoo offered hot air balloon rides and horse-riding displays by famous jockeys. Munich kept its zoo restaurant open until 11 P.M. during the summer, and during the darkest days of the interwar period, it considered installing a roller coaster.[79] Farther afield, the Manchester zoo supplemented its income with merry-go-rounds, a shooting range, and a race course.[80]

The Berlin zoo was so embedded into the social life of the city that major charities and other social organizations, including the Berlin Gymnastic Society and the Belzig lung sanitarium, held annual meetings, garden parties, and fundraisers there.[81] When a flood devastated Würtemberg in 1895, the zoo held a fundraiser featuring the leading ladies of the theater, who sold flowers and refreshments.[82] Every Berliner knew that the place to be on the Day of Sedan, Germany's national holiday commemorating victory over France in the 1870–71 war, was the Berlin zoo, which hosted a lavish celebration.[83]

Even a single page of a Berlin newspaper on one nondescript day, August 31, 1895, reveals the zoo's place of prominence in Berlin's social life. One ad announced a large military double concert featuring the music corps of the Second Guards Artillery regiment. Another advertised Carl Hagenbeck's Somali Expedition, highlighting its nine ostriches, four camels, fourteen antelopes, and one donkey. A third advertised the restaurant located in the zoo, offering breakfast, lunch, dinner, fine wine, and salon rooms that could be booked for "parties large and small."[84] As these advertisements attest, the zoo appealed to visitors to enjoy the many aspects of the zoo apart from animals—music, food, comradery, and the intriguing display of Somalis. To project onto the Berlin zoo's past our image of today's zoos as simply sites of captive animals with some light refreshment options would be to terribly distort the role that the zoo played in Berlin's social life. The Berlin zoo was much more than animals.

In his 1897 account of Berlin, the influential essayist Alfred Kerr described a typical summer's evening:

> Around ten in the evening, one heads to the zoological garden for an hour or so. To listen to music. To take in the cool evening air, have a sip of Selters mineral water with wine, and admire young women. One occasionally leaves the display halls and visits the Kalmucks. They aren't going to be in Berlin much longer. A nighttime peace falls on the half-dark paths of this old, massive park, and there, behind a wooden barrier, on a moonlit patch of land, there they are. A tall chap in priestly garb smokes a cigarette and enjoys the evening air. Other younger chaps are also smoking, enjoying the evening air. They are a merry, elegant, good-natured, kindly, mischievous people, not at all unlike ourselves.[85]

This delightful quote tells us much about the zoo's place in Berlin at the end of the nineteenth century. With its cool air and various diversions—in this case none of which were animals—the zoo was a refuge from city life that could be enjoyed for an hour or two late at night. The zoo was a central gathering point for Berliners in their leisure time, a stage on which life in Germany's first city played out, and a site where Berliners formed their impression of the broader world. A visitor to the zoo at the turn of the century, witnessing the long queues to enter its gates, the packed restaurant, the sold-out music concerts, and the many Berlin celebrities in the crowds, could hardly have suspected that the zoo's golden age was about to come to a rapid end.

4

An End to the Sighing of the Animals

GERMANS AT THE END OF the nineteenth century had every reason to be optimistic about the century ahead. In a mass migration, nearly half of the population of 60 million had changed their place of residence, heading primarily toward urban centers where the industrial might of the German empire required their labor. Berlin was clearly one of the winners from this transfer of humanity, achieving a population of 4 million by 1920 that would rank it the third largest city in the world after New York and London.[1]

Huge industrial enterprises such as Borsig, Siemens, and Schwartzkopf vaulted Berlin to the top spot on Germany's list of most industrialized cities.[2] Adults improved their financial situation in their new urban homes; their children reaped the rewards of a country increasingly focused on their well-being. Public education, for one thing, had made major advances in the nineteenth century. By roughly the 1880s, virtually every child of elementary school age had access to free schooling, and illiteracy was all but non-existent.[3] The population boom at the end of the nineteenth century combined with medical advances that drastically reduced infant mortality translated into a remarkably youthful population. One-third of the German population on the eve of the Great War was under sixteen years of age.[4] Crowded living quarters and frequently depressing working conditions were, to be sure, a reality for most of the working class, but decent wages, vacation time, and improving health care meant that most Germans could be satisfied with their lot in life or, at a minimum, could expect great things for their children. The roller-skating craze that overtook Berlin in 1900 seemed to symbolize the optimistic, easygoing urbanity of the city at the dawn of a new century. People from all walks of life strapped on their roller skates, and arm-in-arm with their friends, giddily took in the sights of the booming metropolis.

City administrators systematically established infrastructure to accommodate the deluge of humanity. Public health, especially mass vaccination, was one of the clearest examples of a strategy to ensure that crowds of humans could safely live together, but there were many other examples of communal politics. Improved housing, a healthier water supply, sewer systems, expanded fire and police departments, orderly cemeteries—all of these became a focus for European cities in the late 1800s.[5] New facilities such as swimming pools, parks, and sporting venues, both amateur and professional, also sprang up. Civic administrations further subsidized public libraries, museums, and orchestras.

Heading into the twentieth century, the Berlin zoo was a cultural site that the city and Prussian state believed to be of crucial importance to the young, urban, frequently transient German population. It was also, by all accounts, home to a spectacular collection of animals. In 1905, Stanley Smyth Flower undertook a seven-week trip through European zoos in an advisory capacity for the recently founded zoo in Egypt. The report that he submitted afterward was not quite the scientific analysis that the Egyptian authorities expected but was instead filled with his emotional responses to the zoos he encountered. Given the head start that London had, it is striking that the Berlin zoo impressed him even more than the London zoo did: "Berlin possesses the richest Zoological Gardens in Europe, and an immense collection of animals; at a first visit it appears to the visitor that it would be easier to enumerate the kinds not represented, than those that are."[6] The bourgeois goal of its founders, to educate the general public about the natural world in order to achieve a more enlightened population, seemed even more relevant in the crush and squalor of early twentieth-century Berlin than in 1844. And it was to those arguments that the Berlin zoo board would turn when the zoo faced the twin crises of World War I and its disastrous economic aftermath.

The long-serving German chancellor Otto von Bismarck's patchwork alliance system among the major European powers lasted nearly twenty-four years after his abrupt dismissal in 1890, but it unraveled with breath-taking speed in the summer of 1914. A mere thirty-seven days elapsed from the assassination of Austrian archduke Ferdinand in Sarajevo on June 28, 1914, to the German attack on Belgium on August 4. The "spirit of 1914" consumed Germany that summer, especially in the capital, where a frenzied crowd that rivaled those in St. Petersburg and Paris welcomed the news about mobilization. The great novelist Thomas Mann was one of those Germans swept up in the excitement, writing that the war was a defense of German high culture against the sham democracies of the West and, in his view, their base cultural offerings designed for the masses: "Germanness, that is: culture, soul, freedom, art, and not: society, the right to vote, and literature."[7] As the war dragged on, however, the public's enthusiasm for war waned. The British naval blockade began to take a devastating toll on the German population, as did the bleeding

Soldiers on leave view an elephant at the Berlin zoo during World War I. Photos from this period are a rarity. *Landesarchiv Berlin, F Rep. 290 II 12063*

at the fronts. Of the 15.6 million German men between seventeen and fifty eligible to be called up for service, roughly 85 percent of them, or 13.2 million, had been drafted by war's end.[8]

It fell to Ludwig Heck, who had become director of the Berlin zoo in 1888, to lead the zoo during World War I and the years immediately following, when the zoo faced its most trying time since its founding years. Born in Darmstadt in 1860, Heck studied the natural sciences at universities in Strasbourg, Giessen, Berlin, and Leipzig before becoming director of the Cologne zoo. Following a nationwide search for the Berlin zoo director, which attracted applications from a wide spectrum of society, including writers, spa managers, and menagerie owners, the board selected Ludwig Heck to lead Germany's flagship zoo. Heck went on to enjoy an illustrious career of nearly forty-three years in that role—becoming the longest-serving director in the zoo's history—before stepping down in favor of his son, Lutz. Heck the elder became the face of the zoo, regularly featured with "his" animals on the cover of zoo publications, and a fixture in Berlin society. Because of his role in saving the zoo, official zoo histories revere him, conveniently omitting his deep devotion to Hitler and his ideology toward the end of his life.[9]

In 1916, Ludwig Heck turned to the emperor with a plea to help the zoo survive the war: "Since the beginning of war, the situation of the zoological garden, which is currently under state supervision, has been exceptionally unfavorable. Our income has declined precipitously. At the same time, it has not been possible, despite considerable austerity measures, to reduce our expenses in accordance with reduced income. Notably, all articles that we require on a daily basis have become more expensive."[10] Heck then explained to the emperor that the zoo's shortfall in 1914 had been 33,000 marks and had risen to 138,000 in 1915. A similar shortfall was expected in 1916. The only way for the zoo to remain open, Heck maintained, was with the help of a state-sponsored interest-free loan of 200,000 marks. Persuaded by Heck's eloquent and urgent plea, the emperor obliged. When the war continued into 1918, Heck approached the emperor again, requesting another interest-free loan of 250,000 marks. This loan, too, the emperor granted.

The emperor approved both of the requests because he believed in the zoo's importance to the local population, although he personally had little interest in the zoo. He visited it on but two occasions, neither

Berlin zoo director Ludwig Heck (left) and a leading organizer of ethnographic displays, John Hagenbeck (right), beside a group from south Asia on display at the zoo around 1931. With a tenure of forty-three years, Ludwig Heck remains the longest-serving director in the zoo's history. A firm supporter of Nazism, on his eightieth birthday he was presented with the Goethe medal personally by Hitler. *Bundesarchiv, Bild 102-12796*

of which related to the zoo directly. Once was because it offered the best acoustic location to listen to the bells of the newly constructed Kaiser Wilhelm Memorial Church across the road. The second was to attend a lecture in the zoo's marble hall by Duke Adolf Friedrich of Mecklenburg, who had recently returned from traversing Africa. The hall made quite an impression on the kaiser, who described it as "splendid"; he was much less enthusiastic about the okapi brought back by Friedrich, which the kaiser called a "hideous cow," wondering why everyone was "making such a fuss about it."[11]

At some German zoos, including Berlin's, most animals survived the war; the situation in others was utterly catastrophic. The Hannover zoo began the war in a favorable situation, negotiating a contract with the local garrison to purchase those horses that were no longer fit for service. As a result, the zoo had a steady supply of meat during the first years of the war. Indeed, the Hannover zoo was able to sell its surplus meat to zoos in Leipzig, Frankfurt, Cologne, and Halle.[12] As of 1916, however, as the effects of the Allied naval blockade of Germany started to take hold, the situation in Hannover deteriorated drastically. Of the thirty-four monkeys it owned at the outbreak of war, only one was alive by 1919. The big cats fared little better, with five of eighteen surviving the war.[13] Halle's zoo had to contend with a mild popular uprising in 1917 when locals questioned the zoo's provision of meat to the lions and tigers while the population made do with turnips. The zoo used the local newspaper to reassure the public: "Widespread is the opinion that the large cats are fed with meat that would otherwise be made available to the population. This opinion is simply wrong. I want to make it clear that animals in the zoological garden are fed exclusively with the meat of fallen animals—that is, animals that have died. This meat is not only unappetizing to humans, it is strictly forbidden to feed it to humans on health grounds."[14]

At the Leipzig zoo, the elephant Nelly had to be euthanized after months of inadequate nourishment. This once-favorite animal of the public ended up being slaughtered and offered up in a popular local restaurant to Leipzigers, the trunk quickly becoming a sought-after delicacy. A Leipzig daily advised people to brush aside any misgivings they might have about eating elephant: "Some might not be able to get over their prejudice against the unknown. Whoever has tasted the elephant, though, knows how delicious it is!"[15] The dearth of food meant that most of the zoo's monkeys and seals died, too, while parrots suffered because it was no longer possible to import nuts.

The European conflagration also caused the demise of the Frankfurt zoo. With twelve of its keepers at the front and prices of foodstuffs soaring, feeding the animals became an impossibility; the zoo could no longer function as an independent entity and ceded its management to the city of Frankfurt.[16] This was not a panacea, however, as the zoo continued to suffer. Despite using every available green space to grow hay and peas for the animals, the zoo could only delay the inevitable. Weaker animals and those that could be easily purchased again following the war were sacrificed for the more valuable creatures, but this strategy, too, proved insufficient. The popular orangutans and chimps died, as did the elephant Fanny, who received a poetic obituary in the local newspaper ending with a swipe at the British foes responsible for her death:

> May it never be forgotten.
> She was a good girl,
> A daughter of India who was a victim of Lloyd George.[17]

German authorities saw zoos not only as a source of comfort for a population in miserable times but also as institutions that could assist the war effort. The Leipzig zoo's contribution was relatively modest, breeding angora rabbits in order to harvest their wool, whereas the Frankfurt zoo received 20,000 marks from the Prussian Ministry of War to breed animals for domestic consumption. The management of the Frankfurt zoo converted the insectarium into a chicken coop to breed new species of chickens and to deliver eggs to the German population. Zookeepers grew mushrooms in what had been the bird pavilion, and beside the elephant pavilion they planted vegetables and herbs, particularly those used for medicinal purposes. Information plaques provided instructions to visitors on how they could grow the plants themselves. The Hessian Association of Rabbit Breeders donated examples of the twenty-four known types of rabbits to the zoo, which then placed them in cages in the former beer hall. The zoo management encouraged visitors to purchase rabbits eight to twelve weeks old for their own breeding purposes, thereby providing a source of food during the lean war years. In the camel enclosure, the zoo raised goats for milk.[18]

Without a similar food production role for the broader war effort, the management at the Berlin zoo focused its attention on the herculean task of saving its animals. Although attendance at the Berlin zoo had increased in the last year of the war, it was insufficient to cover the exorbitant costs of feeding the animals and keeping them warm.[19] For certain animals, like seals and sea lions, the price of fresh fish was simply prohibitive. In all zoos in Germany, almost all of these animals died.[20] In general, the tireless efforts of Heck to secure money and rations meant that his zoo in Berlin could avoid euthanizing the animals, a process that was becoming commonplace elsewhere. "Unlike London, which was in nowhere near as dire a situation as we were, nor as cut off from the world," he wrote in his 1938 memoirs, "we did not shoot a single animal."[21]

It is difficult to know whether the war itself or the financial crisis of the immediate postwar years proved more crippling to the Berlin zoo. As a result of the Treaty of Versailles, Germany lost 10 percent of its population and 13 percent of its territory, including 80 percent of its iron reserves and 63 percent of its zinc mines.[22] Runaway inflation that began during the war and steadily worsened after it compounded the staggering industrial losses. By 1923, the German government was issuing paper money in ludicrously large denominations of 10 million, 20 million, and 50 million marks, frequently without printing on the reverse side so that the notes could at least be used for scrap paper when they proved valueless in a few weeks' time. On September 21, 1923, the unthinkable occurred: Germany issued its first billion mark note. An average Berliner must have gone mad trying to negotiate even ordinary tasks during the vagaries of the inflationary period. To name but one instance: A Berlin streetcar ticket in 1923 cost 3,000 marks on July 16; it was 6,000 marks two weeks later, 10,000 marks on August 6, 50,000 marks on August 14, and 100,000 marks on August 20.[23] The worthless currency also discouraged German manufacturers. The largest dairy producer in the city, Bolle, which prior to the war had been producing 1 million liters of milk per day for the Berlin population, produced only 25,000 liters a day during the inflationary era.[24]

The economic crisis took its toll in other ways, too. Unemployment in Berlin doubled between October and November 1923, when nearly 360,000 people were looking for work; outside the city, farmers routinely shot and killed Berliners who had fanned out into the countryside to steal crops, particularly potatoes.[25] Ludwig Heck complained that the zoo in 1920 was "surviving on alms"[26] and speculated that its seventy-eight-year existence might come to an end without state intervention. In a letter to the Prussian Academy of Sciences requesting its support for the zoo's application for funds from Prussian and Berlin authorities, Heck wrote:

> The Berlin Zoological Garden has offered considerable support to science in its long history.... Above all, the zoo's role in providing material to excite broad sections of the population, and attract the youth to thoughtful consideration of nature, cannot be overestimated.
>
> Its closing would spell the demise of all zoological gardens in Germany. We can only fervently hope that the zoo, in its current desperate plight, will be granted a financial subsidy that will secure its existence.[27]

Even with the support of the Prussian Academy of Sciences, the state was not immediately forthcoming with funds;[28] in the meantime, the zoo's losses mounted, exceeding 1 million marks in 1920 and rising to 1.625 million marks in 1921.[29] By 1922, the zoo's situation had deteriorated to the point that it had to close. The zoo's board announced the shattering news in November: "The Zoological Garden is a non-profit enterprise constituted as a shareholding corporation. The hardships have become so severe, that the Garden, which during these unfavorable times has suffered dreadfully, must shut its doors this winter. Its reopening can only take place with a subvention of 25–30 million marks. Should this not be forthcoming, the fate of the Garden and its animal collection will be sealed."[30]

While it awaited its fate, the zoo had little choice but to implement major cost-saving measures; some animals were given away and others were grouped together to reduce heating costs. The municipal government also granted the zoo permission to raise funds from the public, an unlikely source of philanthropy given the runaway inflation. As it turned out, however, Berliners became the saviors of the zoo. Newspapers pleaded with the Berlin public to dig into their pockets, with headlines blaring "The Zoo in Distress!" and "Help the Zoo!" Even though Berlin residents were in dire straits themselves, they contributed 10 million marks to the zoo, allowing it to open again by March 30, 1923. The zoo, like much of Germany, would nevertheless be on shaky ground until the introduction of the new currency, the Rentenmark, in 1924.[31]

The catastrophic inflation of the early 1920s caused zoos elsewhere in Germany to close. Dresden, Breslau, Munich, and Hannover all had to close their zoos, sometimes for short periods, such as six months for the Dresden zoo, and sometimes for longer; Hannover shut for nearly two years and Breslau closed for six.[32] In most cases, the zoos' animals were sold to cover at least some of the operating shortfall. Such was the situation for the Munich zoo, which sold its collection to the Nuremberg zoo for nearly 2 million marks.[33]

Some politicians, such as the Hannoverian senator H. Grote, saw little reason to reopen the zoos:

> People always say that the Zoological Garden is an extremely important cultural institute for the youth. I do not share this opinion. In my view, the Zoological Garden is first and foremost a center of entertainment.... It is true, of course, that the youth head there and look at animals. But from the Reformation, and up to the era of Goethe and Schiller, there were no zoological gardens in Germany and our culture has nevertheless risen steadily.[34]

As no zoo closed permanently during the Weimar era, the vast majority of German society apparently did not share Senator Grote's views. Not only did cities consider them to be vital to the well-being of the population, offering people fresh air and park-like settings and drawing them closer to the natural world, zoos were now considered vital to the protection of animal species. When the Munich zoo reopened in 1927, for example, the local newspaper boasted that it would be a "giant breeding farm for exotic and endangered animals."[35] It was now no longer sufficient to simply pique popular interest in the animal world.

The time had come for zoos themselves to play a leading role in species preservation through education and breeding programs.

The contemporary perception that animals are worthy of preservation, regardless of whether those animals directly benefit humanity, is a recent phenomenon. For most of human history, few people, including those involved with zoos, were terribly bothered if animals were hunted to extinction or their habitats destroyed to the point that the species was no longer viable. Even though a large number of robust zoos were already in existence in the late nineteenth and early twentieth centuries, they did little to protect endangered species, many of which went extinct, including Steller's sea cow (1850), the Cape lion (1865), the Labrador duck (1875), the North American passenger pigeon (1907), the Pyrenean ibex (1910), the Carolina parakeet (1914), the Barbary lion (1922), and the Syrian wild donkey (1927).[36] The marsupial Tasmanian wolf (thylacine) lasted somewhat longer, until 1936, when the last one died in a zoo in Hobart, Australia.

For the most part, breeding wild animals in captivity is a balanced affair requiring detailed biological knowledge, appropriate enclosures, a sufficient number and type of animal, and infusion of new blood to avoid inbreeding. Not all animals are well suited for it. But the quagga, the southernmost African zebra type, distinguished by a horse-like front half, a striped rear half, and the tail of a donkey, had proven to breed easily under human guidance. Still, since preservation of a species for its own sake was simply not in the mental framework of late nineteenth-century Europeans, it too went extinct, in 1883, the result of a massive hunting spree by white settlers who viewed the animal as competition for the grasslands where they grazed their cattle.[37] The second-to-last of its kind on earth died in the Antilopenhaus in the Berlin zoo, the last in the Amsterdam zoo.[38] It is now difficult to find any traces whatsoever of this animal, which once existed by the millions. Only twelve hides, fourteen skulls, and seven skeletons exist in all the world's natural history museums.[39]

Although European zoos from the outset saw their mission in bridging the divide between nature and the city dweller, only gradually, in the last decades before the turn of the century, did they come to consider playing a direct a role in the preservation of species, and then only sporadically. The widespread emphasis in zoos on breeding to preserve an endangered species is a post–World War II phenomenon.

The first European attempts to bring a species back from the brink involved the Berlin zoo, at least indirectly. The Père David deer, named after the French missionary who had studied the species in an animal sanctuary south of Beijing in 1856, had gone extinct in the wild by the beginning of the twentieth century, a result of both a catastrophic flood in 1895 that wiped out the bulk of the herd and the upheaval of the Boxer Rebellion, during which the Chinese hunted the animal for food. The duke of Bedford acquired the remaining eighteen David deer from European zoos, all of whom had descended from three in the Berlin zoo, and bred a herd at his Woburn Abbey wildlife refuge that numbered ninety by the outbreak of World War I. Since that time, through breeding at wildlife reserves and zoos, the number of David deer has increased to the point that it has been reintroduced into China, where several thousand live in monitored wildlife reserves.[40] This achievement is worth stating plainly: All of the David deer currently on Earth descended from the last remaining three in the Berlin zoo in the 1870s.[41]

The other major conservation effort in the early part of the twentieth century involved Europe's largest land mammal, the European bison, or wisent. For much of German history, the wisent held a place of almost mythical standing. From the epic poem the *Nibelungenlied* (Song of the Nibelungs we know that as far back as the medieval era young males demonstrated their masculinity by hunting the creature.[42] The last wisent in the wild was shot wandering through a German forest in 1755, leaving about 700 in a reserve in Bialowies, Poland, almost all of which were killed in the chaos following World War I. In 1921, Kurt Priemel, director of the Frankfurt zoo, established the International Society for the Preservation of the Wisent, which aimed to pool the resources of zoological gardens throughout Europe to save an animal perilously close to extinction. Almost every zoo in possession of wisents was represented at the founding meeting held in Berlin.[43] Priemel recognized the need for this international cooperation in order to be successful, stating at the founding of the society: "All our efforts toward the noble goal of nature preservation will remain piecemeal unless they are based in internationalism. Nature preservation is today not only an unavoidable requirement of our era, it is a science that now enjoys widespread scholarly recognition."[44] At the time of the founding of the society, there were only fifty-six wisents left in the world, four of which were in the Berlin zoo, three bulls and one fragile cow.

Lutz Heck, the soon-to-be director of the Berlin zoo, was deeply interested in the preservation of the wisent and other species, many of which, like the bear, moose, lynx, and beaver, had all but disappeared from central Europe. In his 1941 book *Auf Tiersuche in Weiter Welt* (Searching for Animals Far Afield), which was as much a political treatise as an account of his time in the African savannah, Heck wrote: "I too advocated for the preservation of endangered animals, those creatures that were the last of their kind . . . . I felt it not only my duty to engage myself in the protection of threatened species, it was something I felt passionately about. I undertook everything within my power to turn thoughts about preserving the animal world into action."[45] Heck took it upon himself to build a photographic record of every remaining wisent, traveling with his camera to zoos and reserves in Holland, Denmark, Sweden, England, Hungary, Germany, and Poland. The number of wisents rose steadily through a combination of efforts: the introduction of bison, an animal almost indistinguishable from the wisent, from the United States to assist with European breeding in the 1930s; a catalogue of breedable wisents published by European, Asian, and US zoos; and the assistance of the New York Zoological Society, which reserved lands for breeding purposes.[46]

Hermann Göring, the forest supervisor and German game supervisor during the Nazi era, provided a boost to the wisent in 1934 when he created Germany's first wildlife park in Schorfheide, where he placed wisents and twenty bison that he had received from the Canadian government. The plaque at the entrance of the reserve harkened back, in typical Nazi fashion, to a bygone Germany, one untainted by the scourge of modernity, an earthly cradle and animal paradise: "Once, primeval big game animals made their way through Germany's forests. The hunt was used by our forefathers as a test of courage. In 1934 German Game Supervisor Hermann Göring established a game preserve on this site. Wisents, moose, wild horses, beavers, and other wildlife find here a sanctuary, and give witness to the richness of animal life in a Germany not yet ruled by man."[47] By 1941, there were 105 wisents on Earth, half of which resided in Germany.[48] Forty years later, the European bison herd had grown to 2,459 and was reintroduced into the wild in the forests of eastern Poland.[49] Through a concerted effort based at the Berlin zoo, but involving many other countries, an animal for which all hope had been lost is now no longer endangered.

One of the clearest examples of zoos' new focus on the preservation of species comes from the refounding of *Der Zoologische Garten*, a monthly journal established in 1859 and headquartered at the Frankfurt zoo.[50] In the years immediately following World War I, the journal, like much of Germany, floundered as a result of the economic downturn. In 1922, it finally shut down. Six years later, however, when the Weimar Republic had at least temporarily stabilized, the journal was restarted, not strictly as a journal for the zoos of Germany but as a collaborative effort of nearly all the major central European zoos.[51] The new editors emphasized the cultural and scientific role of zoos, in particular the furnishing of animals for zoological study. For much of the history of German zoos, animals contributed long past their death as objects of study by scientists associated with natural history museums, who were grateful for this biological material that their institutions could scarcely have afforded on their own.

By the 1920s, however, science had become interested not only in form and function of animals, for which cadavers served their purposes well, but increasingly in physiology and animal psychology. The study of living animals no longer fell to the amateur but became a mainstream scientific pursuit attracting such notable German zoologists as Wolfgang Köhler, whose study of apes revealed their high degree of intelligence; Oskar Heinroth, who helped establish ornithology as a legitimate field of scientific inquiry; Ernst Matthes, who discovered the newt's ability to smell; and Karl von Frisch, who proved that blood-sucking insects had the ability to distinguish color.[52] These scientists agreed that it was preferable to study living animals in the wild, but for practical reasons this was simply not possible. It fell to zoos to provide the living specimens for scientific study for some of Germany's leading scientists.

Apart from a focus on species preservation, the journal *Der Zoologische Garten* continued its historic mandate to provide logistical information on the basic care of zoo animals, including how cages should be heated and lit, animal diet, best practices in animal transport, and so on. It

featured articles on comparative anatomy, animal psychology, parasi-
tology and pathology, vaccinations, and habitat conservation. The editors dedicated significant space in the journal to articles on habitats of
species at risk, including whales, fur-bearing animals, tropical birds,
penguins, and animals designated as European natural monuments.[53]
Responding to the general public, who were increasingly sympathetic
to the plight of animals, the publication also aspired to reach a broader
audience than in the past. "May our new journal," wrote one of the editors, "succeed in winning the esteem of scientists as well as the hearts
of animal friends!"[54]

The changing perception of animals in the first decades of the twentieth century was evident elsewhere, including in a publication read by
tens of thousands of Berliners every year. At the turn of the century, the
Berlin zoo's guidebooks informed visitors bluntly if a given animal was
on the brink of extinction, with little indication that such an occurrence
was to be lamented. At that time, visitors could expect that several species of zebra on display, the Tasmanian marsupial wolf (thylacine), and
the white tail gnu would in due course be extinct in the wild.[55]

Zoo publications a few decades later were markedly different.
Visitor's guides portrayed the possibility of an animal—any animal—
going extinct as a tragedy and a sharp critique of the modern, especially European, world. In a souvenir publication from 1927, showcasing
photographs of the zoo taken with the new Zeiss Ikon camera, the
authors are no longer matter of fact about the devastation of animal life.
After indicating that the hippo had been hunted to extinction in Egypt
and Nubia, the authors wrote: "Everywhere it is the same curse of our
nature-devastating European civilization. It brings with it remarkable
technical achievements, better weapons and the like, but not refined
attitudes."[56]

Publications aimed at schoolchildren were even more upfront about
the dangers that humans posed to the animal world. Referencing one
German animal on the brink of extinction, zoo director Lutz Heck
wrote in 1931:

The black stork is protected legally as a "natural monument"
(*Naturdenkmal*), as are all animals and plants threatened with extinction. Nobody is permitted to shoot them or take their eggs.

Unfortunately it must be said that we make life difficult for not only the black stork but the white stork, too. It seems like we must make use of every inch of earth. That we can't leave alone a single swamp, mire, or moor. Nor a single fallow field or heather.[57]

Heck used the entry on the zebra to make children further aware of the dangers of civilization:

Africa was originally an animal paradise, in which comparatively few humans, the negroes, lived. With their simple weapons, arrows and spears, they could not do much damage to the animal world. Back then there were innumerable herds of elephants, buffalos, giraffes, antelopes, and zebras. Until the whites arrived with their firearms. They managed to render vast sections of Africa animal-less. The curse of European civilization![58]

These same publications also boasted when an animal had been reintroduced to the wild, including swans into the Havel River in eastern Germany and two types of deer into the Grunewald.[59] Indeed, the reintroduction of native species became central to the zoo's mission. In its annual report for 1929, the zoo board explained its role in bringing animals to the public rather than the other way around: "We continue to fill our city parks, where possible, with indigenous animals in order to excite and teach the general public who reside in more distant parts of the city about zoology. In this way, we can counter the alienation from nature that big cities cause."[60]

Paul Matschie was a curator at the Berlin Zoological Museum, the forerunner of the Natural History Museum and an institution separate from the zoo (although it welcomed the zoo's dead animals for study). He was a close friend of Ludwig Heck and an ardent proponent of the need to educate the public on species preservation. Matschie's own research focused on species variation that occurred depending on habitat, such as the subtle differences in appearance between leopards from West Africa and those from East Asia, or between Sumatran and Siberian tigers. He introduced the idea of geographic variation in his lavishly illustrated 1899 book *Lebende Bilder aus dem Reiche der Tiere* (Living Images from the Animal Kingdom), in which Ludwig Heck wrote: "I agree entirely with my friend Matschie, that characteristics of the species go hand in hand with the natural geography."[61] The friendship between Heck and Matschie was rooted, at least in part, in their joint alarm at the cavalier manner in which humans were devastating the animal world. "Relentlessly, humans strive to put every speck of land to their use," wrote Matschie in the introduction to the book. "The number of species that have been exterminated is reaching frightening levels . . . . Even into our own era, there is hardly any attention paid in schools to living things. Pupils who leave school with their certificate are perhaps able to give a talk in Greek, but are not able to differentiate between a sparrow and a chickadee."[62]

In the interwar period, when Germany's financial catastrophe threatened all zoos, many leading figures associated with zoos publicly espoused their indispensable role in the preservation of species. Werner Sunkel, an eminent ornithologist, argued that nature conservation was as much a part of zoos as their traditional roles, such as educating the public on natural history and providing an oasis in the crowded urban environment. "We stand in awe of the 'living fossils' in zoos," Sunkel wrote in 1919, "the largest and most unspoiled animals: elephants, giraffes, rhinos, and the large wild cattle." Sunkel left no doubt as to the reason that the existence of these "natural monuments," as he called them, was threatened: "They and many others face extinction . . . . As the interesting remains of a nearly extinct fauna, they deserve our protection from destruction by Man and his culture, from eradication at the hands of 'the Lord of Creation.'" Zoos, he believed, played a crucial role in reorienting the public away from an attitude of dominance over animals to one of stewardship.[63]

Alongside lofty arguments about preserving elephants and other exotic animals from around the world because they were part of "life on earth," zoos also promoted protection of German animals, a cause that zoo directors believed could be more readily understood by the zoo-going public. On this account, zoos had their work cut out for them. The director of the Halle zoo lamented that most of his visitors could not distinguish between a heron and a stork, and he was annoyed that few, even among the educated classes, bothered to read the labels on the cages.[64] Acquiring and displaying German animals also had its challenges. Whereas only a phone call to a professional animal trader was needed to start the acquisition of attractions like an elephant or a meerkat, zoos often had to wait months to obtain the far-less lucrative otter, hawk, or woodpecker. Even then, zoo personnel tended to rely on personal friends to deliver local animals. Once at the zoo, German animals posed their own problems. Lions were easier to keep alive in captivity in early twentieth-century Germany than deer, whose sensitive digestive systems caused them to succumb more frequently to disease.[65]

Zoo experts believed that labels on cages could achieve some of the educational goals about the need to protect species, but the format in place fell far short of doing so. Typically, labels on the cages of threatened German species indicated the seasons when a hunting ban applied to the animal. The rationale for the ban, however, was frequently lacking, an omission that frustrated the Halle zoo director, Friedrich Hauchecorne:

> Untold times I have stood by the birds of prey cage at the Berlin zoo and had to explain to visitors the phrasing on the label: "Protected from 1 March to 1 October." It is crucial to make clear the rationale for these protective measures . . . . I am of the opinion that the public can be brought around to the idea of conservation by emphasizing the beauty and majesty of animal life.[66]

Hauchecorne here points to a change in the human view of animals. Whereas preservation efforts in the past were justified on the basis of an animal's utility to humans—typically for sustenance or for clothing—the new efforts eschewed this category and emphasized an intrinsic value of the animal, its beauty and its idiosyncratic way of being, regardless of utility. In Hauchecorne's view, hunters, collectors, and those who made their living from forestry and agriculture posed the greatest threat to domestic wildlife and would be the most difficult audience to convince. Still, he believed that zoos provided the ideal opportunity to reach that audience, given the large number of country dwellers who visited them. Urban dwellers, he felt, needed less convincing of the need for conservation efforts, given their "longing for nature."[67]

Although zoos were the most visible of the sites dedicated to preserving wildlife, they were not the only ones. Private animal parks began to appear in the late nineteenth century, often tracing their roots to the philanthropy of noblemen. In England, the duke of Bedford and Baron von Rothschild established large, well-known wildlife parks in, respectively, Woburn and Tring. In the Caucasus, Prince Alexander von Oldenburg founded a wildlife refuge on his estate. By far the most intriguing private animal park, however, was Friedrich Falz-Fein's wildlife refuge in Askania-Nova in the steppes of southern Russia, an area that became a pilgrimage site for academics and laypeople interested in animals. The land, located near the mouth of the Dneiper River, a half-day wagon ride from the village of Kachowka, had been in German hands for more than three generations when Falz-Fein decided to establish a refuge for animals. At his behest, large numbers of animals from various continents were brought to Askania-Nova in 1888—a bison and fifty-two Canada geese from North America; a kangaroo from Australia; a maras from South America; zebras, antelopes, and gnus from Africa, the best-represented continent; and from Europe the Przewalski wild horses. Unlike the better-known mustang, whose ancestors had been domesticated, the Przewalski horse was the only truly wild horse in existence and remains so to this day.[68]

The refuge soon became home to a massive collection of thousands of animals in dozens of species. Eleven years before Hagenbeck popularized the "open-air" zoo concept in Stellingen, Askania-Nova allowed its animals to roam freely across the vast enclosure, with virtually no human surveillance. The occasional professor or zoo director who entered the enclosure to study the animals did so at his own risk. Karl Soffel, a German scientist who went to Askania-Nova in 1911, was awestruck by the sight of so many animals sharing the same space and the ability of the southern animals to adapt to the northern climate. "It is quite something," he wrote "to see the colorful zebras and African antelopes, ostriches, etc. tromping about in the snow."[69] He believed that the freedom to range resulted directly in improved breeding prospects: "Most of the mammals and birds here reproduce: camels, antelopes (whose current herd size of 30 started with one pair), zebras, gnus, even the painfully shy Saigas and mufflons."[70] Askania-Nova was even represented at the Paris world's fair, winning a prize in the botanical garden category.[71]

The connection between Askania-Nova and the Berlin zoo ran through the zoo's director. Ludwig Heck met Falz-Fein in 1889, the

year after Askania-Nova was founded, and immediately formed a last-
ing bond with him: "This relationship developed in the course of time
into a heartfelt and true friendship," wrote Falz-Fein's stepson, "which
lasted undimmed until Friedrich's last days. The love of nature and of
animals brought these two men together.... I have rarely in my life
encountered individuals so strongly connected to each other as Professor
Heck and Friedrich."[72] Heck visited the refuge for the first time in 1901,
delighted in particular by the Przewalski horses, the only such horses
to be found in private ownership.[73] Heck and Oskar Heinroth, the
director of the new aquarium at the zoo, became regular visitors to the
wildlife refuge in the Russian steppes, both of them amazed by the
opportunity to observe a wide variety of animal life if not in the wild,
then not quite in captivity either. When Falz-Fein returned to Berlin
for medical treatment toward the end of his life, Heck and Heinroth
visited him frequently in the hospital. On his good days, Friedrich went
to the zoo.[74] Given his admiration for Askania-Nova and his eventual
support for Nazism, it is perhaps unsurprising to find that Heck was
horrified by the nationalization of the refuge under the Bolsheviks. He
recalled one incident that further cemented his negative view of the
Communists: "During Friedrich's time there was a veterinarian named
Ivanov who resided in Askania-Nova for quite a while, and who successfully bred horses with artificial insemination. According to witnesses,
he was sent by the Soviets to west Africa in order to—and this is in
keeping with that Godless movement—produce an offspring between
a human and a monkey."[75]

Highlighting its efforts at species conservation, the Berlin zoo today
likes to style itself as "Noah's Ark on the Spree River." This fundamental
transformation of the Berlin zoo, from an institution to express human
dominance over nature into one that instilled its visitors with respect
for animal life, began during the dire years of the Weimar Republic and
continued in the more stable years that followed. The Berlin zoo was at
the center of a public and scientific dialogue around the intrinsic worth
of animals and about the pitfalls of European civilization. The age of
serving up surplus animals at gala dinners was long past.

Having survived the worst years of the Weimar Republic, the Berlin
zoo began a steady ascent to its former glory. Newspaper headlines in
1925 raved about the "flourishing zoo" and delighted in the expansion

of the animal collection, one of the largest in the zoo's history.[76] The zoo could count again on the fixed subvention from the city for school visits (34,000 RM; i.e., Reichsmarks) that had been part of the zoo's mandate since 1895.[77] Attendance reflected the zoo's improved fortunes:

1924	1,535,012 visitors
1925	1,698,354 visitors
1926	1,606,036 visitors[78]

By 1926 the zoo had achieved the same level of financial stability it had enjoyed in the prewar era,[79] allowing it to increase its animal collection for the first time since World War I. First on the list of new acquisitions was a giraffe from the former colony of German East Africa, a rarity as most zoos obtained giraffes from the Sudan. The zoo also added the nearly extinct Cyprus wild sheep (mouflon), Scottish Highland cattle (exhibited for the first time in Germany), various species of English cattle, a puma from California, and a banteng from Southeast Asia, the first of these cattle to be exhibited alive in Europe.[80] Likely due to a summer that saw the most rain since 1889, attendance slipped in 1927, down nearly 200,000, but rebounded again in 1928 to an all-time high of 1,766,546.[81] Not surprisingly, the economic depression of 1929 caused attendance to fall again, but it was still robust at more than 1.5 million visitors.[82]

For many domestic and international organizations, the rejuvenated zoo was the destination of choice for their conventions. A banquet was held there in July 1929 for 400 US physicians in Berlin attending an annual meeting.[83] In the fall, 30,000 visitors attended the exhibit of "What, how, and where does the housewife purchase?" put on by the Greater Berlin Association of Housewives. General Motors held three car shows at the zoo over 1929–30. Other exhibitors included the Hackebeil book publishing house, the German Dental Association, and the League of German Hairstylists.[84]

The strong attendance in the latter half of the 1920s was due in large part to the reintroduction of the human zoo, those ethnographic showcases that had proven so successful in the nineteenth century. John Hagenbeck, half-brother of Carl Hagenbeck, organized a show of South

Asians in 1926, the first such show to be held at the Berlin zoo in twenty-five years. John was as much a showman as his brother, parading the more than 100 Indians and their nine elephants down Berlin's trendy Ku'damm on the way to the zoo, the unusual procession attracting all manner of onlookers who might well have echoed the *Vossische Zeitung's* reaction: "What a delight!"[85] According to the zoo's annual report, the show, held in a new hall specifically designed to host human exhibits, "resonated with the general public, even though there had been protests in some 'Indian' circles about putting their countrymen on display."[86] With its elephants, buskers, and snake charmers, the show was reminiscent of the Sinhalese show that had taken place in the Berlin zoo in 1885, but with nearly twice as many participants.[87]

The following year, the zoo hosted a group from the Italian colony of Tripoli, the first time that the zoo had independently organized an exhibit of humans. A last-minute complication caused the zoo's director of operations, Dr. Freyer, to head to Rome to deal with colonial authorities there and the zoo director Ludwig Heck to plead his case with the

People from Tripoli enact a market scene in a structure that the Berlin zoo constructed for the 1927 ethnographic display of North Africans. The dwarf Said (front right) was one of the main attractions. *Berlin Zoo Archive*

Italian embassy in Rome. Even the German foreign minister, Gustav Stresemann, became involved.[88] Italian authorities finally agreed to the display of their colonial subjects in Berlin on three conditions: (1) that it would be made clear to the public the advantageous situation in which Tripoli has found itself under Italian authority, (2) that an Italian interpreter would be present at the show, and (3) the show's participants would not be permitted close contact with the Berlin population.[89]

The new exhibit hall that had housed the Indian show went through an extensive reworking to convert it into a north African village, complete with a market square, a mosque with a seventeen-meter-high minaret, cafés, a pantomime theater, fountains, and hay-covered feeding troughs.[90] Those on display exhibited their various talents in making crafts of leather, ivory, and pearls in the bazaar-like atmosphere. As was the case in past shows, the visitors put on displays of both daily life and milestone events in the life of north Africans. The wedding re-enactment with its belly dancers, Bedouins on horseback, and lively music proved popular, prompting one Berlin newspaper to exclaim: "It's as if a fairy tale has come to life!"[91] Although attendance at the Tripoli show would not reach the lofty heights of the 1883 Sinhalese show, it still drew in large numbers, peaking at 78,000 visitors on one Sunday in September 1927.[92] The show left Berlin several weeks earlier than planned, but this was no reflection on the show's popularity; the early closing can be blamed on the rainfall that had plagued Berlin for weeks and showed no sign of letting up.[93]

The Tripoli show billed itself as representative of north African rather than "Arab" life, a situation that was immediately clear to visitors because of the presence of another group on display beside the Arabs. Twenty-four Jews took up residence in the Berlin zoo in the summer of 1927. Playing traditional African instruments, including hand drums and a version of the bagpipes, the Jews were the talk of the town. A local daily enticed people to the show with the headline: "The beautiful Camilla and the dwarf Said." The "dwarf" in question worked in the fabricated coffeehouse as a waiter, "carrying 2 hundred-weights with ease."[94] For Camilla, Berlin newspapers had nothing but unrestrained praise: "No one can argue that the star of the troupe is Camilla, a picture-perfect 22-year-old Jewish girl, possessing facial features of the nobility, but with an Oriental flair."[95] Berlin's love affair with the African Jew Camilla is

Representatives of the Sara people from Chad pose at the Berlin zoo in 1931. This group, the last to be exhibited before World War II, caused a sensation because of the wooden discs inserted into the females' lips and the three dwarf men who accompanied the visitors. *Berlin Zoo Archive*

noteworthy, given that at the same time across the country in Munich, Hitler was rebuilding the Nazi party.

The last major display of humans in the Berlin zoo was the so-called Sara Kaba Lip Negroes in 1931, an exhibit that had more in common with the smaller circus freak show than with the zoo's more elaborate ethnographic showcases. The group had proved popular with the public when put on display in various German zoos the previous year, allowing the Berlin zoo board to be reasonably confident that their presence in Berlin would be a windfall.[96]

The troupe, which had no animals, consisted of nine female Africans from Chad, in whose bottom and top lips had been inserted wooden discs measuring up to 21 cm in diameter, and three dwarf men.[97] Posters around Berlin highlighted the African women's unusual appearance by forefronting the lips and accentuating them by way of a gaping mouth. At the time, German academics believed that men in the village had imposed the lip plates on the women so as to render them unattractive and therefore less likely to be targeted for theft by neighboring villages.[98]

Even today, anthropologists disagree as to the reason behind the lip plates. Some argue that they are an ornamentation that enhances female beauty, others that the lip size has a bearing on the bride's cattle price. The *Vossische Zeitung* again promoted a humane, empathetic response to the show, as it had done during the nineteenth-century shows, writing that the "Lip-Negroes" could take comfort in the fact that "they appeared as unusual to us as we did to them."[99] Although we lack attendance figures for the show, it appears that it was fairly successful, netting the zoo a profit of 18,000 RM.[100]

The show was also popular elsewhere in Europe, including Basel, Switzerland, where the zoo had for decades actively courted human exhibits to increase its financial ability to purchase exotic animals. The Basel zoo had exhibited humans, for example, long before it acquired its first elephant.[101] In the vast majority of calendar years that the zoo hosted displays of humans, between 20 and 25 percent of the entire attendance for that year came during the ethnographic exhibits, although these shows rarely lasted more than two weeks.[102]

A comic strip that appeared in the *Basler Helgen*, a weekly illustrated magazine with a circulation of nearly 60,000, reveals in striking fashion some popular perceptions around the African women with lip discs. The reader follows the protagonist, Dr. Babbedipfi, a well-dressed but otherwise average Basler, over the course of nine panels as he visits the display of African women at the Basel zoo. The initial panels show him purchasing his ticket at the kiosk, then heading into the zoo where he meets one of the African women with a lip disc sitting on the grass. He takes her behind a hut where he kisses her. In the next panel, he is swearing his devotion to her in an improvised marriage ceremony. This erotic attraction, however, has consequences for Dr. Babbedipfi, who finds himself confined on a table while his new wife inserts a disc into his lip. When he emerges from the procedure, he is still dressed as the well-to-do European, but now sporting an ugly expression on his face and a lip to match his wife's. In the final two panels, the reader learns Dr. Babbedipfi had been dreaming. He rises from bed, proceeds to the zoo, and, with an expression of sheer delight on his face, watches the African women from a safe distance.[103] Both he, and presumably the readers, are to be relieved that the Basler did not end up adopting African ways.

While acknowledging the erotic attraction of foreign women, the message behind the lighthearted comic strip was clearly a negative one, namely, that disaster awaited those who developed an overly familiar relationship with foreign people. Although this comic strip is but one response in Basel to the exhibit of lip-disc women, it is nevertheless a useful point of comparison to Berlin, where the shows of foreigners had received an overwhelmingly positive response and where romantic relationships between Berliners and "exotic" peoples *had* developed. It is difficult to imagine that a similar comic strip about the Jewish sensation Camilla would have been possible in Berlin.

The days of the human zoo were drawing to an end, however, not because of any widespread criticism of the shows—communist newspapers were the only ones in the interwar period to consistently attack the shows—but rather because they were falling prey to the medium of film, a much more cost-efficient way to bring the world to many more Germans. During the first years of the interwar period, zoos in Germany and the human zoo were part and parcel of the film industry. The famous director Fritz Lang filmed a movie in Hagenbeck's Stellingen zoo in 1919, taking advantage of both the exotic locale and the foreign extras. Film, not human displays, would now deliver the exotic to Germans; it is no coincidence that the promoters of the ethnographic exhibits, like the Hagenbeck firm, moved into film early on.[104] The most visible sign of the times was the sale of the Berlin zoo's purpose-built display hall for human shows to a developer who made it into Berlin's most luxurious cinema, the "Ufa-Palast am Zoo."

The zoo attempted in the aftermath of World War II to resurrect the shows with a display of Lapps in 1952 and Africans the following year, but neither of the shows resonated with the public. (Nevertheless, a compelling image of postwar Germany is a Lapp family with children tending a reindeer, the bombed-out aquarium in the background, and a number of Berliners looking on.) An extravagant show of Indians at Hagenbeck's zoo in Stellingen, planned for 1957 to mark the fiftieth anniversary of the zoo, was scrapped.[105] It is likely that the shows would have ended at this point either way, but the advent of long-distance tourism made it a certainty. Although the performances that natives put on for tourists in the postwar period were as contrived as what had once been in zoos, the fact that they were performed in their homeland gave—and gives—for many tourists at least the illusion of authenticity.

Berliners observe a family of Lapps in the zoo in 1952, with the ruined aquarium in the background. The attempt to resurrect the "human zoo" in the postwar era failed largely because of the advent of film and long-distance tourism. *Landesarchiv Berlin, F Rep. 290 0018042*

Cinema was not the only new form of entertainment to threaten the zoo's viability. Car ownership had increased exponentially in the 1920s, allowing Germans to partake of entertainment options even farther afield. In 1922, there were only 17,000 cars in Berlin. Seven years later, the 82,000 cars on the streets of Berlin made a traffic light on Potsdamer Platz—Europe's first—a necessity.[106] The enormous growth in sporting events also concerned the zoo's directorship. With the establishment of the German Football League in 1900, soccer started to professionalize and become more popular, although it would be some time before it reached the heights of popularity that England was experiencing. Still, by 1913, the "German Stadium" in Berlin's Grunewald area could hold 33,000 spectators and was to be the showpiece of the 1916 Olympics.[107] (Those Olympics were canceled because of World War I but would return to Germany in 1936. The "German Stadium" was razed to make way for the Nazi monumental Olympic Stadium.) In 1928, the zoo dedicated its annual art display held in the Antilopenhaus to the "Art of Sport" in order to, as the zoo board phrased it, "remind the sport-going public of the zoological garden."[108]

Faced with these tremendous pressures from new forms of entertainment, many German zoos turned to all types of gimmicks to attract visitors. Several other zoos hosted human exhibits as did Berlin but were required to supplement them with circus-like entertainments. During the interwar era, the Dresden zoo hosted fire-eaters and lion tamers; Nürnberg held fireworks displays; and the Frankfurt zoo established a movie theater and a spa around the naturally occurring hot springs, hosted beauty contests, and offered horse-riding lessons.[109] Leipzig loaned out its carnivorous cats during the Weimar era for film productions like the *Tiger from Eschnapur* and, like Dresden, offered the public many animal *acts* as a circus might, rather than static, educational displays.[110] Once again in German history, the Berlin zoo was an outlier. It alone stands out during the Weimar period for having sufficient income from visitors and city subsidies to avoid resorting to base entertainments.

Nevertheless, in the new entertainment environment, the zoo's leadership had to find ways of maintaining its relevance. Since film had undercut its ethnographic shows, the zoo looked elsewhere to boost attendance.[111] Ironically, the zoo would turn to a source of entertainment that it had neglected for some time: animals. "It appears that the time for such ethnographic displays of peoples has passed," the zoo's board wrote in 1927. "Countries and the people who inhabit them and their traditions are being brought closer through picture and cinema.... We have decided, therefore, that in the future we will be focused more on animal-catching expeditions."[112] And the zoo did indeed return to its roots, squaring off with the array of new entertainments in the capital by sending trappers to Africa to acquire marquee animals to replace the humans in the zoo.

Until the 1920s, the Berlin zoo, like many zoos in the Western world, had relied on animal traders like Carl Hagenbeck to fill its enclosures. The need to keep the animals alive on the journey from the place of captivity to their European destination required a certain expertise and differentiated the zoo from the Berlin zoological museum, which sought only dead specimens and could, therefore, conduct its own expeditions with relative ease. In 1908, for example, an expedition went out from the museum to Cameroon, returning a year later laden with alcohol-filled jars containing 68 mammals, 1,354 birds, 124 reptiles and amphibians, 62 fish, and 11,742 arthropods, of which roughly 11,000 were insects.[113]

The 1920s saw major zoos in Europe and the United States embark on their own expeditions, which served the dual purpose of eliminating their payments to intermediaries and increasing the number of showpiece animals. The US National Zoo undertook major expeditions during that decade to Tanganyika, the Dutch East Indies, and Liberia, acquiring animals by the thousands.[114] The Berlin zoo's first major animal-acquiring expedition took place in 1925 under the guidance of the zoo director's son, Lutz Heck. After an eighteen-day journey from Berlin, Heck and his group arrived in Abyssinia, today's Ethiopia. Having spent several months in the interior collecting monkeys, zebus, and turtles, the group returned to the inland town of Diredaua to load the collection onto five train wagons bound for the coast, where they were transferred onto small boats and rowed out to a French steamer. On the stormy voyage back to France, a pair of porcupines escaped from a damaged crate and jumped overboard, while an ostrich died when it was knocked over by a wave. Heck and the sailors tossed the bird into the Mediterranean between Corsica and Sardinia, one member of Heck's crew remarking as the bird floated away: "I would love to see the faces of the coast dwellers when this sea monster washes ashore!"[115] According to Heck, the monkeys screeched in delight at the sight of the French coast when the steamer neared its destination after a voyage of nearly three weeks. As it turned out, their celebration was premature. Another 110 hours by train awaited them from France to the Berlin zoo, where Heck delivered the fruits of his African journey: over 100 species of birds and animals.[116]

Two years later, Heck and his crew returned to Africa with a single purpose: to capture a rhino. This prized possession was beyond the reach of most zoos that could not afford the price tag of 30,000 marks.[117] On the long journey to Africa, Heck had time to dwell on the rhino's reputation for fierceness. Tales had made their way back to Germany from Africa of an animal that killed humans for pleasure, that ran at trains and derailed them when they were introduced into Africa, and whose skin was so thick that walking sticks were made of it.[118] Since the tranquilizer dart would not be invented until the 1950s, Heck might have had good reason to be concerned. Using the same procedure for capturing dangerous animals as had been prevalent in the nineteenth century, he waited for an adult rhino to come into sight with its offspring nearby and then shot the adult. With some surprise, but not a hint of remorse, Heck reported that the young male rhino hardly even broke from its grazing to notice the death of its mother.[119] Elated, Heck telegrammed back to Berlin: "Rhino, juvenile, male, caught by myself. Everyone healthy." Heck transported the rhino, now named "Mtoto," the Swahili word for child, and consuming nearly twelve liters of milk per day, to Geneva and then by train over the alps. Admiring his acquisition months later, Heck expressed a view common at the time—that he had, in fact, improved the rhino's life:

> As I stand today in front of the rhino enclosure in our garden and observe the magnificent, grown-up, healthy and beautiful animal, now five times as heavy as the infant we caught back then in the bush, I have that pleasant feeling of a hunter and researcher, who has accomplished a difficult task. And I am convinced that the rhino, which is no longer harassed by ticks, and which will never be inflicted with an infectious disease, is quite content in the Berlin Zoo.[120]

Along with the rhino, Heck had acquired for the zoo five giraffes, nine zebras, one white-beard gnu, one gazelle, three hippos, monkeys, meerkats, porcupines, two lions, one leopard, four ostriches, and twenty-four other species of birds.[121]

Heck the elder displayed the exotic new animals that his son had acquired in cages, as had been common practice at German zoos for nearly a century. Carl Hagenbeck's founding of a zoo in Stellingen near Hamburg in 1909, however, brought about a revolutionary change to this once unquestioned approach to animal exhibits. Although German zoos up to that point had installed a handful of barless enclosures that displayed animals in their re-created habitat, the vast majority of them still exhibited animals by their taxonomy in cages and tended to organize themselves in broad categories like mammals, birds, and reptiles. Zoos had approached the display of animals as humans had intellectually conceived the animal world: the Linnaean system of distinct groups based on related traits. Hagenbeck's new zoo broke the rules, employing exclusively natural habitat enclosures and hidden barriers like moats to separate animal and visitor, and displaying animals not by taxonomic commonalities but by habitat or geography. The shock of at least one famous visitor to the unprecedented scene was likely not unusual. "Thomas Edison walked around a group of trees to suddenly confront a lion face-to-face with nothing, apparently, to separate them," wrote one observer. "It scared the daylights out of the old inventor."[122] Hagenbeck completed the illusion of displaying animals in the wild by painting elaborate panorama backdrops of, for example, the African savannah or of the frozen Arctic. Hagenbeck also had viewing platforms installed so visitors could take in the expansive vistas. It was, as one author has written, "an imaginary universe that visitors could inhabit in the presence of wild animals."[123]

Tapping into what he perceived as increasing public pity regarding animals in cages, Hagenbeck famously proclaimed that his zoo would bring an end to the "sighing of the animals."[124] The experiment resonated with the public, more than a million of whom visited the zoo in its first year in operation. An exuberant Kaiser Wilhelm II was among them, exclaiming to Hagenbeck and his sons on his first visit to the park in June 1908: "Good morning, comrades! I already know your zoo from the cinema, but my brother *ordered* me to see it in person, so now show me what you've get here!"[125]

Zoo directors, on the other hand, reacted harshly to what they saw as a watering-down of the scientific mission of zoos. For them, Hagenbeck's zoo, a private enterprise without any connection to the state, was synonymous with a circus. Zoo directors throughout Germany boycotted his animal-trading business after his park opened.[126] When Hagenbeck proposed the establishment of one of his zoos in Berlin, the board of the Berlin zoo stated in no uncertain terms that it considered Hagenbeck's zoos to be sites of second-rate entertainment. In a letter to Admiral Friedrich von Hollmann, the zoo board outlined the fundamental differences between the Berlin zoo and what that zoo considered Hagenbeck to be: a dangerous imposter:

> Hagenbeck's animal show foregoes any systematic overview, employs theatrical lighting effects, and has a very small animal collection. The character of his undertaking is such that it causes a certain excitement in the lower masses that a zoological garden cannot match. As a consequence, these animal parks are a dangerous competitor for zoological gardens.

Should Hagenback establish an animal park in Berlin with state or municipal support, the Berlin zoo, widely acknowledged as the best in the world, would be badly damaged ....

As Vienna, Paris, and Hamburg have demonstrated, even large cities are not able to support two zoological gardens.

The zoo directors ended the letter with an appeal about the zoo as a public good:

With respect to the point that the Berlin zoological garden, like all zoological gardens, is run as a non-profit organization, I would like to highlight especially that Hagenbeck's enterprise is a private business, that exists solely for his personal benefit.[127]

Hagenbeck's death in 1913 meant that the Berlin zoo was able to avoid competition in its own backyard, but it would be unable to resist indefinitely the new model of zoo that his park near Hamburg represented. The zoo visitor's guide for 1926, still defiant, marked one of the last times that the zoo justified the traditional manner of displaying animals: "The management [of the zoo] has strived for decades to display animals which form a cohesive unit in the natural world beside one another. In this way, the visitor will have the correct impression of what is related in the natural world."[128] In other words, the zoo leadership believed that animal classification, identifying how seemingly disparate animals could nevertheless belong to the same species, was more important for understanding the animal kingdom than displaying unrelated animals together in a free enclosure, and certainly more important than misplaced concepts of the animal's "happiness." It was useful, then, to display animals by species—cattle, deer, antelope, rodents, and so on. By the end of the 1920s, however, with Hagenbeck's panorama park now approaching its twentieth year, the Berlin zoo responded directly to the Hagenbeck challenge by constructing its own free-ranging enclosures for related animal groups.[129]

One of the key obstacles the zoo faced in moving toward the new system of displaying animals was the reticence of the long-serving zoo director, Ludwig Heck. Ever fearful of his zoo being reduced to a circus-like entertainment venue, Heck opposed the move toward natural habitat enclosures because he believed it would incline the zoo toward collecting only those animals suited for such a display. In the end, he was forced to relent because of the public's overwhelmingly positive reaction to Hagenbeck's model. "Admittedly, these types of displays can be sensational," he wrote in a prominent Berlin daily, "and we will therefore also be taking steps in this direction, as soon as we have the financial means to do so."[130]

By 1931, the Berlin zoo had constructed from scratch its first enclosure without fences. It is likely that Heck's son, Lutz Heck, who would become the zoo's director two years later, influenced his father in this direction. "For me personally," he wrote in an official zoo publication, "the implementation of large enclosures without fences is a heartfelt desire."[131] However he may have felt about it personally, the younger Heck was aware that there had been a change in the public's view of animals that necessitated the new display methods, writing in a widely circulated zoo publication: "Getting rid of the cages corresponds to the sensitivities of today's visitor."[132]

Ludwig Heck and his fellow zoo directors had not been able to stop the Hagenbeck revolution from affecting their zoos, which now had to reconsider their fundamental nature. A bourgeois emphasis on *Bildung*, the education of a person as a whole, which was of central importance to the zoo's founders, was still present, especially in the case of schoolchildren. However, the demonstration of human prowess and exalting man's role in nature so prevalent in the mid-nineteenth century had all but been eclipsed in the 1920s by nature conservation and an increasing emphasis on the value of animal life in and of itself, rather than in terms of utility to humans. Scientists did not require an elaborate argument to justify a wide-ranging international effort to preserve the wisent; it was simply self-evident that the animal should be saved from extinction. In removing the bars from many zoo cages in the postwar period, zoos began a different narrative about the animals, one relating to their freedom and happiness rather than one about human dominance.[133] They had little choice. Not only had Hagenbeck's model proved enormously profitable but zoo-goers had become increasingly uncomfortable with seeing caged animals with little room to roam.

In his lyric poem about a caged panther at the Paris Jardin des Plantes, the great Czech-Austrian playwright Rainer Maria Rilke wrote:

From seeing the bars, his seeing is so exhausted
That it no longer holds anything anymore.
To him the world is bars, a hundred thousand bars
And behind the bars, nothing.[134]

When he wrote the poem in 1902, his was a solitary voice expressing concern about the way the animal might perceive its own captivity. Thirty years later, even the staunchest opponents of Hagenbeck's theme park were reshaping their zoos to accommodate new, fenceless enclosures and, by extension, the visitors' sympathy for animals. New zoos, like the one in Warsaw that was established in 1927, aware of the major shift taking place in the display of animals, followed the Hagenbeck model from the outset.[135]

By 1932, the Berlin zoo had appeared to come through the worst. During the war and the postwar period, the kaiser, the city of Berlin, and especially the residents of the German capital had financially supported the zoo. It was a flourishing, modernizing zoo, housing more species than almost any other zoo in the world and spearheading international efforts at species conservation. And Berlin itself had swelled to its historical peak of 4.3 million people, before witnessing a steady decline due to war and division. Today, nearly ninety years later, Berlin still has not achieved the population it had on the eve of World War II.[136]

But Germany was about to change in dramatic fashion. After years in the political wilderness, Adolf Hitler led his National Socialist German Workers' Party to a stunning electoral breakthrough in 1930. No longer able to ignore Germany's largest party, the aged president Paul von Hindenburg appointed Hitler chancellor in January 1933, a humiliating act for the field marshal and hero of the Battle of Tannenberg considering Hitler's lowly corporal rank. Hitler immediately outmaneuvered the naive old guard around him and consolidated his power. In rapid fashion, Hitler used the ill-advised arson attack on the German parliament by Marinus van der Lubbe, who had ties to the Communist party, as a pretext to pass the enabling act, which clamped down on civil liberties, thereby securing for himself dictatorial power. He launched a boycott of Jewish businesses, barred Jews from public service, smashed trade unions, burned Jewish books, banned the Social Democratic Party, and began work on the Autobahn—all within five months of taking power. Like so many intellectuals of that era, Lutz Heck, the Berlin zoo director, was swept up in a wave of national renewal and excitement about what the Nazis meant for his own research. And like so many of them, he would sacrifice his institution on the altar of Nazi ideology.

5

The Nazi Ox: The Zoo and Hitler's Worldview

AS GERMANS TOOK TO THE streets in November 1918 to protest against the government that had brought them an interminable war, Wilhelm II recognized that however Germany emerged from that war, it would not include him. The last German kaiser abdicated on November 9, 1918, and fled by train the following day to Holland, where he spent the rest of his life. The dramatic and abrupt end to the Hohenzollern ruling dynasty opened the door for the first democracy on German soil. The Weimar Republic, named after the city in eastern Germany where the constitution was signed (Berlin at the time was too chaotic), was not doomed from the outset, but it did experience an initial five years that soured even reasonable people on democracy. The runaway inflation that crippled the economy and caused life savings to evaporate was only part of the problem. Many Germans came to associate democracy with lawlessness, given that paramilitary organizations murdered more than 300 politicians, including the eminent foreign minister Walter Rathenau.[1]

Dozens of small right-wing parties established themselves during those turbulent years, including the National Socialist German Workers' Party (Nazi Party) in 1920. As the Weimar Republic stabilized after 1925, however, these parties found fewer and fewer Germans attracted to their radical platforms. In the 1928 general election, the Nazis earned a humiliating 2.63 percent of the popular vote.[2]

The Nazis then made a strategic decision to focus on the rural, middle class, and youth votes, given the entrenched loyalty of the working class to the Communist and Socialist parties.[3] The strategy paid off even before the Great Depression of 1929 further swung the pendulum back toward the parties of radical solutions, resulting in a stunning electoral breakthrough for the Nazis in 1930 when they captured the second most seats in the German parliament. Two years later, the Nazis had gained the support of 37.3 percent of voters, the highest percentage of any party. No longer able to ignore the political force the Nazis had become, President Paul von Hindenburg reluctantly appointed Adolf Hitler chancellor on January 30, 1933, much to the excitement of Sturmabteilung (Storm Division—SA) troops who had gathered for a torchlight parade below the balcony of the president's office.

The Nazi seizure of power meant an almost immediate deterioration in the lives of anyone whom the Nazis deemed a political or racial opponent. Although Hitler bullied and harassed those who did not agree with his worldview, he stopped short of murder during his first eighteen months in power. That changed on June 30, 1934, with his rampage against the paramilitary SA and other opponents of the regime in what became known as Night of the Long Knives. The Nazis murdered again on November 9, 1938, during *Kristallnacht* (Night of the Broken Glass), which resulted in the deaths of nearly 100 Jews, and then again, during the genocidal six years of World War II.

Paradoxically, the Nazis treated animals much better than they did some of their co-citizens. The banner that hung over the podium at a Nazi-hosted 1934 international conference on animal protection was a very public message about the place of animals in the Nazi world: "Entire epochs of love will be needed to repay animals for their value and service."[4] Far from simply paying lip service to their desire to end cruelty to animals—from the higher orders to the lowly crustaceans—the Nazis moved rapidly once in power to pass animal-protection legislation. In the first year of Hitler's chancellorship, the Nazis restricted experiments on animals and passed an animal protection law that was likely the strictest in the world, prescribing up to two years in prison for anyone who as much as mistreated an animal.[5] Those who flouted the law risked the power of Hermann Göring, the Prussian minister of the interior, making good on his threat to send any individuals who still thought they could continue to treat animals as inanimate property to the recently opened concentration camp at Dachau.[6] The Nazis showed little of this concern for Jews in the same year, when they burned Jewish books, limited Jews in public schools and universities, curtailed their presence in the medical field, and barred them from the civil service.

Over the next several years, the Nazis enacted further laws that established nature reserves; required restaurants to drop crabs and lobsters, one by one, into rapidly boiling water so as to bring their suffering to a rapid end;[7] and outlawed cockfights, bullfights, and the clipping of dogs' ears. They banned hunting with traps and buckshot and outlawed vivisection, the first German government to do so despite decades of pleas from animal protection societies.[8] (The Nazis also prohibited kosher butchering, but this was more of an attack on Jews than it was an animal-protection measure.) In that same period, the Nazis continued to target Jews by criminalizing relations between Jews and non-Jews and stripping them of their citizenship. The Nazis clearly did not have their fellow Jewish citizens in mind in the preamble to the Law for the Protection of Animals, which expressed the Nazi desire to "awaken and strengthen compassion as one of the highest moral values of the German people." [9]

The elevated place of animals in the Nazi belief system was initially a boon to zoos, which benefited from state funding and moral support of such leading figures as Hitler and Göring. As with other ostensibly progressive aspects of the Nazi regime, however, such as its war on cancer and its "green" conservation policies,[10] the Nazis soon sacrificed animal protection on the altar of conquest and genocide. The regime dismissed Jewish cancer researchers from their posts and ignored conservation areas when the land was needed to build the Autobahn or for troop maneuvers.[11] And animals in Germany, whether in the wild or in captivity, soon suffered a similar fate to the one the Nazis inflicted on humans.

The Berlin zoo was shaped into a Nazi institution by Lutz Heck, the son of the long-serving former director, who succeeded his father in 1932, one year before the Nazis seized power. As destiny would have it, Lutz Heck was born in the zoo, in 1892, the third child of Ludwig and Margarete Heck. He later recalled eagerly eavesdropping on the conversations between his father and the members of the scientific community who regularly visited their home, spellbound by the tales of gorillas, which were still considered half-mythical animals. The younger Heck was also deeply influenced by encounters with German colonialists, as he recalled years later:

> Other people also came to our house, men who were surrounded by an air of adventure. They were the colonial fighters. Wissmann and Rochus Schmidt, family friends that were so close to us that I addressed them as "uncle," were part of that group. The magnificent uniforms of the Protection Troops with the tall yellow boots made quite an impression on us youth. But their stories were truly breathtaking—their battles with the indigenous populations, their bold voyages of exploration into foreign lands, the acquisition of large swaths of land for Germany, and then the hunt on top of that. They hunted large, dangerous animals—buffalo, lions, and elephants! Their tales sparked my imagination in a way that even those thrilling stories of Indians could not, as here the heroes stood before me in flesh and blood. In the sparkle in their eye, in their vivid words and in their booming laughter, I lived out their adventures with them.[12]

The wide-eyed boy did indeed go on to become an African adventurer like those he so admired.

As a member of a short-range artillery formation, Heck was part of Germany's war effort from the first mobilization orders in August 1914 to his discharge from the army in January 1919. His memoirs are curiously silent on his wartime duty, focusing much more on his childhood and the turbulent Weimar era.[13] As a student in the natural sciences at the University of Berlin following the war, Heck experienced firsthand the street fighting so prevalent in the interwar period. While sitting at his preferred study desk at the Zoological Museum in Invalidenstrasse, he witnessed a column of "workers filled with hatred" marching down the street equipped, Heck noted with alarm, with brand-new weapons. The demonstration was a turning point for him. "Like many academics back then," he wrote years later, "I hardly bothered myself with domestic politics. This demonstration stirred something in me."[14] Heck left his microscope and headed out to join a group of volunteer irregulars

Lutz Heck succeeded his father as director of the Berlin zoo. Serving in that role from 1932 until his flight from Berlin in 1945, he molded the zoo into a Nazi institution. *Landesarchiv Berlin, F Rep. 290 II 5299*

to combat the socialists in the streets. He remained in uniform for ten days, fighting in the center of the city near Alexanderplatz and city hall until order had been restored.

After completing his doctorate in 1922, Heck worked at the zoo in Halle for two years before returning to the Berlin zoo, rising to assistant director in 1927 and director five years later. His hostility to the organized working classes, so much in evidence in the 1920s, helped to lay the foundation for his acceptance, and then embrace, of Nazism in the 1930s. So too did his father's influence. The elder Heck's writings are often indistinguishable from Nazi propaganda, as in these 1938 observations of man and nature:

> Today's study of human beings is no longer a distant subject relegated to academics publishing in exclusive journals. Today our national socialist state rests—no, not rests—it lives and breathes research on human beings. We Germans are the first people in the world that has

deliberately and categorically based its laws and public institutions on the natural sciences. And in so doing we Germans have achieved that which researchers and academics have been requesting with increasing urgency ... : Eugenics. A goal-oriented, healthy population policy based on the natural sciences. Prophets and visionaries in the Second Reich preached to the deaf. In that bygone republic, it was indeed the opposite that occurred. The useless person with a hereditary defect, the wretched pest, they were all encouraged to reproduce, were fattened up, and mollycoddled, all because they had the right to vote. There were fewer and fewer individuals with healthy genes, capable people of quality, and this physical and mental deterioration of the body of our nation proceeded year after year in gigantic leaps. Then at the last hour, one is tempted to say at the last minute, the Third Reich arrived and with it, insight and a course reversal. All other nations are a great distance from these ideas; we Germans, on the other hand, are again ahead in the world.[15]

The elder Heck concluded his memoirs with unreserved praise for Hitler and his biological worldview: "As a result of our upheaval and then rebirth, our exceptional Führer and his hardly less exceptional assistants have lifted a real weight from my shoulders, in that they have organized our state—the first in the world!—on the basis of the natural sciences, on the basis of blood and soil."[16] He added a telling passage that offers an important glimpse into the type of household in which Lutz Heck grew up: "My sons have often said to me of late: You were a National Socialist, you preached to us national socialist worldviews, long before the word was in use."[17] It was precisely these passages that would later cause a furor among a number of zoo shareholders, who vowed to disrupt the unveiling of the elder Heck's bust at the zoo in 1954. Katharina Heinroth, the first postwar director of the Berlin zoo, called on the police to provide extra security at the ceremony.[18] The bust of Ludwig Heck, ardent supporter of Hitler's racial schemes, was unveiled without incident and remains in the zoo.

Ludwig Heck and his son were not the only scientists to transpose their thoughts on animal breeding and population control onto the human world. In Britain, Francis Galton, Charles Darwin's nephew, who was involved with selective breeding of domesticated animals in order to increase their productivity, soon argued for the selective breeding of humans based on class. He believed that "intelligent pairing" of the upper and educated classes would result in, as was the case for cattle, a healthier race; reproduction among the lower classes was to be discouraged.[19] The renowned German zoologist Ernst Haeckel and the biologist Alfred Ploetz took this logic beyond class and into the realm of racial hygiene, arguing for some form of guided human reproduction in order to avoid the deterioration of the nation.[20]

The German "father" of breeding Alsatian dogs, Max von Stephanitz, was one of the most outspoken proponents of applying the concepts around animal breeding to the human world. Founder of the Union of German Alsatians in 1899 and its president from 1901 until his death in 1936, Stephanitz was an ardent promoter of the dog that became iconic in the Third Reich. His 1921 book, *Der deutsche Schäferhund in Wort und Bild* (The German Alsatian in Word and Image), promoted concepts that would become widespread under the Nazis. The dangers of mixing races, he argued, applied as much to humans as it did to dogs. The presence of "bastard blood" could lead only to the deterioration of the species, as he argued using France as an example: "How the French people will mentally and morally deteriorate from the unions between French women and 'colored' Frenchmen . . . during the war will be revealed in twenty years and beyond. History has shown over and over that mixing with a foreign race can cause a people of high-standing to decay. Let us animal breeders at least draw a lesson from that experience."[21]

Perhaps the most controversial of the German natural scientists was the world-renowned Austrian ornithologist Konrad Lorenz. Joining the Nazis in 1938, just three months after the Austrian union with Germany, seemed to require little thought on his part. Lorenz wrote afterward: "As a natural scientist, I have, of course, always been a National Socialist."[22] Like many other scientists, Lorenz saw lessons for humans in the animal world. He was intrigued by Oskar Heinroth's studies of birds, which had revealed many of their courting behaviors to be inborn, and he generalized Heinroth's conclusion to other animals, including humans. Mixing races, he argued, would "genetically confuse" human beings, causing a deterioration in the quality of the race. A strong supporter of eugenics, Lorenz believed that humans could be produced like objects in a factory, complete with quality control.[23] Because most of our sources on Lorenz's Nazi past appeared after his death in 1989, his fervent support for Hitler's racial ideology was unknown in 1973 when he was awarded the Nobel Prize in physiology or medicine.

Ludwig Heck's son, Lutz Heck, joined those scientists who believed that the future belonged to Nazism, and he used every opportunity to argue its case. During his 1935 trip to Canada sponsored by Hermann Göring to collect bison and moose, Heck attempted to excite Canadians, primarily German expatriates, about the benefits of National Socialism in order to, as he phrased it, "counteract" the negative images in the Canadian press.[24] He also talked fondly of the political views of his close friend, Baron Kruedener, a German who had emigrated to Canada ten years earlier and had become a game warden in Alberta. "From my conversations with him," wrote Heck in his fascinating account *Auf Urwild in Kanada* (On the Hunt for Ancient Game in Canada), "I know that during his rare visits to the city, he never passes up an opportunity to drop in on the pharmacist Paul Abele, the leader of the district group for the [Nazi Party], and chat for a while about Germany. I can still see his face, lit up with joy, because my guide and I greeted him on the platform of the train station in Edmonton with 'Heil Hitler!' "[25] (Accused of spying during the war, Paul Abele was sent to Ontario in 1940 and incarcerated. As was the case with many "enemy aliens," the charges against him were never proven.) When Heck returned to Germany, his ties to the Nazis became closer. On May 1, 1937, he joined the Nazi Party as member number 3934018,[26] and the following year he was awarded the title of honorary professor on the occasion of Hitler's birthday.[27]

Heck's most important political ally was Hermann Göring, the Nazi point person on nature conservation. Göring became forest supervisor of the German Reich and German game supervisor on July 3, 1934, and, in typical fashion, browbeat his fellow cabinet member, education minister Bernhard Rust, to acquire the nature conservation portfolio. One of Göring's subordinates reported the one-sided phone call as follows: "Listen Herr Rust, what is with Nature Protection? I'm really the only one who is involved with it. Don't you agree that it should be transferred over to me? . . . How's that? The forest and the animals belong to me. Nature Protection fits much better with me than it does with you. . . . Isn't that true? You agree? . . . Thanks!"[28]

Göring would have been well known to the German public through the many short documentaries about him that ran before the main attraction in movie theaters throughout Germany. The image of Göring as a jovial nature lover, frolicking with his birds, dogs, and—the animal for which he was best known—lions, would have been at least as common in the Third Reich as that of the commander in chief of the Luftwaffe in his ill-fitting uniform.[29] A popular Nazi postcard of Göring, for example, did not portray him in his military role but in a casual, fatherly embrace of one of his pet lions.[30] Although it would not happen until the penultimate year of the war, Göring would eventually assume a direct supervisory role over the Berlin zoo when he replaced the Prussian cultural minister as the oversight authority. When Göring assumed that role he broke a tradition that had gone back to the cabinet order of 1841, which assigned oversight over that flagship cultural institution to the Prussian minister of finance and the Prussian minister of culture.[31]

Hermann Göring embraces one of his pet lions in 1938. Although best known as commander in chief of the Nazi air force, Göring was also responsible for nature preservation in Nazi Germany. In this capacity, he became a close friend of the Berlin zoo director Lutz Heck, who furnished him with young lions from the zoo and retrieved them once they became too dangerous to continue to be housed in Göring's private residence. *Library of Congress LC-USZ62-138273*

On April 3, 1941, Lutz Heck began reporting directly to Göring when he took over the Nature Protection Division in Göring's Reich Forestry Office (Reichsforstamt),[32] a high public office that any zoo director would have considered a feather in his cap. Heck deeply admired Göring for his efforts to conserve nature. In *Auf Tiersuche in weiter Welt* (Searching for Animals Far Afield), written in 1941 when the Nazis were at the height of their power, Heck was effusive in his praise of Göring who, he claimed, fought with "all his might" for animal protection laws. "The Reichsmarschall's heartfelt love for our wild animals," he added "is evidenced by the fact that he transformed words into actions. He helped reintroduce the moose, that primeval and largest of German cervines, into those areas where it once lived and from where it was displaced."[33] Heck was a frequent and welcome guest on Göring's private game preserve in Schorfheide and over time developed a personal bond with him. In fact, the relationship was so close that Heck personally went to Göring's villa, rather than sending one of his staff, to collect Göring's lions when they became too big to live with Göring.[34] The head of the SS's pseudo-academic branch to research the Aryan race, known as the Ahnenerbe, wrote that both Lutz and his brother Heinz Heck, director of the Munich zoo, enjoyed Göring's "absolute confidence."[35]

Heck reveled in the friendship of other leading Nazis, including propaganda minister Joseph Goebbels. Goebbels's diary entry from May 14, 1937, speaks volumes of Heck's proximity to the Nazi leadership:

> In the afternoon with Magda and the children to Lanke [a lake in southwest Berlin]. Director Heck from the zoo releases some animals there. A tame fawn, two deer, two swans, wild ducks with offspring and a number of others, too. The children are ecstatic. It is indescribable.... We converse about art with Dr. Heck over coffee. He is a very fine and educated man. A true animal-lover.[36]

In 1943, a good friend of Heck, Eduard Tratz, director of the natural history museum in Salzburg who held the SS officer title of Obersturmbannführer because of his association with the academic branch of the SS, brought Heck to an SS meeting in order to facilitate his application to join the organization. Tratz made clear to Heck that the SS would have "warmly welcomed" an application from him but, for unknown reasons, Heck did not follow up with the application.[37]

Heck was attracted to Nazism in large part because of its message that humans were part of, and subject to, the laws of nature. Heck's studies led him to conclude that the human world functioned in essentially the same manner as the animal world, that there was a hierarchy of both animal and human races, and that humans, like animals, could perish if civilization encroached too far into the environment. He viewed his role as that of bringing Germans closer to nature through his zoo so that they might come to see that humans were but an extension of the animal world. By displaying a wide variety of animals, he hoped to impress upon the visitor the enormous diversity of life on earth, which would in turn "affect their soul." This thinking lay behind his much imitated Kinderzoo initiative, in which children and their parents would be permitted close enough to touch animals like young elephants, lions, bears, and monkeys. Such a sensory experience of the animal, he believed, would lead them to see the rightness of the Nazi worldview:

> Such encounters between human and animal, living thing to living thing, prods an individual ... to think beyond the personal, and leads him toward the laws of nature. Understanding the variety of animals will allow him to recognize the variety of human races. Knowledge about the rise and propagation of certain animal species up to a zenith and their subsequent descent because of a change to their genetic endowment and frequently too because of environmental changes, will cause the visitor to draw comparisons with the fate of peoples, which are subject to similar laws ....
>
> As a result of research in the natural sciences, our genius Führer Adolf Hitler has understood that the well-being and success of a people rests on biological principles. For the first time in the history of humanity, a statesman has recognized that the laws of natural sciences are decisive in the education and development of a people. For the first time in our Fatherland, concepts like hereditary health, race, and attachment to the land are dominating the thoughts of our statesmen.[38]

A child feeds ducks at the Berlin zoo during the 1930s. Lutz Heck, the Berlin zoo director during the Nazi era, promoted these types of close encounters between people and animals so that zoo visitors might better understand the Nazi view that humans were subject to the laws of nature. *Bundesarchiv, B 145 Bild-P020412*

As director of Germany's largest and most popular zoo, Heck was in a powerful position to transmit the Nazi message to the public, something that deeply concerned others in Germany's zoological community. Richard Lehmensick, the long-serving director of the parasitological lab at the University of Bonn, lamented the ascent of "race studies" and the demise of pure biological research, and he spoke out against zoos diving headlong into the latest pseudo-science. Writing a year after the Nazis had seized power, Lehmesick argued forcefully for zoos to remain apolitical:

> Lately, there have been a number of voices calling for zoological gardens to more frequently, and conscientiously, integrate into the great biological movement of our day. I am not able to join this chorus.... It is a not entirely healthy trend lately in the natural sciences to privilege "biological" problems over zoology and botany. Physiological problems, the study of race, and instruction in heredity dominate the

field. Knowledge of form and classification is second class.... With regards to our zoological gardens in particular, they exist above all to spread understanding and joy about the *lifeform, the animal itself*.[39]

Lehmensick could not, however, stop the tide of Nazi racial science that consumed almost all public institutions in Germany.

Historians have long wondered how, precisely, Heck spent the war years. In *The Zookeeper's Wife*, the engrossing 2007 novel about the efforts of the director of the Warsaw zoo and his wife to shield Jews during World War II, author Diane Ackerman damns Lutz Heck with her description of his actions at the Warsaw zoo:

> Heck invited his SS friends to a rare treat: a private hunting party right on the zoo grounds, a spree that combined privilege with the pell-mell of exotic animals even a novice or soused gunman could bag.... Heck and a cadre of fellow hunters arrived on a sunny day full of drink and hilarity, elated by army victories, laughing as they roamed the grounds, shooting penned and caged animals for sport.... The savagery didn't serve hunger or necessity, it wasn't a political gambit, the doomed animals weren't being culled because they'd become too abundant in the wild. Not only was the SS ignoring their value as ... creatures with unique personalities, the men didn't even credit animals with basic fear or pain.[40]

Since the novel was based on the unpublished diary of Antonina Zabinska, the zookeeper's wife of the title, there is some reason to believe her account, but hard evidence is lacking. After the war, the director of the Lodz zoo claimed that Heck had arrived at the Warsaw zoo in late November 1939 to oversee the theft of valuable animals for the Berlin zoo. All others were to be shot. The Lodz zoo director scarcely hid his scorn for Heck: "As far as I can tell from the documents to which I have had access, he robbed suppressed peoples, with no regard for longstanding acquaintances or joint work in the area of nature conservation (to which he had ostensibly dedicated his life)."[41] Other of his actions during the war certainly suggest his contempt for the subjected populations of eastern Europe. Heck returned from a 1942 visit to the Bialowies nature reserve in eastern Poland with six slave laborers to work in the zoo.[42]

Perhaps for these reasons, his children have refused to discuss their father's past. Official histories of the zoo are similarly silent, neglecting to mention Heck's close ties to the Nazis or that he spent any time in eastern Europe during the war.[43]

We know for certain that Heck took a great interest in Polish fauna after the Nazi invasion of Poland in 1939. Heck hoped to use the beavers from Poland to breathe life into the German population of the species, which was perilously close to extinction.[44] He also indicated openly his support for the new nature reserve that Göring established in Bialowies. We know as well that Heck traveled with the Wehrmacht to Askania-Nova, the wildlife refuge in the southern Ukraine that had so captivated his father, and met with Alfred Rosenberg, the Nazi minister for the occupied territories. Rosenberg and leading members of the SS tasked Heck with transforming the refuge into a German nature reserve. Along with this administrative process, Heck arranged for the transfer back to the Berlin zoo the collection of rare wild horses, known as Przewalski horses, for which Askania-Nova was rightly famous. Although Heck later claimed that he sequestered the horses to protect them from the war, nearly 70 percent of those transferred from the eastern front died in German zoos and wildlife parks from aerial bombardment or deprivation.[45]

Heck's subsequent actions suggest that his wartime activities in eastern Europe were far from benign. At the end of April 1945, as the Red Army approached the Tiergarten, Berlin's central park that bordered on the zoo, Heck abandoned the zoo that had been an integral part of his family for over fifty years and fled the beleaguered city. As a parting blow to the Berlin zoo and the animals he claimed to hold close to his heart, Heck transferred 600,000 RM of the zoo's funds to a Swiss bank account before he left. When his successor contacted him in Munich in December requesting repayment, Heck protested that the payout was due to him and refused to discuss the matter further.[46]

Like many Nazi administrators in the conquered territories of eastern Europe, Lutz Heck believed that Hitler had presented Germans with an unprecedented opportunity to reshape a landscape. Those delicate lands, for too long in "inferior" Slavic hands, were to be forged into a setting becoming of the German conqueror, with German plants and animals to complement the hearty German peasant in the East. In a

1942 article, Heck wrote approvingly of Heinrich Himmler's plans to reshape the natural world in the occupied territories:

> When the Reichsführer SS was appointed as Reich Commissioner for the Strengthening of the German National Character in order to expand [to] the East, he was not only thinking of the establishment of German villages and cities, but also of shaping the landscape which was to serve as the new homeland for many Germans. The keen eye of the Reichsführer SS saw that the transformation of the landscape provided the opportunity for the creation of a German East. Tasked by the Führer with introducing this large-scale plan to the East, the Reichsführer SS used the occasion to communicate with the Reich Forest Supervisor as the highest office for nature conservation.... The transformation of the landscape is considered one resource for German population policies.[47]

Heck was positively exuberant about the prospects of reshaping the natural world of eastern Europe, applying to the German Research Society in 1941 for a grant entitled "Transforming the Flora and Fauna of the Newly Reforested Eastern Areas."[48] Heck recognized in Nazism a singular opportunity to advance his research. It was his devotion to Nazism and belief in the ability of humans to change the course of evolution that led him to his most ambitious project yet: raising an animal from the dead.

On a clear September day in 1938, several heavy trucks drove into a game preserve in East Prussia known as Romintern, along a dirt road and into a fifty-hectare clearing enclosed by a fence, a small portion of the vast area that served as Hermann Göring's favorite hunting grounds.[49] There, under the guidance of Lutz Heck, zoo staff unloaded seven massive crates, lined them up near the gate, and opened them, their contents storming out into the German countryside. Observers stared in disbelief at the scene unfolding before them. What they were witnessing, it seemed, had not occurred in Germany in more than 400 years.[50] The following morning, just after daybreak, Forest Supervisor of the Reich and German Game Supervisor Hermann Göring came to visit the aurochs. At great personal risk, Heck and his co-workers attempted unsuccessfully to herd the enormous animals out from the wooded area into the sunny clearing. Still, even a brief glimpse of them was enough to move Göring, who remarked on the strength and beauty of the animals and proclaimed that they would forever have a sanctuary in his German woods.[51]

The aurochs, an animal resembling (but much more massive than) the bull familiar to most people from the bullfights of Spain and Latin America, is the ancestor of today's modern cattle. It once roamed a vast territory from Korea to England, taking in swaths of Africa and India, and left an indelible impression on early people in Lascaux, in southwest France, and in eastern Spain, who painted its image on their cave walls.[52] The most famous hunting scene in the medieval epic poem, and later Wagnerian inspiration, the *Nibelungenlied*, involves the aurochs (also known as the ur): "After that, he defeated one wisent and one moose, four aurochs and one Schelch [which appears to be a mythical animal]." Julius Caesar, during his campaign in the German lands, was struck by the size of the beast, reporting upon his return that it approached that of an elephant.[53] Even Germany's author laureate, Goethe, was fascinated by the aurochs and helped the Jena zoological museum to acquire several of its fossils found near Haßleben.[54]

It is from these long-ago images and from well-preserved skeletons, including one collected by Charles Darwin from the Burwell swamps,[55] that we know almost certainly what the animal looked like, even down to its reddish-blackish color. Distinguished by its massive horns and size, attaining nearly six feet in height at the shoulder and a weight of 3,300 pounds, it was considerably larger than today's Angus or Hereford bull. As a result of hunting and the encroachment of civilization on its traditional grounds, the aurochs went extinct, first in Asia and north Africa, and finally in Europe. The last aurochs on Earth, a cow, died in 1627 in a wooded area fifty-five kilometers south of Warsaw, where today a large rock with a makeshift plaque marks the site where the aurochs vanished. The last bull had died seven years earlier; one of its horns had been adorned with gold ornamentation and presented to the Polish king Sigismund III, who used it as his hunting horn. Swedish armies under Gustavus Adolphus captured the horn as booty during their invasion of Poland in 1655 and donated it to an armory in Stockholm, where the last trace of this once plentiful animal has resided ever since.

Lutz Heck was obsessed with fauna that had a long history in the German lands, especially those that were extinct or endangered, such as the European bison (wisent), bears, beavers, moose, and the aurochs.[56] Having accepted the fringe biological premise that the descendants of earlier species contained at least a critical mass of hereditary genetic material (*Erbmasse*) from their ancestors, Heck set about "breeding back" the largest of the extinct German animals, the aurochs, an undertaking that would dominate his interest for nearly fifteen years. Heck believed that by selectively breeding modern, half-domesticated cattle, he could find the right genetic mix and produce an aurochs for the first time in more than 400 years. He was utterly convinced that making an animal "un-extinct" in this manner was possible: "The magnificent wild animal lives on in the genes of its descendants."[57] Heck collaborated with his brother Heinz Heck, director of the Munich zoo, who also used language as if lifted from *Jurassic Park*: "No animal is completely extinct or lost forever, when there remains in living form even the slightest amount of its genetic material."[58]

While on a trip to Corsica, Heck became intrigued by cattle with coloring that matched that of the aurochs in cave paintings. Heck purchased them and arranged for their transport to the Berlin zoo. When the cattle did not produce the desired offspring, Heck continued his Europe-wide search for suitable breeding material, beginning with bulls that had been bred for bullfighting in southern Europe. These animals, he believed, would be better suited to his purpose than domesticated cattle because they would possess aurochs-like qualities—savageness, a fighting spirit, aggressiveness—all traits that Heck evidently admired.[59] Heck attended a bullfight for the first time in Arles in the south of France, leading him to purchase cattle from nearby Carmague, an island in the mouth of the Rhone River. In 1932, he traveled to the Spanish cities of Madrid, Cordoba, Seville, and Malaga seeking suitable animals in any venue that dealt with cattle. In Malaga, he attended cattle auctions. In Madrid, he met with the Association of Fighting-Animal Breeders. And in all cities he woke early so as to position himself at a point where he was certain to observe an array of cattle: "In the morning, I stood outside the slaughterhouses just before sunrise and studied the cattle that had been brought in from the countryside."[60]

After much deliberation, Heck determined that the most suitable cattle for back-breeding were those found in the ranch of Juan Conradi near Seville because they possessed strikingly similar characteristics to the aurochs. Their coloring was a deep black with a red tinge along the back. The contours of the body strongly resembled those of the prehistoric paintings found in the cave Abrigo de los Toros in Spain. Their horns were massive and tilted forward, their backs long with minimal flex. Heck purchased an adult bull, a juvenile male, one adult cow, and one juvenile cow and transported them to the Berlin zoo, where he proceeded to breed more than 100 calves with the French cattle purchased earlier. The unusual cattle were a sensation in the German capital, attracting such artists as Moritz Pathé, who produced exquisite paintings of them.[61] The arrival of the cattle in the zoo was also reported with some fanfare by the Berlin daily *Vossische Zeitung,* although it seemed self-evident to the author that, contrary to Heck's lofty claims, there was no possibility of breeding an animal back from extinction, only of producing a facsimile thereof: "By crossbreeding several primitive races of cattle, the Zoo wants to gradually breed an animal that closely resembles the aurochs, the ancestor of all cattle races."[62] The zoo visitor's guide of 1934 written by Lutz Heck paints a different story, telling its visitors that the zoo was "single-mindedly" pursuing the retro-breeding of the aurochs.[63]

After nearly ten years of concerted effort, Heck succeeded in breeding an animal in 1938 that, if not the aurochs, bore a striking resemblance to it. Heck bred six more in the zoo before releasing the seven animals into Göring's nature preserve in eastern Prussia, to the utter delight of both men. The animals survived the first war years and the harsh winters, doubling their numbers by 1941.

It is no coincidence that Heck's experiment with raising an animal from the dead took place during the Nazi era.[64] For although Nazism depended on the advanced technology, large bureaucracies, and factory production of modernity, it also eschewed them, glorifying the preindustrial era and the noble life of the peasant. This image was prevalent in Nazi plans for the occupied East, where the ideal German settler was tough-minded, frugal, close to the land, and undistracted by the trappings of urban life, an image that received frequent play in Nazi songs, organizations, and textbooks.[65] The Nazi-as-Romantic resonates in the story of the aurochs, a primeval creature from an era when Germany was raw and pure. For Heck, the project to restore a strong, gigantic alpha-beast from the German past never had a practical purpose, such as increasing the gene pool for modern domesticated cattle.[66] It was always the act itself, the creation process, that mattered to him and, by extension, to his Nazi masters like Hermann Göring. The 1939 zoo visitor's guide, written by Heck, relates this idea of breeding for no other end than to restore, on some level, German greatness:

> Within ten years, we succeeded in breeding-back from modern-day primitive races the extinct aurochs, which once was found all over Germany. Native German fauna was enriched, in altruistic fashion, by placing one bull and five cows of the newly bred Aurochs into the Imperial Nature Preserve Romintern. In so doing, an animal species which was extinct in the German landscape, was brought back to life by a well-thought-out plan and introduced into German woods.[67]

After the war, Heck acknowledged the appeal of acting in a deity-like fashion: "Again and again my brother and I were asked why we undertook the backbreeding of the aurochs, and in particular what practical purpose it served. To those questions I could only answer that we undertook the backbreeding of the [aurochs] out of the sheer pleasure of conducting such a novel experiment in heredity."[68] The height of the aurochs' existence in the distant past, nearly 10,000 to 11,000 years ago, at a time when Germanic tribes roamed central Europe in awe of the creature that ruled the misty forests and fields, appealed to Heck and other Nazis who romanticized a primeval past. "Under the Third Reich," Heck wrote exuberantly in his memoirs, "the extinct aurochs lives again as a German wild animal."[69] In Heck's view, the aurochs, like Germany, had risen again under the Nazis.

At the end of the war, as the Red Army methodically pushed the Nazi invaders back toward the capital of their ever-shrinking empire, the Nazis made certain that their aurochs would not become a communist war trophy. Göring personally shot the remaining aurochs in his game reserve.[70] The current European herd of more than 3,000 "Heck Cattle" that roam central Europe, including those at the formal breeding ranch

Aueroxenreservat Spreeaue south of Berlin, are descended from the herd at the Munich zoo run by Heinz Heck.

It was not many years after the end of the Second World War that scientists uniformly dismissed Heck's achievement, even going a step further to condemn it. In 1951, the Union of German Zoo Directors resolved that their organization would offer no financial or other support for breeding back extinct species since it was not only a scientific impossibility but took away resources from the pressing issue of preserving threatened animals.[71]

The story of the aurochs lays bare the close ties between the Nazis and the Berlin zoo, yet for decades after the war, the zoo denied any wrongdoing during the Nazi era, rejecting in particular accusations that it dispossessed Jews, and Jews alone, of shares that the zoo had issued from its establishment in 1844 to help raise operating funds. In the face of a concerted effort by Werner Cohn, a sociology professor at the University of British Columbia and the son of a Jewish shareholder, the zoo was forced to confront its past. Cohn had spent much of his childhood at the zoo, using the free admission that was the only tangible benefit of a share in the zoo. That is not to say that the shares were not valuable. Although they did not pay cash dividends, the limited number of them, around 4,000, made them exclusive throughout most of their history, frequently proving difficult to purchase as they were passed down through generations. A share in the Berlin zoo today is worth about 7,000 euros.[72] The board attempted to dismiss Cohn's query about the nature of the sale of his father's zoo share in August 1938 to one Ferdinand Kallmeyer. In a sharply worded letter, the zoo's lawyer indicated that there was neither "pressure, compulsion, or duress" in the transaction between his father and Kallmeyer.[73]

Shortly after the board responded to Cohn, the zoo's CEO Hans-Peter Czupalla revealed the zoo's management to be anything but sympathetic to the plight of Jews in Nazi Germany. Hiding behind the standard refrain of the far right that the Jews were just one of a number of Nazi victims and, anyway, wasn't it time to move on, Czupalla said in an interview with the *Süddeutsche Zeitung* that he "preferred to look to the future, and not constantly at the past." "Even murder," he added "has a statute of limitations." (He was right that the German legal code of 1871 has a statute of limitations for murder, but Germany removed the statute in 1979 for crimes against humanity.) He also suggested that Nazi victims who demanded restitution were crying over spilled milk: "My family sold a valuable carpet," he told the reporter "for a sack of potatoes. I can't exactly take it back from the farmer today." Finally, in response to Cohn's claim that Jews were historically important to the zoo, both as shareholders and general supporters, Czupalla responded in macabre fashion that the zoo had been completely demolished in 1945: "Not a solitary Jewish citizen has contributed to this zoo, the one that you see before you today. This one has been built up by more recent citizens. I say that without pathos or pride, but simply as fact."[74]

Faced with overwhelming public pressure to investigate its anti-Semitic past, the zoo agreed in 2002 to have its files examined by Monika Schmidt, a researcher associated with the Center for Research on Anti-Semitism at the Technical University of Berlin. There, much to the "surprise" of former directors Hans Frädrich and Heinz-Georg Klös, who claimed that the zoo's archive had been destroyed during the war, Schmidt found the complete minutes of the meetings of the zoo's board of directors from the 1930s.[75] Those files reveal a zoo complicit, bordering on zealous, in its efforts to march lockstep with Nazi racial policies.

In its annual report for 1933, the zoo's board stated matter-of-factly: "The members of the board, Justice Georg Siegman and Lawyer Walter Simon, resigned their seats of their own accord." The board's account, to be generous, omitted important context around the resignation of the two Jewish members. In 1933, the zoo's board of directors was a who's who of prominent Berlin society, including the former mayor of Berlin, Arthur Scholtz; the director of the Prussian State Library and the board's chairman, Hugo Krüß; and Karl Gelpcke, director of the Hamburg Hypothekenbank in Berlin and president of the Berlin Chamber of Industry and Commerce.[76] In late April 1933, the same month that the Nazis organized their first major anti-Semitic action, the boycott of Jewish shops and businesses, the zoo board met for its annual general meeting. Gelpcke, the chairman of the board, looked kindly on the request of a female shareholder to remove any non-Aryans from the board and promised to hold a general assembly in the near future with new elections for the board. Unsurprisingly, it turned out that the shareholder had had close ties to the Nazi Party and had been put up to the request by the party's local branch. One Jewish shareholder was furious with Gelpcke's response, writing to the board: "On behalf of a number of shareholders, I write to the board with reference to our last general assembly, requesting that the board keep politics away from the Garden.... The Zoological Garden is a venue for science and for socializing and has always kept its distance from politics. The shareholders are comprised of Aryans and non-Aryans and both have the <u>same</u> goal in mind: the well-being of the zoo."[77]

Ignoring the letter, two members of the board consulted with Reich Commissar for the Economy Otto Wagener, who informed them that the board's contingent of four Jews was disproportionately high relative to the Jewish population of Berlin. Only two would be permitted. Since one of the Jewish members, von Schwabach, had close ties to the banking house of S. Bleichröder, he was temporarily spared. The board made clear its intentions for the remaining Jewish board members: "Actions must be undertaken so that Herr von Simpson and one of the two lawyers resign from their position." In May 1933, one of these lawyers, Walter Simon, did indeed resign from the board, though considering the board's position, it was hardly on his own accord as the board later claimed. In September, the board continued to marginalize its Jewish members by promoting two Nazis to vacant positions: Willi Luther from the justice department and the police captain Fritz Kummertz. Aware of the futility of his situation, the Jewish board member Georg Siegmann resigned his seat in the fall of 1933.

Unexpectedly, Gelpcke did not press for the immediate removal of the two remaining Jews, but they too would be ousted eventually as the board became an instrument of the Nazis. What is revealing about the board's stance here is that these two had converted to Christianity. Only in the warped Nazi ideology that equated religion with race could these two individuals be considered Jewish. In 1936, the shareholders elected ardent Nazis to the board: the retired SS brigade leader Ewald von Massow, the high-ranking Dresden Bank official Karl Rasche, and Eugen Fischer, the director of the Kaiser Wilhelm Institute for Anthropology, Human Heredity, and Eugenics and one of the most devoted followers of Nazi racial policies, who could frequently be found in the field taking cranial measurements of Sinti and Roma.

The fate of Simon and Siegmann, the two Jewish board members who were forced from their positions in 1933, is unknown but may be reasonably surmised. Walter Simon remained a lawyer in Germany until 1936, at which point he disappeared from the historical record until January 19, 1942, when the Nazis deported him and his wife to Riga; they were not heard from again. Georg Siegmann was deported with his wife to Terezin in the occupied Czech lands on July 16, 1942, and from there to Auschwitz. They, too, have left no record.[78] They were only four among the 55,000 Berlin Jews whom Nazis deported to the East and murdered.[79] The centuries-old Jewish community in Berlin, once numbering nearly 170,000, or almost one-third of the entire German Jewish population, had been reduced by half through Jewish emigration by 1942 and then wiped out in the most frenzied period of the Holocaust that followed thereafter.[80]

"Aryanizing" the board was but one manifestation of Nazi racial policies at the Berlin zoo. Shortly thereafter, Jewish shareholders would be targeted. From 1938, they were no longer permitted to bequeath their shares nor sell them on their own. They could only sell them back to the zoo. Acting under the auspices of the Reich stock law of 1937, the zoo began dispossessing Jews of their shares, offering them below market value. The zoo typically purchased shares from Jews at a reduced price of 300 RM and sold them to non-Jews for 370 to 380 RM a share.[81] It is difficult to know for certain how many of the zoo's 4,000 shares were owned by Jews, but there is anecdotal evidence to suggest that Jews made up a sizable portion of the shareholders. It is reasonable to assume, for example, that the number of shares sold in 1938 (10 percent) and 1939 (15 percent) were primarily from Jewish shareholders.[82] In this period just before the Nazi state forced all Jews to give up their financial holdings, the zoo turned a profit of roughly 7,000 RM from forcing Jews to sell their shares below market value.

Having removed Jews from the board and dispossessed Jewish shareholders of their shares, both of which were behind-the-scenes transactions, the board moved toward a much more public expression of its anti-Semitism. At a meeting on March 29, 1938, the board agreed in principle that Jews should be prevented from visiting the zoo, but it was unclear how to accomplish this in practice. The minutes reveal the board's uncertain position: "At the conclusion [of the meeting], the chair came back to the question of admitting non-Aryans to the zoo, a question that was of utmost urgency to the board. After a lengthy discussion, which brought up the fact that a second playground had been installed for Jewish children, that Jews were no longer allowed seats at the concert pavilion, etc., it was decided to ask the party for advice."[83] Lutz Heck was one of the driving forces behind prohibiting Jews from visiting the zoo in early 1938, several months before the Nazi Party banned Jews from all cultural institutions in November 1938.[84] In response to the board's request, Hans Ammon, co-director of the Berlin zoo and committed National Socialist, sent a letter to the Düsseldorf zoo (and presumably other German zoos, although only the Düsseldorf letter has survived) requesting information on whether the zoo reserved entry exclusively to Aryans, and if so by what method. In the reply, which indicated that the zoo had yet to address the matter, the mayor of Düsseldorf added his own view, writing that he considered the restriction of Jewish entry to the zoo "a pressing matter."[85]

One day before the Night of the Broken Glass in November 1938, the board began taking concrete steps to prevent Jews from visiting the zoo. Ammon and Gelpcke proposed that commencing in January 1939, the zoo would have signs hanging at all entrances reading "Jews are not welcome here." Ammon also recommended that as of the new year, Jews would not be permitted to purchase season tickets. The board passed both proposals unanimously. As it turned out, however, events in Nazi Germany would render these initiatives pointless. Following the Nazi-organized rampage against Jewish businesses and places of worship in November 1938, the Nazis took their attack against Jews into other areas of society, banning them from all public cultural sites and various city-run installations, including public squares, museums, cabarets, movie theaters, swimming pools, skating rinks, and sports venues. They also forbade them to enter the government district bordered by Wilhelm Street, Voss Street, Leipzig Street, and Unter den Linden.[86] By the end of 1938, several weeks before the board had planned to institute measures to marginalize Jews gradually, the Nazi Party banned Jews entirely from visiting the zoo. At a general assembly in April 1939, two days after the boardroom had been renovated (which included swapping a picture of the kaiser for one of Hitler), Ammon could barely disguise his pleasure at the exclusion of Jews: "Ladies and gentlemen, the general clean-up and removal of dust from this room is in a way symbolic of the year that has just passed .... [The zoo] has always been important as the lungs of Berlin, offering fresh, clean air. I find, though, that since November 1938, our air here has become much cleaner than it had been."[87] Jews, who had consistently supported the Berlin zoo as patrons and shareholders, were now banned.

In 2011, after more than sixty years of denial, the zoo finally acknowledged its complicity in Nazi racial policies by placing a plaque on its signature building, the Antilopenhaus. It reads: "Due to the support of its Jewish shareholders, the Berlin Zoological Garden grew to become a cultural and societal centre of the city. Under National Socialist rule, they were discriminated against, persecuted, deprived of their rights, and dispossessed. They were forced to divest their shares, including their shares in the zoo. As Jews, they were refused entry to the Berlin Zoological Garden. In sadness and unending memory."[88] Werner Cohn, who had fought a decades-long battle for the zoo to recognize its role as abettor to Nazi policies, was not present at the unveiling. Whether he was invited is not clear. It is reasonable to assume, however, that he would have been underwhelmed by the plaque, which uses passive voice throughout and allows some of the anti-Semitic zoo leaders, among them Ammon, Heck, and Gelpcke, to remain in the historical shadows. The plaque was also a token gesture compared to Cohn's claim that, given the appreciation of the shares over seventy years, the zoo owed dispossessed shareholders the equivalent of $10 million, a sum that Cohn wished to see delivered to the Tel Aviv zoo.[89]

As the story of the zoo's battle with Cohn so clearly reveals, the zoo's long-standing claim that only its photo archive survived the war—a claim that the zoo directorship also made to me when I asked for access to its files in 2009—is no longer credible. Not only does Schmidt's work on the zoo's support for Nazi racial policies indicate that a substantial set of documents did indeed survive, ones that were released only under duress, but there are also other indications that the zoo is in possession of a valuable historical collection that it refuses to share. In 1994, for example, in the zoo's own journal *Bongo*, the director, Hans Frädrich, wrote: "In Berlin, two fortunate events came together. Despite the chaotic war years and those of the immediate postwar period, a large part of the historical material remained intact, or was able to be secured at literally the last minute. These documents found in my predecessor Heinz-Georg Klös an admirer and enthusiastic compiler."[90]

The zoo's failure to deal with its Nazi past was also on prominent display at the unveiling of a bronze bust to Lutz Heck in March 1984, one year following the death of the ninety-one-year-old former director. Mention of Heck's desire to ban Jews from the zoo, his complicity in the dispossession of their shares, his close ties to leading Nazis, his use of slave labor, and orders to slaughter animals in occupied eastern Europe were entirely absent from the ceremony. In place of an honest evaluation of the zoo's Nazi past, the zoo chose to fete him for establishing the fenceless enclosures in the park. The director of the zoo further praised his role in nature conservation and his authorship of many very popular books. Heck's son attended the ceremony, offering tales from growing up in the "Villa Heck" that showed his father's bonhomie.[91] Heck's bust, like his father's, continues to occupy a place of prominence at the zoo, far overshadowing the one modest plaque that the zoo believes atones for its sins against Jews.

The Berlin zoo is not alone among German zoos in whitewashing the Nazi past. The official histories of other prominent German zoos avoid the topic almost entirely. None, with the exception of a history of the Leipzig zoo, mention that Jews were banned from the premises after 1939.[92] The Jewish director of the Breslau zoo, Hans Honigmann, realized before most of his colleagues where Nazi racial rhetoric would lead, and he resigned his post at the zoo in 1934. He spent the rest of his life in exile in the United Kingdom and died in Scotland, where he had found a position at the University of Glasgow.[93] The exception among German zoos is the Munich zoo, which, under the leadership of Heinz Heck, maintained a cool relationship with the Nazis. Heinz Heck was the only German zoo director not to join the Nazi Party,[94] a model that seemed to be emulated throughout the zoo: Only five of the ninety Munich zoo employees joined the Nazi Party. Heck's disdain for the Nazis became self-evident—and a sharp contrast to his brother's conduct at the Berlin zoo—at the end of the war, when the Wehrmacht placed a streetcar on its side across the Thalkirchner Bridge leading to Munich to slow the advance of American troops. Heinz Heck led Lelabati, one of the zoo's elephants, to the bridge and had her drag away the streetcar.[95]

6

Animals among the Beasts: The Zoo Descends into War

FROM THE TIME HITLER BECAME chancellor of Germany in 1933 to the outbreak of war in 1939, the Berlin zoo, increasingly an instrument of the Nazis, rose to unprecedented heights. Its territory increased substantially when, in 1935, following years of pressure from Lutz Heck, Göring transferred to the zoo 21,000 square meters of land in the Tiergarten, which was under Prussian jurisdiction. The zoo used the land to establish vast fenceless enclosures, [1] including the showpiece thirteen-meter-high artificial craggy mound for mountain goats, constructed with sandstone from the Elbe River.[2] The zoo also had a colossal collection of animals, both in numbers and species: 1,263 mammals in 433 species, and 2,653 birds in 853 species.[3]

Attendance at the Berlin zoo reflected its rising fortunes. Hitler's first year in power saw 979,000 visitors to the zoo, a number that grew to 1.265 million in 1934, 1.61 million in 1935, and a staggering 1.75 million in 1936. Although the trajectory had been rising throughout the first half of the 1930s, several events in 1936 contributed to the one-year jump of nearly 400,000 visitors. The pavilion for the big cats that dated to 1871 was torn down and replaced by a spectacular lion enclosure made from 12,000 liters of sandstone that became the industry standard for free-ranging animal pens. The 2,000-square-meter enclosure also represented best practices of the day. Wooden walls could be inserted to separate animals if need be; accommodations for the keepers were discreetly tucked away behind the faux mountain, its water moats practically invisible to visitors; and three surfaces were heated, allowing the lions a refuge from the cold.[4] The zoo administration also believed that the reasonable entry prices and close connections to the Nazi mass tourist organization Kraft durch Freude (Strength through Joy)—including placing posters and replicas of animals in the organization's show windows throughout Berlin—had boosted the numbers.[5]

The third year of Hitler's dictatorship was also a landmark one for the zoo in other ways. It acquired two gorillas and three juvenile chimps, helping to fill the hole left by the death of the enormous, and enormously popular, gorilla Bobby. Heck had returned from Canada with five bison and one moose for the zoo, but animals were not the only fruits of Heck's Canada trip. He exhibited his photographs of the unspoiled Canadian nature he encountered during Berlin's "green week," a public event organized by the city to educate Berliners on environmental issues.[6] Apart from gorillas and moose, the zoo also acquired four of the extremely rare Australian marsupial wolf. In addition to the animal acquisitions, the zoo had had notable success in breeding animals. The male Indian elephant Orje was born in April and became a drawing card for the zoo. Three moose, one Siberian tiger, and a male orangutan, an extreme rarity in captivity at the time, were also born at the zoo. A series of twenty-two radio shows broadcast information on all of the zoo's new animals to an eager public.[7]

Clearly, though, the zoo profited immensely from Berlin's hosting of the XI Olympic Games from August 1 to 16, 1936. Well aware of the unique opportunity afforded by the huge international event, Heck integrated the zoo's programming into that of the Games. He held a gala opening of the new lions' enclosure one week before the Games commenced to take advantage of the influx of visitors, and the zoo held regular concerts by the Schutzstaffel (SS), Sturmabteilung (SA), army, and air force bands during the first two weeks of August, all of which, according to the zoo's annual report, attracted a diverse audience.[8] The zoo also reached out to the athletes, establishing in the Olympic village on the outskirts of Berlin a mini-zoo that showcased such German animals as geese, ducks, swans, black and white storks, and deer.[9] The German animals shared the spotlight in the village with a kangaroo that the Australian Olympic team had brought along and would donate to the Berlin zoo at the conclusion of the games.

Although the Olympics accounted for much of the zoo's attendance spike, the board's decision to construct a new exhibit to highlight Germany's indigenous animals also attracted visitors. The zoo built large enclosures for lynx, foxes, the retro-bred aurochs, and boars. The new exhibit included a farm setting that showcased goats, sheep, chickens, and geese. Beavers, otters, bears, and wolves were also to have a place of prominence in what zoo management called the "German Zoo."[10] Although it might be tempting to see Nazi ideology behind the German Zoo, given that there is no scientific reason to display animals based on the way humans have divided the globe politically, the idea of exhibiting animals native to Germany had been circulating at the Berlin zoo long before the Nazis came to power. The 1906 zoo visitor's guide indicated the zoo's hope to have the equivalent of a "German Zoo" in place before too long: "Native birds of prey and animals of prey will eventually be displayed in a separate section of the garden along with the entire spectrum of our animal world, including insects, amphibians, and fresh water fish. It will be a great collection of animals from the fatherland."[11]

Nevertheless, the image of German children at the Berlin zoo viewing nearly extirpated central European animals like the otter, beaver, moose, and lynx accorded well with the role of nature in the Nazi concept of Germanness. *Heimatlehre*, or instruction in the homeland, a movement founded by Konrad Guenther, became a key component of childhood education in the Third Reich, through which Germans were to feel at one with plants, trees, and animals that inhabited German lands. The Nazis saw in this movement a harking back to the era of Goethe and Alexander von Humboldt, visioning an almost romantic sensibility for the natural world rather than the clinical observation of it by biologists, whom the Nazis believed to be guilty of distancing Germans from nature.[12] For the Nazis, the connection between nature and Germans was not simply one of aesthetics but related directly to their viability as a nation. Although nature was subverted to the war's ends, the Nazi ideal was nevertheless a German people aware of their place in creation. "The natural beauty of our German fatherland," said Hitler "its diverse plant and animal life must remain preserved for our people: It is the source of power and strength for our national socialist movement."[13] Again and again, Hitler ranted about creating in the occupied eastern territories "gardens and orchards." His interest was not only in carving manicured landscapes out of raw nature in eastern Europe but also in taming the "wild" population there as well.[14]

Nazi propagandists feted Hitler as an unparalleled nature lover, one who was most at home in his mountain retreat. "To marvel at nature, from which all life springs, gives [Hitler] immense pleasure," wrote Ludwig Zukowsky in 1941.[15] Germans saw in Hitler a man with an abiding affection for animals that reached from his Alsatian Blondi to the rest of the animal world, visible in his proclamation about being their self-appointed defender: "I have always said that there is nothing more noble than to be the lawyer for those who cannot defend themselves well—in the new Reich there is to be no more animal torture!"[16]

While the keen Nazi interest in animals and nature helped the zoo enjoy a golden era under Hitler, the 1930s also witnessed the first time in the long history of German zoos that animal protection societies, as well as individual concerned citizens, leveled sustained disapproval at them for their treatment of animals. Prior to this point, the Berlin zoo had been criticized on occasion—notably in 1889 when vivisection opponents attacked the zoo for wishing to euthanize the rogue elephant Rostom—but had not been the focus of animal protection societies' efforts. Those organizations were more preoccupied with humane butchering, proper animal husbandry, and protecting pets. Indeed, Carl Hagenbeck, who had made animals into an unabashed entertainment spectacle at his new park in Stellingen, was elected by an overwhelming majority to the Hamburg animal protection society, with only one vote opposed.

German zoos in the interwar period increasingly found themselves on the defensive as Germans expressed concern for the well-being of animals in zoos in terminology that would resonate today. More and more visitors complained that animals "suffered emotionally" from their confinement, while zoo directors were cognizant that visitors came to pity lions, tigers, and bears as they paced back and forth along the perimeter of their enclosures. Other visitors believed the animals to be homesick for their native lands.[17]

Zoos tried to ease these concerns by explaining that animals did not comprehend the world the way humans did. "Behind bars" did not have the same connotation for an animal as it did for a human prisoner who had been incarcerated and who might reasonably expect a return to a free life. An animal, according to K.W. Muth, a prominent German zoo official, simply did not think that way.[18] He also explained away an animal's constant pacing not as a result of boredom, which was the conclusion to which most visitors had come, but rather the animal's inner drive toward physical exercise, which can take the form of repetitive motions.[19] Zoo proponents had nevertheless to be cautious about how far they would take this line of thinking. Ever since Alfred Brehm's influential *Tierleben* (*Life of Animals*) was published in the 1860s, a significant section of the population had come to believe that animals could experience emotions in a similar way to humans. The idea of animals as tame and human-like was perhaps nowhere more evident than at the Frankfurt zoo, where zookeepers would remove the animals from their cages and saunter about the zoo with them so that the public could engage with the animals. Along the paths of the zoo, visitors encountered chimps, elephants, seals, and antelopes. Karl Neiß and his pride of lions were especially popular. The zoo director, George Steinbacher, finally brought an end to the practice in the late 1930s because of the potential harm to both animals and visitors, much to the dismay of the zookeepers who enjoyed the tips they received from the public.[20]

Popular books in the Nazi period, such as Ludwig Zukowsky's *Tiere um große Männer* (Great Men and Their Animals), spread the message about the fundamental similarities of humans and animals: "All of the positive virtues of the human heart, be it courage, loyalty, gratitude, patience, and last but not least, love, can be found in the same measure, if not even more developed, in animals."[21] (The author, a longtime employee of the Frankfurt zoo who wrote unabashedly of his admiration for Hitler, went on to become director of the Leipzig zoo in 1957.)[22] Thus, zoo proponents were not able to simply argue that animals were not humans and therefore not capable of suffering emotionally in captivity. Given prevailing attitudes, this line of reasoning would have fallen on deaf ears.

For these reasons, those involved with zoos returned to long-standing arguments in favor of zoos: Far from harming species, zoo directors pointed out, zoos protected species, particularly endangered ones. German zoos frequently trumpeted the breeding programs that had saved the wisent from extinction.[23] The general public, zoo proponents also argued, received their education about the natural world largely through zoos, and this education was vital to the human condition. Urban centers had destroyed the symbiotic relationship between humans and nature, removing from people the ability to see the diversity of the natural world and its interdependence. Zoos could return to humanity some of the "reverence for God's creations" that had once been so self-evident.[24] Children in particular, they felt, could learn to appreciate animals only by viewing the living creatures in a zoo. How else could people be motivated to fight against the whale hunt, elephant poaching, or the "senseless seal slaughter"?[25] To the point, many German zoos in the 1930s established separate areas where children were permitted to touch not only domesticated animals but young wild animals as well.[26] Zoos also returned to an egalitarian argument—that they provided those without the means to travel to exotic lands the possibility of seeing foreign animals.

In an open letter to the director of the Leipzig zoo after his visit there in 1936, Jakob von Uexküll, a prominent biologist at the University of Hamburg, questioned the fundamental premise of zoos. Revisiting some of the criticisms of Hagenbeck's panorama zoo in Stellingen, he suggested that the mock nature in animal enclosures served simply to dupe the visitor rather than serve any practical purpose for the animals. He used the example of the Leipzig zoo's artificial climbing mound for baboons to make his point. The mound was an attractive landscape for visitors to view and imparted to them some sense of the animal in a "natural" environment, but the climbing surfaces were less than ideal, designed more for mountain goats that tended to spring from foothold to foothold rather than for monkeys that preferred to clamber.[27] In his response, the Leipzig zoo director, Karl Max Schneider, corrected some of Uexküll's assumptions about the climbing surface but accepted his fundamental reproach of the zoo: that it existed for humans and not for animals. "On the one hand," he wrote, "there is a demand to orient the zoo according to the animal. On the other, following the idea of an 'animal paradise,' there is pressure to exhibit the animal so that the visitor parts with a delightful impression. Personally, I would say that [the zoo] needs to be conceived for humans."[28] Creating zoos that catered to humans rather than animals, Schneider argued, achieved a higher purpose—to instill in visitors a deeper understanding of their role as guardians of the earth. They would understand that they have been entrusted as caretakers of nature and that the biblical "brother's keeper" applies to the animal world, too. After all, he suggested, who was to benefit from the nature protection laws that Germany had recently enacted? Surely, they existed because the animal itself had an intrinsic value, regardless of its role in human life. The director concluded by asking provocatively: "Would we enact nature protection laws and work to preserve certain species if we knew that humans were, sooner or later, going to go extinct? I believe that, yes, we would still do it. For the sake of our brothers. To protect life itself."[29]

Beyond increased societal concern about animals in captivity, the Berlin zoo found itself suddenly looking old in a world of modern entertainments. Even in the banner Olympic year, the zoo was unable to compete with that dramatic new advance in the entertainment industry—film. Germany's leading studio, UFA, had been established in 1917 and within a short time started producing films at a furious pace; in 1922, for instance, it produced 474 new films.[30] Germany's censors banned *All Quiet on the Western Front*, based on Erich Maria Remarque's great pacifist novel, but it nevertheless attracted 400,000 viewers to an illegal showing by the Social Democratic Party. Berliners streamed into the city's marquee movie houses—the Kolobri on Belle-Alliance-Platz, the Rivoli on Bergmannstrasse, and the City on Friedrichstrasse.[31] In 1936 alone, the movie theaters of Berlin reported a total attendance of more than 61 million in a city of roughly 4 million. The competition from this popular new medium seemed to irritate the zoo's management, who felt it necessary to point out what they considered the more noble undertaking of their enterprise: "When one learns that 61 million people visited Berlin's movie theaters, then it is to be hoped that visits to our zoo, where a systematic collection of live animals from around the world is presented to the visitor, will increase."[32] Television was not yet the competition that it would become, but that day was not far off. In 1936, a select subsection of the German public was able to receive the limited TV broadcast of the Berlin Olympics.[33] Radio outstripped TV for most of the Third Reich, as 16 million people had purchased the reasonably priced *Volksempfänger* (People's Receiver) by 1941.[34]

Partly in response to the pressure from other entertainment options, Lutz Heck became a champion for building a second zoo in Berlin. Unlike the Berlin zoo, which aimed to showcase the sheer diversity of animal life, the Tierpark (animal park), which Heck envisioned for the Grunewald, the enormous wooded area in the west of the city, was to exhibit herd animals in vast enclosures so as to impart to the population knowledge about the animal world and the "joy" the animals offered.[35] The new animal park was to be divided into five geographic regions: Africa, where giraffes, zebras, ostriches, and the big cats would be displayed in a steppe-like environment; Asia, focusing on tigers and deer; Australia, showcasing kangaroos, emus, and various marsupials; America, where bears, bison, and mountain sheep would be on display; and Europe, with an emphasis on German animals. The border on one side of the European enclosure was to be the Havel River, allowing anyone on the other side of the river and outside the park to view German wildlife among the trees. This aspect seemed particularly important to Heck, who wrote with a certain degree of triumphalism: "The great animal park with its new ideas and aims will be established with state funds, and will be called <u>The German National Animal Park</u>."[36] Heck expected the concept to resonate with the German public, predicting up to 100,000 visitors on Sundays, many of them arriving in Volkswagens, which he described as the "car of the future."

Heck's proposal for a second zoo in the German capital soon backfired in dramatic fashion. In 1937, Hitler instructed his architect and confidante Albert Speer to reshape Berlin, converting its irregular street patterns and overlapping architecture into a city of clean, straight boulevards and grandiose buildings to project the might of "Germania," the new capital of the German Reich. When he appointed Speer general inspector of construction, Hitler explained his vision of a central artery: "To bring to the chaos of Berlin's built environment a major thoroughfare, one that is worthy of the national socialist movement and the essence of the German imperial capital."[37] Hitler envisioned a north-south axis 5 kilometers long and 120 meters wide running from Tempelhof airport in the south through the center of the city and

terminating at a future northern train station. Germany's megaloma-
niacal buildings were to line the street, including a triumphal arch to
honor World War I veterans that was to be similar to but significantly
larger than Paris's Arc de Triomphe, and the Volkshalle, a massive
domed hall to house state functions of more than 180,000 people.

Hitler and Speer were under no illusions that such a massive project
could be completed overnight, expecting the triumphal unveiling to
take place in 1950.[38] But almost immediately on receiving his orders
from Hitler, Albert Speer identified the Berlin zoo as an obstacle to
Nazi plans for the city, something of which Heck was unaware when
he championed an animal park in Grunewald in August 1937. Several
months earlier, Speer had already contacted the Prussian finance minister requesting information on any new building permits for the zoo,
telling the minister that "a relocation of the zoo was planned to accommodate the reshaping of the Imperial Capital."[39] One month later, the
chief building inspector for Prussia wrote: "Speer informed me today,
that he was told by Göring, that there was to be only <u>one</u> zoo in Berlin,
and that it is to be in Grunewald."[40] Speer subsequently contacted the
mayor of Nürnberg, which had recently relocated its zoo, to help him
gauge the cost of moving the Berlin zoo across the city. The projected
cost of 4.7 million RM apparently did not dissuade Hitler's architect.[41]

Predictably, Heck was aghast when he learned that Speer had hijacked
his plan for a second zoo. He wrote a lengthy plea to the Prussian
finance minister in which he outlined the need to maintain the Berlin
zoo at its current location. Heck worried about the future of some of
the zoo's iconic buildings—the elephant pagoda, the ostrich house in
the form of an Egyptian temple, and the Antilopenhaus, a Byzantine
temple. He also stressed that the Berlin zoo had transitioned toward
fenceless enclosures at the beginning of the 1930s, rendering the argument about greater space at Grunewald moot: "The Berlin zoo is already
well on its way with the expansion of its fenceless enclosures. Such
enclosures already exist for elephants, lions, bears, monkeys, cattle,
deer, horses, seals, wolves, pigs, mountain goats, and numerous smaller
animals. The lion enclosure is the largest anywhere. Paris modeled its
seal basin on Berlin's."[42]

Heck also appealed to Nazi sensibilities, suggesting that exposure to
the zoo would instill in visitors a sense of the place of humans in the

natural world and, equally important, lead them toward key aspects of Nazi ideology, such as the need for sufficient agricultural land to feed a population and the dangers of race mingling: "In its present form, the Berlin Zoological Garden offers not only an overview of the animal world, but brings home to the visitor issues like food supply, manners of living, and heredity. The fact that large sections of the garden exhibit only indigenous animals, both wild and tame, increases the bond to the living creatures of the Heimat."[43] Heck also highlighted the role that the zoo played in the health of Berlin's citizens, referring to the zoo as the "lungs of Berlin" and citing statistics to demonstrate that more Berliners took advantage of the natural splendor in the zoo than they did in the surrounding Tiergarten park. Attendance on a typical summer day at the zoo ranged between 7,000 and 10,000; on discounted days, attendance rose to more than 80,000. Directly contradicting his earlier assertion that Berliners would gladly drive their new Volkswagens to a second zoo, Heck doubted that these numbers would be achieved in Grunewald, given that Berliners would be less inclined to head to the outskirts of the city, especially in the evening. Heck concluded his letter with a message from his father, who had led the zoo for over forty years: "Relocating the zoological garden would mean the destruction of an incomparable masterpiece."[44]

Shortly thereafter, and just two days before Germany invaded Poland, Hans Ammon, the chairman of the zoo's board, wrote to the Chief Construction Council for Berlin, forcefully stating his position: "Our board is unanimous, indeed it is our firm conviction, that for the well-being of the entire Berlin population, the Berlin zoological garden must remain at its current location. Only at this location can it fulfill its mandate to contribute to the health and education of the public."[45]

The zoo director's arguments to keep the zoo in Berlin's center were no match for Speer's ego, however, especially since Speer had earlier that year successfully moved the zoo in Nürnberg, the spiritual home of Nazism, to accommodate his monumental architecture. The Nürnberg experience should have caused the Berlin zoo leadership great concern, for the new Nürnberg zoo, which Hitler visited in May 1939, had been considerably pared down, forcing it to ship many of its animals far afield.[46] Two months after the outbreak of war, Speer made it clear at a meeting with Heck that the Grunewald project would be proceeding but in a watered-down version of the original plan. Concerned about preventing Berliners from enjoying the wooded areas of the Grunewald, Speer proposed that pavilions would be erected near the S-Bahn station and other enclosures would be scattered throughout the Grunewald. Admission could then only be charged to view the exotic animals in the pavilions, while the rest of the displays would be, as Speer phrased it, "accessible to anyone." Heck responded to the Nazi Party's first architect stating the obvious: "The zoo would then most likely become a ward of the state."[47]

The European conflagration brought a rapid end to the brewing feud between Speer and Heck as the Nazi regime and zoo directors throughout Germany turned their attention to preparing zoos for wartime. Nazi officials recognized that zoos were instrumental to the well-being of the German population during wartime, issuing a decree in October 1939 that protected them from many of the war's deprivations until the very end. They received preferential treatment in the delivery of meat from abattoirs, and initially their employees were exempt from military service.[48]

Like other leading Nazis, Lutz Heck believed that animals were intrinsic to the war effort. He enjoyed receiving letters from German soldiers at the front, for they confirmed to him the role of animals in human existence. According to Heck, these letters contained countless stories of German soldiers buoyed by their encounter with indigenous animals in the many far-flung locations in which they had found themselves during the war. Heck believed that animals would see Germany's military personnel through the ordeal: "In my view, occupying oneself with the animal world is the best way to lead a healthier life, and in particular to balance out the demands of the fight."[49] The importance of animals for soldiers took other forms, too. In response to multiple requests from the armed forces, the Berlin zoo provided to naval crews, military airfields, and crews staffing defensive bunkers a host of animals, including young brown bears, coatis, raccoons, dogs, parrots, lambs, peacocks, and pheasants presumably as a distraction and comfort in time of war.[50]

The Berlin zoo, its location at the outset of the war comfortably away from the fronts, played surrogate to other zoos, absorbing all of the animals from the Saarbrücken zoo, which found itself on the western front, as well as those animals from the Warsaw zoo that had survived the merciless German bombing of the Polish capital. Needless to say, space constraints meant that the Berlin zoo could be only a temporary holding pen before the animals were dispersed among other zoos.[51] The crowded conditions made the care of animals challenging in that first winter of the war, as did the unusually harsh winter. In Duisburg, zoo authorities complained that they had "rarely" had to deal with such a long spell of cold weather, while zoos in Frankfurt, Hamburg, Dresden, and Hannover noted with alarm that temperatures had dipped to -26 degrees Celsius. In Halle and Munich, cold temperatures forced many of the subtropical animals to remain almost exclusively indoors. Giraffes and apes were typically spending only fifteen minutes outside each day before returning to their building.[52] Maintaining large buildings at a comfortable indoor temperature was still relatively easy at this point of the war because coal was not yet in short supply, but as the war dragged on zoos would be forced to consolidate animals into fewer and fewer buildings to save on heating costs. The majority of German zoos were able to avoid animal losses during the cold winter of 1939–40, with the exception of Königsberg in East Prussia, which lost almost all of its water fowl when the temperature dropped from +2 to -21 degrees Celsius overnight.[53]

In January 1940, four months after the outbreak of hostilities, Hermann Göring, in his capacity as Reich minister for air transport and commander in chief of the air force, ordered zoos to undertake the necessary defensive preparations in case of aerial attack. Zookeepers reinforced fences around animal pens so that escape was all but impossible. In addition, the Berlin zoo established "observation stations" at various pens, either steel pillboxes or semi-subterranean bunkers, from which zoo personnel could observe the pens during an aerial bombing.[54] Göring made clear that predatory animals that managed to escape their pens during a bombardment—and could not be immediately recaptured—were to be shot.[55]

The tension between Göring's two portfolios was on display several months later when he issued further guidelines for securing Germany's zoos. As commander in chief of the air force, he was responsible for organizing air defense of Germany, including shelters and evacuation plans for civilians. It fell to him, for example, to approve of the air raid shelter for 150 people that was installed under the Berlin zoo's artificial panoramic mountain for mountain goats.[56] Yet, as forest supervisor, he was responsible for sustaining Germany's forests and wildlife, the latter closely tied to the conservation efforts of zoos. As somewhat of a compromise, he ordered that only the bare minimum of predatory animals were to be kept in zoos. "Of those animals who would present a clear danger to the public in the event of an aerial attack (for example, bears and lions)," he wrote to all German zoos in the spring of 1940, "as much as possible, only those that are necessary for breeding are to be kept. Surplus animals are to be eliminated in due course." Zoos were to make arrangements with the proper authorities so that the pelts and meat of those animals that were to be killed could be used for human consumption. Endangered animals, such as the European bison, wild horses, and mountain zebras, as well as animals that would be expensive to replace, were to be relocated to nearby nature reserves. All other animals could remain in the zoo.[57]

Somewhat surprisingly, the Reich Ministry of Finance did not expect zoos to absorb the costs of these state-required (as compared to war-caused) "damages." In 1941, the ministry awarded 250,000 RM jointly to zoos in Cologne, Munster, Duisburg, Düsseldorf, and Wuppertal for the animals lost to relocation or shooting. (Curiously, Berlin was not on the list of zoos receiving funding in 1941, although it certainly experienced animal losses.)[58] In 1942, when plunder from conquered territories was keeping the German economy afloat, the Ministry of Finance paid nearly 125,000 RM to German zoos for similar damages.[59]

In the meantime, and counterintuitively, attendance at the Berlin zoo climbed significantly. Having dropped in 1939 to 1.59 million, nearly 200,000 off its remarkable year in 1936, attendance at the zoo steadily increased in the first years of the war. In 1940, it reached 1.84 million, surpassing the Olympic year, and in 1941, with Germany now officially at war with the world, the zoo fell just shy of 2 million visitors. Accommodating these large crowds during wartime presented a host of challenges. For example, an aerial bombing the previous year had destroyed thirty public washrooms in the park, leaving only two functioning toilets. Predictably, visitors were relieving themselves in the bushes, causing Lutz Heck to plead with the city's construction department to install more toilets.[60]

A zookeeper surveys the damage in September 1941 following one of the first Allied bombings of the zoo. An animal corpse is in the background. This damage would pale in comparison to that caused by the November 1943 bombings. *Berlin Zoo Archive*

City-sponsored visits by schoolchildren, which rose more than 50 percent in the first few years of the war, brought many visitors to the zoo, as did special programming for members of the Wehrmacht. Any wounded soldier recovering at the Berlin military hospital was permitted free entry to the zoo. "Wehrmacht Days," events jointly sponsored by the zoo and Strength through Joy for all military personnel stationed in and around Berlin, were well attended, attracting between 6,000 and 8,000 to each event. And the summer concert series continued uninterrupted through the war. It is remarkable that until 1941 the war was of almost no consequence to the Berlin zoo. Even though many of its zookeepers were at the front, the remaining zoo staff fed the 2,749 animals representing nearly 1,100 species on a regular basis.[61] This is not to say that it was straightforward for amateurs to step in to feed the animals in place of the regular zookeepers. Katharina Heinroth, wife of the aquarium director, wounded her finger when trying to feed meat to the crocodiles in 1943. When her fever reached 105.8 Fahrenheit from the subsequent infection, her husband, fearing the worst, called Katharina's mother to her bedside. But an experimental drug saved the life of the woman who would go on to become the first postwar director of the Berlin zoo and the first female German zoo director.[62]

The zoo continued to purchase animals during the war just as it always had, including three of which the zoo was particularly proud: a sable antelope, a hartebeest, and a bushbuck. The year 1941 was also an important one for births in the zoo, with the arrival of wisents, one male giraffe, two Kamchatka bears, a zebra, a Shetland pony, a yak, a zebu, and camels. As a result, the zoo, which had already acquired animals from other zoos (either legitimately from German zoos seeking refuge for their animals or illicitly from eastern European zoos), was bursting at the seams.[63] While the Nazis murdered their way across the Soviet Union, the zoo's visitor guide of 1941 has not a single reference to the war and indeed indicates that the zoo will be open the same hours as in peacetime: 7 A.M. to 11 P.M. in the summer, and 9 A.M. to 7 P.M. in the winter.[64]

For the first three years of the war, German cities had been spared the terrible fate of the European cities Germany had bombed, including Rotterdam, Warsaw, and Coventry. That changed in 1942 when the Royal Air Force (RAF) began its massive bombing campaign against German cities, starting with Essen and Cologne, Lubeck and Rostock, and leading to the horrendous firebombing of Hamburg in July and August 1943, during which more than 30,000 people died in the city inferno that reached 1,400 degrees Celsius.[65] Three months later, on Monday and Tuesday, November 22 and 23, Air Chief Marshal Harris of the RAF sent 764 aircraft to the German capital to, as he said, "burn [the enemy's] black heart out."[66] Nearly 2,500 tons of bombs were dropped over Berlin in a twenty-two-minute period,[67] forcing more than 150,000 people to evacuate their homes in a swath ranging from the Tiergarten in the center of the city to the suburb of Spandau. Most of Berlin's iconic cultural buildings—the state opera, the German Theater, the National Gallery, Humboldt University, the armory (Zeughaus), St. Hedwig's church, the Charité Hospital, the "Red" City Hall, Charlottenburg Palace—were bombed out or reduced to ashes; the big railway stations were badly damaged, and the Ku'damm, the trendy shopping street, was in flames.[68] One eyewitness described the devastation in his diary the night following the raid: "We have lived through an indescribable experience and survived what seemed like the end of the world."[69] With the exception of a few subway lines, public transportation in the city center effectively came to a halt.[70]

The following night the RAF returned again to the German capital. And again three nights later. By the end of the week, nearly half a million Berliners were homeless, an inauspicious beginning to the Battle of Berlin, which would continue for the next four and a half months and claim 50,000 lives.[71] For one diarist, Berlin was no longer recognizable: "Corpses, corpses, rubble and buildings in flames: there seems to be nothing else in the city."[72] Joseph Goebbels, who in February 1943 had whipped the audience in Berlin's athletic arena Sportspalast into a frenzy with his rhetorical question "Wollt ihr den totalen Krieg?" (Do you want total war?) seemed surprised when total war found the German capital in November:

> What I saw was truly shattering. The whole Tiergarten quarter has been destroyed, so has the section round the zoo. While the outer facades of the great buildings are still standing, everything inside is burned to the ground ... you see nothing but remnants of walls and debris.... Groups of people scamper across the streets like veritable ghosts. How beautiful Berlin was at one time and how rundown and woebegone it now looks![73]

Aware of the increasing danger to the capital from the skies, the Berlin zoo administration had begun prior to 1943 to evacuate its animals to zoos in Germany and German-occupied Europe, in Augsburg, Breslau, Frankfurt, Halle, Cologne, Copenhagen, Prague, and Vienna. In total, nearly 500 of the zoo's animals found shelter in other zoos, only one of which, the giraffe Rieke, would be returned to the Berlin zoo following the war.[74]

Still, thousands of animals remained in the zoo, located at the center of the area targeted by the RAF, to await their fate.[75] That first massive raid killed more than 700 animals, nearly one-third of the zoo's remaining collection within fifteen minutes of the first bomb falling, including a rhino, a chimp, three lions, two tigers, two giraffes, and half of the antelope and deer herd.[76] Ursula Gebel, a resident in the center of Berlin, captured the terrible animal carnage in her diary:

That afternoon . . . I had been at the elephant enclosure and had seen the six females and one juvenile doing tricks with their keeper. That same night, all seven were burnt alive. The entire zoo was destroyed by bombing. The hippopotamus bull survived in his basin [but] all the bears, polar bears, camels, ostriches, birds of prey, and other birds were burnt. Every enclosure, except the animal hospital, was destroyed. The tanks in the aquarium all ran dry, the crocodiles escaped, but like the snakes they froze in the cold November air. All that survived in the zoo was the bull elephant named Siam, the bull hippopotamus, and a few apes.[77]

From Eduard Tratz, Lutz Heck's close friend, we have one of the most detailed accounts of the Allied bombing's devastating effect on the zoo. In a letter to his friends three days after the bombing, he wrote:

Lutz and his family are still alive. His residence, however, is gutted. The same is true for the administration building and those buildings around it. The animals have been largely annihilated. Among the elephants, only "Siam" has survived, the others lie scorched and charred under the rubble of the elephant pavilion. The carnivore pavilion is almost entirely a victim of the flames. Only its bears are still alive. A giraffe survived as well. Miraculously, all of the apes are still alive, including the gorilla "Pongo."

An Abu Markub [the Egyptian name for a large, stork-like bird known as the shoebill] sits with several pelicans, black from grime, and flamingos out in the open, as their pavilion was set ablaze during the second night of bombing. Some cattle, deer, the sea lions, several antelopes, kangaroos, etc. are still alive. The park itself makes a bleak impression, as the majority of the enclosures have been destroyed. The aquarium received a direct hit in the Hall of Crocodiles on the second night of terror and was completely destroyed.

It was about half past ten in the morning when Lutz Heck and I arrived at the ruins of the aquarium. The vision was like something from Dante: writhing giant lizards, wounded from the blast, tossing about in foot-deep water, and behind them the open gate glowing fiery red.[78]

The next day, clean-up crews herded escaped monkeys, antelopes, deer, and birds, scampering among the still smoldering ruins and the strewn animal corpses, back into their pens. Zookeepers ushered the pygmy hippo, whose pen had been destroyed, into the only warm, wet place available—the men's bathroom at the entrance facing the train station.[79] A veterinary group descended onto the zoo to salvage what they could from the corpses. They spent a week butchering the elephant corpses to make into soap and fertilizer, while zoo personnel feasted for two days on a soup they made from a crocodile tail.[80]

Throughout Berlin, rumors abounded that animals escaped during the bombing and were fanning out across the city, hiding in parks and alleyways. One diarist recorded the types of wild stories that made the rounds in the winter of 1943:

> Crocodiles and giant snakes are supposed to be lurking in the hedge-rows of the Landwehr canal. An escaped tiger made its way into the ruins of the Café Josty, gobbled up a piece of *Bienenstich* pastry it found there—and promptly died. Some wag, who drew uncomplimentary conclusions regarding the quality of Josty's cake-making, was sued for libel by the *Konditorei*'s owner. The Court ordered a post-mortem of the dead animal which found, much to the satisfaction of the confectioner, that the tiger's death had been caused by glass splinters found in its stomach.[81]

In his autobiographical *Die Galeere* (The Galley), published in 1949, Bruno Werner, a journalist, described the tumult in Berlin's central Wittenbergplatz that his friend encountered following one of the bombings:

> George tried to use the sidewalk, but it was blocked with furniture and suitcases.... He stumbled over clothes and lampstands with their cords which had been dragged through the dirt. He suddenly noticed that some people were moving to get out of the way of something, while others were stepping over a grey body in the middle of the road. It was a dead crocodile that had presumably escaped from the zoological garden or had been flung there by the explosions.... People walked over it without looking. Everyone was in a hurry.[82]

Lutz Heck dismissed such stories as pure rumor, insisting that only monkeys, a few small animals, and birds—but no dangerous animals—had escaped the zoo during the bombing.[83] Allied bombing destroyed not only animals but most of the zoo's iconic, famously expensive buildings, the ones that had put it on the map of Europe in the nineteenth century. The elegant Antilopenhaus, where the monarchs of Germany, Russia, and Austria-Hungary had had breakfast back in 1872, was shattered beyond recognition. The pile of rubble became the tomb of eighteen animals. All that remained of the magnificent elephant pagoda, which had once attracted visitors from all over Europe, was one corner tower. In the ruins of this one-time Berlin architectural icon lay the bodies of seven charred elephants. The main restaurant and the monkey house were badly damaged but still operational.

The devastation of November 1943 meant that there was little cause for celebration the following year when the zoo marked 100 years of its existence. The Reich minister for education acknowledged the muted anniversary in his letter of congratulations to Heck: "All segments of

One of the few trees left in Berlin stands in front of the ruins of the elephant pagoda around 1946. Given the exorbitant cost, zoo management decided against restoring this once iconic building. *Landesarchiv Berlin, F Rep. 290 0000455*

the population, but in particular scientists, have found the immense suffering of this unparalleled cultural institution of the Reich's capital due to the terror attacks to be extraordinarily painful."[84] At the outset of the war, there had been more than 4,000 animals in the Berlin zoo. When Red Army soldiers entered the zoo in May 1945, only ninety-one animals remained.[85]

The zoo, once a tranquil oasis and refuge from the clamor of the city, became the stage on which the hellish closing act of the Third Reich played out. Because of the zoo's close proximity to one of the city's three flak towers, the Red Army targeted the area around the zoo. Nearly 10,000 civilians and wounded soldiers descended on the massive tower seeking refuge from the ferocious battle. Commoners huddled beside Knights' Cross holders and high-ranking party officials in the hot, crowded hallways of the bunker that Goebbels had ordered the German army to defend to the last man. Fighting was intense not only in and around the zoo but under it as well, as German and Russian troops battled in the tunnels of the Zoological Garden subway stop.[86] The zoo itself was a wasteland of craters, ruined buildings, animal corpses, and shells of tanks. The Volkssturm, the hastily organized militia of teens and senior citizens that was to defend Berlin against the Red Army, dug anti-tank trenches throughout the zoo and erected tank hurdles with fallen trees and bits of fencing.[87] None of these meager defenses mattered, of course, in the face of a well-equipped Red Army little inclined to show mercy after the horrors of the Nazi invasion of the Soviet Union.

The Berlin zoo may have suffered disproportionately due to its proximity to the government district of Hitler's empire, but other zoos in Germany fared little better. The zoos in Frankfurt, Cologne, and Hannover had been damaged—but not yet destroyed—by aerial bombardment in 1941. The Leipzig zoo was struck a few weeks after the first massive air raid on Berlin in November 1943, wiping out many of the signature buildings and a significant portion of the animal collection. Heinrich Dathe, who after the war became the first director of the new zoo in East Berlin, recalled the night: "The carnivorous cats remained remarkably indifferent. For most of the animals, the air attack seemed to be nothing more than a thunderstorm. Only the chimps jumped around like mad. Their pavilion had been destroyed, and they all ran away screaming hysterically."[88] The Breslau zoo managed to avoid the destruction of war until 1944, when the Russians devastated it, along with the rest of the Hitler-ordained "Fortress Breslau." An artillery shell that landed near the aviary released the exotic bird collection, which took to the air in a burst of color over the gray, scarred landscape, those birds of paradise in this instance terribly misnamed. Following the destruction of the enclosures and given the paltry provisions available, the zoo management sent out a commando to euthanize the carnivorous animals. They went systematically around the zoo. First they shot the wolves, then the brown bears, who had initially approached them in delight expecting food, then the polar bears, whose coats ran red. They then proceeded to kill the lions, leopards, tigers, and hyenas. Standing among the carnage with some of the animals still howling, the zookeepers, who had worked with the animals for years, wept.[89]

And finally, the Dresden zoo was destroyed in the incineration of that city in February 1945, a scene that rightly caused Kurt Vonnegut, who was present at the bombing, to suggest that humans might just have to accept with resignation our fate, which is to kill each other on a regular basis. "And so it goes," his refrain after every senseless death in *Slaughterhouse-Five*, which seems almost juvenile when Vonnegut first uses it, becomes unbearable by the end. The protagonist, Billy Pilgrim, destabilized by witnessing the Dresden firebombing, finds comfort in his alien abduction to Tralfamadore, where the odd, but kindly, Tralfamadorians place him in their zoo for observation. Pilgrim is much happier in the confines of the Tralfamadorian zoo than he ever was on earth; in the Tralfamadorian zoo he can escape a world of war. The same could not be said for the animals of the Dresden zoo, the vast majority of which were killed in the destruction of February 1945. Elephants trumpeted and ran madly in all directions after a phosphorous bomb struck their pavilion. One was blown across the moat that ringed off its enclosure from visitors. Now freed, but too terrified to run, the elephant stood trembling on one spot. Nearby, a young elephant cow lay on its back, its stomach torn open. The monkey house had also received a direct hit, killing many and causing others to flee. One gibbon emerged from the wreckage, surprised, it seemed, that it no longer had hands, to be met by a zookeeper with a pistol who shot him. In this scene, as in

The once majestic House of the Antelopes stands without animal life in 1952. Of all the major pavilions from the nineteenth century, only the House of the Antelopes would be restored. *Landesarchiv Berlin, F Rep. 290 0012818*

the thousands of others that played out across the city over those two days in February 1945, Gerhart Hauptmann's phrase about the bombing he witnessed is tragically poignant: "He who has forgotten how to cry can learn to do so again in Dresden." Some of the monkeys, as if eager to put as much distance between themselves and the madness of the human city, fled to the Ore Mountains of Saxony some 100 kilometers away, where they were spotted in the summer.[90]

As the bombs rained down on their city and the fields of Europe became soaked in the blood of their friends and family, Berliners headed to the zoo in greater numbers than they ever had. Other German zoos also found themselves receiving an almost unmanageable number of visitors during the worst years of the war. The Halle zoo had twice as many visitors in 1943 as in 1939.[91] In 1942, the sixty-four-year-old Leipzig zoo achieved the highest attendance figures in its history, welcoming nearly 840,000 visitors.[92] Despite a devastating bomb attack in October 1943 on the Hannover zoo, which saw many of the animals simply leap out over the destroyed fencing, another in spring 1944 which destroyed the monkey pavilion, and a complement of zookeepers thinned by call-ups to the front, the zoo remained open until 1944, welcoming nearly 10,000 visitors a month. This attendance is even more remarkable when one considers that the city was under almost constant attack and visitors to the zoo were required to evacuate it when the air raid siren sounded.[93] The story was similar in Frankfurt, where the greatest attendance in the zoo's history occurred in 1943.[94] These surprising figures suggest that once the fine line between civilization and savagery had been crossed, Germans headed to the zoo not only as a refuge and distraction from wracked nerves and the devastation around them but also to take comfort in the presence of animals, which were blameless in the disaster.

7

The Hippo and the Panda: A Tale of Two Zoos

THE SECOND WORLD WAR HAD turned the clock back on Berlin some 700 years. On the once bustling Alexanderplatz and Gendarmenmarkt, Berliners planted potatoes, vegetables, wheat, and poppies.[1] Raw sewage ran in the streets, much to the delight of the rats. Mounds of garbage, growing taller by the day, attracted swarms of flies. Ghostly, starving people made their way among the timbers, broken glass, and water pipes that thrust up through the streets like the tentacles of some underground monster, passing thousands upon thousands of corpses.

At the center of the ruined city was the spectacle of the Berlin zoo. With only 91 animals remaining of the 4,000 at the beginning of the war, few marquee animals beyond the sickly elephant Siam, a former director who had absconded with funds, and the basic infrastructure in tatters, the Berlin zoo had effectively come to an end. Its terrain was no longer identifiable as that of a zoo. Bomb craters, fallen trees, rubble piles, and the charred shells of trucks and tanks had replaced the elegant pathways and exotic buildings. The hastily dug graves of twenty-eight zoo workers and countless animals added a macabre series of mound-patches to the zoo's wartime quilt. (The human corpses would be exhumed the following year and reburied in proper Berlin cemeteries.)[2]

Animals lay dead in their cages in black pools of blood. In the former cage of the largest gorilla in Europe lay two dead SS men. Nearby, another corpse sat with a machine gun on his knee.[3]

Against these tremendous odds, the Berlin zoo opened to the public two months after the end of the war, piles of rubble still towering over the makeshift cages. It would take brigades of "rubble women," those women who cleaned up from the devastation of war because men were in short supply, several more months to remove the debris, but even a decade after the end of the war, the ruins of some of the zoo's buildings still showed the scars of the eighteen-month bombing of the city.[4] The most visible reminder of the war was the massive flak tower that lay just beyond the zoo's northern fence in full sight of its visitors. The tower, one of three reinforced concrete defensive structures that resembled battleships placed around Berlin to halt the Red Army advance, was targeted for detonation in 1947, an act that was expected to generate such explosive power that the zoo temporarily moved all of its animals to another section as a precaution. But the tower was only partially damaged by the attempted demolition, and it continued to provide a grim backdrop to the zoo into the 1960s, when a British detonation crew flooded the structure and dropped depth charges into it to destroy it definitively.[5]

Katharina Heinroth, a zoologist and wife of the former aquarium director, had been tending to the zoo since the war's end, and in August 1945, the public education department at Berlin city hall asked if she would be willing to assume the directorship of the zoo. Although she was hesitant because of the disastrous postwar situation, Heinroth agreed, thus becoming the first female director of a German zoo.[6] Heinroth deserves much credit for caring for the zoo on a day-to-day basis during those dire days, pitching in to do everything from feeding animals to removing the rubble, but she herself recognized the important role of the occupation authorities in bringing the zoo back to life. Every Monday, the "fatherly," as Heinroth described him, Colonel Robert Nunn of the British occupation authority and Heinroth drove around the grounds of the zoo as she pointed out the desperate state of disrepair of most of the buildings. Nunn responded by providing cement, roofing supplies, and corrugated iron.[7] The Soviet authorities, who jointly administered the conquered city with Britain, France, and

Post–World War II *Trümmerfrauen* (rubble women) clean up some of the damage from the horrendous aerial bombings. In the background is the destroyed monkey pavilion. *Berlin Zoo Archive*

the United States, did their part, too, frequently providing the zoo with their dead horses for animal feed. This Soviet concern for the zoo is not all that surprising. From the account of Konstantin Simonov, a Soviet diplomat, we know that the Soviet soldiers were particularly fond of the zoo. Simonov himself was much more moved by the sight of the dead animals he encountered when he entered the zoo in May 1945 than he was by the dozens of human corpses.[8]

Many of the ninety-one animals that survived the war were sickly from deprivation or had been badly wounded in the bombings. Siam, the male elephant, was the main attraction in spite of the festering wound around his tusk. Other animals that drew visitors included a troupe of baboons, the female chimp Suse, two brown bears, a pair of lions, and the hippo Knautschke, who had been born in the zoo in 1943. The yak Philipp seemed destined to die from a grenade splinter in his side, but a last-minute operation saved him. Such an operation, in the era before tranquilizers, was no easy task. The yak had to be led into a narrow corral, then bound with rope while the operation was performed. The sole representative of ankole cattle, native to East Africa, was an attraction both because of its long, curved horns and the unusual natural pattern on its forehead in the shape of a swastika.[9] Still, even though the zoo in the immediate postwar period was primarily a makeshift shelter among the ruins for a handful of animals, by 1946 more than a million Germans had visited it since the war's end.[10]

Just as the zoo was emerging, tentatively, from the catastrophe of war, international events dealt it another major setback. In 1948, in response to the western Allied introduction of a separate currency into their zones of Germany, the Soviet Union blocked all land access to West Berlin. The Allies responded to the Soviet blockade with what was up to that point the largest airlift in history, supplying a city of 2.2 million people with food, coal, and building supplies. The airlift allowed Berliners to avoid starvation, but the winter of 1948–49 was by no means an easy one. Allied air forces were at best able to deliver only 8,000 tons of supplies per day, considerably lower than the 12,000 tons daily that West Berlin required prior to the blockade.[11] The Allies on the ground in West Berlin were understandably eager to reduce superfluous costs and maximize territorial use. Colonel Mande, the new British commander for the Tiergarten district, ordered the zoo to cut down all of its trees for use as heating fuel, to plant spinach on any free space, and to rid itself of display animals to make way for chicken coops to feed the population. Heinroth opposed the order, arguing to the Berlin senate that such actions would bring an end to the zoo. The senate agreed that the trees in question were national monuments and

Katharina Heinroth, the first postwar director of the Berlin zoo, arrives at Tempelhof airport in Berlin following her return from Indonesia to purchase animals using private donations. Her tireless efforts saved the zoo in the early years following the war. *Landesarchiv Berlin, F Rep. 290 0041192*

sided with her that the animals could remain in the zoo, but only if she could feed them without disadvantaging Berliners. Heinroth arranged to acquire for the zoo the corpses of domesticated animals that were not suitable for human consumption as well as scraps from local abattoirs.[12] Like past directors, she also came to rely on Berliners, large numbers of whom brought their own food for the animals, along with coal briquets to help provide heat, as the almost treeless Berlin had little firewood.[13] The Berlin zoo, on the verge of closing for good for the third time in its existence, had been saved by a devoted population and a wily director.

Apart from restoring the zoo after the war, Heinroth introduced a major change to its manner of business that would have a profoundly positive effect on the animals: She curtailed the practice of public feeding of the animals. Zoo authorities had long considered the well-established practice to bond the public to animals and thereby fulfill the zoo's mandate to raise popular interest in the natural world. Although it is difficult to imagine from today's vantage point, Heinroth struggled with the decision because of its importance to visitors, even though she was aware of the cost in animal lives. "My heart becomes heavy," she wrote in her memoirs, "when I think of 'Aunty Zebra,' the young woman who brought a tasty bite to a zebra every morning before going to her job at the bank. Or the female usher from the cinema, who every afternoon went to 'her' parrot and fed him nuts and talked to him for a while.... To take this life pleasure away from them was really not easy."[14] She nevertheless recognized the necessity of the measure: "The advantages of the ban on public feeding of the animals soon revealed themselves: The incidents of death from overfeeding or intestinal infections came to an end. The health of our charges was significantly better than before. It was no longer possible, as had happened in the past, for someone to unknowingly cause the death of our polar bear by giving him salt herring to eat."[15] However, Heinroth's feeding ban applied only to the more delicate animals. It was not until 1960, following the death of an elephant that visitors had overfed, that the Berlin zoo banned public feeding of all animals.[16]

By the time Heinroth retired at the end of 1956, the zoo had emerged from the rubble to once again take its place as Germany's flagship zoo. The reconstruction of the Antilopenhaus, the zoo's first major exotic building of the nineteenth century, marked the end of the instability that had characterized the postwar decade. Heinroth also oversaw two other major building projects: the elephant house and the hippo complex, both completed in 1956.[17] By that year, the zoo's collection had grown to 2,000 animals, half of its pre-war size, but nevertheless a remarkable feat given its disadvantageous situation after the war.

Although Heinroth had certainly left the zoo in good shape, her successor, Heinz-Georg Klös, still needed to secure the financial stability of the zoo. In order to do so, he adopted the common practice of acquiring popular animals that would entice visitors through the gates. Immediately upon being named director, he set about acquiring for the zoo monkeys, carnivores, zebras, seals, and elephants. It was his belief that these animals were necessary to raise money for two other categories of animals—those of scientific interest, often disparaged by visitors as "the Director's animals," and those animals that were unlikely to attract the public but merited a place in the zoo by virtue of their endangered status. The wombat, which spends most of its day sleeping in a corner of its cage, was one example of the former category. The Hawaiian goose or the trumpeter swan fell into the latter.[18] The iconic animals, elephants and monkeys in particular, helped to increase the zoo's annual attendance by more than 400,000 by the end of the 1960s.

Under Klös the zoo's territory expanded by nearly 60,000 square meters, primarily in the area bordered by the S-Bahn railway lines and the Landwehr canal. However, he did not always use this space for the vast enclosures that had become common in zoos by then. Demonstrating at least mild opposition to the Hagenbeck style of zoo that exhibited animals in fenceless enclosures, he preferred to "systematically" display the animals in related groups. Such a display, he believed, would allow visitors to learn about the commonalities among related animals rather than to view a contrived wilderness that imparted little knowledge. The primary disadvantage of the "systematic" approach is that it constrains the space in which to display the animals. Mindful of this major disadvantage, Klös combined cages where possible to allow for somewhat more space and avoided acquiring animals for which wider spaces were an absolute necessity.[19] The zoo still developed enclosures with mock nature but arranged them by individual species. Such was the case of the 2,000-square-meter lion enclosure; when it opened in 1965, it was the largest in the world.[20]

Under Klös's guidance, and in keeping with its historical mission, the zoo engaged in a sweeping public education campaign. Old signage indicating the species of the animal in Latin was replaced with information in English, French, German, and Latin about the animal's biology, characteristics, and habitat. Beginning in 1968, the zoo produced 475,000 visitor's guides annually, and it acknowledged the international community with its first English guide in 1969. The zoo also prepared a guide especially for schoolteachers so they could educate themselves about the animals prior to a class visit. Zoo personnel gave public talks in local high schools and in the popular Urania educational institute. The zoo continued its massive radio campaign, too. Its radio show *Friendship with Animals*, which started under Katharina Heinroth's directorship as a Sunday show, aired more than 750 times during the zoo's 125th anniversary year in 1969.[21] The anniversary also provided the occasion for the German postal service to issue four commemorative stamps depicting orangutans, pelicans, gaurs (Indian bison), and zebras. One of the stamps portrayed a mother orangutan teaching her offspring to walk while the father rested his arm reassuringly on the mother; another showed a pelican watching over its offspring in a nest. On the other stamps, a zebra galloped with its foal, and a gaur and its offspring gazed off in the distance.[22] The zoo strategically chose to portray animals with their offspring so that the general public would be convinced of the animals' happiness in captivity. Animals in despair, presumably, would not mate.

By the end of the 1960s, the Berlin zoo had taken its place once again alongside the largest and most varied zoos in the world, and it was attracting as many visitors as it ever had. In 1970, it drew 1.9 million people, edging out 1941 as the best attendance year in its existence.[23] What is perhaps even more surprising, considering that just a few decades earlier the zoo lay in rubble with barely an animal collection, the zoo was able to attract these large numbers when across town another zoo was doing the same thing.

After reunification, it was commonplace for East Germans to mock their regime's claim of "Weltniveau" (world-class) status, which it applied to any moderately successful undertaking. The East Berlin Tierpark (to distinguish it from the original West Berlin zoo, I will refer to the "Tierpark" [animal park] when discussing the zoo in East Berlin) was one of the few communist undertakings truly deserving of the description. A staggeringly successful societal project, it would go on from its modest start in 1955 to become the best attended zoo in Germany two years later.

Before the establishment of the Tierpark, the larger, historic zoos of Dresden and Leipzig held pride of place among the zoos in that part of Germany under Soviet occupation. In a workshop for "new teachers" (Neulehrer)—young people untainted by the Nazi past who were not much older than their students and were hastily prepared for the classroom—the director of the Leipzig zoo outlined the importance of zoos as sites of public education. He considered animal "kindergartens" to be crucial in creating a bond between children and animals, and he believed that zoos were uniquely qualified to convey the sense of tragedy when animals go extinct.[24] The Dresden zoo in the years immediately following the war drew between 500,000 and 1 million visitors a year, more than all sporting events in the city and more than

Visitors gather around the polar bear enclosure at the East Berlin Tierpark in 1960. Thousands of East Germans volunteered during the construction of the Tierpark, making it one of East Germany's most successful societal projects. *Landesarchiv Berlin, F Rep. 290 0069104*

all theater and other cultural events combined.[25] Given that the majority of visitors came from the working class, the Dresden zoo director Wolfgang Ullrich lamented that the Socialist Unity Party of Germany, East Germany's ruling party, had not included zoos in its initial Five Year Plan.[26]

In January 1953, when two Germanies existed but few Germans thought that the division would be permanent, Paul Wandel, the minister of education, science, and culture in the East German government, wrote to the mayor of East Berlin proposing a zoo in the communist half of the capital:

> It appears to me that a zoological garden in the democratic sector of Berlin is an urgency. The Biological Station of the Young Pioneers has established the framework for a collection of animals from our German homeland, but this is a long way from fulfilling the needs of both the youth and adult population that a zoological garden can.[27]

The mayor of East Berlin, Friedrich Ebert, responded positively to Wandel's suggestion, also foreseeing the zoo as a place for animals "from our German homeland."[28] Wilhelm Pieck, the first East German president, added his voice and political weight to the debate, publicly claiming that the prospect of a child in the eastern zone never seeing an elephant or lion was "unbearable" to him.[29] Although the zoo from its establishment two years later hosted exotic animals from other parts of the world, the initial focus on animals from the homeland likely stems from East Germany's Cold War rhetoric that it represented the entirety of Germany. The party's emphasis on German animals was to reinforce the idea that the communist regime was not simply relinquishing the western half of the country despite the increasingly entrenched camps.

The Berlin population, however, did not always see the division the way the politicians did. During a public meeting in East Berlin about a potential zoo in that part of the city, residents spoke out against the plan, pointing out that Berlin already had a zoo. In the pre–Berlin Wall era, when Berliners could move with relative ease across the city, the division would have been far less in evidence than our perceptions of it today, and thus it is understandable that many considered a second zoo in a moderately large city an extravagance.[30]

Despite public misgivings, East Berlin's ruling authority, the Magistrat, approved the construction of a zoo in East Berlin, a project to be headed up by the city's Department of Culture. The city donated 100,000 deutsche marks (DM) to start with, but the bulk of the funds were to be raised by a lottery (nearly 500,000 DM) and by admission fees to cultural events (200,000 deutsche marks (DM)).[31] Members of the communist youth group, the Young Pioneers, also flooded the city, collecting change from their classmates and subway riders.[32] The project clearly struck a chord with the population in the eastern zone, who supported the new Tierpark both financially and with their labor. Businesses, both state run and private, and party organizations raised funds to buy animals, often with a sly reference to their type of industry. One "people's-owned" factory that produced refrigeration equipment donated a polar bear to the zoo. Another factory that built bedroom furniture provided the zoo with several storks. The Ministry for Heavy Industry raised funds for an elephant.[33]

The Tierpark instantly became a massive societal project, on a par with Stalin's showpiece boulevard in East Berlin known as Stalin

Boulevard, with its beautiful modern apartment buildings, cafés, shopping outlets, movie theaters, and lush gardens. One of the Tierpark's directors of volunteers captured the parallels between the two projects, in admittedly awkward fashion:

> You all know about those days when we were building Stalin Boulevard. Every Berliner whose heart and soul was behind the project took pride when he walked along the boulevard, saying to his family: You see, over there in the seventh floor, I put those three bricks in place!
>
> Similarly, there are today many businesses, and many individuals from all branches of society who can already say with a certain amount of pride: Part of that elephant's trunk belongs to me; I contributed so that we could acquire the elephant.
>
> It was the case that in a certain business, one department would raise funds for a foot, another for the trunk, and so on.[34]

On one of East Germany's most visible stages, the Third Party Conference of the Socialist Unity Party, Chairman Walter Ulbricht praised the East Berlin zoo as an example of a grassroots initiative and a model for the rest of the republic.[35]

In typical East German fashion, an elaborate propaganda effort to justify the East German state accompanied the opening of the Tierpark. On Friday, July 1, 1955, the director, Heinrich Dathe, gave a lecture to invited guests followed by a private viewing of the grounds. The grand opening took place two days later, when a massive parade of thousands of individuals made its way along Stalin Boulevard toward the entrance of the zoo. The parade consisted of more than 100 Young Pioneers (some of them dressed up as Chinese and East Indians); 200 workers involved with the construction of the zoo; dozens of flags of the communist movement, Germany, and Berlin; large pictures of the mayor of East Berlin; representatives from the many industries that had aided with construction or sponsored animals; and banners reading, "We open today our Berlin Tierpark!" and "All of Germany welcomes the Berlin Tierpark!" Camels, donkeys, and ponies were scattered throughout the parade.

The most blatantly propagandistic part of the procession involved a historical re-enactment portraying the aristocratic, landowning family that had once lived on the land now occupied by the people's zoo. A horse pulled a carriage with a typical Junker family and its footman. The message could hardly be missed. What had once been private lands in the hands of barons was now public property for a peaceful educational project, the "loveliest zoo in all of Germany," as one banner read.[36] When President Wilhelm Pieck cut the ribbon, 500 balloons and thousands of doves took to the air and bands struck up a tune.[37] Thirty thousand Berliners streamed into the Tierpark that afternoon to visit the capital's latest attraction.[38]

The Tierpark's area of nearly 160 hectares made it the largest area of any zoo in the world, more than four times larger than the zoo in the western half of the city and considerably larger than the Bronx zoo in New York City, which measured 100 hectares.[39] Although it had a modest collection highlighted by one lion, two polar bears, and two Indian elephants, the vast, tastefully manicured grounds attracted large crowds. In 1956, the first full year it was open, nearly 1 million people visited Germany's newest zoo. The following year, 1.45 million passed through its gates, surpassing its West Berlin counterpart and even the Frankfurt zoo, at the time the most popular one in Germany. The Munich zoo, in contrast, first reached 1 million visitors in 1967, and by 2009 still had not drawn 1.5 million visitors in a year.[40] Ho Chi Minh and the East German prime minister Otto Grotewohl were two notables among the Tierpark's visitors in that 1956 banner year.[41]

The Tierpark quickly gained standing beyond Germany's borders. "This facility," wrote a journalist for the *Welt am Sonntag* in 1959, "is probably the only product of the division that is assured its place in a reunited Berlin."[42] The journalist continued with unabashed enthusiasm, referring to the East Berlin zoo as "a small Versailles" and praising the polar bear enclosure: "The most imposing facility is surely the polar bear pit, the largest of its kind anywhere. In front of a gray backdrop, ten white bears pose in remarkable fashion on a craggy arctic landscape—built in part from the ruins of the Reichsbank."[43] In 1960, Major General Dalton, director of the London Zoo, and his wife visited the Tierpark, leaving a flattering message in the guestbook: "Our visit gave us much pleasure, and we learned much that we can apply to the reconstruction of the London Zoo."[44] Other official visits that year included zoologists from Czechoslovakia, naturalists from Sweden, a professor from Sofia, the director of games and fisheries in Sudan, the directors of the Caracas zoo and of the Nepal zoo, and Heinz Heck, grandson of Ludwig Heck, former Berlin zoo director, and chief zoologist at the Catskills Game Farm in New York.[45]

The Tierpark director was well aware that the modest collection of animals would not enthrall the public for long. Since it had a plentiful supply of exotic animals and was ideologically close to the German Democratic Republic (GDR), Vietnam was East Germany's preferred supplier of animals. The Vietnamese government may well have considered that providing the Tierpark with animals was the least it could do to repay East Germany for its aid over the years. Having established official relations with the Democratic Republic of Vietnam in 1950, in the midst of the Vietnamese struggle against their French colonial masters, East Germany went on to provide substantial financial and in-kind aid to Ho Chi Minh's communist country throughout the Cold War. In the 1950s, East German assistance took on many forms, including sending members of East Germany's Ministry for State Security to help train Vietnamese secret police officers and producing Vietnamese currency in East Germany.[46] The ruling Vietnamese Workers Party was also thankful for East German assistance in building a publishing house where the party printed its leaflets, newspapers, and other official documents, and for East German expertise and financial aid in revamping the aged hospital in Hanoi.[47] East German support for Vietnam became even more pronounced during the Vietnam War, when East Germany provided more humanitarian assistance to the war-torn country than any other European Soviet bloc country.[48]

Even though East Germany had well-established links with Vietnam by the time the Tierpark was established, arranging transport of the animals was by no means easy. For one, East Germany had no merchant vessels to speak of, forcing it to hire Polish and Czech ships. As the animals awaited transport in Vietnam while East Germany searched for available vessels, the Vietnamese government became increasingly agitated, threatening to begin charging East Germany for the animals that were languishing dockside. Care for the animals during the long sea voyage also proved problematic because the East Germans believed, mistakenly, that regular sailors with good intentions could look after them. As the East German organizer of one transport reported in justifying the absence of expert zookeepers: "The sailors on these ships are more than happy to take on the tasks of [animal care.]"[49] Enthusiasm soon proved no substitute for veterinary knowledge. All three of the pythons on the first transport died before they reached Berlin.

After several years of negotiations and many false starts, a gala celebration took place on March 18, 1958, in the East German embassy in Hanoi to mark the gift of a substantial number of animals from Vietnam to East Germany, attended by the president of the Fatherland Front of Vietnam (an organization of the party to implement its social programs), a representative of Vietnam's foreign ministry, and Vietnam's ambassador to the GDR. The transport, which consisted of animals that the GDR could not otherwise afford, included one elephant (named Unity), two deer (one named Dien Bien Phu), four monkeys, two bears, one porcupine, three pythons, one turtle, three pigs, two parrots, and several exotic birds.[50] A Polish ship sailed for four weeks with the animal cargo to the East German port of Wismar, where workers herded the animals into seventeen crates which they then loaded into four trucks bound for East Berlin.[51] Following the shipment from Vietnam, the Tierpark director arranged for the transport of a tiger from China, an elephant from India, and polar bears from Russia. In those early years, the arrival of animals frequently outpaced the Tierpark's ability to accommodate them; many of these acquisitions, even five years after the zoo opened, were still in provisional pens. The seven lions, two Chinese tigers, and other wild cats were being kept in converted Czech train wagons into the late 1950s.[52]

The Tierpark received a boost in 1958 when the German Academy of Sciences (Deutsche Akademie der Wissenschaften) established a research station there. From the conception of the Tierpark, Heinrich Dathe had hoped to attract a research center in the zoo, given the plentiful supply of animals available for observation.[53] The Center for Vertebrate Research (its interest a reflection that the Tierpark housed exclusively vertebrates at the time) examined the behaviors and health of various vertebrates, with a special emphasis on birds. Researchers were particularly interested in biophysics of flight and the mechanics of nighttime vision. For all that the researchers studied living animals, there was no substitute for dissecting the organs of dead animals, which the Tierpark delivered up for research purposes. Indeed, the scientists were pleased at how much their collection of eyes had grown in the first year in operation.[54] As such, the research institute was not so terribly different from the Natural History Museum of Berlin, which for most of its history had been the main recipient of carcasses from the Berlin

In 1961, Heinrich Dathe, the only director in the history of East Berlin's zoo, the Tierpark, holds up an Asian black bear cub that had been born in the zoo. The Tierpark became one of East Germany's flagship cultural institutions and an important propaganda counterpoint to the original West Berlin zoo during the Cold War. *Bundesarchiv, Bild 183-82785-0001*

zoo. Scientists were also actively involved with cataloguing the animals, from the growth cycle of their teeth to life expectancy and breeding frequency.[55] The center, which collaborated closely with similar institutes in the Soviet Union, was prodigious in its output, producing more than 140 scientific publications in its first decade, including four books.[56]

More than any other single figure, Heinrich Dathe shaped the Tierpark into an East German icon. Born in 1910 in Reichenbach, the only child of a middle-class family, Dathe earned his PhD from the University of Leipzig in the natural sciences, focusing on zoology and botany, much to the dismay of his office-oriented father, who had hoped his son would pursue a legal career.[57] In 1932, while still a doctoral candidate, Dathe joined the Nazi Party. Since this was an era when the party's fortunes were rising but it was not yet in power, Dathe avoided the "March violets" label that old-time Nazis disparagingly applied to those Germans who jumped on the bandwagon in the spring of 1933.[58] Dathe joined the Nazis before it was politically expedient to do so, and he remained a party member until the end of the war. And like many who joined the Nazi movement, Dathe later downplayed the significance of his party affiliation.

In his 2001 memoirs, Dathe was eager that his reputation as one of East Germany's most respected public figures remain untarnished. Dathe asserted that he joined the party as an uncertain youth who was influenced by Nazi rhetoric about the humiliation of Versailles and promises of restored national glory. The fact that some of his professors supported the Nazis also factored into his decision.[59] Missing in his account was any mention of misgivings about his party affiliation as the regime came to power and revealed its true colors. He moved directly from his membership in the Nazi party to his wartime service on the western front, omitting mention of any of the Nazis' very public anti-Semitic measures. Perhaps most revealing of Dathe's attempt to whitewash his own past, he neglected to mention that he was the director of the Nazi Party chapter (*Ortsgruppe*) at the Leipzig zoo, a crucial position within the Nazi apparatus to organize the party at the grassroots level.[60] An Ortsgruppe director was typically responsible for all aspects of the Nazi Party in his locality, including budget, press releases, membership, and the organization of three or four lower party administrative units known as cells.

As if it atoned for his Nazi involvement, Dathe pointed out that he published the work of Jewish scholars in his journal *Zoologischer Garten* during the war and found ways to invite Israeli scholars to international conferences he hosted after the war against the East German regime's wishes.[61] Dathe was grateful to the communist regime after the war for accepting him in spite of his Nazi affiliation, and he returned the favor with steadfast loyalty, if not in party membership. Dathe thus joined a growing list of East German functionaries whose Nazi past the communists chose to ignore when it was convenient for them to do so.[62]

The future Tierpark director experienced World War II firsthand, both as a soldier for six years on the western front, where he was badly injured in one arm, and as an observer to the devastation of Leipzig and the bombing of the Leipzig zoo while on leave in February 1944.[63] When the war ended in 1945, the British army took Dathe prisoner and confined him in a prisoner-of-war camp in Italy for the next two years.[64] Although he remembers the English treating them "very fairly," the prospect of years in the camp followed by an uncertain future in a homeland reduced to rubble caused him to contemplate suicide. He later claimed that he took the unexpected appearance in his camp of a small, red-headed bird known as a woodchat shrike as a sign from above and dropped all thoughts of ending his life.[65] Dathe became something of a celebrity in the camp, giving ornithology lectures that attracted more than 2,000 listeners. Once released, Dathe took in the sights of Italy, spending pleasant days in the Rome zoo and at Vesuvius and Pompeii before returning to the Soviet Occupied Zone of Germany.[66]

Dathe became assistant director of the Leipzig zoo in 1950 and held the position until 1954, when he received word that he had been promoted to Tierpark director. Dathe could scarcely believe his good fortune of being given the singular opportunity to build a zoo from scratch. His salary was modest at the outset and would remain so throughout his time as director, but the perks in his contract were exceedingly generous. The party provided him a house on the zoo's grounds, twenty-four days of vacation, preferential vacation times in the labor union–owned villa, and journals and newspapers from both sides of the Iron Curtain in translation that were typically inaccessible to East German researchers.[67] Dathe went on to become one of the most celebrated East German citizens, winning the National Prize of the GDR in 1965, the Gold Star for Friendship among Nations, and the Gold Medal of Conservation, awarded to him by the Zoological Society of San Diego.

Dathe was not only one of the most celebrated GDR citizens but also one of the most loved. East Germans gave him the credit he was due for guiding the Tierpark through major construction projects, including the Alfred-Brehm Pavilion, built in 1963, which housed indoor tropical animals, and the elephant pavilion, which had been under discussion from 1976 but was not completed until September 1989, weeks before the Berlin Wall fell.[68] Beyond the Tierpark itself, Dathe's outreach efforts paid considerable dividends. Due in no small measure to his immensely popular Sunday radio show *Overheard in the Tierpark*, which over the course of the GDR's history ran exactly 1,774 times, virtually every East German knew Heinrich Dathe and admired his deep affection for animals.[69] Of the many stories of his animal rescue efforts, one in particular was talked about in living rooms and coffee shops across the country. Nearly fifty years before the arrival of Knut, the polar bear born in the West Berlin zoo that became a cultural phenomenon, the East Berlin zoo had its own bear that swept to national attention and distracted the public from the wall that had been constructed months earlier. For the first time in European history, and only the second time worldwide, a sun bear had been born in captivity. The birth of Evi caused a sensation in the city and around the globe; other zoos were both shocked and envious that the Tierpark, in only its sixth year, had bred a sun bear. Dathe basked in the festive atmosphere and the international accolades. The shock was therefore the more severe when he received a call that the mother bear had hurled the cub against a wall. Berliners were glued to their radios as they followed the fortunes of the tiny bear, which then moved into Dathe's house in Paddington-like fashion. Images of the bear taking his bottle, playing soccer with an apple, and frolicking in his first bubble bath caused children across the country to ask their parents for a pet bear. Having nursed her to health, Dathe returned Evi to the bear enclosure in the Tierpark, where she lived to the age of thirty-five—at the time, the oldest sun bear in the world.[70]

In another instance, a woman confined to bed because of illness was unable to join the thousands of Berliners streaming to the Tierpark to see Chi-Chi, the panda loaned from China in 1958. When Dathe learned of her profound sadness, he packed Chi-Chi into a crate and drove the panda across the city to the woman's apartment building. With the help of his assistants, he dragged the crate up four stories and into her modest quarters. Dathe described the scene that followed: "On the face of the woman who looked deathly ill spread a satisfied, happy smile. We laid her hand on the pelt of the precious animal, who could not have been more genteel. That was the greatest reward for our efforts. The episode confirmed for me and strengthened me in my mission to acquaint humans with other living creatures, with our brothers in different dress."[71] The blockbuster 2003 movie *Goodbye Lenin* imagined a kinder East Germany with the respected East German cosmonaut Siegmund Jähn as its leader, but the movie could just as easily have featured Heinrich Dathe instead.

Dathe and his western counterpart, Katharina Heinroth, enjoyed a close friendship that originated in the interwar period when they both studied at the Leipzig zoo. On his insistence, she was the only western zoo director who was permitted entry into the GDR to attend the opening ceremonies of the Tierpark. Their friendship was most evident in 1956 when a baboon escaped from the western zoo and found its way across the sector boundary into an East Berlin park. Dathe personally corralled the baboon into a carry-cage, filled out the endless bureaucratic forms, and drove the animal back to its western home.[72]

Somewhat surprisingly, the construction of the Berlin Wall in August 1961 did not noticeably disadvantage the Tierpark. It is true that it lost the majority of its West Berlin visitors, but attendance was robust even without the Berliners from the western zones. The regime did, however, prevent West Germans from attending the Tierpark's gala celebration marking its tenth anniversary.[73] Although it slowed considerably, exchanges of personnel and knowledge between the city's two zoos did not end entirely after 1961. Indeed, when the West Berlin zoo held a public opening of its new bird pavilion in 1962, Dathe showed up unannounced, to the great surprise of his West Berlin colleagues, who insisted he take his seat in the front row. Dathe recalled, "My presence was without doubt quite a sensation."[74] The wall also made animal transports to East Berlin more cumbersome. For example, a British airline was prepared to fly to Tempelhof, West Berlin's main airport, with an elephant destined for the Tierpark, but refused to fly to East Berlin. Although photographers salivated at the prospect of an elephant making its way through the opening at Checkpoint Charlie, it was not to be. The East Germans found another airline willing to fly the large, delicate cargo to East Berlin.[75]

Dathe remained director of the Tierpark as the two Berlins—and two Germanies—united in 1990, but his tenure after that was brief. Using a clause in the unification treaty that prevented individuals over sixty years of age from being employed by the new German public service, the government pensioned off the eighty-year-old in December 1990 and evicted him from his residence on the Tierpark grounds. Less than one month later, Dathe died of cancer.

For many East Germans, Dathe's treatment was emblematic of the heavy-handed western takeover of the East. Fear was widespread that the West would dismantle the Tierpark, in the same manner that it had instantly shut down nonproductive factories, throwing large numbers of East Germans out of work, and had replaced entire university departments with western academics. Journalists from the communist newspaper *Neues Deutschland;* leading members of the revamped Communist Party, the Party of Democratic Socialism; and thousands of Berliners attended Dathe's funeral,[76] where Pastor Werner Braune highlighted the importance of the Tierpark for the East in his eulogy: "There is today a tendency to wind down everything. It would be a mistake to fundamentally alter the Tierpark. Berlin is large enough to support it and other similar institutions.... We would be throwing overboard not only the Tierpark, but the love of the population of our city for a facility built by thousands."[77]

Although Dathe clearly supported the socialist Germany, he kept a low public profile about his politics. The party, on the other hand, politicized the Tierpark from its inception. As one of East Germany's most successful public projects and an icon that resonated across the republic, the Tierpark featured prominently in the Socialist Unity Party's view of itself and the country.

The party founded the Tierpark for many of the reasons that zoos had been founded in the past—to preserve rare species, to educate the public about the natural world, and to provide an oasis to offset the harsh urban environment. To these, however, must be added the reasons idiosyncratic to divided Berlin. The party intended the zoo in the East German capital to serve a variety of propagandistic purposes.

The Ministry of Culture, for one, outlined the role the zoo could play in educating the public about the global communist movement: "In the purchase and exchange of animals, and through diverse cultural activities, the friendly relations between the GDR and the peace-loving peoples of the world will be strengthened."[78] The Tierpark's deputy director echoed the importance of the zoo for creating citizens aware of the communist struggle: "The result of the many voluntary contributions and gifts of animals both domestically and from abroad is that the Berlin Tierpark is not only a symbol of the Berlin population's will to rebuild, but it is at the same time an expression of international solidarity."[79] When Vietnam donated thirty animals to East Germany, the Communist Party made certain to emphasize the broader significance of the gesture: "This gift, and the enrichment of our Tierpark with rare animals of tropical Vietnam are an expression of practical acts in the service of friendly relations among our peoples. We are delighted that these brotherly bonds will be in future even tighter, and even more fruitful for both of our peoples in our fight against global imperialism."[80]

The establishment of a zoo in the eastern zone also aimed to reduce the number of easterners who visited the original zoo in the West, still a relatively easy journey for most Berliners in this era before the Wall. The strategy more than succeeded. Not only did the percentage of East Berliners visiting the West Berlin zoo drop from 20.3 percent in 1954 to 16.6 percent in 1955,[81] but the Tierpark also attracted many West Berliners to the Soviet zone. In 1957, about 40 percent of the 1.5 million visitors to the Tierpark came from the West. Even the landmark millionth visitor to the Tierpark was a West Berliner.[82]

Time and again, East Germany's flagship zoo became a stage on which the ideological battle with West Germany played out. In 1958, there was great fanfare around the arrival at the Tierpark of Chi-Chi, a giant panda from China. Chi-Chi, one of only four pandas of this type in zoos worldwide, attracted nearly 400,000 visitors during her three weeks in Berlin.[83] The Tierpark's director boasted that socialist solidarity allowed the rare creature to be put on display in East Germany instead of the West. US Secretary of State John Foster Dulles, he claimed, had denied the panda entry into the United States.[84] The panda was indeed a coup for the Tierpark, as a panda would not be seen in Berlin for another twenty-two years, when the western zoo finally acquired one.

A few years after the success of Chi-Chi, an alarmed Dathe wrote to Berlin city hall requesting more funds for the Tierpark in light of increased competition from the western zoo. With its new monkey pavilion, he claimed, the original zoo in the West was much better able to host a large collection of monkeys. When Dathe determined that the western zoo was about to acquire twenty-two chimps, he feared that business in his Tierpark would dry up. "There is a very real possibility," he wrote, "of a mass movement of peoples to the western zoo."[85] When further funds were not forthcoming, Dathe again played the Cold War card. He matter-of-factly informed city hall that shrinking the Tierpark's budget would require him to reduce the zoo's animal collection by about 60 percent, including buffalos, chimpanzees, elephants, and antelopes. "I likely do not have to go into the predictable negative foreign propaganda," he wrote "that such a situation in Berlin's Tierpark would bring upon the GDR."[86] The pleas eventually proved effective. A few years later, the Tierpark had a state-of-the-art heated monkey pavilion that allowed the zoo for the first time to exhibit chimpanzees and orangutans year round rather than only in the summer months.[87]

In 1964, Dathe and his wife joined a safari in Tanganyika, Uganda, and Kenya that had been organized by the Frankfurt zoo.[88] At a total cost of nearly 6,000 DM for both Dathe and his wife, the enormously expensive trip had to be approved at the highest levels of the Communist Party, which asked Dathe to campaign on behalf of the GDR in return: "During conversations with colleagues and on other similar occasions, Dathe and his wife are obligated to discuss the achievements of the GDR."[89] The party also insisted that Dathe join the group in Cairo, thereby avoiding a trip through West Germany.

The Tierpark even trumped the western zoo at its own propaganda game. In 1962, in a show of solidarity with a city recently enclosed by the Berlin Wall, US Attorney General Robert Kennedy visited West Berlin, preceding his brother John F. Kennedy's visit and his "Ich bin ein Berliner" speech by nearly one year. One of the highlights of Robert Kennedy's visit was a ceremony at the Berlin zoo where Kennedy, in the presence of the mayor and future West German chancellor Willy Brandt, donated an American bald eagle. Eager to match the counterpart across the Wall, the East Berlin Tierpark acquired bald eagles on its own and became the first European zoo to breed them.[90]

In almost every public pronouncement, the party trumpeted the fact that the Tierpark owed its existence to the efforts of thousands of volunteers and a large number of private donations. In the year following the erection of the Berlin Wall, which had been constructed to stem the tide of East Germans fleeing to the West (and therefore the regime's most public admission of its inferiority), Dathe took pains to highlight the number of cultural events that occurred at the zoo—twenty-four concerts, three fashion shows, and nine "colorful" afternoons dedicated to children—and reminded Berliners in his official press release that the zoo was a "truly socialist cultural venue, established by the people, for the people, and used by the people."[91] In 1971, the Ministry of Culture tasked the zoos of the republic with educating the "socialist" person, focusing in particular on inculcating youth with an awareness of the natural world and the country's ties, illustrated through the animal collection, to world communism. The regime pointed to the Tierpark's youth wing as a stellar example: "The Youth Club of the Tierpark, with currently over 400 members, not only offers our youth from all backgrounds a sensible way to spend their leisure time, it also contributes to the development of a socialist person, whose work extends to our socialist brother lands."[92]

In 1979, Minister of Culture Siegfried Wagner delivered a speech at a meeting of directors of GDR zoos with the lofty title "Zoos in a Developed Socialist Society." He boasted that the nine zoos in the GDR had developed over the previous thirty years into "zoos of a socialist type," ones that were, he continued "fundamentally different from those in the capitalist world."[93] Although the regime contrasted the communist zoo with the inferior product in the West, it was by no means clear what the difference was. Wagner seemed to imply in his major 1979 speech that the western zoos exploited animals for their sheer entertainment value when he claimed that "the sole purpose" of GDR zoos "lay in public education and relaxation, animal protection, and research."

The regime's official support of zoos was rooted in its belief that communism, a more peaceful ideology than capitalism, required humans to be in harmony with nature. The minister of culture referred to one

US attorney general Robert F. Kennedy donates an American bald eagle to the West Berlin zoo in 1962. The East Berlin zoo would trump its western counterpart in Cold War propaganda by breeding bald eagles first. *Landesarchiv Berlin, F Rep. 290 0080492*

of the regime's ideological founders in discussing the role of zoos in the GDR: "Friedrich Engels has already pointed out the extent to which humans and nature form a union, and are reliant on one another: 'And so with each step we are forced to recall that we in no way dominate nature as a conqueror rules a foreign land, or as someone who is somehow removed from nature. Rather, we of flesh and blood and brains belong to nature, are part and parcel of nature, and our entire dominance over it is based in recognizing and properly applying its laws.' "[94] The East German regime also recognized the basic role that zoos played as entertainment that could compete with that offered in the West. The slogan "Everything for the good of the people," which appeared throughout the GDR, also underlay the rationale for zoos. The Tierpark was to make people delighted with their lot in life, confident in the victory of socialism, and, where progress had been made in preserving endangered species, generally optimistic about the future.[95]

The party's strong support for East German zoos helped them to considerably outstrip other entertainment venues. In 1972, they received 12.6 million visitors. Six years later that number rose to 14.1 million. As a point of comparison, the highest East German soccer league, the Oberliga, drew only 2.1 million fans in the same year.[96] Or another way of putting it: East German zoos alone had more visitors than zoos in *all* of Germany in the pre-war period.[97] By the time the East German regime collapsed in 1990, the Tierpark had received more than 90 million visitors.[98]

The massive interest in zoos was not solely an East German phenomenon. Both sides of the Iron Curtain experienced a boom in zoos during the Cold War. Following World War II, new zoos sprang up in the West in Braunschweig, Dortmund, Erfurt, Stuttgart, and Gelsenkirchen, and in the eastern cities of Cottbus, Magdeburg, Schwerin, Rostock, and East Berlin. By 1960, zoos in Germany were welcoming three times as many visitors as they had in the pre-war period.[99] From the time of its shaky reopening in 1945 until the unification of Germany in 1990, West Berlin's zoo drew about 80 million visitors, a number that fell below attendance at its East Berlin counterpart but was by every other measure a resounding success.[100]

It is difficult to know for certain the reasons behind the German fascination with zoos. On the one hand, zoos had exerted a strong attraction on Germans, if not since their establishment, then at least since the

1870s. Germany had more zoos than any other European country by the dawn of the twentieth century. On the other hand, it is hard not to link the explosion in German zoo attendance to the war. The 2,500 doves that party officials released at the opening of the Tierpark were on one level typical East German propaganda, a frequently employed tactical symbol to differentiate East Germany from the West German war-mongering heir to the fascists. In this case, however, the propaganda did capture something deeper about the Tierpark. It represented an idyllic world, at harmony with nature, far from the ravages of twentieth-century warfare. In East Berlin, the 90 million visitors over thirty-five years came to see a scene of tranquility, a modest collection of domestic and exotic animals in a vast, pastoral setting. Clearly, the Tierpark satisfied some deep need in the East Berlin population.

Was this a need simply for relaxed entertainment? Perhaps, but it seems unlikely that this would be the entire explanation. East Germany had other entertainment venues, from circuses to festivals, sporting events, cinemas, and theater. None of these could compete with zoos.

The hippo Knautschke delights his audience. Having been dragged from the rubble following a bombing in World War II, Knautschi, as Berliners called him, became a symbol of the city's resurrection. *Landesarchiv Berlin, F Rep. 290 0044542*

East Germans, like their western counterparts and Germans that had gone before them, sought out animals more than almost any other option to fill their free time.

An event four years after the end of the war helps to capture the deeper significance of the zoo for Berliners, and since this was an era when residents could move about their zoned-off city freely, it has explanatory potential for both sides of the Iron Curtain. In 1949, desperate to acquire new animals but lacking the funds to do so, the Berlin zoo made an arrangement with the Leipzig zoo to lend Berlin its two female hippos to breed with Berlin's male hippo, Knautschke, who had been born in the zoo in 1943 and later in the war was pulled from the rubble beside his dead mother. The agreement specified that the first offspring would be the property of the Leipzig zoo, and the second would belong to Berlin. The first mating was effortless, producing a baby hippo for the Leipzig zoo in 1950. Although the second mating took longer, it too was successful, producing a female that would reside in Berlin. Word of the hippo's birth spread throughout the city, bringing a child-like joy to a population that had had so little in which to delight. When the zoo director announced that the baby hippo's name would be revealed publicly, the actor Walther Groß, a household name from the cabaret circuits, led a huge crowd through the streets of Berlin and into the zoo for the naming ceremony. The scene of the newly named Bulette romping in the water beside her father Knautschke, the baby who had survived the fire-bombing of 1943 and in the last months of the war had been pulled from the rubble in miraculous fashion, enchanted the droves of Berliners who turned out. The infant hippo resonated with the people around her, a people who survived against the odds of war and blockade to find themselves in a different, less troubled Germany. There was every indication that Bulette would have a better life than her father, war-scarred Knautschke; Germans fervently hoped the same for their own children.[101]

Epilogue: Of Trams and Tortoises

WHEN VLADIMIR LENIN AND HIS Bolsheviks seized power in 1917, millions of Russians fled to cities as far-flung as Shanghai, New York, and Istanbul to escape the unfolding regime of terror. The mass exodus also led to an influx of Russians to Berlin, either to take temporary advantage of Berlin's advantageous position on the east–west rail corridor or to make Berlin their permanent home. In 1923, roughly 360,000 Russians lived in the German capital, among them some of the most notable names in Russian literature: Ilya Ehrenburg, Maxim Gorky, Boris Pasternak, and Vladimir Nabokov.[1] Most of the émigrés arrived at the burgeoning Zoological Garden train station and for convenience settled into apartments in close proximity to it.

It is because of this confluence of historic events that Nabokov came to spend many of his days in the zoo during his fifteen-year stay in Berlin, forming impressions that found their way into his literary works. In his short story "A Guide to Berlin," published on Christmas Eve 1925, an unnamed narrator sits in a typical Berlin pub, telling his visibly bored companion about his morning outing.[2] The narrator describes the minutiae that he encounters as he takes the tram to the zoo: the pattern of snow on utility pipes that lay on the streets awaiting their installation by city workers, the thickness of the tram conductor's fingers, and the texture of the tortoise's tongue that he observes once he arrives at the zoo. "That's a very poor guide," the nonplused listener responds to the narrator. "Who cares about how you took a streetcar and went to the Berlin zoo? . . . What do trams and tortoises matter?"[3]

If the companion had been paying attention, he would have noticed that the narrator had already answered both parts of his question. The rhythms of daily life matter because they shape our understanding of our world, oftentimes in ways that only future historians are able to decipher. "In the objects around us [is] the fragrant tenderness," explains the narrator, "that only posterity will discern and appreciate in the far-off times when every trifle of our plain everyday life will become exquisite and festive in its own right."[4] A tram ride, although typically banal, could well have a profound effect on someone's life, perhaps due to the interaction with the conductor, the advertisements in the car, or another passenger that one might meet. The narrator also makes clear why tortoises in the zoo matter. Referring to the zoo as Eden, he suggests that the magnetic power of zoos relates to a human longing: "If churches speak to us of the Gospel, zoos remind us of the solemn and tender beginning of the Old Testament."[5]

These two aspects that Nabokov highlights in his narrator's day tour of Berlin—the zoo as a site of reflection on humanity's place in life on earth, and the crucial role of daily habits in forming broader human views of their reality—have been at the heart of this history of the Berlin zoo. Throughout time, the Berlin zoo was not simply the site of the occasional leisurely outing but a destination that became integrated into the daily life of the city's inhabitants—and one that helped them to understand their place in both the human and the animal world. What would have been clear to any visitor throughout the Berlin zoo's history, for example, is the extent to which the zoo, and by extension its surrounding metropolis, occupied exalted status in Germany. During the late nineteenth century, while other zoos floundered, the Berlin zoo was the best customer of the animal magnate Carl Hagenbeck. It alone among German zoos was not required to resort to circus-like entertainments to secure its bottom line, even during the worst of the Weimar years. When the Cold War framework foisted another zoo on the capital, both zoos flourished, together attracting more than 3.5 million visitors a year.[6] Hagenbeck's admittedly spectacular zoo on the outskirts of

Hamburg, in contrast, spelled the end of Hamburg's original municipal zoo. "I believe that no city has more zoo-friendly residents than Berlin," Katharina Heinroth, the Berlin zoo's first post–World War II director, wrote in her memoirs.[7] And, at least in Germany, history confirms her observation.

Another mental image that Berliners in the late nineteenth and early twentieth centuries would have brought away from a visit to the zoo was that they were *not* colonizers. This negative finding is significant because it stands in stark contrast to the message that other prominent zoos communicated. European zoos of that era typically represented an expression of power, conquest, and justification of imperialism. Unlike US zoos, with their unobtrusive buildings integrated into pastoral settings, European zoos featured grandiose buildings, frequently in British colonial style, appearing to celebrate imperial conquest.[8] The London Zoo, which showcased the reach of the British empire by the multitude of animals on display from the colonies, is perhaps the prime example of an "imperial zoo," but this theme presents itself in other zoos, farther afield, as at the Tokyo zoo, which the Japanese government used during World War II to teach visitors about countries that it had taken over, and to celebrate "animal-soldiers" like horses and carrier pigeons that aided in conquest.[9] Although the Berlin zoo had exotic buildings, notably the elephant pagoda, the Antilopenhaus, and the Egyptian-style ostrich building, they simply reflected the animals' countries of origins and could hardly be expressions of German imperialism given that they showcased countries under British rule. Moreover, the Berlin zoo was established nearly forty years before the first association to promote a German imperial presence abroad, the German Colonial Association, came into being, or its more radical sibling under Carl Peters, the Society for German Colonization. It is true that Germany did not have much of a colonial presence to speak of, but even after 1884, when the zoo was able to acquire animals from Germany's colonies, the zoo never became a propaganda piece for colonialism. The fact that the Colonial Society banned shows from Germany's colonies after the zoo first displayed colonial subjects from Samoa in 1900 reveals that there was a discomfort with the promotion of colonialism at the zoo. During the nineteenth century, the Berlin zoo did not celebrate conquest over other peoples or promote the acquisition of colonies.

After roughly the 1870s, a visitor to the Berlin zoo would also have been unlikely to come away with the notion that humans were the masters of creation, that they had fulfilled some destiny to exert dominance over nature, including its animals. Lichtenstein, the Berlin zoo's first director, for all of his efforts to promote knowledge of the natural world, tended to agree that animals existed for humans to do with as they pleased. By the early twentieth century, however, the zoo had undergone a complete reversal, sharply criticizing the cavalier attitude of past Europeans toward animals and reorienting its work toward species preservation. Even during the Nazi era, while Hitler aimed to tame the landscape of the eastern territories, the zoo contributed to making German lands *more* wild through its introduction of an aurochs-like animal and other species and drawing public awareness to German animals on the brink of extinction.

Given these perceptions that the Berlin zoo helped to form, can the history of the Berlin zoo instruct us on the difficult question of the historic roots of Nazism? On this most important of issues, our conclusions can be suggestive, but, because of the confluence of factors that must be taken into account, perhaps that is their limit. Geoff Eley and David Blackbourn's strong criticism of the notion that Germany was uniquely preordained to a radical racial regime is based in the idea that the revolutions of 1848 did not, in fact, fail. The middle class may not have swept away the old regime as had happened in England, but they wielded enormous economic and cultural power. And their cultural perceptions, particularly their understanding of other peoples and cultures, was by no means exclusively rooted in paternalism and dominance. True, Heinrich von Treitschke, a very influential German historian of the nineteenth century and a rabid anti-Semite, dismissed Jews as "nothing but German-speaking orientals"; Jacobsen whipped his Inuit showmen; and the eminent anthropologist Rudolf Virchow observed dispassionately as his measuring instruments induced a fit of hysteria in his female Inuit subjects, but some of the striking images around the exhibits of humans suggest that not all Germans shared these views: German women weeping for their African boyfriends; a Berliner sharing a smoke with a Calmuck and reflecting on a common humanity; letters to major newspapers referring to the humans in the zoo as "equals." The subtext of the display of humans may well have been that racial differences exist, that race was indeed a concept, but that is not the whole story. Many Berliners were genuinely open to and curious about foreigners and saw them as equals. If the human zoos are an indication—and it is worth remembering that, in some cases, virtually every inhabitant of the city saw them—then the idea that Germans were somehow predisposed to authoritarianism and conquest of other peoples seems even further outdated.

In more recent times, a young polar bear at the Berlin zoo encapsulated the idea woven throughout the zoo's history that Berliners were aware of the pitfalls of their civilization. Born on December 5, 2006, to Tosca, a polar bear who had been captured in the Canadian wilderness and paraded around East Germany in the state circus before arriving in the Berlin zoo with the collapse of communism, Knut became a global sensation when his mother rejected him—the last victim of communism, went the black humor at the time. People from far beyond Germany's borders became fixated on the fate of the wobbly, helpless creature. Against the desires of animal rights groups who believed that

Zookeeper Thomas Dörflein looks at his charge, the polar bear Knut, in 2007. Knut became a global sensation and a symbol of the environmental movement until his death in 2011. *Landesarchiv Berlin, F Rep. 290 0027809_C*

humans should not intervene with Knut because they would be producing an "unnatural" bear, the Berlin zoo decided to use its keepers as surrogates for his mother. Newspapers around the world snapped pictures of Thomas Dörflein, the zookeeper tasked with raising Knut, as he cuddled the bear, gave him his bottle, and mock-wrestled with him. Dörflein became an intimate part of the Knut story, which made the news of his sudden death of a heart attack at age forty-four in September 2008 all the more shocking. Knut followers flocked to his graveside to pay their respects.[10]

Other animals, such as Bobby the gorilla and Knautschke the hippo, were beloved in Berlin, but Knut was known around the world. Sigmar Gabriel, the German minister of the environment (and since 2009 leader of the Social Democratic Party), was among the first to visit Knut. Italian prime minister Romano Prodi interrupted his state visit to drop in on the sensation. Knut appeared on the front page of *The Guardian*.[11] Annie Liebowitz joined the pilgrimage to the Berlin zoo, photographing Knut for the green issue of *Vanity Fair*. On the cover of that issue, Knut sits on an ice floe in a stylized Arctic looking up longingly, hopefully at the determined face of Leonardo di Caprio.

With the help of Liebowitz, Knut became the symbol of the environmental movement, the World Wildlife Fund panda for a new generation. He not only drew attention to the dangers to the Arctic of runaway greenhouse gas emissions,[12] but he soon also became a reminder of all wildlife threatened by our poisoned seas and clear-cut forests. Knut broke down cultural barriers. On this, it seemed, the whole world could agree: For the sake of little bears like Knut, we must stop our environmental devastation.

Then, as suddenly as his first keeper, Knut died. It was March 19, 2011, a beautiful spring Saturday, at 3:22 P.M., in front of some 700 visitors. One of the witnesses who watched in horror as the scene developed described an epileptic-type attack: "All of a sudden he stood up, then came down and for the next two minutes spun around in a circle."[13] Knut appeared to lose his balance and fell into the pool in his enclosure, floating to the surface minutes later, paws first. The zoo was cleared of its visitors so that they would not witness the grim task of removing the corpse, which in itself was daunting. Almost all of the water from the pool needed to be drained, and a crane brought in to lift the bear.[14] The zoo's curator of bears, Heiner Klös, announced at a hastily improvised press conference that the cause of death was a mystery. It would later be determined that Knut died from an infection that had eroded the lining of his brain.

An outpouring of grief followed Knut's death. "This is terrible," said the mayor of Berlin with conviction. "We had all taken him into our hearts."[15] Facebook groups such as "RIP Knut—We love you forever" sprang up. Thousands of Berliners left candles, flowers, and handwritten notes at the zoo's gates. Knut's death even rivaled major international catastrophes for headlines, such as the Fukushima nuclear meltdown in Japan a week after Knut's death and the ongoing bombing of Libya. Given these global crises, the Berlin zoo director wondered if the widespread grief over Knut's death was somewhat over the top. "I, too, liked Knut," he told a leading German daily "but more than 20,000 are dead in Japan, and there is now a war in north Africa."[16] Anxious to avoid public hysteria, the zoo quietly transported Knut's corpse to Berlin's Natural History Museum, where it was stored in the basement. In 2014, the taxidermied Knut joined Bobby, the zoo's iconic gorilla, on display at the museum.[17]

Why, we might reasonably ask, did Knut strike such a chord? A good part of the answer lies in the manner by which animals give us pause about our supposedly advanced societies. "As we gaze into the mirror [that wilderness] holds up for us," writes the American environmental historian William Cronon, "we too easily imagine that what we behold is Nature when in fact we see the reflection of our own unexamined longings and desires."[18] At numerous points in the zoo's history, Berliners came to relate deeply with the animals (and peoples) on display, visibly craving a reconnection with nature. Berliners rallied around their zoo animals like no other urban residents, rescuing them during World War I, then again during the inflationary era between the wars. They saved the animals they could during the horrors of World War II and after the war when the Soviets squeezed the city during the Berlin blockade. Thousands of East Germans pitched in to construct the Tierpark and visited it in droves for years afterward.

And so it was with Knut. In saving a little bear rejected by his mother, it seemed that Germans, and many other peoples from around the world, had a chance to do their part, however small, to right a wrong of centuries, to love what had been for too long unloved.

Raising Knut was a belated apology to the natural world. The Berlin zoo's long and storied history helps us to see that humans, having demonstrated beyond doubt their ability to subdue nature, came to view it with nostalgia. Can it be purely coincidence that the profound connection of Berliners to their zoo intensified through the bloody twentieth century? Even in the first postwar year, nearly 1 million Berliners visited what was surely the saddest zoo in existence. Those animals, in their pacifism, seemed to satisfy, even partially, a longing for a simpler time and a more tranquil world.

NOTES

Introduction

1. Joachim Oppermann, "Tod und Wiedergeburt: Über das Schicksal einiger Berliner Zootiere," *Bongo* 24 (1994): 80–81; Lutz Heck, *Animals: My Adventure* (London: Methuen, 1954), 77.
2. Oppermann, "Tod und Wiedergeburt," 81.
3. Ludwig Heck, *Papa Heck und seine Lieblinge* (Berlin: Naumann, 1931).
4. Bernhard Blaszkiewitz, "Vom Spitzhörnchen zum Orang-Utan—Hundert Jahre Primatenhaltung in Zoologischen Gärten," *Bongo* 13 (1987): 55–56.
5. "Gorilla 'Bobby' aus dem Berliner Zoo tot," *Schwedter Tageblatt*, August 2, 1935, p. 3.
6. Heck, *Animals*, 77.
7. Heck, *Papa Heck*, entry three, unpaginated.
8. See the excellent discussion in Richard Bulliet, *Hunters, Herders, and Hamburgers* (New York: Columbia University Press, 2005).
9. Richard Bulliett's enchanting *The Camel and the Wheel* (New York: Columbia University Press, 1990), reveals the importance of this beast of burden for the history of the Mideast.
10. Kathleen Kete, *The Beast in the Boudoir: Pet-Keeping in Nineteenth Century Paris* (Berkeley: University of California Press, 1994). As Kete so cuttingly summarizes: "faithful dogs took the place of faithless people" (25). Keith Thomas, one of the most influential scholars of animal-human relations, used pets and other animals to trace the changing attitudes of humans toward the animal world. See Keith Thomas, *Man and the Natural World: Changing Attitudes in England,*

1500–1800 (London: Allen Lane, 1983). Jennifer Mason investigates pets and middle-class America in *Civilized Creatures: Urban Animals, Sentimental Culture and American Literature, 1850–1900* (Baltimore: Johns Hopkins University Press, 2005). Pets are also central in James Serpell, *In the Company of Animals: A Study of Human-Animal Relationships* (Cambridge: Cambridge University Press, 1996). More generally on the advent of animal rights groups as a reflection of human sympathies to animals, see Rob Boddice, *A History of Attitudes and Behaviours towards Animals in Eighteenth- and Nineteenth-Century Britain* (Lewiston: Mellen, 2009). Nigel Rothfels's pioneering work on zoos remains indispensable: *Savages and Beasts: The Birth of the Modern Zoo* (Baltimore: Johns Hopkins University Press, 2002). An important compilation of animals in human history is Linda Kalof and Brigitte Resl, eds., *A Cultural History of Animals*, 6 vols. (Oxford: Oxford University Press, 2007).

11. Harro Strehlow, "Zoological Gardens of Western Europe," in *Zoo and Aquarium History*, ed. Vernon Kisling Jr. (New York: CRC Press, 2001), 85.

12. Strehlow, "Zoological Gardens," 84.

13. Annelore Rieke-Müller, "Die Gründung Zoologischer Gärten um die Mitte des 19: Jahrhunderts im deutschsprachigen Raum," in Lothar Dittrich, Dietrich von Engelhardt, and Annelore Rieke-Müller, *Die Kulturgeschichte des Zoos* (Berlin: VWB, 2001), 83, 240.

14. Richard Burkhardt, "Constructing the Zoo: Science, Society, and Animal Nature at the Paris Menagerie, 1794–1838," in *Animals in Human Histories*, ed. Mary Henninger-Voss (Rochester, NY University of Rochester Press, 2002), 233.

15. Harriet Ritvo, *The Animal Estate: The English and Other Creatures in the Victorian Age* (Cambridge, MA: Harvard University Press, 1987), promotes the idea of the "imperial zoo." Recently, Takashi Ito has taken issue with this view in *London Zoo and the Victorians, 1838–1859* (Woodbridge: Boydell Press, 2014).

16. Harriet Ritvo, "The Order of Nature," in *New Worlds, New Animals*, ed. R. J. Hoage and William Deiss (Baltimore: Johns Hopkins University Press, 1996), 45.

17. Donna Mehos, *Science and Culture for Members Only: The Amsterdam Zoo Artis in the 19th Century* (Amsterdam: Amsterdam University Press, 2006), 11.

18. Horst Gleiss, *Unter Robben, Gnus und Tigerschlangen* (Wedel: Natura et Patria Verlag, 1967), 14.

19. Stanley Smyth Flower, *Report on Mission to Europe, 1905* (Cairo: National Printing Department, 1906), 10–11.

20. Annelore Rieke-Müller and Lothar Dittrich, *Der Löwe brüllt nebenan* (Cologne: Böhlau, 1998), 43–44.

21. Rachel Poliquin, *The Breathless Zoo: Taxidermy and the Cultures of Longing* (University Park: Pennsylvania State University Press, 2012), 19.

22. John Berger, *About Looking* (New York: Vintage International, 1991), 11.

23. Nigel Rothfels, *Savages and Beasts: The Birth of the Modern Zoo* (Baltimore: Johns Hopkins University Press, 2002), 1.

24. Hergé, *Tintin in the Congo* (London: Egmont, 2005), 27.

25. "South Africa Fights Rhinoceros Poachers," *New York Times International Weekly*, August 9–10, 2014, 14.

26. Because of their ability to shed light on human history, animal-human studies have gained much credence in recent years. Harriet Ritvo deserves special mention here for moving animal studies into mainstream academia. In *The Animal Estate,* Ritvo illuminates concepts such as social status and empire through animal-human examples like pet-keeping, breeding of domesticated animals, and the London zoo. Britons recognized the London zoo, she argues, for what Sir Stamford Raffles and other founders in the London Zoological Society intended it—"the emblem of British domination over its colonial empire" (231). Although it did not set out to investigate animals per se, Jared Diamond's sweeping blockbuster *Guns, Germs, and Steel: The Fates of Human Societies* (New York: W. W. Norton, 1997) could hardly have argued more eloquently for the importance of animals in human history. The close proximity of Europeans to domesticated animals—a scenario that could not be replicated by the aboriginal peoples of the Americas because of the absence of animals that could be domesticated—led to the transfer of animal diseases to Europeans, with the Europeans subsequently developing immunities. It was the absence of those immunities, a result simply of the randomness of distribution of the earth's fauna, that proved so devastating to the peoples of the Americas.

27. Books directly about the Berlin zoo have mostly been written by the Berlin zoo's Klös family dynasty: Heinz-Georg Klös, *Von der Menagerie zum Tierparadies: 125 Jahre Zoo Berlin* (Berlin: Haude & Spenersche, 1969); Heinz-Georg Klös and Ursula Klös, *Der Berliner Zoo im Spiegel seiner Bauten, 1841–1989* (Berlin: Heenemann, 1990). A slightly updated version of *Von der Menagerie* is Heinz-Georg Klös, Ursula Klös, and Hans Frädrich, *Die Arche Noah an der Spree, 1844–1994: 150 Jahre Zoologischer Garten Berlin* (Berlin: FAB Verlag, 1994). More academic treatments of German zoos in general are found in Lothar Dittrich and Annelore Rieke-Müller, *Der Löwe brüllt nebenan*; Christina Wessely, *Künstliche Tiere: Zoologische Gärten und urbane Moderne* (Berlin: Kulturverlag Kadmos, 2008); Mitchell Ash, ed., *Mensch, Tier und Zoo: Der Tiergarten Schönbrunn im internationalen Vergleich vom 18. Jahrhundert bis heute* (Vienna: Böhlau Verlag, 2008).

28. Subsequent authors have challenged their idea that zoos originated in the bourgeois environment, pointing to their location in royal residences and the fact that not all zoos originated from bourgeois initiatives, as was the case with the Munich zoo. See Annelore Rieke-Müller and Lothar Dittrich, *Der Löwe brüllt nebenan*, 4–7.

29. Alexandra Richie, *Faust's Metropolis: A History of Berlin* (New York: Carroll & Graf, 1998).

30. Wolfgang Ribbe, *Geschichte Berlins,* 2 vols. (Berlin: Berliner Wissenschafts Verlag, 2002).

31. It is a similar phenomenon in the United States, where the zoo visitorship of 130 million is more than attendance at baseball, football, and hockey games combined. Elizabeth Hanson, *Animal Attractions: Nature on Display in American Zoos* (Princeton, NJ: Princeton University Press, 2004), 2; Arnold Arluke and Clinton Sanders, *Regarding Animals* (Philadelphia: Temple University Press, 1996), 1.

Chapter 1

1. Lothar Dittrich, "Fürstliche Menagerien im deutschsprachigen Raum ab den 1760er Jahren bis zur Gründung der Zoologischen Gärten Mitte des neunzehnten Jahrhunderts," in *Die Kulturgeschichte des Zoos*, ed. Lothar Dittrich, Dietrich von Engelhardt, and Annelore Rieke-Müller (Berlin: Verlag für Wissenschaft und Bildung, 2001), 70.

2. Mary Henninger-Voss, *Animals in Human Histories* (Rochester: University of Rochester Press, 2002), 231.

3. Helmut Zedelmaier and Michael Kamp, *Hellabrunn: Geschichte und Geschichten des Münchner Tierparks* (Munich: Bassermann, 2011), 17.

4. Harro Strehlow, "Zoological Gardens of Western Europe," in *Zoo and Aquarium History: Ancient Collections to Zoological Gardens*, ed. Vernon Kisling (New York: CRC Press, 2001), 89.

5. The notable exception here was the royal menagerie at Vienna-Schönbrunn, established in 1752 and still the site of the oldest continuous public display of exotic animals. Dittrich, "Fürstliche Menagerien," 70.

6. Harro Strehlow, "Zoos and Aquariums of Berlin," in *New Worlds, New Animals*, ed. R. J. Haage and William Deiss (Baltimore: Johns Hopkins University Press, 1996), 63. When the Berlin zoo was founded in 1844, it became the second example after Vienna of a transition from a sovereign's private menagerie into the more systematic and public exhibits of a zoo. See Strehlow, "Zoological Gardens," 83–89.

7. Dittrich, "Fürstliche Menagerien," 75.

8. Harro Strehlow, " 'Das Merkwürdigste auf der Insel waren mir die lebendigen Thiere': Ein Besuch Christian Ludwig Brehms in der Menagerie auf der Pfaueninsel im Oktober 1832," *Bongo* 24 (1994): 31; Heinz-Georg Klös, *Von der Menagerie zum Tierparadies: 125 Jahre Zoo Berlin* (Berlin: Haude & Spenersche, 1969), 21–23.

9. Strehlow, "Das Merkwürdigste," 31.

10. Strehlow, "Das Merkwürdigste," 38.

11. Sigrid Dittrich, "Exoten an den Höfen von Renaissancefürsten und ihre Darstellung in der Malerei," in *Die Kulturgeschichte des Zoos*, ed. Lothar Dittrich, Dietrich von Engelhardt, and Annelore Rieke-Müller (Berlin: Verlag für Wissenschaft und Bildung, 2001), 12.

12. Klös, *Von der Menagerie*, 17. In the original German: Um das Rhinzeros zu sehen (<u>erzählte</u> mir mein Freund), beschloss ich auszugehen.

13. Strehlow, "Zoological Gardens of Western Europe," 81; Florence Pieters, "The Menagerie of the White Elephant in Amsterdam," in *Die Kulturgeschichte des Zoos*, ed. Lothar Dittrich, Dietrich von Engelhardt, and Annelore Rieke-Müller (Berlin: Verlag für Wissenschaft und Bildung, 2001), 60.

14. Hinrich Lichtenstein, *Reisen im südlichen Africa in den Jahren 1803, 1804, 1805 und 1806* (Berlin: C. Salfeld, 1811), vol. 1, p. 5. This passage appears on page 4 of the English translation of this book, *Travels in Southern Africa in the Years 1803, 1804, 1805 and 1806* (London: Henry Colburn, 1812).

15. Lichtenstein, *Reisen im südlichen Africa,* vol. 1, 412.

16. Annelore Rieke-Müller, "Angewandte Zoologie und die Wahrnehmung exotischer Natur in der zweiten Hälfte des 18. und 19. Jahrhundert," *History and Philosophy of the Life Sciences* 17 (1995): 476.

17. Lichtenstein, *Reisen im südlichen Africa,* vol. 2, 573–574.

18. Lichtenstein, *Reisen im südlichen Africa,* vol. 1, 248.

19. Lichtenstein, *Reisen im südlichen Africa,* vol. 2, 318.

20. Lichtenstein, *Reisen im südlichen Africa,* vol. 1, 396–397. This passage is from the English translation *Travels in Southern Africa in the Years 1803, 1804, 1805 and 1806* (London: Henry Colburn, 1812), 244–245.

21. Gottfried Mauersberger, "Der Gründer des Berliner Zoologischen Gartens, Martin Hinrich Lichtenstein (1780–1857): Eine biographische Skizze," *Bongo* 23 (1994): 7.

22. Mauersberger, "Der Gründer des Berliner Zoologischen Gartens," 17.

23. Annelore Rieke-Müller and Lothar Dittrich, eds., *Der Löwe brüllt nebenan: Die Gründung Zoologischer Gärten im deutschsprachigen Raum 1833–1869* (Cologne: Böhlau Verlag, 1998), 54.

24. Mauersberger, "Der Gründer des Berliner Zoologischen Gartens," 29–30.

25. Paul Lawrence Farber, *Finding Order in Nature* (Baltimore: Johns Hopkins University Press, 2000), 35.

26. David Blackbourn, "Germany and the Birth of the Modern World," GHI Lecture delivered May 17, 2012, p. 13, http://www.ghi-dc.org/files/publications/bulletin/bu051/009_bu51.pdf.

27. Andrea Wulf, *The Invention of Nature: Alexander von Humboldt's New World* (New York: Knopf, 2015), 193.

28. Walter Bußmann, *Zwischen Preußen und Deutschland. Friedrich Wilhelm IV. Eine Biographie* (Berlin: Siedler Verlag, 1990), 340.

29. Andreas Daum, *Wissenschaftspopularisierung im 19. Jahrhundert: Bürgerliche Kultur, naturwissenschaftliche Bildung und die deutsche Öffentlichkeit, 1848–1914* (Munich: Oldenbourg, 1998), 276.

30. Laura Dassow Walls, *The Passage to Cosmos: Alexander von Humboldt and the Shaping of America* (Chicago: University of Chicago Press, 2009), 218.

31. Walls, *The Passage to Cosmos*, 218.

32. Ilse Jahn, "Zoologische Gärten—Zoologische Museen: Parallelen ihrer Entstehung," *Bongo* 24 (1994), 23.

33. Rieke-Müller and Dittrich, *Der Löwe brüllt nebenan*, 22.

34. GStA, HA Rep. 76, Va Sekt. 2, Tit X, Nr. 49, Folio 9, July 20, 1833, letter from Lichtenstein to the king.

35. GStA, HA Rep. 76, Va Sekt. 2, Tit X, Nr. 49, Folio 9, July 20, 1833, letter from Lichtenstein to the king.

36. GStA, ZMBS I, Blätter 63–64. Undated letter from Lichtenstein to his wife.

37. Rieke-Müller and Dittrich, *Der Löwe brüllt nebenan*, 37.

38. GStA, ZMBS I, Blatt 59, September 3, 1883, letter from Lichtenstein.

39. GStA, ZMBS I, Blatt 61, September 17, 1883, letter from Lichtenstein to his wife.

40. GStA, ZMBS I, Blätter 74–77, October 18, 1883, letter from Lichtenstein to Herr von Maltzahn, Intendant of royal palaces and gardens.

41. GStA, ZMBS I, Blatt 74–77, October 18, 1883, letter from Lichtenstein to Herr von Maltzahn, Intendant of royal palaces and gardens.

42. GStA, ZMBS I, Blatt 65, October 8, 1883, letter from Lichtenstein to his wife. GStA, ZMBS I, October 18, 1883, letter from Lichtenstein to the king.

43. GStA, ZMBS I, Blatt 68, October 14, 1883, letter from Lichtenstein to his wife.

44. GStA, ZMBS I, October 18, 1883, letter from Lichtenstein to the king.

45. Mauersberger, "Der Gründer des Berliner Zoologischen Gartens," 16.

46. Donna Mehos, *Science and Culture for Members Only: The Amsterdam Zoo Artis in the 19th Century* (Amsterdam: Amsterdam University Press, 2006), 82–102.

47. Mehos, *Science and Culture for Members Only*, 24.

48. David Barclay, *Friedrich Wilhelm IV and the Prussian Monarchy 1840–1861* (Oxford: Oxford University Press, 1995), 42.

49. Barclay, *Friedrich Wilhelm IV*, 42.

50. Bußmann, *Zwischen Preußen und Deutschland*, 346.

51. Barclay, *Friedrich Wilhelm IV*, 43.

52. Barclay, *Friedrich Wilhelm IV*, 66.

53. Ulrike Leitner, ed., *Alexander von Humboldt/Friedrich Wilhelm IV, Briefwechsel* (Berlin: de Gruyter, 2013), 434.

54. Bußmann, *Zwischen Preußen und Deutschland*, 350.

55. Bußmann, *Zwischen Preußen und Deutschland*, 348.

56. Alexandra Richie, *Faust's Metropolis: A History of Berlin* (New York: Carroll & Graf, 1998), 129; Julius Schoeps, "Berlin wird Weltstadt," in *Berlin: Geschichte einer Stadt*, ed. Julius Schoeps (Berlin: be.bra verlag, 2001), 59.

57. Günter Richter, "Zwischen Revolution und Reichsgründung," in *Geschichte Berlins*, ed. Wolfgang Ribbe (Berlin: Berliner Wissenschafts-Verlag, 2002), 605.

58. Schoeps, "Berlin wird Weltstadt," 60.

59. Schoeps, "Berlin wird Weltstadt," 58; Richie, *Faust's Metropolis*, 126.

60. Malve Gräfin Rothkirch, *Der "Romantiker" auf dem Preussenthron* (Düsseldorf: Droste, 1990).

61. Barclay, *Friedrich Wilhelm IV*, 28.

62. Bußmann, *Zwischen Preußen und Deutschland*, 436.

63. See Eva Heinecke, *König Friedrich Wilhelm IV von Preußen und die Errichtung des Neuen Museums 1841–1860 in Berlin* (Halle: Universitätsverlag Halle-Wittenberg, 2011).

64. Friedrich Wilhelm, deeply devoted to his Protestant faith, spent his reign building breakwaters of religion against the revolutionary storm, some of them, like the towering Cologne Cathedral, not just metaphorical. A regent by the grace of God, he famously refused the imperial crown offered to him by the liberal Frankfurt delegates as a "dog collar." Barclay, *Friedrich Wilhelm IV*, 74, 194–195.

65. Klös, *Von der Menagerie*, 28.

66. Rieke-Müller and Dittrich, *Der Löwe brüllt nebenan*, 120. Cattle, one of the most likely species for cross-breeding with foreign species, were initially in short supply at the Berlin zoo. There were only two species of cattle from 1844 to 1867, when a third was added. See Heinz-Sigurd Raethel, "Der Berliner Zoo und seine Rindersammlung 1843–1991," *Bongo* 20 (1992): 45.

67. Rieke-Müller and Dittrich, *Der Löwe brüllt nebenan*, 115.

68. Harriet Ritvo, "The Order of Nature," in *New Worlds, New Animals*, ed. R. J. Hoage and William Deiss (Baltimore: Johns Hopkins University Press, 1996), 44–47.

69. Klös, *Von der Menagerie*, 36.

70. GstAD, I. HA Rep. 89 Nr. 31823 GZ, Blatt 3, June 30, 1841, letter from the king to Lichtenstein.

71. GstAD, I. HA Rep. 89 Nr. 31823 GZ, Blatt 4, August 18, 1841, letter from Ladenberg, Lichtenstein, and Lenne to the king.

72. GstAD, I. HA Rep. 89 Nr. 31823 GZ, Blätter 13–14, September 8, 1841, letter from the king; GStAD, I. HA Rep. 89 Nr. 31823 GZ Blätter 28–29, February 13, 1843, letter from the king to Minister of State Eichhorn.

73. GstAD, I. HA Rep. 89 Nr. 31823 GZ, Blätter 25–27, December 4, 1842, draft letter from Eichhorn to the king.

74. Klös, *Von der Menagerie*, 35.

75. Mauersberger, "Der Gründer des Berliner Zoologischen Gartens," 15.

76. GstAD, I. HA Rep. 89 Nr. 31823 GZ Blatt 30, August 13, 1843, letter from Alexander von Humboldt to the king.

77. See Hans Frädrich and Harro Strehlow, "Der Zoo und die Wissenschaft," *Bongo* 24 (1994): 161–180.

78. Strehlow, "Zoos and Aquariums of Berlin," 65.

79. On this area of the Tiergarten as raw nature, see Mauersberger, "Der Gründer des Berliner Zoologischen Gartens," 15.

80. Klös, *Von der Menagerie*, 31.

81. Klös, *Von der Menagerie*, 34.

82. Klös, *Von der Menagerie*, 34.

83. On Richard Lepsius, see Hartmut Mehlitz, *Richard Lepsius: Ägypten und die Ordnung der Wissenschaft* (Berlin: Kulturverlag Kadmos, 2011).

84. GstAD, I. HA Rep. 89 Nr. 31823 GZ Blätter 31–35, July 26, 1843, letter from Lichtenstein to unknown.

85. GstAD, I. HA Rep. 89 Nr. 31823 GZ Blätter 31–35, July 26, 1843, letter from Lichtenstein to unknown.

86. Richie, *Faust's Metropolis,* 150.

87. Richie, *Faust's Metropolis,* 150.

88. GstAD, I. HA Rep. 89 Nr. 31823 GZ Blätter 44–51, March 27, 1845, letter from Eichhorn to the king.

89. Klös, *Von der Menagerie,* 38.

90. Schoeps, "Berlin wird Weltstadt," 57.

91. Ilja Mieck, "Von der Reformzeit zur Revolution" in *Geschichte Berlins,* ed. Wolfgang Ribbe (Berlin: Berliner Wissenschafts-Verlag, 2002), 576.

92. GstAD, I. HA Rep. 89 Nr. 31823 GZ Blätter 55–58, July 10, 1846, letter from Eichhorn to the king.

93. In contrast, the zoos in Frankfurt and Cologne were far less dependent on the support of individuals employed by the state. See Rieke-Müller and Dittrich, *Der Löwe brüllt nebenan,* 224.

94. GstAD, I. HA Rep. 89 Nr. 31823 GZ Blätter 55–58, July 10, 1846, letter from Eichhorn to the king.

95. Jutta Buchner, *Kultur mit Tieren* (Münster: Waxmann Verlag, 1996), 154.

96. Two weeks after the zoo's grand opening, an industrial fair in the armory exhibited nearly 520,000 thalers worth of goods from more than 600 Berlin manufacturers. Schoeps, "Berlin wird Weltstadt," 58.

97. Mustafa Haikal and Jörg Junhold, *Auf der Spur des Löwen: 125 Jahre Zoo Leipzig* (Leipzig: Zoo Leipzig, 2003), 80.

98. On the origins of these German zoos, see Horst Gleiss, *Unter Robben, Gnus und Tigerschlangen* (Wedel: Natura et Patria Verlag, 1967); Mustafa Haikal and Winfried Gensch, *Der Gesang des Orang-utans: Die Geschichte des Dresdner Zoos* (Dresden: Edition Sächsische Zeitung, 2011); Ludwig Baumgarten, *Chronik Zoologischer Garten Halle* (Halle: Zoologischer Garten Halle GmbH, 2001); Victor Goering, *Die Entwicklung des Zoologischen Gartens zu Frankfurt a.M. von 1858 bis 1908* (Frankfurt: Kommissionsverlag, 1908); Lothar Dittrich and Annelore Rieke-Müller, *Ein Garten für Menschen und Tiere* (Hannover: Verlagsgesellschaft Grütter, 1990); Peter Mühling, *Der alte Nürnberger Tiergarten 1912–1939* (Nürnberg: Druckhaus, 1987).

99. Goering, *Die Entwicklung des Zoologischen Gartens zu Frankfurt a.M,* 5–6.

100. Dittrich and Rieke-Müller, *Ein Garten für Menschen und Tiere,* 19–20.

101. GstAD, I. HA Rep. 89 Nr. 31823 GZ Blätter 55–58, July 10, 1846, letter from Eichhorn to the king.

102. GstAD, I. HA Rep. 89 Nr. 31823 GZ Blätter 55–58, July 10, 1846, letter from Eichhorn to the king. Underlined in original.

103. GstAD, I. HA Rep. 89 Nr. 31823 GZ Blätter 55–58 July 10, 1846, letter from Eichhorn to the king.

104. Harriet Ritvo, *The Animal Estate: The English and Other Creatures in the Victorian Age* (Cambridge, MA: Harvard University Press, 1987), 211.

105. GstAD, I. HA Rep. 89 Nr. 31823 GZ Blätter 77–84, May 17, 1846, letter from executive committee to the king. In 1855, more than 22,000 pupils visited the zoo.

106. See Annelore Rieke-Müller, "Die Gründung Zoologischer Gärten um die Mitte des 19: Jahrhunderts im deutschsprachigen Raum," in *Die Kulturgeschichte des Zoos*, ed. Lothar Dittrich, Dietrich von Engelhardt, and Annelore Rieke-Müller (Berlin: VWB, 2001), 90.

107. GstAD, I. HA Rep. 89 Nr. 31823 GZ Blatt 59, July 21, 1846, letter from the king to Eichhorn.

108. Klös, *Von der Menagerie*, 44.

109. Klös, *Von der Menagerie,* 45.

110. Klös, *Von der Menagerie,* 45.

111. Jonathan Sperber, *The European Revolutions* (Cambridge: Cambridge University Press, 2005), 110.

112. Klös, *Von der Menagerie*, 45.

113. Klös, *Von der Menagerie*, 39.

114. The first three zoo guides, from 1844, 1849, and 1851, contain almost word-for-word identical descriptions. The order in which the animals are presented is, however, different based on new pathways through the zoo. LA-B, Nat 6, *Der Führer im zoologischen Garten zu Berlin. Beschreibung der Tiere* (Berlin: L. Wehl & Comp., 1849, 1851).

115. On the German approach to nature, see in particular David Blackbourn, *The Conquest of Nature* (New York: W. W. Norton, 2006).

116. Farber, *Finding Order in Nature*, 11; Rachel Poliquin, *The Breathless Zoo* (University Park: Pennsylvania State University Press, 2012), 116.

117. Farber, *Finding Order in Nature*, 51.

118. Jahn, "Zoologische Gärten," 14.

119. Jahn, "Zoologische Gärten," 16.

120. Jahn, "Zoologische Gärten," 9.

121. Hannelore Landsberg, "Das erste Zootier des Museums—eine Mandrill? Die Gründung des Zoologischen Gartens und dessen Bedeutung für die Sammlungen des Zoologischen Museums der Berliner Universität," *Bongo* 24 (1994): 98.

122. Landsberg, "Zootier des Museums," 97. Schomburgk's voyage is recounted in detail in his memoir of the trip: Richard Schomburgk, *Reisen in Britisch-Guiana in den Jahren 1840–1844* (Leipzig: J. J. Weber, 1848).

123. Landsberg, "Zootier des Museums," 102.

124. Cornelia Essner, *Deutsche Afrikareisende im neunzehnten Jahrhundert* (Wiesbaden: Steiner, 1985), 76; Mauersberger, "Der Gründer des Berliner Zoologischen Gartens," 20.

125. On this journey, see H. Scurla, *Alexander von Humboldt—sein Leben und Wirken* (Berlin: Verlag der Nation, 1959).

126. Farber, *Finding Order in Nature*, 91. Curiously, only the zoos in Dresden and Hannover were founded by nature societies. Rieke-Müller and Dittrich, *Der Löwe brüllt nebenan*, 226.

127. Daum, *Wissenschaftspopularisierung im 19. Jahrhundert*, 89. The Munich animal protection society was the largest in Europe in 1843, at more than 3,600 members. See Anne Dreesbach, "'Die Gefangenen unserer zoologischen Gärten:' Der Tierpark im Spiegel der Kritik," in *Nilpferde an der Isar: Eine Geschichte des Tierparks Hellabrunn in München,* ed. Michael Kamp and Helmut Zedelmaier (Munich: Buchendorf Verlag), 249. In 1888, the Urania society was founded, complete with public theaters to promote understanding of the natural world through images. The pre-Internet generation of Germans will instantly recognize the "Urania" theater as a site of breathtaking slideshows by modern explorers. These are the voluntary associations at the core of David Blackbourn and Geoff Eley's thoughtful claim that Germany did indeed experience a bourgeois revolution in the nineteenth century in the form of civil society rather than as political power. See David Blackbourn and Geoff Eley, *The Peculiarities of German History* (New York: Oxford University Press, 1984), 190–195.

128. Daum, *Wissenschaftspopularisierung im 19. Jahrhundert*, 346.

129. Rieke-Müller and Dittrich, *Der Löwe brüllt nebenan,* 48; Daum, *Wissenschaftspopularisierung im 19. Jahrhundert*, 339.

130. Although the Hamburg Zoo was eventually closed in favor of Hagenbeck's Tierpark, it was very successful in the nineteenth century, surpassed only by Berlin in its variety of animals. See Hermann Reichenbach, "A Tale of Two Zoos," in *New Worlds, New Animals,* ed. R. J. Hoage and William Deiss (Baltimore: Johns Hopkins University Press, 1996), 52.

131. Annelore Rieke-Müller, "Die Gründung zoologischer Gärten um die Mitte des 19. Jahrhunderts im deutschsprachigm Raum," in *Die Kulturgeschichte des Zoos,* ed. Lothar Dittrich, Dietrich von Engelhardt, and Annelore Rieke-Müller (Berlin: Verlag für Wissenschaft und Bildung, 2001), 89–90.

132. On the importance of illustrations in portraying the "exotic," see David Ciarlo, *Advertising Empire* (Cambridge, MA: Harvard University Press, 2011), 126.

133. Daum, *Wissenschaftspopularisierung im 19. Jahrhundert*, 238, 337.

134. Richie, *Faust's Metropolis*, 126.

135. Farber, *Finding Order in Nature*, 30.

136. Donna Mehos, "The Rise of Serious Science at the Amsterdam Zoo *Artis*," in *Die Kulturgeschichte des Zoos,* ed. Lothar Dittrich, Dietrich von Engelhardt,

and Annelore Rieke-Müller (Berlin: Verlag für Wissenschaft und Bildung, 2001), 109.

137. Quoted in Rieke-Müller, "Angewandte Zoologie," 479.

138. Rieke-Müller, "Angewandte Zoologie," 461–478.

139. Quoted in Richard Leffer, ed. *Deutsche Kolonialzeitung* (Berlin: Verlag des deutschen Kolonialvereins, 1886).

140. Klös, *Von der Menagerie*, 48.

141. GStAD, I. HA Rep. 76 Vc, Sekt 1 Tit XXII Nr. 120, Bd. 2, June 17, 1865, letter from Peters to Herr Dr. von Mühler.

142. Wilhelm Peters, *Naturwissenschaftliche Reise nach Mossambique* (Berlin: G. Reimer, 1862), 1–2.

143. Peters, *Naturwissenschaftliche Reise*, 180–181.

144. The best work on the history of taxidermy is Poliquin, *The Breathless Zoo.*

145. Peters, *Naturwissenschaftliche Reise*, 180–181.

146. Peters, *Naturwissenschaftliche Reise*, 178.

147. GStAD, I. HA Rep. 76 Vc, Sekt 1 Tit XXII Nr. 120, Bd. 2, January 19, 1864, letter from Peters to Herr Dr. von Mühler.

148. Klös, *Von der Menagerie*, 55–56.

149. GstAD, Zoologisches Museum, S I, Verwaltungsakte Gutachten, April 2, 1868, report by Peters on the zoological garden.

150. Schoeps, "Berlin wird Weltstadt," 56.

151. Mieck, "Von der Reformzeit zur Revolution," 590.

152. Schoeps, "Berlin wird Weltstadt," 56.

153. Fr. Fr., "Der zoologische Garten in Berlin," *Die Gartenlaube* (1873): 262, http://de.wikisource.org/wiki/Der_zoologische_Garten_in_Berlin.

Chapter 2

1. "Die Drei-Kaiser-Tage in Berlin," *Illustrirte Zeitung*, no. 1527, October 5, 1872, 247.

2. Georg Horn, "Aus der Drei-Kaiser-Woche," *Die Gartenlaube,* no. 42 (1872): 696.

3. Bismarck's classic maneuvering lay at the root of inviting the three emperors to meet in Berlin. See Jonathan Steinberg, *Bismarck: A Life* (New York: Oxford University Press, 2011), 328.

4. Heinz Georg Klös*, Von der Menagerie zum Tierparadies: 125 Jahre Zoo Berlin* (Berlin: Haude & Spenersche, 1969), 67.

5. "Die Drei-Kaiser-Tage in Berlin," *Illustrirte Zeitung*, no. 1527, October 5, 1872, 250. See also Heinz-Sigurd Raethel, "Das Antilopenhaus im Berliner Zoo—Ein Tierhaus erzählt Geschichte," *Bongo* 14 (1988): 78–79.

6. Heinrich Leutemann, "Beim schwarzen Jack im zoologischen Garten in Berlin," *Die Gartenlaube* 4 (1873): 58.

7. Heinz Georg Klös and Ursula Klös, *Der Berliner Zoo im Spiegel seiner Bauten, 1841–1989* (Berlin: Heenemann, 1990), 58. See also Theodor Knottnerus-Meyer, "Neues vom Zoologischen Garten zu Berlin," *Der Zoologische Garten* 46, no. 2 (1905): 34–36.

8. Klös and Klös, *Der Berliner Zoo im Spiegel seiner Bauten,* 57.

9. May 17, 1891, *VZ,* no. 225, Supplement 1, midday edition, p. 1.

10. Klös and Klös, *Der Berliner Zoo im Spiegel seiner Bauten,* 62.

11. "Der zoologische Garten in Berlin," *Die Gartenlaube* 16 (1873): 262.

12. Raethel, "Das Antilopenhaus," 74.

13. Lothar Dittrich and Annelore Rieke-Müller, *Ein Garten für Menschen und Tiere: 125 Jahre Zoo Hannover* (Hannover: Verlaggesellschaft Grütter, 1990), 13.

14. August Woldt, "Das Elephantanhaus im Berliner zoologischen Garten," *Die Gartenlaube* 52 (1882): 860.

15. Theodor Knottnerus-Meyer, "Neues vom Zoologischen Garten zu Berlin," *Der Zoologische Garten* 46, no. 2 (1905): 34–36.

16. "Das Gründungsfieber der Jetztzeit," *Die Gartenlaube* 36 (1872): 592–593.

17. Dittrich and Annelore Rieke-Müller, *Carl Hagenbeck: Tierhandel und Schaustellungen im Deutschen Kaiserreich* (Frankfurt: Peter Lang, 1998), 30.

18. Carl Hagenbeck, *Von Tieren und Menschen* (Leipzig: Paul List Verlag, 1967), 7. Hagenbeck's memoirs have gone through several editions since they were first published in 1908. The version I have used was issued in the German Democratic Republic. The much abridged English version pales compared to the German version.

19. Dittrich and Rieke-Müller, *Carl Hagenbeck,* 92–93.

20. Dittrich and Rieke-Müller, *Carl Hagenbeck,* 109–110.

21. Haug von Kuenheim, *Carl Hagenbeck* (Hamburg: Ellert & Richter Verlag, 2009), 11.

22. Ludwig Zukowsky, *Tiere um große Männer* (Frankfurt: Moritz Diesterweg, 1938), 106.

23. Kuenheim, *Carl Hagenbeck,* 157.

24. Eric Ames, *Carl Hagenbeck's Empire of Entertainments* (Seattle: University of Washington Press, 2008), 12, 23; Kuenheim, *Carl Hagenbeck,* 6–9; Dittrich and Rieke-Müller, *Carl Hagenbeck,* 233.

25. Herman Reichenbach, "Carl Hagenbeck's Tierpark and Modern Zoological Gardens," *Journal of the Society for the Bibliography of Natural History* 9. no. 4 (1980): 573.

26. Hagenbeck, *Von Tieren,* 25.

27. Hagenbeck, *Von Tieren,* 30.

28. Hagenbeck, *Von Tieren,* 31.

29. Kuenheim, *Carl Hagenbeck,* 51.

30. Hagenbeck, *Von Tieren,* 37.

31. E. Kanngiesser, "Karl Hagenbeck: Ein Erinnerungsbild," *Der Zoologische Garten* 54, no. 5 (1913): 122.

32. Ames, *Hagenbeck's Empire of Entertainment,* 28.

33. Dittrich and Rieke-Müller, *Carl Hagenbeck,* 101.

34. Elizabeth Hanson, *Animal Attractions: Nature on Display in American Zoos* (Princeton, NJ: Princeton University Press, 2004), 80

35. Reichenbach, "Carl Hagenbeck's Tierpark," 574.

36. Annemarie Lange, *Das Wilhelminische Berlin. Zwischen Jahrhundertwende und Novemberrevolution* (Berlin: Dietz, 1988), 59.

37. Nigel Rothfels, *Savages and Beasts: The Birth of the Modern Zoo* (Baltimore: Johns Hopkins University Press, 2002), 49.

38. As quoted in Kuenheim, *Carl Hagenbeck,* 80.

39. Hagenbeck, *Von Tieren,* 111.

40. As quoted in Rothfels, *Savages and Beasts,* 63.

41. Reprinted in Rothfels, *Savages and Beasts,* 66.

42. Hugo von Koppenfels, "Meine Jagden auf Gorillas," *Die Gartenlaube* 25 (1877): 419. Koppenfels's claim was a direct attack on Paul du Chaillu, whose accounts of his encounters with gorillas were brought into question by the academic community. See Monte Reel, *Between Man and Beast* (New York: Doubleday, 2013).

43. As quoted in Rothfels, *Savages and Beasts,* 22.

44. Nigel Rothfels, "Catching Animals," in *Animals in Human Histories,* ed. Mary Henninger-Voss (Rochester: University of Rochester Press, 2002), 210.

45. As quoted in Kuenheim, *Carl Hagenbeck,* 106.

46. Hagenbeck, *Von Tieren,* 162–163.

47. Kanngiesser, "Karl Hagenbeck. Ein Erinnerungsbild," 122; Kuenheim, *Carl Hagenbeck,* 130; Dittrich and Rieke-Müller, *Carl Hagenbeck,* 51.

48. David Blackbourn, *The Conquest of Nature* (New York: W. W. Norton, 2006), 173.

49. As quoted in Kuenheim, *Carl Hagenbeck,* 92.

50. Dittrich and Rieke-Müller, *Carl Hagenbeck,* 31–32.

51. Dittrich and Rieke-Müller, *Carl Hagenbeck,* 116.

52. He may well have been influenced by his recent business partners Barnum and Bailey, who, from the inception of the "greatest show on earth," had incorporated "exotic" peoples, the first of which were Fiji "cannibals." David Ciarlo, *Advertising Empire: Race and Visual Culture in Imperial Germany* (Cambridge, MA Harvard University Press, 2011), 85.

53. Quoted in Stefan Goldmann, "Wilde in Europa: Aspekte und Orte ihrer Zurschaustellung," in *Wir und die Wilden: Einblicke in eine kannibalische Beziehung,* ed. Thomas Theye (Hamburg: Rowohlt, 1985), 243.

54. Anne Dreesbach, *Gezähmte Wilde: Die Zurschaustellung "exotischer Menschen" in Deutschland, 1870–1940* (Frankfurt: Campus Verlag, 2005), 24.

55. Raymond Corbey, "Ethnographic Showcases, 1870–1930," in *The Decolonization of Imagination,* ed. Jan Nederveen Pieterse and Bhikhu Parekh (Ann Arbor: University of Michigan Press, 1995), 66.

56. Dreesbach, *Gezähmte Wilde,* 30.

57. Goldmann, "Wilde in Europa," 256.

58. See Z. S. Strother, "Display of the Body Hottentot," in *Africans on Stage: Studies in Ethnological Show Business,* ed. Bernth Lindfors (Bloomington: Indiana University Press, 1999), 1–40.

59. Dreesbach, *Gezähmte Wilde,* 25.

60. Corbey, "Ethnographic Showcases," 68.

61. Goldmann, "Wilde in Europa," 248.

62. Ames, *Carl Hagenbeck's Empire of Entertainments,* 65. Hagenbeck's company was the largest organizer of shows of exotic peoples in Germany, but it appears that rivals attempted to enter the lucrative trade, to the point of employing imposters. Questions raised by the Berlin anthropological society of Zulus that had been brought in by a Hagenbeck rival quickly led to the show's being terminated. See Sitzung am 20. December 1879, Virchow reporting, *Zeitschrift für Ethnologie* 11 (1879): 400.

63. Goldmann, "Wilde in Europa," 259. See also Corbey, "Ethnographic Showcases," 68, and Dreesbach, *Gezähmte Wilde,* 84.

64. Corbey, "Ethnographic Showcases," 58–60; Bob Mullan and Garry Marvin, *Zoo Culture* (London: Weidenfeld & Nicolson, 1987), 87.

65. Elizabeth Hanson, *Animal Attractions: Nature on Display in American Zoos* (Princeton, NJ: Princeton University Press, 2004), 37.

66. Hilke Thode-Arora, *Für fünfzig Pfennig um die Welt: Die Hagenbeckschen Völkerschauen* (Frankfurt: Campus Verlag, 1989), 21–23.

67. Ursula Klös, "Völkerschauen im Zoo Berlin zwischen 1878 und 1952," *Bongo* 30 (2000): 33.

68. March 12, 1878, *VZ,* Supplement 4, p. 3.

69. Thode-Arora, *Für fünfzig Pfennig,* 146.

70. M. Hoffmann, *Beiträge über Leben und Treiben der Eskimos in Labrador und Grönland: Aus dem Tagebuch des Herrn Carl Hagenbeck in Hamburg mit dem Schiffe "Eisbär" nach Grönland entsandten Herrn Jacobsen* (Berlin: Selbstverlag des Herausgebers, 1880), 4.

71. Klös, "Völkerschauen im Zoo Berlin," 34.

72. March 23, 1878, *VZ.*

73. March 8, 1878, *VZ.*

74. March 8, 1878, *VZ.*

75. December 23, 1884, *VZ,* no. 601, Supplement 1, p. 1.

76. A useful contemporary report on Virchow and the *Fortschrittspartei* is found in "Skizzen aus deutschen Parlamentssälen," *Die Gartenlaube* 32 (1881): 524–528.

77. Andreas Daum, *Wissenschaftspopularisierung im 19. Jahrhundert: Bürgerliche Kultur, naturwissenschaftliche Bildung und die deutsche Öffentlichkeit, 1848–1914* (Munich: Oldenbourg, 1998), 83. Häckel was the most prominent of a number of German scientists who continued Darwin's work, including Fritz Müller, O. Schmidt, and Weismann. See Carus Sterne, "Charles Darwin," *Die Gartenlaube* 19 (1882): 315–318.

78. Thomas Theye, "Optische Trophäen," in *Wir und die Wilden: Einblicke in eine kannibalische Beziehung*, ed. Thomas Theye (Hamburg: Rowohlt, 1985), 26.

79. "Ausserordentliche Zusammenkunft im zoologischen Garten am 7. November 1880," *Zeitschrift für Ethnologie* 12 (1880): 259.

80. March 23, 1878, *VZ*, Supplement 1. Report on Berliner Anthropological Society Meeting of March 16, 1878.

81. March 23, 1878, *VZ*, Supplement 1. Report on Berliner Anthropological Society Meeting of March 16, 1878.

82. March 23, 1878, *VZ*, Supplement 1. Report on Berliner Anthropological Society Meeting of March 16, 1878.

83. March 19, 1879, *VZ*, no. 80.

84. April 12, 1878, *VZ*, Supplement 3, p. 4; April 7, 1878, *VZ*, Supplement 4, p. 1.

85. April 10, 1878, *VZ*, Supplement 1, p. 3.

86. Thode-Arora, *Für fünfzig Pfennig*, 168. Mustafa Haikal and Winfried Gensch, *Der Gesang des Orang-utans: Die Geschichte des Dresdner Zoos* (Dresden: Sächsische Zeitung, 2011), 41.

87. September 22, 1878, *VZ*, Supplement 1, p. 4.

88. September 25, 1878, *VZ*, Supplement 1; September 26, 1878, *VZ*, Supplement 1, no. 226, pp. 1–2; September 27, 1878, *VZ*, Supplement 1, no. 227, p. 3.

89. September 25, 1878, *VZ*, Supplement 1; see also Klös, "Völkerschauen im Zoo Berlin," 37–38. In Breslau, the Nubians were also paraded through town before entering the zoo. See Horst Gleiss, *Unter Robben, Gnus und Tigerschlangen* (Breslau: Natura et Patria Verlag, 1967), 34.

90. As quoted in Klös, "Völkerschauen im Zoo Berlin," 38.

91. September 26, 1878, *VZ*, no. 226, Supplement 1, pp. 1–2.

92. September 26, 1878, *VZ*, no. 226, Supplement 1, pp. 1–2.

93. September 27, 1878, *VZ*, no. 227, Supplement 1, p. 3.

94. October 23, 1878, *VZ*, Supplement 3, p. 2.

95. September 27, 1878, *VZ*, no. 227, Supplement 1, p. 3.

96. September 29, 1878, *VZ*, no. 229, Supplement 2, p. 1.

97. Dreesbach, *Gezähmte Wilde*, 76.

98. October 4, 1878, *VZ*, no. 233, Supplement 3, p. 4.

99. As quoted in Klös, "Völkerschauen im Zoo Berlin," 38.

100. October 2, 1878, *VZ*, no. 231, Supplement 1, pp. 2–3; October 16, 1878, *VZ*, no. 243, Supplement 1, p. 3.

101. February 3, 1886, *VZ*, Supplement 1, p. 2.

102. October 13, 1878, *VZ*, no. 241, Supplement 3, p. 2.

103. February 7, 1888, *VZ*, Supplement 1, p. 3.

104. For a summary of this debate, see Elizabeth Henry Bellmer, "The Statesman and the Ophthalmologist: Gladstone and Magnus on the Evolution of Human Colour Vision, One Small Episode of the Nineteenth-Century Darwinian Debate," *Annals of Science* 56 (1999): 25–45.

105. Report by Virchnow, *Zeitschrift für Ethnologie* 11 (1879): 389–393. See also November 18, 1879, *VZ*, no. 322, Supplement 2, p. 3.

106. December 25, 1878, *VZ*, no. 303, Supplement 4.

107. September 9, 1879, *VZ*, no. 252, Supplement 1, p. 3.

108. September 11, 1879, *VZ*, no. 254, Supplement 1, p. 3.

109. September 30, 1879, *VZ*, no. 273, Supplement 4, p. 1.

110. Hagenbeck, *Von Tieren*, 48.

111. September 23, 1879, *VZ*, no. 266, evening edition, p. 2.

112. September 30, 1879 *VZ*, no. 273, Supplement 1, p. 4.

113. October 7, 1879, *VZ*, no. 280, Supplement 1, p. 2.

114. October 14, 1879, *VZ*, no. 287, p. 2.

115. Dittrich and Rieke-Müller, *Carl Hagenbeck*, 154.

116. October 19, 1881, *VZ*, no. 487, Supplement 1, p. 1.

117. Thode-Arora, *Für fünfzig Pfennig*, 118.

118. Dittrich, Rieke-Müller, *Hagenbeck* 154.

119. Thode-Arora, *Für fünfzig Pfennig*, 76, 119.

120. March, 19, 1879, *VZ*, no. 80.

121. Hoffmann, *Leben und Treiben der Eskimos*, 9. Ames's translation appears on page 36.

122. Hoffmann, *Leben und Treiben der Eskimos*, 9.

123. Hoffmann, *Leben und Treiben der Eskimos*, 16. See also Garth Taylor, "An Eskimo Abroad, 1880: His Diary and Death," *Canadian Geographic* 101, no. 5 (1981): 38–39.

124. Taylor, "An Eskimo Abroad," 40.

125. Hoffmann, *Leben und Treiben der Eskimos,* 17. Also Ames, *Carl Hagenbeck's Empire of Entertainments*, 37.

126. Taylor, "An Eskimo Abroad," 40.

127. Taylor, "An Eskimo Abroad," 38.

128. Dreesbach, *Gezähmte Wilde*, 74.

129. Taylor, "An Eskimo Abroad," 40–41.

130. Klös, "Völkerschauen im Zoo Berlin," 42; Klös, *Von der Menagerie*, 78.

131. Taylor, "An Eskimo Abroad," 43.

132. As quoted in Rothfels, *Savages and Beasts*, 140.

133. Ames, *Carl Hagenbeck's Empire of Entertainments*, 38; Thode-Arora, *Für fünfzig Pfennig,* 35.

134. As quoted in Taylor, "An Eskimo Abroad," 41.

135. "Ausserordentliche Zusammenkunft im zoologischen Garten am 7. November 1880," *Zeitschrift für Ethnologie* 12 (1880): 270.

136. "Ausserordentliche Zusammenkunft im zoologischen Garten am 7. November 1880," *Zeitschrift für Ethnologie* 12 (1880): 270.

137. "Ausserordentliche Zusammenkunft im zoologischen Garten am 7. November 1880," *Zeitschrift für Ethnologie* 12 (1880): 271.

138. Quoted in Klös, "Völkerschauen im Zoo Berlin," 43.

139. Klös, "Völkerschauen im Zoo Berlin," 43.

140. March 29, 1879, *VZ*, Supplement 1, p. 4.

141. Heinrich Steinitz, "Feuerländer in Berlin," *Die Gartenlaube* 44 (1881): 732–734.

142. Quoted in Klös, "Völkerschauen im Zoo Berlin," 44.

143. Quoted in Klös, "Völkerschauen im Zoo Berlin," 44.

144. Thode-Arora, *Für fünfzig Pfenning,* 169.

145. Dittrich and Rieke-Müller, *Carl Hagenbeck,* 159.

146. July 29, 1883, *VZ,* no. 349, Supplement 1, p. 2.

147. July 24, 1883, *VZ,* no. 340, evening edition, p. 1.

148. As quoted in Klös, "Völkerschauen im Zoo Berlin," 46.

149. August 6, 1883, *VZ,* no. 362, evening edition, p. 2. This is the equivalent of 200 tons, the Prussian unit of measurement for beer.

150. August 10, 1897, *VZ,* Supplement 1, p. 4. The crowds might also have been swelled by a concert that same day of the Prussian grenadier regiment under a black Kapellmeister, the only musician, a Berlin daily noted, in the Prussian army. See August 10, 1897, *VZ,* Supplement 1, p. 4.

151. Michael Erbe, "Berlin im Kaiserreich," in *Geschichte Berlins,* ed. Wolfgang Ribbe (Berlin: Berliner Wissenschafts-Verlag, 2002), 694.

152. Dreesbach, *Gezähmte Wilde,* 76; April 22, 1883, *VZ,* no. 389, Supplement 1, p. 2. The train transporting one of these enormous animals to Dresden after the Berlin show nearly derailed when the improperly secured elephant began to sway in its carriage. See September 19, 1883, *VZ,* no. 437, Supplement 1, p. 2

153. August 30, 1883, *VZ,* no. 403, Supplement 2, p. 2.

154. Hagenbeck, *Von Tieren,* 58.

155. September 3, 1884, *VZ,* no. 411, Supplement 1, p. 1.

156. Thode-Arora, *Für fünfzig Pfennig,* 170.

157. August 18, 1885, *VZ,* no. 382, evening edition, Supplement, p. 1.

158. August 23, 1883, *VZ,* no. 381, pp. 3–4.

159. August 23, 1883, *VZ,* no. 381, pp. 3–4.

160. August 23, 1883, *VZ,* no. 381, pp. 3–4.

161. August 23, 1884, *VZ,* no. 393, midday edition, p. 4.

162. Ames, *Carl Hagenbeck's Empire of Entertainments,* 108; Thode-Arora, *Für fünfzig Pfennig,* 50.

163. Dittrich and Rieke-Müller, *Carl Hagenbeck,* 164.

164. February 2, 1886, *VZ,* Supplement 1, p. 2.

165. Jennifer Kramer, *Switchbacks: Art, Ownership, and Nuxalk National Identity* (Vancouver: University of British Columbia Press, 2006), 28.

166. Thode-Arora, *Für fünfzig Pfennig,* 52.

167. Reprinted in Wolfgang Haberland, "'Diese Indianer sind Falsch': Neun Bella Coola im Deutschen Reich 1885/86," *Archiv für Völkerkunde* 42 (1988): 56. Adrian is spelled incorrectly throughout.

168. Haberland, "Diese Indianer sind Falsch," 15.

169. January 27, 1886, *VZ*, Supplement 2, p. 3.

170. Quoted in Haberland, "Diese Indianer sind Falsch," 19.

171. January 29, 1886, *VZ*, Supplement 3, p. 7.

172. February 7, 1886, *VZ*, Supplement, p. 3.

173. Kramer, *Switchbacks*, 31.

174. Quoted in Ames, *Carl Hagenbeck's Empire of Entertainments*, 109.

175. Ames, *Carl Hagenbeck's Empire of Entertainments*, 108–109.

176. Ames, *Carl Hagenbeck's Empire of Entertainments*, 108.

177. June 23, 1886, *VZ*, no. 31, Supplement 1, p. 3.

178. Thode-Arora, *Für fünfzig Pfennig*, 60.

179. Klös, "Völkerschauen im Zoo Berlin," 49.

180. The famous nineteenth-century animal artist Heinrich Leutemann pointed to the absence of animals, women, and children as the primary cause of the show's relatively poor draw. See Kuenheim, *Carl Hagenbeck*, 114.

181. Haberland, "Diese Indianer sind Falsch," 36.

182. February 2, 1886, *VZ*, Supplement, pp. 2–3.

183. August 24, 1895, *VZ*, no. 395, Supplement 1, p. 1.

184. As quoted in Klös, "Völkerschauen im Zoo Berlin," 51.

185. Thode-Arora, *Für fünfzig Pfennig*, 131; Kramer, *Switchbacks*, 37.

186. Kramer, *Switchbacks*, 37.

187. As quoted in Ames, *Carl Hagenbeck's Empire of Entertainments*, 108.

188. Goldmann, "Wilde in Europa," 259.

189. Stefan Goldmann, "Zur Rezeption der Völkerausstellungen um 1900," in *Exotische Welten, Europäische Phantasien*, ed. Hermann Pollig (Stuttgart: Edition Cantz, 1987), 93.

190. Ursula Klös, "Völkerschauen im Zoo Berlin," 61.

191. Ursula Klös, "Völkerschauen im Zoo Berlin," 61

192. June 28, 1900, *VZ*, no. 297, evening edition, p. 3; June 30, 1900, *VZ*, no. 301, evening edition, p. 3.

193. July 20, 1900, *VZ*, no. 335, evening edition, p. 2.

194. Ursula Klös, "Völkerschauen im Zoo Berlin," 61.

195. May 29, 1900, *VZ*, no. 247, evening edition, p. 4.

196. June 1, 1900, *VZ*, no. 252, Supplement 1, p. 2.

197. September 19, 1895, *VZ*, no. 439, Supplement 1, p. 3.

198. June 21, 1900, *VZ*, no. 285, Supplement 1, p. 1.

199. Quoted in Klös, "Völkerschauen im Zoo Berlin," 61.

200. May 27, 1900, *VZ*, no. 244, Supplement 3, p. 2.

201. July 11, 1900, *VZ*, evening edition, p. 2.

202. As quoted in Dittrich and Rieke-Müller, *Ein Garten für Menschen und Tiere*, 46.

203. Cornelia Essner, *Deutsche Afrikareisende im neunzehnten Jahrhundert* (Wiesbaden: Steiner, 1985), 54–56.

204. Carl Peters was one of nineteenth-century Germany's foremost advocates for colonies, authoring dozens of essays and articles promoting German colonial policy. See Christian Geulen, "The Final Frontier," in *Phantasiereiche: Zur Kulturgeschichte des deutschen Kolonialismus*, ed. Birthe Kundrus (Frankfurt: Campus Verlag, 2003), 48.

205. Essner, *Deutsche Afrikareisende*, 66.

206. Falkenstein's account of caring for the gorilla and transporting it back to Germany is found in Paul Güssfeldt, Julius Falkenstein, and Eduard Pecuel-Loesche, *Die Loango-Expedition. Ausgesandt von der Deutschen Gesellschaft zur Erforschung Aequatorial-Africas, 1873–1876* (Leipzig: Verlag von Eduard Baldamus, 1888), 149–169, http://library.si.edu/digital-library/book/dieloangoexpedioogssf.

207. Hans Werner Ingensiep, "Kultur- und Zoogeschichte des Gorillas," in *Die Kulturgeschichte des Zoos*, ed. Lothar Dittrich, Dietrich von Engelhardt, and Annelore Rieke-Müller (Berlin: Verlag für Wissenschaft und Bildung, 2001), 153.

208. Dr. Falkenstein, "M'Pungu," *Die Gartenlaube* 33 (1876): 556.

209. See, for example, the articles on Stanley in issues 1, 4, 5, and 14 of *Die Gartenlaube* 1890.

210. Essner, *Deutsche Afrikareisende*, 114–116.

211. Blackbourn, *The Conquest of Nature*, 177.

212. Ernst von Weber, *Vier Jahre in Afrika* (Leipzig: Brockhaus, 1878).

213. Otto Thamm, *Von Kiel bis Samoa: Reise Erlebnisse des am 16. März 1889 ertrunkenen Obermatrosen Adolph Thamm* (Berlin: Conrads Buchhandlung, 1889).

214. Dr. H. Lange, "Die 'Afrikanische Gesellschaft' und die deutsche Expedition an der Loangoküste," *Die Gartenlaube* 38 (1874): 613–616. *Die Gartenlaube* also ran regular articles on non-German explorers, like David Livingstone. See "David Livingstones Ende," *Die Gartenlaube* 12 (1875): 201–204.

215. March 4, 1886, *VZ*, Supplement 3, p. 5. Same date, evening edition, pp. 1–2.

216. January 13, 1888, *VZ*, Supplement 1, p. 2.

217. "Ausserordentliche Zusammenkunft im zoologischen Garten am 7. November 1880," *Zeitschrift für Ethnologie* 12 (1880): 267–268.

218. August 20, 1883, *VZ*, no. 386, evening edition, Supplement 1, p. 1.

219. August 4, 1887, *VZ*, Supplement 1, p. 2.

220. September 9, 1883, *VZ*, no. 421, Supplement 3, p. 2.

221. January 31, 1886, *VZ*, Supplement 5, p. 12.

222. October 19, 1880, *VZ*, no. 291, Supplement 2, p. 2.

223. August 22, 1884, *VZ*, no. 391, midday edition, p. 3.

224. August 22, 1884, *VZ*, no. 391, midday edition, p. 4.

225. March 23, 1878, *VZ*, Supplement 1. Report on Berliner Anthropological Society Meeting of March 16, 1878.

226. September 17, 1879, *VZ*, no. 260, Supplement 1, p. 4.

227. September 17, 1879, *VZ*, no. 260, Supplement 1, p. 4.

228. August 23, 1883, *VZ*, no. 381, pp. 3–4.

229. October 19, 1881, *VZ*, no. 487, Supplement 1, p. 1.

230. September 18, 1883, *VZ*, no. 435, Supplement 1, p. 2.

231. July 28, 1883, *VZ*, no. 347, Supplement 2, p. 2; July 29, 1883, *VZ*, no. 347, midday edition, Supplement 1, p. 1.

232. Hagenbeck, *Von Tieren*, 63.

233. Hagenbeck, *Von Tieren*, 66.

234. Pollig, "Exotische Welten, Europäische Phantasien," 20–24. As Nigel Rothfels has elegantly summarized, the shows of humans spoke to a "consistently escalating desire of Germans—and, indeed, Europeans more generally—to learn as much as possible about other peoples of the world." Rothfels, *Savages and Beasts*, 90.

235. Alfred Lehmann, "Zeitgenössische Bilder der ersten Völkerschauen," in *Von Fremden Völkern und Kulturen,* ed. Werner Lang, Walter Nippold, and Günther Spannaus (Düsseldorf: Droste-Verlag, 1955), 31.

236. Rudyard Kipling, *The Mark of the Beast and Other Stories* (New York: Signet, 1964), 50

237. Friedrich Gerstäcker, "Civilisation und Wildniß," *Die Gartenlaube* 17 (1855): 224–225.

238. Fritz Kramer, "Eskapistische und utopische Motive in der Frühgeschichte der deutschen Ethnologie," in *Exotische Welten, Europäische Phantasien,* ed. Hermann Pollig (Stuttgart: Edition Cantz, 1987), 67.

239. Hagenbeck, *Von Tieren*, 102. A similar sentiment about the Sri Lankan "paradise" where the Sinhalese do "even less work than they do at the zoo shows" is found in Ludwig Beckmann, "Die Hagenbeck'schen Singhalesen," *Die Gartenlaube* 34 (1884): 566.

Chapter 3

1. Heinz-Georg Klös and Ursula Klös, *Der Berliner Zoo im Spiegel seiner Bauten, 1841–1989* (Berlin: Heenemann, 1990, 70–72.

2. David Ciarlo, *Advertising Empire: Race and Visual Culture in Imperial Germany* (Cambridge, MA: Harvard University Press, 2011), 126.

3. August Woldt, "Das Elephantanhaus im Berliner zoologischen Garten," *Die Gartenlaube* 52 (1882): 860.

4. February 2, 1892, *VZ*, no. 63, Supplement 1, p. 4. Berlin alone among German zoos had two elephants. Most zoos considered themselves fortunate to have one. See, for example, Lothar Dittrich and Annelore Rieke-Müller, *Ein Garten für Menschen und Tiere: 125 Jahre Zoo Hannover* (Hannover: Verlaggesellschaft Grütter, 1990), 68.

5. Klös and Klös, *Der Berliner Zoo im Spiegel seiner Bauten*, 122.

6. Klös and Klös, *Der Berliner Zoo im Spiegel seiner Bauten*, 122.

7. June 14, 1901, *VZ*, no. 273, Supplement 1, p. 1.

8. "Der zoologische Garten in Berlin," *Die Gartenlaube* 16 (1873): 262.

9. Klös and Klös, *Der Berliner Zoo im Spiegel seiner Bauten*, 57.

10. See Edward Said, *Orientalism* (New York: Vintage, 1978), 209. Among Said's harshest critics are Ibn Warraq, Defending the West: *A Critique of Edward Said's Orientalism* (Amherst, NY: Prometheus, 2007), and Robert Irwin, *For Lust of Knowing* (London: Allen Lane, 2006). On the role of intellectual writings on Germany's colonial aspirations, see George Steinmetz, *The Devil's Handwriting: Precoloniality and the German Colonial State in Qingdao, Samoa, and Southwest Africa* (Chicago: University of Chicago Press, 2007), 25.

11. "Der zoologische Garten in Berlin," *Die Gartenlaube* 16 (1873): 266.

12. John Williams, *Turning to Nature in Germany* (Stanford: Stanford University Press, 2007), 8–9.

13. Annemarie Lange, *Das Wilhelminische Berlin. Zwischen Jahrhundertwende und Novemberrevolution* (Berlin: Dietz, 1988), 89; Kristin Poling, "Shantytowns and Pioneers beyond the City Wall: Berlin's Urban Frontier in the Nineteenth Century," *Central European History* 47, no. 2 (2014): 249.

14. Poling, "Shantytowns and Pioneers," 249.

15. Paul Lindenberg, "Aus der Reichshauptstadt," *Die Gartenlaube* 7 (1888): 634.

16. Paul Lindenberg, "Aus der Reichshauptstadt," *Die Gartenlaube* 7 (1888): 634.

17. G. Klausen, "Kinderbelustigung im Zoologischen Garten," *Die Gartenlaube* 22 (1899): 707.

18. Klös and Klös, *Der Berliner Zoo im Spiegel seiner Bauten*, 78–80.

19. "Kleinere Mitteilungen," *Der Zoologische Garten* 33 (1892): 253–259.

20. "Der zoologische Garten in Berlin," *Die Gartenlaube* 16 (1873): 266.

21. All animal costs are taken from November 4, 1887, *VZ*, no. 515, Supplement 1, p. 4.

22. Lange, *Das Wilhelminische Berlin*, 92.

23. June 16, 1900, *VZ*, no. 277, evening edition, p. 3.

24. August 1, 1897, *VZ*, Supplement 1, p. 1; August 22, 1897, *VZ*, no. 392, Supplement 1, p. 3; July 14, 1900, *VZ*, no. 325, evening edition, p. 4; September 8, 1895, *VZ*, no. 421, Supplement 1, p. 2.

25. September 24, 1895, *VZ*, Supplement 2, p. 2; July 28, 1900, *VZ*, no. 349, evening edition, p. 4; September 13, 1891, *VZ*, no. 427, Supplement 1, p. 3.

26. January 15, 1886, *VZ*, Supplement 1, p. 3.

27. February 7, 1892, *VZ*, no. 63, Supplement 1, p. 4.

28. Dittrich and Rieke-Müller, *Ein Garten für Menschen und Tiere*, 66; Christoph Scherpner, *Von Bürgern für Bürger—125 Jahre Zoologischer Garten Frankfurt am Main* (Frankfurt: Zoologischer Garten, 1983), 56.

29. "Kleinere Mitteilungen," *Der Zoologische Garten* 35 (1894): 155.

30. J. Müller-Liebenwalde, "Aus dem Berliner zoologischen Garten," *Der Zoologische Garten* 34 (1893): 363–366.

31. Hildegard von Bülow, "Meine Tierfreundschaft im Dresdner Zoologischen Garten," *Der Zoologische Garten* 46, no. 7 (1905): 193–194.

32. Klös and Klös, *Der Berliner Zoo im Spiegel seiner Bauten*, 82.

33. Harriet Ritvo, "The Order of Nature," in *New World, New Animals*, ed. R. J. Hoage and William Deiss (Baltimore: Johns Hopkins University Press, 1996), 46.

34. Ciarlo, *Advertising Empire*, 29.

35. "Das fünfzigjährige Jubelfest des Berliner zoologischen Gartens," *Der Zoologische Garten* 35, no. 8 (1894): 303.

36. Heinrich Bolau, "Stillstand und Rückzug im Zoologischen Garten zu Hamburg," *Der Zoologische Garten* 44, no. 2 (1903): 35; Theodor Knottnerus-Meyer, "Der Zoologische Garten zu Frankfurt-am-Main," *Der Zoologische Garten* 44, no. 5 (1903): 171.

37. Brehm's *Tierleben* is available online at http://archive.org/stream/brehmstier lebenao4breh#page/n11/mode/2up.

38. Andreas Daum, *Wissenschaftspopularisierung im 19. Jahrhundert: Bürgerliche Kultur, naturwissenschaftliche Bildung und die deutsche Öffentlichkeit, 1848–1914* (Munich: Oldenbourg, 1998), 257.

39. Karl Brandt, "Mutterliebe bei den Tieren," *Die Gartenlaube* 19 (1899): 581.

40. June 14, 1901, *VZ*, no. 273, Supplement 1, p. 1.

41. Helmut Zedelmaier and Michael Kamp, *Hellabrunn: Geschichte und Geschichten des Münchener Tierparks* (Munich: Bassermann, 2011), 11.

42. Oskar Heinroth, "Vesperbrot des Orang-Utan 'Rolf' im zoologischen Garten zu Berlin," *Die Gartenlaube* 28 (1899): 896.

43. Alfred Brehm, "Menschenaffen," *Die Gartenlaube* 3 (1876): 284.

44. Ritvo, 284.

45. June 2, 1900, *VZ*, no. 254, p. 2. To be clear, hunting was still permitted, but it was now to be monitored. See Bernhard Gißibl, "German Colonialism and the Beginnings of the International Wildlife Preservation in Africa," *German Historical Institute Bulletin* 3 (2006): 127–128.

46. See the outstanding new biography, Jane Ridley, *The Heir Apparent: A Life of Edward VII, the Playboy Prince* (New York: Random House, 2013).

47. Article from the *Berliner Tageblatt* in *Der Zoologische Garten* 24 (1883), 92.

48. See Ritvo, "The Order of Nature," 48–49; Anne Dreesbach, "Die Gefangenen unserer zoologischen Gärten—Der Tierpark im Spiegel der Kritik," in *Nilpferde an der Isar: Eine Geschichte des Tierparks Hellabrunn in München*, ed. Michael Kamp and Helmut Zedelmaier (Munich Buchendorf Verlag, 2000), 248–249.

49. GstAD, I. HA Rep. 89 Nr. 31823 GZ Blatt 176. Undated letter to kaiser. Signed: "Mama, a sister."

50. GstAD, I. HA Rep. 89 Nr. 31823 GZ Blätter 178–180. Undated letter from the board of the zoological garden to the king.

51. GstAD, I. HA Rep. 89 Nr. 31823 GZ Blätter 178–180. Undated letter from the board of the zoological garden to the king.

52. GstAD, I. HA Rep. 89 Nr. 31823 GZ Blätter 178–180. Undated letter from the board of the zoological garden to the king.

53. GstAD, I. HA Rep. 89, Nr. 31823 GZ Blätter 175, October 6, 1889, letter from von Zitzewitz.

54. GstAD, I. HA Rep. 89 Nr. 31823 GZ Blätter 178–180. Undated letter from the board of the zoological garden to the king.

55. GstAD, I. HA Rep. 89 Nr. 31823 GZ, Blätter 178–180. Undated letter from the board of the zoological garden to the king.

56. September 12, 1889, *VZ*.

57. GstAD, I. HA Rep. 89 Nr. 31823 GZ, Blätter 178–180. Undated letter from the board of the zoological garden to the king.

58. January 8, 1889, *VZ*, Supplement 1, p. 1.

59. October 3, 1889, *VZ*, no. 462, evening edition.

60. GstAD, I. HA Rep. 89 Nr. 31823 GZ Blatt 182, March 25, 1890, letter from Dr. L Heck to the emperor and Lucanus.

61. February 28, 1892, *VZ*, Supplement 1, p. 4.

62. Adolf Nill, "Eine Elefantentötung in Nills zoologischen Garten in Stuttgart," *Der Zoologische Garten* 35 (1894): 21–27.

63. February 22, 1888, *VZ*, Supplement 1, p. 2.

64. March 20, 1890, *VZ,* no. 133, Supplement 1, p. 1.

65. Renate Brucker, "Tierrechte und Friedensbewegung: 'Radikale Ethik' und gesellschaftlicher Fortschritt in der deutschen Geschichte," in Dorothee Brantz and Christof Mauch ed., *Tierische Geschichte: Die Beziehung von Mensch und Tier in der Kultur der Moderne* (Paderborn: Ferdinand Schöningh, 2010), 268–272.

66. Harriet Ritvo, *The Animal Estate: The English and Other Creatures in the Victorian Age* (Cambridge, MA: Harvard University Press, 1987), 141, 151, 159.

67. Mustafa Haikal and Winfried Gensch, *Der Gesang des Orang-utans: Die Geschichte des Dresdner Zoos* (Dresden: Sächsische Zeitung, 2011), 40.

68. Dittrich and Annelore Rieke-Müller, *Carl Hagenbeck. Tierhandel und Schaustellungen im Deutschen Kaiserreich* (Frankfurt: Peter Lang, 1998), 95–96.

69. "Korrespondenzen," *Der Zoologische Garten* 31 (1890): 123.

70. Ludwig Baumgarten, *Chronik Zoologischer Garten Halle* (Halle: Zoologischer Garten Halle GmbH, 2001), 17.

71. "Bericht über den zoologischen Garten zu Dresden über das Geschäftsjahr von 1. April 1890 bis 31. März 1891," *Der Zoologische Garten* 33 (1892): 55.

72. "Bericht des Verwaltungsrat der Neuen Zoologischen Gesellschaft zu Frankfurt a. M. für 1899," *Der Zoologische Garten* 41 (1900): 248.

73. "Jahresbericht über den zoologischen Garten in Hamburg 1891," *Der Zoologische Garten* 33 (1892): 127.

74. "Miscellen," *Der Zoologische Garten* 21 (1880): 221.

75. "Kleinere Mitteilungen," *Der Zoologische Garten* 35 (1894): 155.

76. March 14, 1879, *VZ*, no. 75, Supplement 1, p. 4.

77. September 29, 1878, *VZ*, no. 229, Supplement 2, p. 1.

78. Mustafa Haikal and Jörg Junhold, *Auf der Spur des Löwen: 125 Jahre Zoo Leipzig* (Leipzig: Zoo Leipzig, 2003), 70–71.

79. Zedelmaier and Kamp, *Hellabrunn,* 24–26.

80. Stanley Smyth Flower, *Report on Mission to Europe, 1905* (Cairo: National Printing Department, 1906), 24.

81. August 7, 1897, *VZ,* Supplement 1, p. 2; June 13, 1901, *VZ,* no. 271, Supplement 1, p. 3.

82. August 20, 1895, *VZ,* no. 387, Supplement 1, p. 2.

83. August 31, 1895, *VZ,* Supplement 1, p. 2.

84. August 31, 1895, *VZ,* Supplement 1, p. 2.

85. Anne Dreesbach, *Gezähmte Wilde: Die Zurschaustellung "exotischer Menschen" in Deutschland, 1870–1940* (Frankfurt: Campus Verlag, 2005), 202.

Chapter 4

1. Elke-Vera Kotowski, "Tanz auf dem Vulkan," in *Berlin: Geschichte einer Stadt,* ed. Julius Schoeps (Berlin: be.bra, 2001), 120.

2. Julius Schoeps, *Berlin: Geschichte einer Stadt* (Berlin: be.bra, 2007), 90.

3. Hans-Ulrich Wehler, *Deutsche Gesellschaftsgeschichte,* vol. 3 (Munich: Beck, 1995), 1279.

4. Wehler, *Deutsche Gesellschaftsgeschichte,* vol. 3, 1252–1253.

5. Wehler, *Deutsche Gesellschaftsgeschichte,* vol. 3, 1255.

6. Stanley Smyth Flower, *Report on Mission to Europe, 1905* (Cairo: National Printing Department, 1906), 15.

7. As quoted in Hans-Ulrich Wehler, *Deutsche Gesellschaftsgeschichte,* vol. 4 (Munich: Beck, 2003), 20.

8. Wehler, *Deutsche Gesellschaftsgeschichte,* vol. 4, 102.

9. Heinz-Georg Klös, *Von der Menagerie zum Tierparadies: 125 Jahre Zoo Berlin* (Berlin: Haude & Spenersche, 1969), 85–110.

10. GStA PK, I. HA Rep. 89, Nr. 31825, November 29, 1916, letter from Heck to His Majesty, the Kaiser and King.

11. Ludwig Heck, *Heiter-Ernste Lebensbeichte: Erinnerungen eines alten Tiergärtners* (Berlin: Deutscher Verlag, 1938), 195.

12. Lothar Dittrich and Annelore Rieke-Müller, *Ein Garten für Menschen und Tiere: 125 Jahre Zoo Hannover* (Hannover: Grütter, 1990), 87.

13. Dittrich and Rieke-Müller, *Ein Garten für Menschen und Tiere,* 87.

14. Ludwig Baumgarten, *Chronik Zoologischer Garten Halle. Teil 1, 1901–1945* (Halle: Zoologischer Garten Halle, 2001), 63.

15. Mustafa Haikal and Jörg Junhold, *Auf der Spur des Löwen: 125 Jahre Zoo Leipzig* (Leipzig: Pro Leipzig, 2003), 111, 119.

16. Christoph Scherpner, *Von Bürgern für Bürger—125 Jahre Zoologischer Garten Frankfurt am Main* (Frankfurt: Zoologischer Garten, 1983), 99.

17. Scherpner, *Von Bürgern für Bürger*, 102.

18. Scherpner, *Von Bürgern für Bürger*, 102.

19. GStA PK, I. HA Rep. 89, Nr. 31825, January 30, 1918, letter from Heck to kaiser.

20. Leopold Epstein, "Bemerkenwertes aus dem Zoologischen Garten zu Frankfurt a. M.," *Der Zoologische Beobachter* 59, no. 1 (1918): 89.

21. As the war brought with it a fear of spies that was indistinguishable from a fear of foreigners, Sinti and Roma (gypsies) in Germany were rounded up and placed in prison, leaving their dancing bears in need of a home. The Frankfurt zoo took in dozens of bears this way, many of whom were euthanized before the end of the war. Scherpner, *Von Bürgern für Bürger*, 100.

22. Wehler, *Deutsche Gesellschaftsgeschichte*, vol. 4, 241.

23. Henning Köhler, "Berlin in der Weimarer Republik," in *Geschichte Berlins,* vol. 2, ed. Wolfgang Ribbe (Berlin: Berliner Wissenschafts-Verlag, 2002), 839–840.

24. Köhler, "Berlin," 844.

25. Köhler, "Berlin," 840–841.

26. BBAW, September 27, 1920, letter from Ludwig Heck, II-XI-125 Akten der Preussischen Akademie der Wissenschaften 1812–1845. Zentrales Archiv der Akademie der Wissenschaften der Deutschen Demokratischen Republik.

27. BBAW, Undated, handwritten note, Berlin Brandenburg Akademie II-VI-25. Verhandlungen der Gesamtakademie.

28. BBAW, November 13, 1922, letter from Ludwig Heck. Berlin Brandenburg Akademie II-VI-25. Verhandlungen der Gesamtakademie.

29. LA-B, A. Pr. Br. Rep. 042, Nr. 3069, May 9, 1922, newspaper article. Title of newspaper illegible.

30. GStA PK, I. HA, Rep. 191, Nr. 4296, November 8, 1922, Abschrift des Actien-Vereins der Zoologischen Gartens zu Berlin.

31. Klös, *Von der Menagerie*, 101–102.

32. Horst Gleiss, *Unter Robben, Gnus und Tigerschlangen* (Breslau: Natura et Patria, 1967), 118–119.

33. Helmut Zedelmaier and Michael Kamp, *Hellabrunn: Geschichte und Geschichten des Münchner Tierparks* (Munich: Bassermann, 2011), 55.

34. Dittrich and Rieke-Müller, *Ein Garten für Menschen und Tiere*, 88.

35. Zedelmaier and Kamp, *Hellabrunn*, 64.

36. Götz Ruempler, "Zoologische Gärten und Naturschutz," *Bongo* 13 (1987): 64.

37. Ruempler, "Zoologische Gärten," 64.

38. Klös, *Von der Menagerie,* 86.

39. Berlin's natural history museum has the "richest" collection: three skulls, one skeleton, and one hide. Joachim Oppermann, "Tod und Wiedergeburt. Über das Schicksal einiger Berliner Zootiere," *Bongo* 24 (1994): 54–56.

40. Ruempler, "Zoologische Gärten," 65–66. See also Ludwig Heck and C. Freyer, *Streifzüge durch den Zoologischen Garten Berlin mit dem Zeiss Ikon-Camera* (Berlin: Verlag des Zoologischen Gartens, 1927), 62.

41. Marvin Jones, "Der Berliner Zoo und der Elaphurus davidianus," *Bongo* 11 (1986): 66.

42. Ludwig Heck, *Papa Heck und seine Liebling* (Berlin: Naumann, 1931), 20.

43. Heinz-Sigurd Raethel, "Der Berliner Zoo und seine Rindersammlung 1843–1991. Teil II," *Bongo* 21 (1993): 43.

44. Christoph Scherpner, *Von Bürgern für Bürger—125 Jahre Zoologischer Garten Frankfurt am Main* (Frankfurt: Zoologischer Garten, 1983), 105.

45. Lutz Heck, *Auf Tiersuche in Weiter Welt* (Berlin: Paul Paren, 1941), 266.

46. Scherpner, *Von Bürgern für Bürger,* 105.

47. Heck, *Auf Tiersuche,* 274.

48. Heck, *Auf Tiersuche,* 270–274.

49. Ruempler, "Zoologische Gärten," 65; see also LA-B, *Werbeheft* 1931, 11.

50. Nyhart considers the journal an early example of environmentalism. See Lynn Nyhart, *Modern Nature* (Chicago: University of Chicago Press, 2009).

51. Kurt Priemel, "Der Zoologischer Garten von 1859: Ein Rückblick," *Der Zoologische Garten* 1, no. 1 (1929): 8.

52. Priemel, *"Der Zoologischer Garten* von 1859," 9–10.

53. Priemel, *"Der Zoologischer Garten* von 1859," 11–12.

54. Priemel, *"Der Zoologischer Garten* von 1859," 8.

55. Lutz Heck, *Zooführer durch den Berliner Zoologischen Garten* (Berlin: Verlag des Aktienvereins des Zoologischen Gartens zu Berlin, 1906), 16, 31, 81 LA-B, Nat 6/1906.

56. Ludwig Heck and Clemens Carl Freyer, *Streifzüge durch den Zoologischen Garten Berlin mit dem Zeiss Ikon-Camera* (Berlin: Verlag des Actien-Vereins des Zoologischen Gartens, 1927), 38.

57. Heck, *Papa Heck,* Entry 10, "Der Schwarze Storch." Unpaginated.

58. Heck, *Papa Heck,* Entry 18, "Das Zebra." Unpaginated.

59. LA-B, *Werbeheft* 1931, 11.

60. LA-B, A. Rep. 001-002/899. Annual report of Berlin zoo for the year 1929.

61. Renate Angermann, "Anna Held, Paul Matschie und die Säugetiere des Berliner Zoologischen Gartens" *Bongo* 24 (1994): 113.

62. Angermann, "Anna Held," 117.

63. Werner Sunkel, "Zoologische Gärten," *Zoologischer Beobachter* 60 (1919): 141–142.

64. Friedrich Hauchecorne, "Naturschutzaufgaben unserer Zoologischen Gärten," *Der Zoologische Garten* 1 (1928): 81.

65. Hauchecorne, "Naturschutzaufgaben," 83.

66. Hauchecorne, "Naturschutzaufgaben," 84.

67. Hauchecorne, "Naturschutzaufgaben," 85.

68. Woldemar von Falz-Fein, *Askania-Nova: Das Tierparadies* (Neudamm: Neumann, 1930), 80.

69. Karl Soffel, "Der Tierpark des Herrn Friedrich Falz-Fein zu Askania-Nova (Sudrüssland) *Zoologischer Beobachter* 56 (1915): 4.

70. Soffel, "Der Tierpark," 4.

71. Falz-Fein, *Askania-Nova*, 81.

72. Falz-Fein, *Askania-Nova*, 82–83.

73. Heinz Heck, "Askania Nova—Ein Besuch vor beinahe 100 Jahren," *Bongo* 23 (1994): 90.

74. Falz-Fein, *Askania-Nova*, 309.

75. Heck, *Heiter-Ernste*, 175.

76. LA-B, A. Pr. Br. Rep. 042, Nr. 3069; *VZ*, June 25,1925, "Aufblühen des zoologischen Gartens."

77. LA-B, A. Rep. 001-002/899. Undated speaking notes.

78. LA-B, A. Rep. 001-002/898. Annual report of Berlin zoo for 1926.

79. LA-B, A. Rep. 001-002/898. Annual report of Berlin zoo for 1926.

80. LA-B, A. Rep. 001-002/898. Annual report of Berlin zoo for 1926.

81. LA-B, A. Rep. 001-002/898. Annual reports of Berlin zoo for 1927 and 1928.

82. LA-B, A. Rep. 001-002/898. Annual reports of Berlin zoo for 1929.

83. LA-B, A. Rep. 032-08, Nr. 303, July 3, 1929, letter from Dr. Madaus to Städtische Bauamt Tiergarten, Berlin.

84. See the correspondence in LA-B, A. Rep. 032-08, Nr. 303.

85. July 1, 1926, *VZ*, "Indien in Berlin."

86. LA-B, A. Rep. 001-002/898. Annual report of Berlin Zoo for 1926.

87. January 9, 1926, *VZ*, no. 413, evening edition. See also Ursula Klös, "Völkerschauen im Zoo Berlin zwischen 1878 und 1952," *Bongo* 30 (2000): 67–69.

88. Klös, "Völkerschauen im Zoo Berlin," 70.

89. Klös, "Völkerschauen im Zoo Berlin," 70.

90. March 30, 1927, *VZ*, no. 151, evening edition, p. 4.

91. June 4, 1927, *VZ*, no. 261, Supplement 1, p. 2.

92. September 5, 1927, *VZ*, no. 49, evening edition, p. 2.

93. August 30, 1927, *VZ*, no. 408, Supplement 1, p. 2.

94. June 6, 1927, *VZ*, no. 255, p. 4.

95. June 6,1927, *VZ*, no. 255, p. 4; July 26, 1927, *VZ*, no. 349, evening edition, p. 4.

96. LA-B, A. Rep. 001-002/899. February 2, 1931, memo from chair of the board of directors to the board.

97. Klös, "Völkerschauen im Zoo Berlin," 78.

98. April 21, 1931, *VZ*, no. 186, Supplement 1, p. 2.

99. April 22, 1931, *VZ*, no. 189, Eevening edition, p. 4.

100. Klös, "Völkerschauen im Zoo Berlin," 78.

101. Balthasar Staehelin, *Völkerschauen im Zoologischen Garten Basel, 1879–1935* (Basel: Basler Afrika Bibliographien, 1993), 44.

102. Staehelin, *Völkerschauen im Zoologischen Garten Basel*, 47.

103. Staehelin, *Völkerschauen im Zoologischen Garten Basel*, 144–146.

104. Anne Dreesbach, *Gezähmte Wilde: Die Zurschaustellung "exotischer Menschen" in Deutschland, 1870–1940* (Frankfurt: Campus Verlag, 2005), 315.

105. Dreesbach, *Gezähmte Wilde*, 318.

106. Kotowski, "Tanz auf dem Vulkan," 122.

107. Annemarie Lange, *Das Wilheminische Berlin. Zwischen Jahrhundertwende und Novemberrevolution* (Berlin: Dietz, 1988), 560, 577.

108. LA-B, A. Rep. 001-002/899. Annual report of the Berlin zoo for the year 1928.

109. Mustafa Haikal and Winfried Gensch, *Der Gesang des Orang-utans: Die Geschichte des Dresdner Zoos* (Dresden: Sächsische Zeitung, 2011), 65; Scherpner, *Von Bürgern für Bürger*, 107, 111–112.

110. Haikal and Junhold, *Auf der Spur des Löwen*, 78, 123.

111. LA-B, A. Rep. 001-002/898. Annual report of Berlin Zoo for 1927.

112. LA-B, A. Rep. 001-002/898. Annual report of Berlin Zoo for 1927.

113. BA, R-1001-3359, January 21, 1910, letter.

114. Elizabeth Hanson, *Animal Attractions: Nature on Display in American Zoos* (Princeton, NJ: Princeton University Press, 2004), 100–125.

115. Lutz Heck, *Aus der Wildnis in den Zoo: Auf Tierfang in Ostafrika* (Berlin: Ullstein, 1930), 53.

116. Heck, *Aus der Wildnis*, 56.

117. LA-B, A. Rep. 001-002/899. Annual report of the Berlin zoo for the year 1928.

118. Heck, *Aus der Wildnis*, 72.

119. Heck, *Aus der Wildnis*, 76. The account of the rhino capture was reissued in 1943 in a publication for Germany's military personnel. See Ludwig Heck and Lutz Heck, *Tiere in Natur und Kunst* (Dresden: Zwinger-Verlag Rudolf Glöß, 1943), 4–34. The capture of giraffes, the other notable animal of the expedition, did not involve the killing of the parent but rather an awkward ambush with a lasso-like device. See Lutz Heck, "Giraffenfang und Giraffenzucht des Berliner Zoologischen Gartens," *Der Zoologische Garten* 9, No. 5 (1937): 191–204.

120. Heck, *Aus der Wildnis*, 77.

121. Heck, *Auf Tiersuche,* 93–118 The total value of the animals was a staggering 175,000 marks.

122. Eric Ames, *Carl Hagenbeck's Empire of Entertainments* (Seattle: University of Washington Press, 2008), 184.

123. Ames, *Carl Hagenbeck's Empire of Entertainments*, 179.

124. Ludwig Zukowsky, *Tiere um große Männer* (Frankfurt: Moritz Diesterweg, 1938), 108.

125. Ames, *Carl Hagenbeck's Empire of Entertainments*, 198.

126. Zedelmaier and Kamp, *Hellabrunn*, 33.

127. GStA PK, I. HA. Rep. 89, Nr. 31824. April 10, 1911, letter from Aktien Verien of zoo to Herr Friedrich von Hollmann.

128. LA-B, Zoo Führer, 1926.

129. LA-B, A. Pr. Br. Rep. 042, Nr. 3071. Undated newspaper article, no author given, entitled "Freianlagen im Zoo."

130. LA-B, A. Pr. Br. Rep. 042, Nr. 3071. August 25, 1929, *Berliner Tageblatt*, "Unser Zoo."

131. LA-B, *Werbeheft* 1931, 8.

132. LA-B, *Werbeheft* 1931, 8.

133. Nigel Rothfels, "Immersed with Animals," in *Representing Animals*, ed. Nigel Rothfels (Bloomington: Indiana University Press, 2002), 216.

134. Translation by Stephen Mitchell, http://www.thefoolsparadise.com/der-panther. Accessed December 2, 2014.

135. Jan Zabinski, "Die Gründung und Entwicklung des Warschauer Zoos," *Der Zoologische Garten* 9, nos. 1/2 (1937): 13.

136. Köhler, "Berlin," 898.

Chapter 5

1. Thomas Vormbaum, *A Modern History of German Criminal Law* (New York: Springer, 2014), 153, footnote 112.

2. Conan Fischer, *The Rise of the Nazis* (Manchester: Manchester University Press, 1995), 90.

3. There is an enormous literature on the Nazi rise to power. Several of the most important include Thomas Childers's work, which emphasizes the importance of religion over class. See *The Nazi Voter: The Social Foundations of Fascism in Germany* (Chapel Hill: University of North Carolina Press, 1983). Detlev Peukert highlights the fact that the Nazis drew from a broad societal spectrum in *The Weimar Republic: The Crisis of Classical Modernity* (New York: Hill and Wang, 1992). Hans Mommsen argues for the importance of structures in Weimar Germany over voting patterns as an explanation for the rise of the Nazis. See his *Rise and Fall of Weimar Democracy* (Chapel Hill: University of North Carolina Press, 1996).

4. Arnold Arluke and Clinton Sanders, *Regarding Animals* (Philadelphia: Temple University Press, 1996), 137.

5. Boria Sax, *Animals in the Third Reich: Pets, Scapegoats, and the Holocaust* (New York: Continuum, 2000), 111.

6. Arluke and Sanders, *Regarding Animals*, 134.

7. Kathleen Kete, "Animals and Ideology: Politics of Animal Protection in Europe," in *Representing Animals*, ed. Nigel Rothfels (Bloomington: Indiana University Press, 2002), 30.

8. Sax, *Animals in the Third Reich*, 113–116; Kete, "Animals and Ideology," 28.

9. Arluke and Sanders, *Regarding Animals*, 136.

10. The seminal work on Nazi cancer research is Robert Proctor, *The Nazi War on Cancer* (Princeton, NJ: Princeton University Press, 2000). For a useful introduction to Nazi environmental policies, see Franz-Josef Bruggemeier, Mark Cioc, and Thomas Zeller, eds., *How Green Were the Nazis? Nature, Environment, and Nation in the Third Reich* (Athens: Ohio University Press, 2005).

11. David Blackbourn, *The Conquest of Nature* (New York: W. W. Norton, 2006), 281.

12. Lutz Heck, *Auf Tiersuche in Weiter Welt* (Berlin: Paul Paren, 1941), 4–5.

13. See Heck, *Auf Tiersuche*, 8–9.

14. Heck, *Auf Tiersuche*, 8.

15. Ludwig Heck, *Heiter-Ernste Lebensbeichte: Erinnerungen eines alten Tiergärtners* (Berlin: Deutscher Verlag, 1938), 208.

16. Heck, *Heiter-Ernste*, 373.

17. Heck, *Heiter-Ernste*, 373.

18. Katharina Heinroth, *Mit Faltern begann's: Mein Leben mit Tieren in Breslau, München und Berlin* (Munich: Kindler, 1979), 222.

19. Aaron Skabelund, "Rassismus züchten: Schäferhunde im Dienst der Gewaltherrschaft," in *Tierische Geschichte: Die Beziehung von Mensch und Tier in der Kultur der Moderne*, ed. Dorothee Brantz and Christof Mauch (Paderborn: Ferdinand Schöningh, 2010), 59.

20. Skabelund, "Rassismus züchten," 59.

21. As quoted in Skabelund, "Rassismus züchten," 66.

22. Eugeniusz Nowak, *Wissenschaftler in turbulenten Zeiten* (Schwerin: Stock & Stein, 2005), 206.

23. Sax, *Animals in the Third Reich*, 125–136.

24. Lutz Heck, *Auf Urwild in Kanada* (Berlin: Paul Paren, 1937), 57. Heck's diary entries from his trip to Canada are reprinted in Ludwig Heck and Lutz Heck, *Tiere in Natur und Kunst* (Dresden: Zwinger-Verlag Rudolf Glöß, 1943), 45–56.

25. Heck, *Auf Urwild*, 61.

26. Kai Artinger, "Lutz Heck: Der 'Vater der Rominter Ure': Einige Bemerkungen zum wissenschaftlichen Leiter des Berliner Zoos im Nationalsozialismus," footnote 8, http://www.diegeschichteberlins.de/geschichteberlins/persoenlichkeiten/persoenlichkeitenhn/491-heck.html.

27. Artinger, "Lutz Heck," 1.

28. Heinrich Rubner, *Deutsche Forstgeschichte 1933–1945: Forstwirtschaft, Jagd und Umwelt im NS-Staat* (St. Katharinen: Scripta Mercaturae, 1997), 111.

29. Ludwig Zukowsky, *Tiere um grosse Männer* (Frankfurt: Verlag Moritz Diesterweg, 1938), 172–175.

30. Mustafa Haikal and Jörg Junhold. *Auf der Spur des Löwen: 125 Jahre Zoo Leipzig* (Leipzig: Pro Leipzig, 2003), 158.

31. BA, R4901/945. February 22, 1945, letter from Prussian Finance Minister Popitz to Göring.

32. Rubner, *Deutsche Forstgeschichte,* 186.

33. Heck, *Auf Tiersuche,* 263.

34. Rubner, *Deutsche Forstgeschichte,* 186.

35. Rubner, *Deutsche Forstgeschichte,* 186.

36. Elke Fröhlich, ed., *Die Tagebücher von Joseph Goebbels*, Part 1, vol. 3 (Munich: Saur, 1987), 145.

37. BA, NS 21/49. May 26, 1943, Aktenvermerk.

38. Heck, *Auf Tiersuche*, 290.

39. Rudolf Lehmensick, "Die Bedeutung von Schule und Universität für den Zoologischen Garten," *Der Zoologische Garten* 7, 1–3 (1934): 288. Italics in original.

40. As quoted in Kitty Millet, "Caesura, Continuity, and Myth: The Stakes of Tethering the Holocaust to German Colonial Theory," in *German Colonialism: Race, the Holocaust, and Postwar Germany*, ed. Volker Langbehn and Mohammad Salama (New York: Columbia University Press, 2011), 96–97.

41. Artinger, "Lutz Heck," 10–11, footnote 61.

42. Monika Schmidt, "Die 'Arisierung' des Berliner Zoologischen Gartens," *Jahrbuch für Antisemitismusforschung* 12 (2003): 221.

43. See Heinz-Georg Klös, *Von der Menagerie zum Tierparadies: 125 Jahre Zoo Berlin* (Berlin: Haude & Spenersche, 1969), 111–132.

44. Artinger, "Lutz Heck," 5.

45. Artinger, "Lutz Heck," 6.

46. BBAW, Bestand Akademieleitung 493. See the December 12, 1945, memorandum of the Aktien-Verein and Heck's response of May 20, 1946.

47. As quoted in Artinger, "Lutz Heck," 5.

48. Artinger, "Lutz Heck," 5.

49. Göring's hunting lodge in East Prussia should not be confused with his game reserve north of Berlin known as Shorfheide. See Frank Uekoetter, *The Green and the Brown: A History of Conservation in Nazi Germany* (New York: Cambridge University Press, 2006), 100–105.

50. Lutz Heck, *Auf Tiersuche in Weiter Welt* (Berlin: Paul Paren, 1941), 220. See also "Nachrichten aus zoologischen Gärten," *Der Zoologische Garten* 11, nos. 1/2 (1939): 35.

51. Heck, *Auf Tiersuche*, 221.

52. Walter Frisch, *Der Auerochs* (Starnberg: Lipp Graphische Betriebe, 2010), 12.

53. Manfred Kriener, "Weg ist weg," *Die Zeit*, April 26, 2010, 5, http://www.Zeit.de/2010/17/Tier-Auerochse?page=all&print=true. Accessed April 26, 2010.

54. Frisch, *Der Auerochs*, 22.

55. Frisch, *Der Auerochs*, 24.

56. Lutz Heck, *Auf Tiersuche*, 195.

57. Kriener, "Weg ist weg."

58. As quoted in Frisch, *Der Auerochs*, 59.

59. Heck, *Auf Tiersuche*, 200.

60. Heck, *Auf Tiersuche*, 214.

61. Frisch, *Der Auerochs*, 150.

62. March 7, 1931, *VZ*, no. 308, Supplement 1, p. 2.

63. LA-B, Nat 6/1934 *Führer durch den Zoologischen Garten Berlin*, 33.

64. There were efforts by German scientists during this era to breed back the Polish wild horse, but these efforts were not as sustained nor as successful as they

were with the aurochs. See Otto Antonius, "Zur Rückzüchtung des polnischen Wildpferdes," *Der Zoologische Garten* 10, nos. 1–2 (1938): 102–107.

65. Blackbourn, *Conquest of Nature*, 296.

66. The Nazis did fund legitimate research to improve animal breeding, including cattle, but Heck's work was not part of it. See Ute Diechmann, *Biologists under Hitler* (Cambridge, MA: Harvard University Press, 1996), 150, and Susanne Heim, *Plant Breeding and Agrarian Research in Kaiser-Wlhelm-Institutes, 1933–1945* (Dordrecht: Springer, 2008).

67. LA-B, Nat 6/1939, *Führer durch den Zoologischen Garten Berlin*, 54. It appears that Heck's figures are off here, as, by his own earlier account, seven were released into the Prussian woods.

68. As quoted in Kai Artinger, "Lutz Heck: Der 'Vater der Rominter Ure': Einige Bemerkungen zum wissenschaftlichen Leiter des Berliner Zoos im Nationalsozialismus," 9, footnote 48, http://www.diegeschichteberlins.de/geschichteberlins/persoenlichkeiten/persoenlichkeitenhn/491-heck.html.

69. Heck, *Auf Tiersuche,* 223.

70. Kriener, "Weg ist weg," 7.

71. Artinger, "Lutz Heck," 4.

72. Steffi Kammerer, "Im Gehege des Vergessens: Was wurde aus Aktie 1114?" *Süddeutsche Zeitung*, October 12, 2000, 1, Berlin-Seite, http://www.hagalil.com/archiv/2000/10/zoo-aktie.htm.

73. Kammerer, "Im Gehege des Vergessens," 1. Werner Cohn has made available the full text of the letter from the zoo's lawyer, Dr. Richard Lehmann, from April 4, 2000, on his website www.wernercohn.com/zoo.html.

74. Kammerer, "Im Gehege des Vergessens," 2.

75. Sylke Heun and Peter Schubert, "Die langen dunkeln Schatten der Vergangenheit: Eine Studie belegt erstmals, wie jüdische Zoo-Aktionäre in der Nazizeit systematisch ausgegrenzt wurden," *Die Welt*, October 6, 2002.

76. Schmidt, "Die 'Arisierung' des Berliner Zoologischen Gartens," 212. Seigman and Simon mentioned in the board's report for 1933 were Jews, as were two other members of the board: Ernst Kritzler and Paul Julius von Schwabach. The latter two, however, had converted to Christianity.

77. Schmidt, "Die 'Arisierung' des Berliner Zoologischen Gartens," 215. Underline in original.

78. Schmidt, "Die 'Arisierung' des Berliner Zoologischen Gartens," 218.

79. Michael Philipp, "Mythos Germania," in *Berlin: Geschichte einer Stadt*, ed. Julius Schoeps (Berlin: be.bra, 2007), 155.

80. Henning Köhler, "Berlin in der Weimarer Republik," in *Geschichte Berlins,* vol. 2, ed. Wolfgang Ribbe (Berlin: Berliner Wissenschafts-Verlag, 2002), 884.

81. Schmidt, "Die 'Arisierung' des Berliner Zoologischen Gartens," 223.

82. Christine Schmitt, "Zoo stellt sich der Geschichte," *Jüdische Allgemeine*, April 21, 2011, http://www.juedische-allgemeine.de/article/view/id/10223. It is also

likely not irrelevant that two neighborhoods in close proximity to the zoo, Charlottenburg and Wilmersdorf, had the highest percentage of Jews in the population of Berlin. See Christian Engeli and Wolfgang Ribbe, "Berlin in der NS-Zeit," in *Geschichte Berlins,* vol. 2, ed. Wolfgang Ribbe (Berlin: Berliner Wissenschafts-Verlag, 2002), 953.

83. Schmidt, "Die 'Arisierung' des Berliner Zoologischen Gartens," 226.

84. Kammerer, "Im Gehege des Vergessens," 3. Wolf Gruner from the Berlin Centre for Antisemitic Research claims to have in his possession a document that demonstrates Heck's desire to ban Jews from the zoo.

85. Schmidt, "Die 'Arisierung' des Berliner Zoologischen Gartens," 227.

86. Engeli and Ribbe, "Berlin in der NS-Zeit," 958.

87. Schmidt, "Die 'Arisierung' des Berliner Zoologischen Gartens," 229.

88. Thomas Loy, "Gedenktafel für jüdische Zoo-Aktionäre enthüllt," *Der Tagesspiegel,* June 28, 2011, http://www.tagesspiegel.de/berlin/ns-geschichte-gedenktafel-fuer-juedische-zoo-aktionaere-enthuellt/4334750.html.   Accessed April 9, 2012.

89. Kammerer, "Im Gehege des Vergessens," 2.

90. Hans Frädrich, "Der Spurensuche zum Geleit," *Bongo* 24 (1994): 4.

91. "Jahresbericht 1984," *Bongo* 9 (1985): 127.

92. See Haikal and Junhold. *Auf der Spur des Löwen,* 168; Ludwig Baumgarten, *Chronik Zoologischer Garten Halle,* Teil 1, 1901–1945 (Halle: Zoologischer Garten Halle GmbH, 2001); Lothar Dittrich, and Annelore Rieke-Müller, *Ein Garten für Menschen und Tiere: 125 Jahre Zoo Hannover* (Hannover: Verlaggesellschaft Grütter, 1990); Horst Gleiss, *Unter Robben, Gnus und Tigerschlangen* (Breslau: Natura et Patria Verlag, 1967); Mustafa Haikal and Winfried Gensch, *Der Gesang des Orang-utans: Die Geschichte des Dresdner Zoos* (Dresden: Sächsische Zeitung, 2011); Christoph Scherpner, *Von Bürgern für Bürger—125 Jahre Zoologischer Garten Frankfurt am Main (*Frankfurt: Zoologischer Garten, 1983).

93. Gleiss, *Unter Robben,* 175.

94. Evelyn Gottschlich, "Wiedereröffnung und Zerstörung," in *Nilpferde an der Isar: Eine Geschichte des Tierparks Hellabrunn in München,* ed. Michael Kamp and Helmut Zedelmaier (Munich: Buchendorf Verlag, 2000), 137.

95. Helmut Zedelmaier and Michael Kamp, *Hellabrunn: Geschichte und Geschichten des Münchener Tierparks* (Munich: Bassermann, 2011), 84.

Chapter 6

1. Lutz Heck, "Nachrichten aus zoologischen Gärten," *Der Zoologische Garten* 8 (1936): 239.

2. H. Steinmetz, "Nachrichten aus zoologischen Gärten," *Der Zoologische Garten* 12 (1940): 335–336.

3. Lutz Heck, "Nachrichten aus zoologischen Gärten," 239.

4. BA, R 4901/1694. Geschäftsbericht, Actien-Verein des zoologischen Gartens zu Berlin für das Jahr 1936, erstattet am 27. April 1937.

5. BA, R 4901/1694. Geschäftsbericht.

6. Lutz Heck, "Nachrichten aus zoologischen Gärten," 242.

7. BA, R 4901/1694. Geschäftsbericht.

8. BA, R 4901/1694. Geschäftsbericht.

9. BA, R 4901/1694. Geschäftsbericht.

10. H. Steinmetz, "Berlin: Bericht über das Kalenderjahr 1937," *Der Zoologische Garten* 10, nos. 3–4 (1938): 156–157.

11. LA-B, Nat 6/1906. *Zoo Führer*, 78.

12. Der Verlag, "Die Deutsche Heimatlehre und ihr Ziel," *Die Tierwelt*, November 1937, 1.

13. Der Verlag, "Die Deutsche Heimatlehre und ihr Ziel," *Die Tierwelt*, November 1937, 1.

14. David Blackbourn, *The Conquest of Nature: Water, Landscape, and the Making of Modern Germany* (New York: W. W. Norton, 2006), 302–303.

15. Ludwig Zukowsky, *Tiere um grosse Männer* (Frankfurt: Verlag Moritz Diesterweg, 1938), 177.

16. Zukowsky, *Tiere um große Männer*, 179.

17. K. W. Muth, "Tiergärten und Tierschutz," *Der Zoologische Garten* 8 (1935/36), 298.

18. Muth, "Tiergärten und Tierschutz," 298.

19. Muth, "Tiergärten und Tierschutz," 298.

20. Christoph Scherpner, *Von Bürgern für Bürger—125 Jahre Zoologischer Garten Frankfurt am Main* (Frankfurt: Zoologischer Garten, 1983), 125.

21. Zukowsky, *Tiere um große Männer*, 8.

22. Scherpner, *Von Bürgern für Bürger,* 122.

23. Karl Max Schneider, "Vom Daseinsrecht der Zoologischen Gärten," *Der Zoologische Garten* 8, nos. 7–9 (1936): 174.

24. Schneider, "Daseinsrecht," 174.

25. Schneider, "Daseinsrecht," 174.

26. Karl Max Schneider, "Der neue Leipziger Tierkindergarten," *Der Zoologische Garten* 8, nos. 7–9 (1936): 274–282.

27. J. V. Ueküll, "Tierparadies im Zoo: Brief an den Direktor des Leipziger Zoologischen Gartens," *Der Zoologische Garten* 12 (1940): 18–19.

28. Karl Max Schneider, " 'Tierparadies im Zoo': Antwort auf den Brief des Herrn Baron Jakob von Ueküll," *Der Zoologische Garten* 12 (1940): 195.

29. Schneider, " 'Tierparadies im Zoo,' " 195.

30. Hans-Ulrich Wehler, *Deutsche Gesellschaftsgeschichte*, vol. 4 (Munich: Beck, 2003), 481.

31. Heinz Knobloch, *Eine Berliner Kindheit: Zwischen Olympia und Luftschutzkeller* (Berlin: Jaron, 1999), 198.

32. BA, R 4901/1694. Geschäftsbericht.

33. Wehler, *Deutsche Gesellschaftsgeschichte*, vol. 4, 482.

34. Wehler, *Deutsche Gesellschaftsgeschichte*, vol. 4, 839.

35. BA, R 4901/1694. August 23, 1937, letter from Heck to undisclosed recipient.

36. BA, R 4901/1694. August 23, 1937, letter from Heck to undisclosed recipient. Underline in original.

37. Michael Philipp, "Mythos Germania," in *Berlin: Geschichte einer Stadt*, ed. Julius Schoeps (Berlin: be.bra, 2007), 152.

38. Christian Engeli and Wolfgang Ribbe, "Berlin in der NS-Zeit," in *Geschichte Berlins*, vol. 2, ed. Wolfgang Ribbe (Berlin: Berliner Wissenschafts-Verlag, 2002), 994.

39. BA, 4901/1694. June 5, 1939, letter from Speer to Prussian Finance Minister.

40. BA, 4901/1694. September 25, 1937, memorandum from Generalbauinspektor

41. BA, 4901/1694. May 22, 1939, letter from mayor of Nürnberg to Generalbauinspektor für die Reichshauptstadt.

42. BA, 4901/1694. August 12, 1939, letter from Heck and Ammon to Prussian finance minister.

43. BA, 4901/1694. August 12, 1939, letter from Heck and Ammon to Prussian finance minister.

44. BA, 4901/1694. August 12, 1939, letter from Heck and Ammon to Prussian finance minister.

45. BA 4901/1694. August 30, 1939, letter from Hans Ammon to Herr Oberbaurat Stephan.

46. Peter Mühling, *Der alte Nürnberger Tiergarten 1912–1939* (Nürnberg: Druckhaus, 1987), 111–112.

47. BA, 4901/1694. November 29, 1939, Protocol of meeting between Albert Speer and Lutz Heck.

48. Lothar Dittrich and Annelore Rieke-Müller, *Ein Garten für Menschen und Tiere: 125 Jahre Zoo Hannover* (Hannover: Verlaggesellschaft Grütter, 1990), 127; Scherpner, *Von Bürgern für Bürger,* 127.

49. Ludwig Heck and Lutz Heck, *Tiere in Natur und Kunst* (Dresden: Zwinger-Verlag Rudolf Glöß, 1943), 3.

50. H. Steinmetz, "Nachrichten aus zoologischen Gärten," *Der Zoologische Garten* 12 (1940): 342–343.

51. Steinmetz, "Nachrichten aus zoologischen Gärten," 342.

52. See the entries on Duisburg, Hannover, Halle, and Frankfurt in "Unsere Tiergärten im Winter 1939/40," *Der Zoologische Garten* 13 (1941): 15–33; Heinz Heck entry on München-Hellabrunn, "Unsere Tiergärten im Winter 1939/40," *Der Zoologische Garten* 13 (1941): 72–73.

53. Hans-Georg Thienemann, entry on Königsberg, "Unsere Tiergärten im Winter 1939/40," *Der Zoologische Garten* 13 (1941): 33.

54. Heinz-Georg Klös, *Von der Menagerie zum Tierparadies: 125 Jahre Zoo Berlin* (Berlin: Haude & Spenersche, 1969), 116.

55. BA, R2/4749. January 1940 (exact date illegible) from Reichminister der Luftfahrt und Oberbefehlshaber der Luftwaffe.

56. LA-B, A Rep. 032-08, Nr. 297. February 26, 1940, letter from Actien Verein to Construction Police of the Reich Capital.

57. BA, R2/4749. April 10, 1940, Richtlinien für die Durchführung der Räumung zoologischer Gärten, Tierparks, Tiergärten und Heimattiergärten. Issued by the Reichsforstmeister.

58. BA, R2/4749. May 13, 1941, letter from Reichsforstmeister to Reich Minister of Finance.

59. BA, R2/4749. May 5, 1943, memorandum.

60. LA-B, A. Rep. 032-08, Nr. 297. April 17, 1942, letter from Heck to construction police.

61. Heimatmuseum Charlottenburg, uncatalogued. *Geschäftsbericht für das Jahr 1941.* Presented at general assembly on May 15, 1942.

62. Katharina Heinroth, *Mit Faltern begann's: Mein Leben mit Tieren in Breslau, München und Berlin* (Munich: Kindler, 1979), 128.

63. H. Steinmetz entry on Berlin "Nachrichten aus zoologischen Gärten," *Der Zoologische Garten* 13 (1941): 307–311.

64. LA-B Nat 6/1941, Lutz Heck, *Wegeweiser durch den Zoologischen Garten Berlin*, 11.

65. Wehler, *Deutsche Gesellschaftsgeschichte*, vol. 4, 931.

66. Robin Neillands, *The Bomber War: The Allied Air Offensive against Nazi Germany* (New York: Overlook Press, 2001), 283–284.

67. Martin Middlebrook, *The Berlin Raids: R.A.F. Bomber Command Winter 1943–44* (New York: Viking, 1988), 112.

68. Engeli and Ribbe, "Berlin in der NS-Zeit," 1012.

69. Hans-Georg von Studnitz, *While Berlin Burns* (Englewood Cliffs, NJ: Prentice Hall, 1964), 137.

70. Dieter Borkowski, *Wer weiß, ob wir uns wiedersehen: Erinnerungen an eine Berliner Jugend* (Frankfurt: Fischer, 1980), 78–79.

71. Neillands, *The Bomber War*, 283–284; Philipp, "Mythos Germania," 155.

72. Helga Schneider, *The Bonfire of Berlin* (London: Heinemann, 1995), 70.

73. As quoted in Roger Moorhouse, *Berlin at War: Life and Death in Hitler's Capital, 1939–1945* (London: Bodley Head, 2010), 321–322.

74. Klös, *Von der Menagerie*, 116.

75. Klös, *Von der Menagerie*, 119.

76. Klös, *Von der Menagerie*, 119. Heinroth, *Mit Faltern begann's*, 130–131.

77. Moorhouse, *Berlin at War*, 323.

78. BA, NS 21/49. November 26, 1943, letter from Tratz to friends and acquaintances.

79. Klös, *Von der Menagerie*, 121.

80. Klös, *Von der Menagerie*, 122.

81. Studnitz, *While Berlin Burns*, 140.

82. As quoted in Michael Philipp, "Mythos Germania," 155.

83. Klös, *Von der Menagerie*, 121.

84. BA, R 4901/945 July 31, 1944, letter from Reich Minister for Science, Upbringing, and Education to Heck.

85. Klös, *Von der Menagerie*, 130.

86. Helmut Altner, *Berlin Dance of Death* (Staplehurst: Spellmount, 2002), 157–159.

87. Heinroth, *Mit Faltern begann's*, 139.

88. Mustafa Haikal and Jörg Junhold. *Auf der Spur des Löwen: 125 Jahre Zoo Leipzig* (Leipzig: Pro Leipzig, 2003), 174.

89. Horst Gleiss, *Unter Robben, Gnus und Tigerschlangen* (Breslau: Natura et Patria Verlag, 1967), 180–181.

90. Mustafa Haikal and Winfried Gensch, *Der Gesang des Orang-utans: Die Geschichte des Dresdner Zoos* (Dresden: Sächsische Zeitung, 2011), 90–92.

91. Ludwig Baumgarten, *Chronik Zoologischer Garten Halle*, Teil 1, *1901–1945* (Halle: Zoologischer Garten Halle GmbH, 2001), 164.

92. Haikal and Junhold, *Auf der Spur des Löwen*, 155.

93. Dittrich and Rieke-Müller, *Ein Garten für Menschen*, 130.

94. Scherpner, *Von Bürgern für Bürger*, 128–129.

Chapter 7

1. Christian Engeli and Wolfgang Ribbe, "Berlin in der NS-Zeit," in *Geschichte Berlins,* vol. 2, ed. Wolfgang Ribbe (Berlin: Berliner Wissenschafts-Verlag, 2002), 1021.

2. Katharina Heinroth, *Mit Faltern begann's: Mein Leben mit Tieren in Breslau, München und Berlin* (Munich: Kindler, 1979), 146.

3. Alexandra Richie, *Faust's Metropolis: A History of Berlin* (New York: Carroll & Graf, 1998), 605.

4. Heinz-Georg Klös, *Von der Menagerie zum Tierparadies: 125 Jahre Zoo Berlin* (Berlin: Haude & Spenersche, 1969), 300.

5. Heinz-Georg Klös and Ursula Klös, *Der Berliner Zoo im Spiegel seiner Bauten 1841–1989* (Berlin: Heenemann, 1990), 218.

6. She would be confirmed as director one month later by the zoo's new board of directors. Heinroth, *Mit Faltern begann's*, 148–150.

7. Heinroth, *Mit Faltern begann's*, 153.

8. Richie, *Faust's Metropolis*, 605.

9. Heinroth, *Mit Faltern begann's*, 153.

10. Klös and Klös, *Der Berliner Zoo,* 218.

11. Wolfgang Ribbe, "Vom Vier-Mächte-Regime zur Bundeshauptstadt," in *Geschichte Berlins,* vol. 2, ed. Wolfgang Ribbe (Berlin: Berliner Wissenschafts-Verlag, 2002), 1096.

12. Heinroth, *Mit Faltern begann's*, 169–170.

13. Heinroth, *Mit Faltern begann's*, 260.

14. Heinroth, *Mit Faltern begann's*, 261.

15. Heinroth, *Mit Faltern begann's*, 261.

16. Klös, *Von der Menagerie*, 220–221. Not until 1968 did the Munich zoo ban visitors from feeding animals, out of concern for humans rather than animals. In that year, a young girl had been killed while feeding an elephant. Helmut Zedelmaier and Michael Kamp, *Hellabrunn: Geschichte und Geschichten des Münchner Tierparks* (Munich: Bassermann, 2011), 107.

17. Klös and Klös, *Der Berliner Zoo*, 221–224.

18. Klös, *Von der Menagerie*, 176.

19. Klös, *Von der Menagerie*, 147.

20. Klös, *Von der Menagerie*, 150.

21. Klös, *Von der Menagerie*, 262–263; Heinroth, *Mit Faltern begann's*, 226.

22. Klös, *Von der Menagerie*, 269, 297.

23. Heinz-Georg Klös, Hans Frädrich, and Ursula Klös, *Die Arche Noah an der Spree: 150 Jahre Zoologischer Garten Berlin. Eine tiergärtnerische Kulturgeschichte von 1844 bis 1994* (Berlin: FAB Verlag, 1994), 471. These attendance figures do not include the aquarium. If aquarium attendance is included, the overall figure rises to 2.6 million in 1970.

24. BA, SAPMO, DR 2/11. July 9, 1948, Protokoll der Sitzung Neulehrerfortbildung. Referent: Herr Professor Schneider.

25. BA, SAPMO, DY 30/IV 2/9.06/101. February 13, 1962, Information über eine Beratung des Gen. Siegfried Wagner, Leiter der Abt. Kultur beim ZK, mit der Fachkommission für Zoologische Gärten beim Ministerium für Kultur am 10.2.1961.

26. BA, SAPMO, DR 2/11, March 3, 1952, "Die Bedeutung der zoologischen Gärten für die Volksbildung und die Wissenschaft," report by Wolfgang Ullrich.

27. BA, SAPMO, DR 2/4119. January 28, 1953, letter from Wandel to Friedrich Ebert, mayor of Berlin.

28. BA, SAPMO, DR 2/4119. February 2, 1953, letter from Ebert to Wandel.

29. Jürgen Mladek, *Professor Dathe und seine Tiere* (Berlin: Das Neue Berlin, 2010), 42.

30. Heinrich Dathe, *Lebenserinnerungen eines leidenschaftlichen Tiergärtners* (Munich: Koehler & Amelang, 2001), 219.

31. LA-B, C. Rep. 121/188. August 27, 1954, Magistratsbeschluss Nr. 690.

32. LA-B, C. Rep. 121, Nr. 29. Stenographisches Protokoll der ersten Zusammenkunft der Gemeinschaft der Förderer des Tierparks und der Leitung des NAW Gross-Berlin am Mittwoch, dem 28. März 1956.

33. LA-B, C. Rep. 121, 176. Undated lecture by Heinrich Dathe, "Der Tierpark Berlin—ein neuer Platz für wilde Tiere in Berlin."

34. LA-B, C. Rep. 121, Nr. 29. Stenographisches Protokoll der ersten Zusammenkunft der Gemeinschaft der Förderer des Tierparks und der Leitung des NAW Gross-Berlin am Mittwoch, dem 28. März 1956.

35. LA-B, C. Rep. 121, Nr. 29. Stenographisches Protokoll der ersten Zusammenkunft der Gemeinschaft der Föderer des Tierparks und der Leitung des NAW Gross-Berlin am Mittwoch, dem 28. März 1956.

36. LA-B, C. Rep. 121/188. Undated. Organisationsplan für den Festzug; June 4, 1955, letter from Erdmann, Leitung des NAW Gross-Berlin an Direktor Beck, Märkisches Museum.

37. Mladek, *Professor Dathe*, 51.

38. Dathe, *Lebenserinnerungen*, 258.

39. Dathe, *Lebenserinnerungen*, 220.

40. Helmut Zedelmaier and Michael Kamp, *Hellabrunn: Geschichte und Geschichten des Münchener Tierparks* (Munich: Bassermann, 2011), 89.

41. LA-B, C. Rep 121, Nr. 178. December 21, 1957, Bericht über die Entwicklung des Tierpark Berlin im Jahr 1957.

42. May 3, 1959, *Welt am Sonntag*, clipping in LA-B, C. Rep. 121, Nr. 174.

43. May 3, 1959, *Welt am Sonntag*, clipping in LA-B, C. Rep. 121, Nr. 174.

44. LA-B, C. Rep. 121, Nr. 174. July 4, 1960, Kurzbericht über den Besuch von Ausländern und Westdeutschen.

45. LA-B, C. Rep. 121, Nr. 174. July 4, 1960, Kurzbericht über den Besuch von Ausländern und Westdeutschen.

46. Christina Schwenkel, "Affective Solidarities and East German Reconstruction of Postwar Vietnam," in *Comrades of Color: East Germany in the Cold War World*, ed. Quinn Slobodian (New York: Berghahn, 2015), 272.

47. Bernd Schaefer, "Socialist Modernization in Vietnam: The East German Approach," in *Comrades of Color: East Germany in the Cold War World*, ed. Quinn Slobodian (New York: Berghahn, 2015), 96–97.

48. Schwenkel, "Affective Solidarities," 272.

49. BA, DY 6/ vorl. 1905. November 8, 1956, letter from Krebs to Ministry for Foreign Affairs.

50. BA, DY 6/vorl. 1905. May 5, 1958, letter from Büro des Präsidiums to Dathe.

51. BA, SAPMO, DY 6/1905, January 27, 1958, letter from Ministry for Foreign Affairs to Presidium of National Council.

52. BA, SAPMO, DY 6/1905, January 27, 1958, letter from Ministry for Foreign Affairs to Presidium of National Council.

53. BBAW Bestand Akademieleitung, Nr. 39, November 4, 1957, letter from Prof. Dr. Streseman to DAW.

54. BA, DF/F/50051, January 23, 1960, Jahresbericht 1959 der Zoologischen Forschungsstelle im Berliner Tierpark.

55. BBAW Bestand Akademieleitung, Nr. 39, September 24, 1958, Ordnung der Aufgaben der Befugnisse und der Arbeitsweise der Zoologischen Forschungsstelle der Deutschen Akademie der Wissenschaften zu Berlin.

56. BBA AKL 1969-1991, Nr. 557, Bestand Akademieleitung 1969–1991, December 3, 1970, Dathe report.

57. Dathe, *Lebenserinnerungen*, 47.

58. BA, DY 30/ J IV 2/3/1028, January 14, 1964, Vorlage für das Sekretariat des ZK der SED.

59. Dathe, *Lebenserinnerungen*, 86–87.

60. Eugeniusz Nowak, *Wissenschaftler in turbulenten Zeiten* (Schwerin: Stock & Stein, 2005), 291.

61. Dathe, *Lebenserinnerungen,* 87–88.

62. The best recent book on the subject is Henry Leide, *NS-Verbrecher und Staatssicherheit: Die geheime Vergangenheitspolitik der DDR* (Göttingen: Vandenhoeck & Ruprecht, 2005).

63. Dathe, *Lebenserinnerungen*, 141.

64. BA, DY 30/J IV 2/ 3A, September 1, 1967, Vorlage an das Sekretariat des Zentralkomitees der SED.

65. Mladek, *Professor Dathe*, 28.

66. Dathe, *Lebenserinnerungen*, 176.

67. LA-B, C. Rep. 121, Nr. 45, November 30, 1954, Dathe contract.

68. BA, DY 27/7896, November 7, 1985, *Neues Deutschland*.

69. Lothar Heinke, "Der Arche-Typ. Ein Leben für den Tierpark Fredrichsfelde: Vor 100 Jahren wurde der Zoologe Heinrich Dathe geboren. Seine Zeit als Direktor ist bis heute legendär," November 7, 2010, *Der Tagesspiegel*.

70. Mladek, *Professor Dathe,* 89.

71. Heinke, "Der Arche-Typ. Ein Leben für den Tierpark Fredrichsfelde."

72. Heinroth, *Mit Faltern begann's*, 240.

73. LA-B, C. Rep. 121, 176, September 22, 1964, letter from Stadtrat Ernst Hoffmann to Dathe.

74. LA-B, C. Rep. 121, Nr. 174. 24.12.162, Bericht über einen Besuch im Zoologischen Garten West-Berlin am December 8, 1962, by Dathe.

75. LA-B, C. Rep. 121, 176, August 12, 1963, clipping from *Die Welt*, "Amerikaner und Sowjetsoldaten treffen sich vor Affenkäfigen."

76. Nowak, *Wissenschaftler*, 300.

77. Mladek, *Professor Dathe*, 165.

78. LA-B, C. Rep. 121, Nr. 178, August 20, 1956, letter from Ministerium für Kultur to Magistrat.

79. BA, DY 6/ vorl. 1905, September 11, 1956, letter from H. Erdmann to Solidaritätsausschuss für Korea und Vietnam.

80. BA, DY 6/vorl. 1905, May 5, 1958, letter from Büro des Präsidiums to Dathe.

81. "Vor Tieren geht der Schlagbaum hoch," August 7, 1956, *Frankfurter Allgemeine Zeitung*. Clipping held in LA-B, C. Rep. 121, 176.

82. LA-B, C. Rep. 121, 176. Undated talk by Dathe, "Der Tierpark Berlin—ein neuer Platz für wilde Tiere in Berlin."

83. LA-B, C. Rep. 121, Nr. 178, December 18, 1958, Pressemitteilung Nr. 115/58.

84. LA-B, C. Rep. 121/23, August 5, 1958, letter from Dathe to Frau Stadtrat Blecha.

85. LA-B, C. Rep. 121, Nr. 178, April 27, 1960, letter from Dathe to Stadtrat Frau Blecha.

86. LA-B, C. Rep. 121, Nr. 178, November 5, 1960, Memorandum regarding telephone conversations with Dathe on the outlook for Berlin's Tierpark.

87. LA-B, C. Rep. 121/23, July 22, 1964, news release.

88. BA, DY 30/ J IV 2/3/947. Protocol Nr. 9/64 of the Secretariat of the Central Committee's sitting on January 29, 1964.

89. BA, DY 30/ J IV 2/3/1028, January 14, 1964, Submission for the Secretariat of the Central Committee of the SED.

90. Mladek, *Professor Dathe*, 120.

91. LA-B, C. Rep. 121, Nr. 340, December 28, 1962, news release Nr. 131/62 by Dathe.

92. LA-B, C. Rep. 121, Nr. 782, January 16, 1976, terms of reference for the Berlin Tierpark.

93. BA, RR 1/5720, March 3, 1979, Siegfried Wagner speech "Die Tiergärten in der entwickelten sozialistischen Gesellschaft."

94. BA, RR 1/5720, March 3, 1979, Siegfried Wagner speech "Die Tiergärten in der entwickelten sozialistischen Gesellschaft."

95. LA-B, C. Rep. 121, 176, May 7, 1962, Presseinformation.

96. Michael Horn and Gottfried Weise, *Das Grosse Lexikon des DDR-Fussballs* (Berlin: Schwarzkopf & Schwarzkopf, 2004), 420.

97. Dathe, *Lebenserinnerungen,* 220.

98. Mladek, *Professor Dathe,* 7.

99. LA-B, C. Rep. 121, 176. Undated talk by Dathe "Der Tierpark Berlin—ein neuer Platz für wilde Tiere in Berlin."

100. Klös, Frädrich, and Klös, *Die Arche Noah an der Spree*, 471. These attendance figures do not include the aquarium.

101. Knautschke went on to sire twenty-four offspring. Heinroth, *Mit Faltern begann's,* 174–177.

Epilogue

1. Sascha Krejsa, "'Vormittags war ich im Zoo.' Der Berliner Zoo als literarischer Ort. Deutsche und russische Schriftsteller im Zoo der 20er Jahre am Beispiel von Kurt Tucholsky und Vladimir Nabokov." Undergraduate thesis, Potsdam University, 2011, 11.

2. Barton Johnson, "A Guide to Nabokov's 'A Guide to Berlin,'" *Slavic and East European Journal* 23, no. 3 (1979): 354.

3. Vladimir Nabokov, "A Guide to Berlin," *New Yorker*, March 1, 1976, 28.

4. Nabokov, "A Guide to Berlin," 27.

5. Nabokov, "A Guide to Berlin," 28.

6. There are other indications of the Tierpark's popularity; for example, in 1957, the Tierpark benefited from an astounding 81,000 volunteer hours; "Zwischen

Kängaruh und Transparenten," *Die Deutsche Zeitung*, May 30, 1959. Clipping in LA-B, C. Rep. 121, Nr. 174.

7. Katharina Heinroth, *Mit Faltern begann's: Mein Leben mit Tieren in Breslau, München und Berlin* (Munich: Kindler, 1979), 260.

8. Elizabeth Hanson, *Animal Attractions: Nature on Display in American Zoos* (Princeton, NJ: Princeton University Press, 2004), 23.

9. Ian Jared Miller, *The Nature of the Beasts: Empire and Exhibition at the Tokyo Imperial Zoo* (Berkeley: University of California Press, 2013), 105.

10. "Tod eines Eisbären: RIP Knut," *Spiegel Online* March 20, 2011, http://www.spiegel.de/panorama/gesellschaft/tod-eines-eisbaeren-r-i-p-knut-a-752059-druck.html.

11. Thomas Schmidt, "Die Bärenmarke," *Zeit Online*, March 28 2007, http://www.zeit.de/2007/14/Knut/komplettansicht?print=true.

12. Roger Boyes, "The Abandoned Cub Who Faces Death Sentence because He Will Grow Up a Softie," *The Times* (London), March 20, 2007.

13. Stefan Jacobs and Johannes Radke, "Eisbär Knut: Tod eines Superstars," *Der Tagesspiegel*, March 19, 2011, http://www.tagesspiegel.de/berlin/berliner-zoo-eisbaer-knut-tod-eines-superstars/3968216.html.

14. "Tod eines Eisbären: RIP Knut," *Spiegel Online*, March 20, 2011, http://www.spiegel.de/panorama/gesellschaft/tod-eines-eisbaeren-r-i-p-knut-a-752059-druck.html.

15. Stefan Jacobs and Johannes Radke, "Eisbär Knut: Tod eines Superstars," *Der Tagesspiegel*, March 19, 2011, http://www.tagesspiegel.de/berlin/berliner-zoo-eisbaer-knut-tod-eines-superstars/3968216.html.

16. "Zoodirektor kritisiert Knut-Hysterie," *taz*, March 27, 2011, http://www.taz.de/!68087/ Accessed November 17, 2014.

17. Constanza Nauhaus, "Der ausgestopfte Eisbär Knut ist zurück," *Die Welt,* July 28, 1914, http://www.welt.de/regionales/berlin/article130647011/Der-ausgestopfte-Eisbaer-Knut-ist-zurueck.html Accessed November 17, 2014.

18. As quoted in Thomas Lekan, "The Nature of Home: Landscape Preservation and Local Identities," in *Localism, Landscape, and the Ambiguities of Place: German-Speaking Central Europe, 1860–1930*, ed. David Blackbourn and James Retallack (Toronto: University of Toronto Press, 2007), 165.

BIBLIOGRAPHY

Archives

Archiv der Berlin-Brandenburgischen Akademie der Wissenschaften (BBAW)
Archiv der Berliner Gesellschaft für Anthropologie, Ethnologie und Urgeschichte
Archiv des Berliner Zoos (photo only)
Bundesarchiv (BA)
Geheimes Staatsarchiv Preußischer Kulturbesitz (GStA)
Heimatsmuseum Charlottenburg
Landesarchiv Berlin (LA-B)

Newspapers

Schwedter Tageblatt (1935)
Vossische Zeitung (VZ) (1878–1931)

Journals

Bongo (1985–2000)
Der Zoologische Garten (1873–1942)
Die Gartenlaube (1855–1890)

Books and Articles

Altner, Helmut. *Berlin Dance of Death*. Staplehurst, UK: Spellmount, 2002.

Ames, Eric. *Carl Hagenbeck's Empire of Entertainments*. Seattle: University of Washington Press, 2008.

Angermann, Renate. "Anna Held, Paul Matschie und die Säugetiere des Berliner Zoologischen Gartens." *Bongo* 24 (1994): 107–138.

Antonius, Otto. "Zur Rückzüchtung des polnischen Wildpferdes." *Der Zoologische Garten* 10, nos. 1–2 (1938): 102–107.

Arluke, Arnold, and Clinton Sanders. *Regarding Animals*. Philadelphia: Temple University Press, 1996.

Artinger, Kai. "Lutz Heck: Der 'Vater der Rominter Ure': Einige Bemerkungen zum wissenschaftlichen Leiter des Berliner Zoos im Nationalsozialismus." http://www.diegeschichteberlins.de/geschichteberlins/persoenlichkeiten/persoenlichkeitenhn/491-heck.html.

Ash, Mitchell, ed. *Mensch, Tier und Zoo: Der Tiergarten Schönbrunn im internationalen Vergleich vom 18. Jahrhundert bis heute*. Vienna: Böhlau Verlag, 2008

"Ausserordentliche Zusammenkunft im zoologischen Garten am 7. November 1880." *Zeitschrift für Ethnologie* 12 (1880): 253–274.

Barclay, David. *Friedrich Wilhelm IV and the Prussian Monarchy 1840–1861*. Oxford: Oxford University Press, 1995.

Bauer-Dubau, Karolin, and Dieter Jung. "Letzte Zufluchtsstätte Zoo." *Bongo* 24 (1994): 181–198.

Baumgarten, Ludwig. *Chronik Zoologischer Garten Halle*. Teil 1, *1901–1945*. Halle: Zoologischer Garten Halle GmbH, 2001.

Beckmann, Ludwig. "Die Hagenbeck'schen Singhalesen." *Die Gartenlaube* 34 (1884): 564–566.

Bellmer, Elizabeth Henry. "The Statesman and the Ophthalmologist: Gladstone and Magnus on the Evolution of Human Colour Vision, One Small Episode of the Nineteenth-Century Darwinian Debate." *Annals of Science* 56 (1999): 25–45.

Berger, John. *About Looking*. New York: Vintage International, 1991.

"Bericht des Verwaltungsrats der Neuen Zoologischen Gesellschaft zu Frankfurt a. M. für 1899." *Der Zoologische Garten* 41 (1900): 248–254.

"Bericht über den zoologischen Garten zu Dresden über das Geschäftsjahr von 1. April 1890 bis 31. März 1891." *Der Zoologische Garten* 33 (1892): 54–58.

Blackbourn, David. *The Conquest of Nature: Water, Landscape, and the Making of Modern Germany*. New York: W. W. Norton, 2006.

Blackbourn, David, and Geoff Eley. *The Peculiarities of German History*. New York: Oxford University Press, 1984.

Blaszkiewitz, Bernhard. "Vom Spitzhörnchen zum Orang-Utan—Hundert Jahre Primatenhaltung in Zoologischen Gärten." *Bongo* 13 (1987): 36–62.

Boddice, Rob. *A History of Attitudes and Behaviours towards Animals in Eighteenth- and Nineteenth-Century Britain*. Lewiston: Mellen, 2009.

Bolau, Heinrich. "Stillstand und Rückzug im Zoologischen Garten zu Hamburg." *Der Zoologische Garten* 44, no. 2 (1903): 33–37.

Borkowski, Dieter. *Wer weiß, ob wir uns wiedersehen: Erinnerungen an eine Berliner Jugend*. Frankfurt: Fischer, 1980.

Boyes, Roger. "The Abandoned Cub Who Faces Death Sentence because He Will Grow Up a Softie." *The Times* (London), March 20, 2007.

Brandt, Karl. "Mutterliebe bei den Tieren." *Die Gartenlaube* 19 (1899): 580–581.

Brehm, Alfred. "Menschenaffen." *Die Gartenlaube* 3 (1876): 44–48.

Brucker, Renate. "Tierrechte und Friedensbewegung: 'Radikale Ethik' und gesellschaftlicher Fortschritt in der deutschen Geschichte." In *Tierische Geschichte: Die Beziehung von Mensch und Tier in der Kultur der Moderne*, ed. Dorothee Brantz and Christof Mauch, 269–285. Paderborn: Ferdinand Schöningh, 2010.

Bruggemeier, Franz-Josef, Mark Cioc, and Thomas Zeller, eds. *How Green Were the Nazis? Nature, Environment, and Nation in the Third Reich*. Athens: Ohio University Press, 2005.

Buchner, Jutta. *Kultur mit Tieren*. Münster: Waxmann Verlag, 1996.

Bulliet, Richard. *The Camel and the Wheel*. New York: Columbia University Press, 1990.

Bulliet, Richard. *Hunters, Herders, and Hamburgers*. New York: Columbia University Press, 2005.

Bülow, Hildegard von. "Meine Tierfreundschaft im Dresdner Zoologischen Garten." *Der Zoologische Garten* 46, no. 7 (1905): 193–201.

Burkhardt, Richard. "Constructing the Zoo: Science, Society, and Animal Nature at the Paris Menagerie, 1794–1838." In *Animals in Human Histories*, ed. Mary Henninger Voss, 231–257. Rochester: University of Rochester Press, 2002.

Bußmann, Walter. *Zwischen Preußen und Deutschland. Friedrich Wilhelm IV. Eine Biographie*. Berlin: Siedler Verlag, 1990.

Childers, Thomas. *The Nazi Voter: The Social Foundations of Fascism in Germany*. Chapel Hill: University of North Carolina Press, 1983.

Ciarlo, David. *Advertising Empire: Race and Visual Culture in Imperial Germany*. Cambridge, MA: Harvard University Press, 2011.

Corbey, Raymond. "Ethnographic Showcases, 1870–1930." In *The Decolonization of Imagination*, ed. Jan Nederveen Pieterse and Bhikhu Parekh, 57–80. Ann Arbor: University of Michigan Press, 1995.

"Das fünfzigjährige Jubelfest des Berliner zoologischen Gartens." *Der Zoologische Garten* 35, no. 8 (1894): 302–304.

"Das Gründungsfieber der Jetztzeit." *Die Gartenlaube* 36 (1872): 592–594.

Dathe, Heinrich. *Lebenserinnerungen eines leidenschaftlichen Tiergärtners*. Munich: Koehler & Amelang, 2001.

Daum, Andreas. *Wissenschaftspopularisierung im 19. Jahrhundert: Bürgerliche Kultur, naturwissenschaftliche Bildung und die deutsche Öffentlichkeit, 1848–1914*. Munich: Oldenbourg, 1998.

"David Livingstones Ende." *Die Gartenlaube* 12 (1875): 201–204.

"Der zoologische Garten in Berlin." *Die Gartenlaube* 16 (1873): 262–266.

Diamond, Jared. *Guns, Germs, and Steel: The Fates of Human Societies.* New York: W. W. Norton, 1997.

Diechmann, Ute. *Biologists under Hitler.* Cambridge, MA: Harvard University Press, 1996.

"Die Drei-Kaiser-Tage in Berlin." *Illustrirte Zeitung*, no. 1527 (October 5, 1872): 231.

Dittrich, Lothar. "Fürstliche Menagerien im deutschsprachigen Raum ab den 1760er Jahren bis zur Gründung der Zoologischen Gärten Mitte des neunzehnten Jahrhunderts." In *Die Kulturgeschichte des Zoos*, ed. Lothar Dittrich, Dietrich von Engelhardt, and Annelore Rieke-Müller, 67–81. Berlin: Verlag für Wissenschaft und Bildung, 2001.

Dittrich, Lothar, and Annelore Rieke-Müller. *Carl Hagenbeck: Tierhandel und Schaustellungen im Deutschen Kaiserreich.* Frankfurt: Peter Lang, 1998.

Dittrich, Lothar, and Annelore Rieke-Müller. *Ein Garten für Menschen und Tiere: 125 Jahre Zoo Hannover.* Hannover: Verlagsgesellschaft Grütter, 1990.

Dittrich, Sigrid. "Exoten an den Höfen von Renaissancefürsten und ihre Darstellung in der Malerei." In *Die Kulturgeschichte des Zoos*, ed. Lothar Dittrich, Dietrich von Engelhardt, and Annelore Rieke-Müller, 9–29. Berlin: Verlag für Wissenschaft und Bildung, 2001.

Dreesbach, Anne. "Die Gefangenen unserer zoologischen Gärten—Der Tierpark im Spiegel der Kritik." In *Nilpferde an der Isar: Eine Geschichte des Tierparks Hellabrunn in München*, ed. Michael Kamp und Helmut Zedelmaier, 246–276. Munich Buchendorf Verlag, 2000.

Dreesbach, Anne. *Gezähmte Wilde: Die Zurschaustellung "exotischer" Menschen in Deutschland, 1870–1940.* Frankfurt: Campus Verlag, 2005.

Engeli, Christian, and Wolfgang Ribbe. "Berlin in der NS-Zeit." In *Geschichte Berlins*, vol. 2, ed. Wolfgang Ribbe, 925–1024. Berlin: Berliner Wissenschafts-Verlag, 2002.

Epstein, Leopold. "Bemerkenwertes aus dem Zoologischen Garten zu Frankfurt a. M.." *Der Zoologische Beobachter* 59, no. 1 (1918): 88–97.

Erbe, Michael. "Berlin im Kaiserreich." In *Geschichte Berlins*, ed. Wolfgang Ribbe, 691–793. Berlin: Berliner Wissenschafts-Verlag, 2002.

Essner, Cornelia. *Deutsche Afrikareisende im neunzehnten Jahrhundert.* Wiesbaden: Steiner, 1985.

Falkenstein, Dr. "M'Pungu." *Die Gartenlaube* 33 (1876): 557–558.

Falz-Fein, Woldemar von. *Askania-Nova: Das Tierparadies.* Neudamm: Neumann, 1930.

Farber, Paul Lawrence. *Finding Order in Nature.* Baltimore: Johns Hopkins University Press, 2000.

Fischer, Conan. *The Rise of the Nazis.* Manchester: Manchester University Press, 1995.

Flower, Stanley Smyth. *Report on Mission to Europe, 1905.* Cairo: National Printing Department, 1906.

Frädrich, Hans. "Der Spurensuche zum Geleit." *Bongo* 24 (1994): 3–6.

Frädrich, Hans, and Harro Strehlow. "Der Zoo und die Wissenschaft." *Bongo* 24 (1994): 161–180.

Frisch, Walter. *Der Auerochs.* Starnberg: Lipp Graphische Betriebe, 2010.

Fröhlich, Elke, ed. *Die Tagebücher von Joseph Goebbels.* Part 1, vol. 3. Munich: Saur, 1987.

Gerstäcker, Friedrich. "Civilisation und Wildniß." *Die Gartenlaube* 17 (1855): 224–225.

Geulen, Christian. "The Final Frontier." In *Phantasiereiche: Zur Kulturgeschichte des deutschen Kolonialismus*, ed. Birthe Kundrus, 35–55. Frankfurt: Campus Verlag, 2003.

Gißibl, Bernhard. " German Colonialism and the Beginnings of the International Wildlife Preservation in Africa." *German Historical Institute Bulletin* 3 (2006): 121–143.

Gleiss, Horst. *Unter Robben, Gnus und Tigerschlangen.* Breslau: Natura et Patria Verlag, 1967.

Goering, Victor. *Die Entwicklung des Zoologischen Gartens zu Frankfurt a.M. von 1858 bis 1908.* Frankfurt: Kommissionsverlag, 1908.

Goldmann, Stefan. "Wilde in Europa: Aspekte und Orte ihrer Zurschaustellung." In *Wir und die Wilden: Einblicke in eine kannibalische Beziehung*, ed. Thomas Theye, 243–269. Hamburg: Rowohlt, 1985.

Goldmann, Stefan. "Zur Rezeption der Völkerausstellungen um 1900." In *Exotische Welten, Europäische Phantasien*, ed. Hermann Pollig, 88–93. Stuttgart: Edition Cantz, 1987.

Gottschlich, Evelyn. "Wiedereröffnung und Zerstörung." In *Nilpferde an der Isar: Eine Geschichte des Tierparks Hellabrunn in München*, ed. Michael Kamp and Helmut Zedelmaier, 112–138. Munich: Buchendorf Verlag, 2000.

Güssfeldt, Paul, Julius Falkenstein, and Eduard Pecuel-Loesche. *Die Loango-Expedition: Ausgesandt von der Deutschen Gesellschaft zur Erforschung Aequatorial-Africas, 1873–1876.* Leipzig: Verlag von Eduard Baldamus, 1888. Accessed July 18, 2014. http://library.si.edu/digital-library/book/dieloangoexpedi00gssf.

Haberland, Wolfgang. " 'Diese Indianer sind Falsch': Neun Bella Coola im Deutschen Reich 1885/86." *Archiv für Völkerkunde* 42 (1988): 3–68.

Hagenbeck, Carl. *Von Tieren und Menschen.* Leipzig: Paul List Verlag, 1967.

Haikal, Mustafa, and Jörg Junhold. *Auf der Spur des Löwen: 125 Jahre Zoo Leipzig.* Leipzig: Pro Leipzig, 2003.

Haikal, Mustafa, and Winfried Gensch. *Der Gesang des Orang-utans: Die Geschichte des Dresdner Zoos.* Dresden: Sächsische Zeitung, 2011.

Hanson, Elizabeth. *Animal Attractions: Nature on Display in American Zoos.* Princeton, NJ: Princeton University Press, 2004.

Hauchecorne, Friedrich. "Naturschutzaufgaben unserer Zoologischen Gärten." *Der Zoologische Garten* 1, nos. 3–4 (1928): 81–87.

Heck, Heinz. "Askania Nova—Ein Besuch vor beinahe 100 Jahren." *Bongo* 23 (1994): 89–90.

Heck, Ludwig. *Heiter-Ernste Lebensberichte: Erinnerungen eines alten Tiergärtners.* Berlin: Deutscher Verlag, 1938.

Heck, Ludwig. *Papa Heck und seine Liebling.* Berlin: Naumann, 1931.

Heck, Ludwig, and Clemens Carl Freyer. *Streifzüge durch den Zoologischen Garten Berlin mit dem Zeiss Ikon-Camera.* Berlin: Verlag des Actien-Vereins des Zoologischen Gartens, 1927.

Heck, Ludwig, and Lutz Heck. *Tiere in Natur und Kunst.* Dresden: Zwinger-Verlag Rudolf Glöß, 1943.

Heck, Lutz. *Animals: My Adventure.* London: Methuen, 1954.

Heck, Lutz. *Auf Tiersuche in Weiter Welt.* Berlin: Paul Paren, 1941.

Heck, Lutz. *Auf Urwild in Kanada.* Berlin: Paul Paren, 1937.

Heck, Lutz. *Aus der Wildnis in den Zoo: Auf Tierfang in Ostafrika.* Berlin: Ullstein, 1930.

Heck, Lutz. "Giraffenfang und Giraffenzucht des Berliner Zoologischen Gartens." *Der Zoologische Garten* 9, no. 5 (1937): 191–204.

Heck, Lutz. *Zooführer durch den Berliner Zoologischen Garten.* Berlin: Verlag des Aktienvereins des Zoologischen Gartens zu Berlin, 1906.

Heim, Susanne. *Plant Breeding and Agrarian Research in Kaiser-Wilhelm-Institutes, 1933–1945.* Dordrecht: Springer, 2008.

Heinecke, Eva. *König Friedrich Wilhelm IV. von Preußen und die Errichtung des Neuen Museums 1841–1860 in Berlin.* Halle: Universitätsverlag Halle-Wittenberg, 2011.

Heinke, Lothar. "Der Arche-Typ. Ein Leben für den Tierpark Fredrichsfelde: Vor 100 Jahren wurde der Zoologe Heinrich Dathe geboren. Seine Zeit als Direktor ist bis heute legendär." *Der Tagesspiegel,* November 7, 2010.

Heinroth, Katharina. *Mit Faltern begann's: Mein Leben mit Tieren in Breslau, München und Berlin.* Munich: Kindler, 1979.

Heinroth, Oskar. "Vesperbrot des Orang-Utan 'Rolf' im zoologischen Garten zu Berlin." *Die Gartenlaube* 28 (1899): 896.

Henninger-Voss, Mary, ed. *Animals in Human Histories.* Rochester: University of Rochester Press, 2002.

Hergé. *Tintin in the Congo.* London: Egmont, 2005.

Heun, Sylke, and Peter Schubert. "Die langen dunkeln Schatten der Vergangenheit: Eine Studie belegt erstmals, wie jüdische Zoo-Aktionäre in der Nazizeit systematisch ausgegrenzt wurden." *Die Welt,* November 6, 2002.

Hirsch, Fritz, and Hennig Wiesner. *75 Jahre Münchner Tierpark Hellabrunn.* Munich: Münchner Tierpark Hellabrunn, 1986.

"Hochzeit bei den Kalmücken." *Die Gartenlaube* 50 (1872): 828.

Hoffmann, M. *Beiträge über Leben und Treiben der Eskimos in Labrador und Grönland: Aus dem Tagebuch des Herrn Carl Hagenbeck in Hamburg mit dem Schiffe "Eisbär" nach Grönland entsandten Herrn Jacobsen.* Berlin: Selbstverlag des Herausgebers, 1880.

Horn, Georg. "Aus der Drei-Kaiser-Woche." *Die Gartenlaube* 42 (1872): 696–698.

Horn, Michael, and Gottfried Weise. *Das große Lexikon des DDR-Fussballs.* Berlin: Schwarzkopf & Schwarzkopf, 2004.

Ingensiep, Hans Werner. "Kultur- und Zoogeschichte des Gorillas." In *Die Kulturgeschichte des Zoos,* ed. Lothar Dittrich, Dietrich von Engelhardt and Annelore Rieke-Müller, 151–170. Berlin: Verlag für Wissenschaft und Bildung, 2001.

Irwin, Robert. *For Lust of Knowing.* London: Allen Lane, 2006.

Ito, Takashi. *London Zoo and the Victorians, 1838–1859.* Woodbridge: Boydell Press, 2014.

Jahn, Ilse. "Zoologische Gärten—Zoologische Museen. Parallelen ihrer Entstehung." *Bongo* 24 (1994): 7–30.

"Jahresbericht 1984." *Bongo* 9 (1985): 127.

"Jahresbericht über den zoologischen Garten in Hamburg 1891." *Der Zoologische Garten* 33 (1892): 124–128.

Johnson, Barton. "A Guide to Nabokov's 'A Guide to Berlin.'" *Slavic and East European Journal* 23, no. 3 (1979): 353–361.

Jones, Marvin. "Der Berliner Zoo und der Elaphurus davidianus." *Bongo* 11 (1986): 63–66.

Kalof, Linda, and Brigitte Resl, eds. *A Cultural History of Animals.* 6 vols. Oxford: Oxford University Press, 2007.

Kammerer, Steffi. "Im Gehege des Vergessens: Was wurde aus Aktie 1114?" *Süddeutsche Zeitung,* October 12, 2000, Berlin-Seite. http://www.hagalil.com/archiv/2000/10/zoo-aktie.htm. Accessed December 8, 2014.

Kanngiesser, E. "Karl Hagenbeck: Ein Erinnerungsbild." *Zoologischer Beobachter* 54, no. 5 (1913): 121–123.

Kete, Kathleen. "Animals and Ideology: Politics of Animal Protection in Europe." In *Representing Animals,* ed. Nigel Rothfels, 19–34. Bloomington: Indiana University Press, 2002.

Kete, Kathleen. *The Beast in the Boudoir: Pet-Keeping in Nineteenth Century Paris.* Berkeley: University of California Press, 1994.

Kipling, Rudyard. *The Mark of the Beast and Other Stories.* New York: Signet, 1964.

Klausen, G. "Kinderbelustigung im Zoologischen Garten." *Die Gartenlaube* 22 (1899): 707.

"Kleinere Mitteilungen." *Der Zoologische Garten* 35 (1894): 155–186.

"Kleinere Mitteilungen." *Der Zoologische Garten* 33 (1892): 219–255.

Klös, Heinz-Georg. *Von der Menagerie zum Tierparadies: 125 Jahre Zoo Berlin.* Berlin: Haude & Spenersche, 1969.

Klös, Heinz-Georg, and Ursula Klös. *Der Berliner Zoo im Spiegel seiner Bauten, 1841–1989.* Berlin: Heenemann, 1990.

Klös, Heinz-Georg, Ursula Klös, and Hans Frädrich. *Die Arche Noah an der Spree, 1844–1944: 150 Jahre Zoologischer Garten Berlin.* Berlin: FAB Verlag, 1994.

Klös, Ursula. "Völkerschauen im Zoo Berlin zwischen 1878 und 1952." *Bongo* 30 (2000): 33–82.

Knobloch, Heinz. *Eine Berliner Kindheit: Zwischen Olympia und Luftschutzkeller.* Berlin: Jaron, 1999.

Knottnerus-Meyer, Theodor. "Der Zoologische Garten zu Frankfurt-am-Main." *Der Zoologische Garten* 44, no. 5 (1903): 137–148.

Knottnerus-Meyer, Theodor. "Neues vom Zoologischen Garten zu Berlin." *Der Zoologische Garten* 46, no. 2 (1905) 33–45, 72–79.

Köhler, Henning. "Berlin in der Weimarer Republik." In *Geschichte Berlins,* vol. 2, ed. Wolfgang Ribbe, 797–925. Berlin: Berliner Wissenschafts-Verlag, 2002.

Koppenfels, Hugo von. "Meine Jagden auf Gorillas." *Die Gartenlaube* 25 (1877): 416–420.

"Korrespondenzen." *Der Zoologische Garten* 31 (1890): 123–125.

Kotowski, Elke-Vera. "Tanz auf dem Vulkan." In *Berlin: Geschichte einer Stadt,* ed. Julius Schoeps, 120–127. Berlin: be.bra verlag, 2001.

Kramer, Fritz. "Eskapistische und utopische Motive in der Frühgeschichte der deutschen Ethnologie." In *Exotische Welten, Europäische Phantasien,* ed. Hermann Pollig, 66–71. Stuttgart: Edition Cantz, 1987.

Kramer, Jennifer. *Switchbacks: Art, Ownership, and Nuxalk National Identity.* Vancouver: University of British Columbia Press, 2006.

Kriener, Manfred. "Weg ist weg." *Die Zeit.* http://www.Zeit.de/2010/17/TierAuerochse?page=all&print=true.

Kuenheim, Haug von. *Carl Hagenbeck.* Hamburg: Ellert & Richter Verlag, 2009.

Landsberg, Hannelore. "Das erste Zootier des Museums—eine Mandrill? Die Gründung des Zoologischen Gartens und dessen Bedeutung für die Sammlungen des Zoologischen Museums der Berliner Universität." *Bongo* 24 (1994): 85–106.

Lange, Annemarie. *Das Wilhelminische Berlin. Zwischen Jahrhundertwende und Novemberrevolution.* Berlin: Dietz, 1988.

Lange, Dr. H. "Die 'Afrikanische Gesellschaft' und die deutsche Expedition an der Loangoküste." *Die Gartenlaube* 38 (1874): 613–616.

Leffer, Richard, ed. *Deutsche Kolonialzeitung.* Berlin: Verlag des deutschen Kolonialvereins, 1886.

Lehmann, Alfred. "Zeitgenössische Bilder der ersten Völkerschauen." In *Von Fremden Völkern und Kulturen,* ed. Werner Lang, Walter Nippold, and Günther Spannaus, 31–38. Düsseldorf: Droste-Verlag, 1955.

Lehmensick, Rudolf. "Die Bedeutung von Schule und Universität für den Zoologischen Garten." *Der Zoologische Garten* 7, nos. 1–3 (1934): 286–289.

Leide, Henry. *NS-Verbrecher und Staatssicherheit: Die geheime Vergangenheitspolitik der DDR.* Göttingen: Vandenhoeck & Ruprecht, 2005.

Leitner, Ulrike, ed. *Alexander von Humboldt/Friedrich Wilhelm IV: Briefwechsel.* Berlin: de Gruyter, 2013.

Lekan, Thomas. "The Nature of Home: Landscape Preservation and Local Identities." In *Localism, Landscape, and the Ambiguities of Place: German-Speaking Central Europe, 1860–1930,* ed. David Blackbourn and James Retallack. Toronto: University of Toronto Press, 2007.

Leutemann, Heinrich. "Beim schwarzen Jack im zoologischen Garten in Berlin." *Die Gartenlaube* 4 (1873): 56–59.

Lichtenstein, Martin Hinrich. *Reisen im südlichen Africa in den Jahren 1803, 1804, 1805 und 1806.* 2 vols. Berlin: C. Salfeld, 1811.

Lichtenstein, Martin Hinrich. *Travels in Southern Africa in the Years 1803, 1804, 1805 and 1806.* London: Henry Colburn, 1812.

Lindenberg, Paul. "Aus der Reichshauptstadt." *Die Gartenlaube* 7 (1888): 107–111.

Loy, Thomas. "Gedenktafel für jüdische Zoo-Aktionäre enthüllt." *Der Tagesspiegel.* June 28, 2011. http://www.tagesspiegel.de/berlin/ns-geschichte-gedenktafel-fuer-juedische-zoo-aktionaere-enthuellt/4334750.html.

Mason, Jennifer. *Civilized Creatures: Urban Animals, Sentimental Culture and American Literature, 1850–1900.* Baltimore: Johns Hopkins University Press, 2005.

Mauersberger, Gottfried. "Der Gründer des Berliner Zoologischen Gartens, Martin Hinrich Lichtenstein (1780–1857). Eine biographische Skizze." *Bongo* 23 (1994): 3–34.

Mehos, Donna. "The Rise of Serious Science at the Amsterdam Zoo Artis." In *Die Kulturgeschichte des Zoos,* ed. Lothar Dittrich, Dietrich von Engelhardt and Annelore Rieke-Müller, 109–115. Berlin: Verlag für Wissenschaft und Bildung, 2001.

Mehos, Donna. *Science and Culture for Members Only: The Amsterdam Zoo Artis in the 19th Century.* Amsterdam: Amsterdam University Press, 2006.

Mehlitz, Hartmut. *Johann August Zeune: Berlins Blindenvater und seine Zeit.* Berlin: Bostelmann & Siebenharr, 2003.

Mehlitz, Hartmut. *Richard Lepsius: Ägypten und die Ordnung der Wissenschaft.* Berlin: Kulturverlag Kadmos, 2011.

Middlebrook, Martin. *The Berlin Raids: R.A.F. Bomber Command Winter 1943–44.* New York: Viking, 1988.

Mieck, Ilja. "Von der Reformzeit zur Revolution." In *Geschichte Berlins,* ed. Wolfgang Ribbe, 405–602. Berlin: Berliner Wissenschafts-Verlag, 2002.

Miller, Ian Jared. *The Nature of the Beasts: Empire and Exhibition at the Tokyo Imperial Zoo.* Berkeley: University of California Press, 2013.

Millet, Kitty. "Caesura, Continuity, and Myth: The Stakes of Tethering the Holocaust to German Colonial Theory." In *German Colonialism: Race, the Holocaust, and Postwar Germany,* ed. Volker Langbehn and Mohammad Salama, 93–119. New York: Columbia University Press, 2011.

"Miscellen." *Der Zoologische Garten* 21, no. 7 (1880): 221–223.

Mladek, Jürgen. *Professor Dathe und seine Tiere.* Berlin: Das Neue Berlin, 2010.

Mommsen, Hans. *The Rise and Fall of Weimar Democracy.* Chapel Hill: University of North Carolina Press, 1996.

Moorhouse, Roger. *Berlin at War: Life and Death in Hitler's Capital, 1939–1945.* London: Bodley Head, 2010.

Mühling, Peter. *Der alte Nürnberger Tiergarten 1912–1939.* Nürnberg: Druckhaus, 1987.

Mullan, Bob, and Garry Marvin. *Zoo Culture.* London: Weidenfeld & Nicolson, 1987.

Müller-Liebenwalde, J. "Aus dem Berliner zoologischen Garten." *Der Zoologische Garten* 34 (1893): 363–367.

Muth, K. W. "Tiergärten und Tierschutz." *Der Zoologische Garten* 8 (1935/36): 297–300.

Nabokov, Vladimir. "A Guide to Berlin." *New Yorker,* March 1, 1976, 27–28.

"Nachrichten aus zoologischen Gärten." *Der Zoologische Garten* 8 (1936): 73–81.

"Nachrichten aus zoologischen Gärten." *Der Zoologische Garten* 11, nos. 1–2 (1939): 32–42.

"Nachrichten aus zoologischen Gärten." *Der Zoologische Garten* 13 (1941): 335–343.

"Nachrichten aus zoologischen Gärten." *Der Zoologische Garten* 12 (1940): 62–65.

Neillands, Robin. *The Bomber War: The Allied Air Offensive against Nazi Germany.* New York: Overlook Press, 2001.

Nill, Adolf. "Eine Elefantentötung in Nills zoologischen Garten in Stuttgart." *Der Zoologische Garten* 35 (1894): 21–27.

Nowak, Eugeniusz. *Wissenschaftler in turbulenten Zeiten.* Schwerin: Stock & Stein, 2005.

Noyes, John. "Landschaftsschilderung, Kultur und Geographie." In *Kolonialismus als Kultur: Literatur, Medien, Wissenschaft in der deutschen Gründerzeit des Fremden,* ed. Alexander Honold and Oliver Simons, 127–142. Tübingen: A. Francke Verlag, 2002.

Nyhart, Lynn. *Modern Nature.* Chicago: University of Chicago Press, 2009.

Oppermann, Joachim. "Tod und Wiedergeburt. Über das Schicksal einiger Berliner Zootiere." *Bongo* 24 (1994): 51–84.

Peters, Wilhelm. *Naturwissenschaftliche Reise nach Mossambique.* Berlin: G. Reimer, 1862.

Peukert, Detlev. *The Weimar Republic: The Crisis of Classical Modernity.* New York: Hill and Wang, 1992.

Philipp, Michael. "Mythos Germania." In *Berlin: Geschichte einer Stadt,* ed. Julius Schoeps, 150–175. Berlin: be.bra, 2007.

Pieters, Florence. "The Menagerie of the White Elephant in Amsterdam." In *Die Kulturgeschichte des Zoos,* ed. Lothar Dittrich, Dietrich von Engelhardt and Annelore Rieke-Müller, 47–66. Berlin: Verlag für Wissenschaft und Bildung, 2001.

Poling, Kristin. "Shantytowns and Pioneers beyond the City Wall: Berlin's Urban Frontier in the Nineteenth Century." *Central European History* 47, no. 2 (2014): 245–274.

Poliquin, Rachel. *The Breathless Zoo: Taxidermy and the Cultures of Longing.* University Park: Pennsylvania State University Press, 2012.

Pollig, Hermann. "Exotische Welten, Europäische Phantasien." In *Exotische Welten, Europäische Phantasien,* ed. Hermann Pollig, 16–25. Stuttgart: Edition Cantz, 1987.

Priemel, Kurt. "*Der Zoologischer Garten* von 1859. Ein Rückblick." *Der Zoologische Garten* 1, no. 1 (1928): 3–12.

Proctor, Robert. *The Nazi War on Cancer.* Princeton, NJ: Princeton University Press, 2000.

Raethel, Heinz-Sigurd. "Das Antilopenhaus im Berliner Zoo—Ein Tierhaus erzählt Geschichte." *Bongo* 14 (1988): 73–82.

Raethel, Heinz-Sigurd . "Der Berliner Zoo und seine Rindersammlung 1843–1991." *Bongo* 20 (1992): 45–54.

Raethel, Heinz-Sigurd. "Der Berliner Zoo und seine Rindersammlung 1843–1991. Teil II." *Bongo* 21 (1993): 39–46.

Reel, Monte. *Between Man and Beast.* New York: Doubleday, 2013.

Reichenbach, Herman. "Carl Hagenbeck's Tierpark and Modern Zoological Gardens." *Journal of the Society for the Bibliography of Natural History* 9, no. 4 (1980): 573–585.

Reichenbach, Herman . "A Tale of Two Zoos." In *New Worlds, New Animals,* ed. R. J. Haage and William Deiss, 51–62. Baltimore: Johns Hopkins University Press, 1996.

Ribbe, Wolfgang. "Vom Vier-Mächte-Regime zur Bundeshauptstadt." In *Geschichte Berlins,* vol. 2, ed. Wolfgang Ribbe, 1027–1210. Berlin: Berliner Wissenschafts-Verlag, 2002.

Richie, Alexandra. *Faust's Metropolis: A History of Berlin.* New York: Carroll & Graf, 1998.

Richter, Günter. "Zwischen Revolution und Reichsgründung." In *Geschichte Berlins,* ed. Wolfgang Ribbe, 605–687. Berlin: Berliner Wissenschafts-Verlag, 2002.

Ridley, Jane. *The Heir Apparent: A Life of Edward VII, the Playboy Prince.* New York: Random House, 2013.

Rieke-Müller, Annelore. "Angewandte Zoologie und die Wahrnehmung exotischer Natur in der zweiten Hälfte des 18. und 19. Jahrhundert." *History and Philosophy of the Life Sciences* 17 (1995): 461–484.

Rieke-Müller, Annelore. "Die Gründung Zoologischer Gärten um die Mitte des 19. Jahrhunderts im deutschsprachigen Raum." In *Die Kulturgeschichte des Zoos,* Lothar Dittrich, Dietrich von Engelhardt, and Annelore Rieke-Müller, eds. Berlin: VWB, 2001.

Rieke-Müller, Annelore, and Lothar Dittrich, eds. *Der Löwe brüllt nebenan: Die Gründung Zoologischer Gärten im deutschsprachigen Raum 1833–1869.* Cologne: Böhlau Verlag, 1998.

Ritvo, Harriet. *The Animal Estate: The English and Other Creatures in the Victorian Age.* Cambridge, MA: Harvard University Press, 1987.

Ritvo, Harriet. "The Order of Nature." In *New Worlds, New Animals,* ed. R. J. Hoage and William Deiss, 43–50. Baltimore: Johns Hopkins University Press, 1996.

Rothfels, Nigel. "Catching Animals." In *Animals in Human Histories,* ed. Mary Henninger-Voss, 182–228. Rochester: University of Rochester Press, 2002.

Rothfels, Nigel. "Immersed with Animals." In *Representing Animals,* ed. Nigel Rothfels, 199–223. Bloomington: Indiana University Press, 2002.

Rothfels, Nigel. *Savages and Beasts: The Birth of the Modern Zoo.* Baltimore: Johns Hopkins University Press, 2002.

Rothkirch, Malve Gräfin. *Der "Romantiker" auf dem Preussenthron.* Düsseldorf: Droste, 1990.

Rubner, Heinrich. *Deutsche Forstgeschichte 1933–1945: Forstwirtschaft, Jagd und Umwelt im NS-Staat.* St. Katharinen: Scripta Mercaturae, 1997.

Ruempler, Götz. "Zoologische Gärten und Naturschutz." *Bongo* 13 (1987): 63–80.

Said, Edward. *Orientalism.* New York: Vintage, 1978.

Sax, Boria. *Animals in the Third Reich: Pets, Scapegoats, and the Holocaust.* New York: Continuum, 2000.

Schaefer, Bernd. "Socialist Modernization in Vietnam: The East German Approach." In *Comrades of Color: East Germany in the Cold War World*, ed. Quinn Slobodian, 95–116. New York: Berghahn, 2015.

Scherpner, Christoph. *Von Bürgern für Bürger—125 Jahre Zoologischer Garten Frankfurt am Main.* Frankfurt: Zoologischer Garten, 1983.

Schmidt, Monika. "Die 'Arisierung' des Berliner Zoologischen Gartens." *Jahrbuch für Antisemitismusforschung* 12 (2003): 211–229.

Schmitt, Christine. "Zoo stellt sich der Geschichte." *Jüdische Allgemeine.* http://www.juedische-allgemeine.de/article/view/id/10223. Accessed April 9, 2012.

Schneider, Helga. *The Bonfire of Berlin.* London: Heinemann, 1995.

Schneider, Karl Max. "Der neue Leipziger Tierkindergarten." *Der Zoologische Garten* 8, nos. 7–9 (1936): 274–282.

Schneider, Karl Max. "'Tierparadies im Zoo': Antwort auf den Brief des Herrn Baron Jakob von Ueküll." *Der Zoologische Garten* 12, nos. 4–6 (1940): 186–195.

Schneider, Karl Max. "Vom Daseinsrecht der Zoologischen Gärten." *Der Zoologische Garten* 8, nos. 7–9 (1936): 173–179.

Schoeps, Julius. "Berlin wird Weltstadt." In *Berlin: Geschichte einer Stadt*, ed. Julius Schoeps, 54–83. Berlin: be.bra verlag, 2001.

Schomburgk, Richard. *Reisen in Britisch-Guiana in den Jahren 1840–1844.* Leipzig: J. J. Weber, 1848.

Schwenkel, Christina."Affective Solidarities and East German Reconstruction of Postwar Vietnam." In *Comrades of Color: East German in the Cold War World*, ed. Quinn Slobodian, 267–292. New York: Berghahn, 2015.

Scurla, H. *Alexander von Humboldt—sein Leben und Wirken.* Berlin: Verlag der Nation, 1959.

Serpell, James. *In the Company of Animals: A Study of Human-Animal Relationships.* Cambridge: Cambridge University Press, 1996.

Skabelund, Aaron. "Rassismus züchten: Schäferhunde im Dienst der Gewaltherrschaft." In *Tierische Geschichte: Die Beziehung von Mensch und Tier in der Kultur der Moderne*, ed. Dorothee Brantz and Christof Mauch, 58–78. Paderborn: Ferdinand Schöningh, 2010.

"Skizzen aus deutschen Parlamentssälen." *Die Gartenlaube* 32 (1881): 224–228.

Soffel, Karl. "Der Tierpark des Herrn Friedrich Falz-Fein zu Askania-Nova (Sudrüssland)." *Zoologischer Beobachter* 56 (1915): 25–63.

Sperber, Jonathan. *The European Revolutions.* Cambridge: Cambridge University Press, 2005.

Staehelin, Balthasar. *Völkerschauen im Zoologischen Garten Basel, 1879–1935.* Basel: Basler Afrika Bibliographien, 1993.

Steinberg, Jonathan. *Bismarck: A Life.* New York: Oxford University Press, 2011.

Steinitz, Heinrich. "Feuerländer in Berlin." *Die Gartenlaube* 44 (1881): 732–735.

Steinmetz, George. *The Devil's Handwriting: Precoloniality and the German Colonial State in Qingdao, Samoa, and Southwest Africa.* Chicago: University of Chicago Press, 2007.

Steinmetz, H. "Berlin: Bericht über das Kalenderjahr 1937." *Der Zoologische Garten* 10, nos. 3–4 (1938): 156–159.

Sterne, Carus. "Charles Darwin." *Die Gartenlaube* 19 (1882): 315–318.

Strehlow, Harro. "Beiträge zur Menschenaffenhaltung im Berliner Aquarium unter den Linden." *Bongo* 12 (1987): 105–110.

Strehlow, Harro. "Beiträge zur Menschenaffenhaltung im Berliner Aquarium unter den Linden. Teil III." *Bongo* 14 (1988: 99–104).

Strehlow, Harro. "'Das Merkwürdigste auf der Insel waren mir die lebendigen Thiere.' Ein Besuch Christian Ludwig Brehms in der Menagerie auf der Pfaueninsel im Oktober 1832." *Bongo* 24 (1994): 31–50.

Strehlow, Harro. "Die Teneriffa-Schimpansen und der Zoologische Garten Berlin." *Bongo* 25 (1995): 47–52.

Strehlow, Harro. "Zoological Gardens of Western Europe." In *Zoo and Aquarium History*, ed. Vernon Kisling Jr., 75–116. New York: CRC Press, 2001.

Strehlow, Harro. "Zoos and Aquariums of Berlin." In *New Worlds, New Animals,* ed. R. J. Haage and William Deiss, 63–72. Baltimore: Johns Hopkins University Press, 1996.

Strother, Z. S. "Display of the Body Hottentot." In *Africans on Stage: Studies in Ethnological Show Business,* ed. Bernth Lindfors, 1–61. Bloomington: Indiana University Press, 1999.

Studnitz, Hans-Georg von. *While Berlin Burns.* Englewood Cliffs, NJ: Prentice Hall, 1964.

Sunkel, Werner. "Zoologische Gärten." *Zoologischer Beobachter* 60, nos. 8–9 (1919): 137–142.

Taylor, Garth. "An Eskimo Abroad, 1880: His Diary and Death." *Canadian Geographic* 101, no. 5 (1981): 38–43.

Thamm, Otto. *Von Kiel bis Samoa: Reise Erlebnisse des am 16. März 1889 ertrunkenen Obermatrosen Adolph Thamm.* Berlin: Conrads Buchhandlung, 1889.

Theye, Thomas. "Optische Trophäen." In *Wir und die Wilden: Einblicke in eine kannibalische Beziehung*, ed. Thomas Theye, 18–95. Hamburg: Rowohlt, 1985.

Thode-Arora, Hilke. *Für fünfzig Pfennig um die Welt: Die Hagenbeckschen Völkerschauen.* Frankfurt: Campus Verlag, 1989.

Thomas, Keith. *Man and the Natural World: Changing Attitudes in England, 1500–1800.* London: Allen Lane, 1983.

Uekoetter, Frank. *The Green and the Brown: A History of Conservation in Nazi Germany.* New York: Cambridge University Press, 2006.

Ueküll, J. V. "Tierparadies im Zoo: Brief an den Direktor des Leipziger Zoologischen Gartens." *Der Zoologische Garten* 12, no. 1 (1940): 18–20.

"Unsere Tiergärten im Winter 1939/40." *Der Zoologische Garten* 13, nos. 1–2 (1941): 1–99.

Verlag, Der. "Die Deutsche Heimatlehre und ihr Ziel." *Die Tierwelt,* November 1937, 1.

Virchnow, Rudolf. "Sitzung am 20. December 1879." *Zeitschrift für Ethnologie* 11 (1879): 400.

Virchnow, Rudolf. "Untitled." *Zeitschrift für Ethnologie* 11 (1879): 389–393.

Vormbaum, Thomas. *A Modern History of German Criminal Law.* New York: Springer, 2014.

Walls, Laura Dassow. *The Passage to Cosmos: Alexander von Humboldt and the Shaping of America.* Chicago: University of Chicago Press, 2009.

Warraq, Ibn. Defending the West: *A Critique of Edward Said's* Orientalism. Amherst, NY: Prometheus, 2007.

Weber, Ernst von. *Vier Jahre in Afrika.* Leipzig: Brockhaus, 1878.

Wehler, Hans-Ulrich. *Deutsche Gesellschaftsgeschichte*, vols. 3–4. Munich: Beck, 1995–2003.

Wessely, Christina. *Künstliche Tiere: Zoologische Gärten und urbane Moderne.* Berlin: Kulturverlag Kadmos, 2008.

Williams, John. *Turning to Nature in Germany.* Stanford, CA: Stanford University Press, 2007.

Woldt, August. "Das Elephantenhaus im Berliner zoologischen Garten." *Die Gartenlaube* 52 (1882): 860–862.

Wulf, Andrea. *The Invention of Nature: Alexander von Humboldt's New World.* New York: Knopf, 2015.

Zabinski, Jan. "Die Gründung und Entwicklung des Warschauer Zoo." *Der Zoologische Garten* 9, nos. 1–2 (1937): 10–18.

Zedelmaier, Helmut, and Michael Kamp. *Hellabrunn: Geschichte und Geschichten des Münchener Tierparks.* Munich: Bassermann, 2011.

Zukowsky, Ludwig. *Tiere um große Männer.* Frankfurt: Moritz Diesterweg, 1938.

INDEX